## ADVERTISEMENT

THE Committee in charge of the Series of JEWISH CLASSICS present herewith, in two volumes, a translation of the Ma'aseh Book together with an Introduction thereto. The collection, known as the Ma'aseh Book, or book of stories or legends, has a long history which is briefly but learnedly sketched in the Introduction. The Ma'aseh Book was read in the Middle Ages by generation upon generation of people, and especially of the women, and while there are many other collections of extracts from the Talmud and other tales taken from ancient Jewish literature, this collection was the most popular. The Committee was fortunate in securing as the translator of this volume the Rev. Dr. Moses Gaster, of London, a distinguished scholar in many fields of Jewish learning and greatly devoted to folklore.

The preceding volumes in this Series have been: "A Selection from the Religious Poems of Solomon Ibn Gabirol," edited by Prof. Israel Davidson and put into English verse by Mr. Israel Zangwill; "Selected Poems of Jehudah Halevi," the text by Prof. H. Brody, the English translation by Mrs. Nina Salaman; "Hebrew Ethical Wills," published in two volumes, text

# THE JPS LIBRARY
# OF JEWISH CLASSICS

# MA'ASEH BOOK

## BOOK OF JEWISH TALES AND LEGENDS
## TRANSLATED FROM THE JUDEO-GERMAN
### *by*
## MOSES GASTER

*two volumes in one*
*Facsimile of original 1934 edition*

*The Jewish Publication Society of America*

PHILADELPHIA   1981 / 5741

# CONTENTS

# INTRODUCTION

The love of the Jews for poetic fiction can be traced as far back as the oldest records of our literature. It can be found in the parables and tales of the Bible, like that of Jotham (Judg. 9.7 ff.), who told the story of the trees choosing a king; or the parables of the prophet Nathan (II Sam. 12.1 ff), who, in rebuking King David, told the story of the poor man's lamb; or that of Jehoash, the king of Israel, who refused to meet Amaziah the King of Judah (II Kings 14.9 ff.); and many more examples can be adduced to show the love of the people in ancient times for the poetical tale. The same holds good also for the Proverbs of Solomon, which in many cases can only be understood as the moral drawn from a story, for each of those tales had a moral significance attached to it. They were lessons told in a manner which appealed to the people's imagination.

In later times legends and tales were told about the life and activity of the great figures of the past. Round each of them a cluster of legends

collected, intended to enhance the moral greatness and wisdom of those personages. Abraham's
goodness, Moses' greatness, David's courage,
Solomon's wisdom, were thus extolled and
magnified through a number of tales in which
those incidents of their life were recounted, in
which they had displayed their characteristic
virtues. These stories endeared the heroes still
more to the people, who always prefer legends
to dry historical facts. The former appealed to
the imagination, kindled a spirit of love and
admiration, set an example of greatness, faith,
endurance, and spiritual strength, which not only
gave pleasure to the reader but was as often a
source of solace and comfort in time of trouble
and sorrow.

Hero worship manifests itself in many ways,
and the form it takes varies with the hero
chosen. The Jewish heroes were not men of
battle, but men of faith. As spiritual leaders of
mankind, they were the objects of veneration;
and thus great scholars, rabbis, the spiritual
leaders, the great sages, from the time of the
destruction of the Temple onwards, were added
to the list of the biblical heroes, of whose personal
life the people wanted to know a little more.
Incidents in their daily life were as many illu-
minating flashes lighting up the personality,

which was otherwise lost in the dimness of the school room, or in the folios of the books which they studied or wrote.

In biblical times a special word was coined to denote a poetical fiction. It was called *Mashal*, that is a parable, an allegory, a story; but in later times the legends and tales were "Actions" performed by the great men, *res gestae*, *Ma'aseh* or, as I would prefer to call them, *Exempla;* and these form a very important part of the midrashic literature. Haggadah, literally translated, means a story "told," whilst Midrash means often the interpretation and study of Holy Writ in the light of the Haggadah. Thus tales and legends, or the *Ma'aseh*, abound in the pages of the Midrash Haggadah. It overflowed into the pages of the Talmud and was also gathered in many collections from olden times.

These tales and legends, these *Ma'asiyyot*, as *Exempla*, formed an essential part of the homiletical discourse on Sabbaths, festivals and other important occasions. The "Lives of the Great" served as the background for the lessons read and the sermons delivered on those specific occasions. The people learned from the lives of the great men how to act in practical life. They were encouraged by the history of the past and they drew conclusions for their own lives, more effective, because of their homeliness and simplicity, than any that oratorical exposition on the part of the preacher or teacher could produce. This practice of weaving legends and parables of old into sermons and homiletical discourses has still survived, and the *Maggid* is the latest exponent of this type of homiletic activity.

This example has been followed by the Church from very early days; and throughout the middle ages, even down to comparatively modern times, many a sermon contained such legends and tales, intended to convey a practical lesson from the life and incidents of the saints and holy men. It is sufficient to mention here the famous collection known as the *Exempla* of Jacques of Vitry.

But these legends and stories led also an independent life. The people liked them for their own sake, and thus collections were made of such stories. Some of them have a moral lesson, drawn from the story, appended at the end, a kind of "moralization," as they are called in the non-Jewish literature; others need not such a moral conclusion, for the story itself is a moral tale and conveys a full lesson to him who reads it.

Broadminded and tolerant as the Jewish spirit is, and recognizing the good and the beautiful wherever found, the Jews did not hesitate to introduce into these collections also stories of non-Jewish origin when they appealed to their poetic inspiration or carried with them similar lessons of a moral and practical character. In such manner they introduced some stories about Alexander the Great, about Roman Emperors and their contemporaries, and in later times, stories of other great men who had come in contact with the Jews for good or for ill, and in which divine providence manifested itself in the protection of the good and in the punishment of the evil. These stories were recounted with glee, whether those who were punished or rewarded were Jews or non-Jews.

The history of the spread of tales from East to West contains an important chapter on the debt which the world owes to the Jews for the prominent part which they took in that dissemination, especially in that of the Indian and Eastern tales in general during the middle ages. Thus the Jews gave and took. There was a constant exchange of the products of the human spirit, of romances and tales, of adages and proverbs.

It is not my intention to follow up the history of these stories here. I must be content with referring in the first place to the introduction to my edition of the *Sefer ha-Ma'asiyyot*, based upon a Ms. discovered by me, containing the largest number of post-biblical tales, and which is probably the oldest collection of this kind.* I have there dealt with all the later collections, of which, however, a few will be mentioned anon when I discuss the sources of the present *Ma'aseh Book*. It suffices therefore to state that there are in existence collections of tales and legends, some taken from the pages of the Talmud and Midrash, others quite independent, all of them practically anonymous. Some have appeared in print from 1516 onwards down to modern times, when many of them were reprinted by Jellinek in his *Bet ha-Midrash*. There are, besides, collections of such tales still in Ms., in public and in private libraries in Oxford, in Paris, and in my own library—which show that the interest in them encouraged men to make and copy such collections. One of them, the Ms. in Oxford, belongs probably to the 12th century.

We have, also, a book in which the stories have been woven together by R. Nissim of Kairuan (10th century), as a book of consolation to his father-in-law for the loss of his son. The book was probably written in Arabic, but has survived in Hebrew form, and has hitherto been considered as one of the oldest collections of this

*The Exempla of the Rabbis*, by Moses Gaster London-Leipzig, 1924.

type, which contain stories and legends also of persons not mentioned in talmudic literature. Of special importance for our purpose is a collection, made by Jacob ibn Habib, of *Ma'asiyyot*, which, as I mentioned before, I would prefer to translate as *Exempla*, taken exclusively from the Talmud, and arranged according to the treatises of that work. It appeared for the first time in Salonica, in the beginning of the 16th century, and was called *'En Ya'akob*. It was then reprinted in Venice in 1546. Thus far the Hebrew collections.

Throughout the ages the Jews have been at least a bilingual nation. They understood Hebrew and spoke at the same time the vernacular, the language of the nations amongst whom they lived; and the number of those who spoke the vernacular among the Jews was always greater than that of those who understood Hebrew well enough to speak or to write. No wonder therefore that we find some of the most important books of the Hebrew literature translated into the language of the people so as to be understood by the masses. To start with, the Bible itself was first translated into Greek and then into other languages, and this happened also in the case of other books, especially those of a popular character, belonging to that wide range of liter-

ature now known as Folklore, the literature of
poetry and fiction.

Many of these tales had also been translated
into the German popular language spoken by
the masses of the Jews, some probably earlier,
some shortly after the Hebrew collections had
appeared in print. Such collections are found
especially in the libraries of Paris and Oxford.
Some are also found among the Mss. of Hamburg
and Munich.

During the 16th century, a large number of
books written in this German popular dialect
were printed in Verona and Basle as well as
in Prague.

Among them there were versions of medieval
romances, like the stories of Arthur and the
Round Table; the so-called Artus Hof; or the
story of Dietrich of Berne, whose combat with
his unrecognized son is probably an echo of an
old Persian tale of a similar character; the story
of Bovo, which is the last redaction of the
English romance of Sir Bevis of Southampton,
and has become the typical title of all such
romantic stories of olden times. This is the origin
of the *Ma'aseh*, now taken to mean an old
grandmother's tale; also a book of animal fables,
the Cow book, had become familiar among the
Jews in such a German translation. Many of

these romances and tales were in rhyme, like
the German and other prototypes. They form
part of the literature of the minstrels, and were
chanted to special tunes well known by the people.
It was the popular literature of the nation, and
was taken over as such by the Jews who dwelt
among them and thence carried further into the
East of Europe, for they were written in the
language understood by the masses, and therefore
enjoyed great popularity.

These productions were, however, not the
starting point of the Judeo-German literature,
by which name I designate all the books written
in the German language in Hebrew characters.
On the contrary, they followed in the wake of
other translations which had been made from
the Hebrew direct. In the first place was the
Bible, in portions and then in its entirety, in
prose and in rhyme. The beginning of this
translation goes father back than any of the
romantic literature. Some of the translations
in rhyme are still in manuscript and are awaiting
publication. Then followed the translation of the
prayers, a large number of which are older than
the time of printing, and among the first to be
printed was the translation of the Jewish historical romance of the destruction of the Temple,
which goes under the name of *Josippon,* a special

version of Joseph Ben Gorion's *Wars of the Jews.*

Almost at the same time there appeared a book of ethical conduct, a book representing the *Musar* type, didactic and moral at the same time, a handbook of the religious and pious life, especially arranged for the benefit of the women. It enjoyed a very great popularity, as is testified by the numerous editions which followed upon one another after the first, which appeared in Prague in 1572. It is ascribed to a certain Moses Henoch and goes under the name of *Brandspiegel* or *Zuchtspiegel* (the mirror of manners and morals). It contains not only maxims of conduct (influenced probably by the famous *Mirror of Kings*, which goes back to the *Secret of Secrets*, ascribed to Aristotle), but also a large number of *Exempla* taken from the talmudic literature. We must record here the fact that an edition of this book appeared in Basle in 1602, printed by Conrad Waldkirch.

As already remarked, the oldest Judeo-German prints appeared in Italy. Prague was almost the second in the order of printing and Basle followed suit. All the books that issued from the presses of Basle were beautifully executed. Characteristic of this literature is further the fact that it is printed in a peculiar cursive Rashi type, somewhat, but not quite, similar to the latter; an

exact copy, no doubt, of the cursive handwriting
of the 15th and 16th centuries. It has been
named *Weiber-Taitsch*, i. e. the German of the
Women, and can easily be distinguished both
from the Rashi and from the square type, whenever they are printed together, e. g. in prayer
books. In modern times, in Poland and in
Russia, the square type has been substituted for
the other, which had held sway for at least three
centuries.

It was thus natural that, after the first necessities had been satisfied by translations from the
Bible of liturgical and historical pieces, books of
moral teaching, the haggadic tales and legends,
should also be taken up and translated.

It must be remembered in this connection that
among the German speaking peoples there cir-
culated about that time a book which enjoyed
great popularity. It was the German version of
the famous collection of ancient tales and
*Exempla* known as *Gesta Romanorum*. The very
title corresponds as closely as possible to the
Hebrew *Ma'aseh* and *Ma'asiyyot*, things done by
some prominent man or woman, or an example
set by great men. It contains short tales and
stories to which, as a rule, a succinct moral or, as
it is called, moralization, is attached. Considering the large number of Mss. and prints in which

that German book has been preserved, it is not
unlikely that it found among Jews also a large
number of readers, just as the other tales and
romantic poems enjoyed a wide popularity among
them, to such an extent that in fact they were
translated, or rather transliterated, into Judeo-
German.

In this case the Jewish literature presented
such a vast material to anyone who wanted to
imitate the German example, that he had no need
to avail himself of that book, but could go to
his own Hebrew literature and provide a book
as rich in stories, as interesting in incidents, as
any other collection, and at the same time give
back to the people its own. He had only to draw
upon the books in existence, especially upon the
above mentioned *'En Ya'akob*, and also upon
some in manuscript, to make a collection far
larger and more interesting to the Jewish public
than any that other literatures could provide.
In fact, some of the tales in the *Gesta* are of
distinctly Jewish origin, and here the Jewish
competitors for popularity could improve upon
those versions, which had been more or less
altered or modified to suit the taste of the
Christian reader. But, on the other hand, they
learned from the *Gesta* to append to the end of
these tales, moral conclusions, that is a kind of

moralization which is often in rhyme. This book, a kind of Jewish *Gesta* or a *Gesta Judaeorum*, was to be the counterpart, the substitute; for the other book, which contained *Ma'asiyyot* of heathen kings and Christian heroes, and thus in the year 1602 a certain Jacob ben Abraham of Mezeritch published a number of rabbinical tales and legends. The book was printed in Basle by Konrad Waldkirch.

The sources are briefly indicated by the editor, in the title page and in the introduction or rather preface printed on the back of the title page in that edition. It will be seen that the author had originally prepared a much larger collection of tales and legends (more than three hundred), but he printed only 254, and allowed the wrong number to stand on the title page, which probably had been printed before the rest of the book had been finished. From the very wording of the title page it is evident that Jacob ben Abraham, by whose orders the book was printed, was probably not the author of the translation of the whole book. He may have compiled it out of the material already in existence, and he may have added some new translations. It was intended to be a powerful competitor of the non-Jewish books which he mentions. Another work which evidently stimulated Jacob ben Abraham to prepare this compilation was, no doubt, the book of moral teaching, the *Brandspiegel*, referred to above. This book contained also a number of tales and *exempla* taken from the talmudic literature and used specifically for inculcating moral lessons. Our author preferred, however, to allow the reader to draw his own conclusions and to apply the lessons to his own life. Moreover his book was to be a book of entertainment purely and simply, yet not without a high moral purpose.

The principal part in this collection is therefore taken up by a number of tales taken directly from the Talmud, or rather from the *'En Ya'akob.* The translator dealt with his material in the same free manner as other popular writers have done before and since. He keeps as close as possible to the original, though he inserts here and there words and sentences intended to explain obscure passages. In accordance with the style of this Judeo-German literature, many technical expressions which had become thoroughly popular have been retained in their Hebrew form, accompanied by a translation into German.

It would be difficult to find the principle which guided him in the compilation of these stories from talmudic sources. The fact that certain treatises have been exhaustively dealt with whilst others have been entirely neglected, points to the same conclusion, namely that originally there may have been in existence in translation a far larger number of such haggadic talmudic tales, perhaps another hundred.

These talmudic stories are not real tales in the strict sense of the word. The element of wonder plays a very small part; we hear very little of supernatural beings; of angels or demons; of fairies, not at all. They are more like the *exempla* or stories which are told of recluses and ascetics in the contemporary Christian literature of the 15th and 16th centuries. The characters appeal to the people as men who were pious and devout, and the ancient Rabbis and sages appear to them always surrounded with a kind of halo as the best and noblest types of the nation. Yet they do not claim supernatural virtue or power to such a degree that their actions could not be imitated by others or that their teaching should be too high to be followed by the masses. They enjoyed no doubt special divine favors obtained by holy living, deep study, nobility of character, and gentleness of heart, which made them worthy to be imitated by the people. They lived in a peculiar atmosphere, appreciated only by those who had been reared in a similar environment of devotion and piety. Hence their attraction especially for the Jews who lived under similar conditions in the East as well as in the West, and more particularly for those who felt that their Bible and their Talmud contained in every detail teachings superior to any other literature in the world. They are a true picture of that inner spiritual life of the Jewish middle classes who found pleasure and spiritual comfort in the lives and the doings of the sages of old.

Of a different type is another group of stories which the compiler added to the rabbinic tales, and which are of a local origin. It is the cycle of legends which originated in the German towns along the Rhine, viz. Speyer, Worms, Regensburg, and Cologne. The central figures are the great masters of talmudic learning who flourished in those towns. Thus we have a cycle of legends concerning Rabbi Samuel the Hasid, or the Pious, which is followed by another about his son, Rabbi Judah the Hasid, or the Pious. Stories are told of Rashi, of R. Jehiel of Paris, and incidentally also a story about Maimonides, probably because in that story the rabbi from Germany plays an equally important role. Here we are transported into a totally different world. It is the atmosphere of the middle ages with its romantic tales, and its love of fantastic incidents.

The heroes have assumed a totally different character, and the miraculous adventures that occur are just as extraordinarily fantastic as those found in the romances of medieval chivalry and adventure. Among them we have also the story of Amram (242), closely connected with one of the churches of Mayence; quite in the style of one of the stories of the Golden Legends of Jacobus a Voragine. The marvelous and unexpected plays an important role. These comprise practically Nos. 158–189. While the source for the former group has been mostly the *'En Ya'akob* and the *Yalkut*, here no doubt the primary source must have been the *Ma'aseh Adonai* and *Ma'aseh Nissim* ascribed to Shamash Yuzpa.

This cycle is followed by another set of tales mostly of an anonymous character. These have been taken from small collections of tales, such as the *Hibbur Ma'asiyyot*, edited by ben Attar, or from other haggadic stories like the *Midrash of the Decalogue*, or the exemplifications of the Ten Commandments, and the *Parables of Solomon*. It is probably not sheer coincidence that every one of these books had been printed in Venice in the first half of the 16th century, which in any case gives us a definite indication as to the probable date when the Judeo-German translation of the bulk of the book could have been made.

The third part, beginning with No. 190, contains additional stories from the above mentioned collections of Midrashim, a few stray ones from the Talmud, and possibly also one or two from the *Musar Book*, and two or three from the *Kaftor va-Ferah* of Jacob Luzzatto, printed in Basle in 1580.

Not a few, however, are popular tales, or are derived from sources which have not yet been completely traced. It is not unlikely that the compiler may have found some in as yet unpublished Hebrew Mss. Among other books which he utilized was the work of Judah the Pious, known as the *Sefer Hasidim*, of which an edition appeared in Basle in 1581, the very place where the 1602 edition of the *Ma'aseh Book* appeared. It is therefore almost certain that the compilation of the book could not have taken place, at any rate in the form in which it appeared in print, earlier than 1581. It was between that date and 1602 that the collection of the material must have been made, and the translation of some parts of the whole, as well as the printing, belongs to that same time.

This is unquestionably the first edition. The arguments which have been adduced in favor of an edition prior to this are far from convincing. On the contrary, everything points to the fact that there was no other edition. In the first place there is no allusion on the title page to any other edition. As a rule when a second edition is made the author tries to praise his work and show the superiority over the previous one. Here no trace of it is found. It reads as a direct invitation to the people to get hold of this book which, as is mentioned in the preface, is to be substituted for other books of a similar kind but not of Jewish origin. Then there is a still more definite proof. Among the sources which are used there is, in the first place, the *Sefer Hasidim* which was printed in Basle in 1581. Then the book of Luzzatto, *Kaftor va-Ferah*, printed also in Basle in 1580 for the first time. From these two the author has taken some stories and chapters. No previous edition exists of Luzzatto's work and, therefore, no one could have printed a book of precisely the same character and with the same contents previous to that publication. Some time must elapse before a Hebrew book is translated and printed, and the time between 1580 and 1602 is far too short for anyone, not only to do the work but also to print it. Moreover no other edition can have appeared in between for the simple reason that books printed in

Judeo-German at that time were not easily reprinted. They had first to find their public, and in the case of the *Ma'aseh Book* it has taken just 100 years before a new edition appeared. If in any Ms. of an uncertain date a reference is made to a *Ma'aseh Book* (cf. *Serapeum*, 1864, 67 sq.), in the first place the date mentioned by Steinschneider, 1580, is given as doubtful, and secondly it need not refer to any printed book at all.

The language of the *Ma'aseh Book* is that formerly spoken by the Jews along the Rhine and in Switzerland, a peculiar dialect which had become the literary language of all the Judeo-German books; and as this became the literature of the women par excellence, the type as well as the language was called *Weiber Taitsch*, i. e. the German of the Women.

The success of the book was very great and, like the *Brandspiegel*, it became a true household book. This was due to the popular style in which it was written and the moral and poetical value of the pieces that it contained. Although the author adhered literally to the wording of the original, yet he took some liberty in rounding off the story, adding some details here and there, making the dialogues more dramatic, and giving to the whole that homely touch which characterizes all popular literature. There is no stiffness or rigidity, and therefore the book appealed to those readers for whom it was intended. Lest any one be tempted to glorify unduly the *Ma'aseh Book*, as a piece of Yiddish literature, it is necessary to remind him that it is in no sense original, every one of its stories being a translation of a Hebrew original, though the sources of a few of them still remain unknown.

It is difficult to trace the whole history of the book. It is not unlikely that the first edition has been thumbed out of existence. This may also have been the fate of other editions of the 17th century, of which hitherto no trace has been found. It may be that the later editions have caused the total disappearance of the earlier one. Only three copies are so far known to exist of the first edition. One is in the British Museum, one in the Buxtorf collection at Basle, a third is in the Zurich library, others I have not yet been able to trace.

But another edition appeared in Amsterdam in 1701, where already changes and alterations had been introduced. The title page has been altered and the preface of the first edition, as well as the index or table of contents at the end, has been omitted.

No sooner were these editions published than

a kind of rival collection made its appearance in Frankfort on the Main in 1703. The difference between this new *Ma'aseh Book* and the old one consists in the insertion at the beginning of a number of stories taken from the Zohar and other cabalistic writings not used by the compiler of the first publication, also from *Shebet Yehudah, Yuhasin, Shalshelet ha-Kabbalah, Yalkut, Zohar Hadash, Noblot Hokmah, 'Emek ha-Melek.*

After these tales the whole of the old *Ma'aseh Book* was incorporated verbatim without a word to indicate this wholesale appropriation of another man's work, a new title page was substituted for the old one and a short preface of the first was omitted. The similarity of these two publications has introduced a certain confusion in the history of the book. It is sufficient, however, to state that the difference between the two editions consists only in the few additional stories placed at the head. The old edition, however, was reprinted again in Amsterdam in 1723, but in order to avoid confusion or to prevent the appearance of its being a direct copy of the 1701 and 1703 editions, the title was altered to *Allerlei Geschichte.*

The Basle edition has in fact 257 stories, though, on account of errors in the numbers (some numbers being omitted and others re-

peated), it happens that the last story is numbered
255 instead of 257. The stories in this edition
correspond almost altogether to those in the
Amsterdam edition of 1723, though here and
there the order is different.*

There is also an edition of the *Ma'aseh Book*,
printed in Homburg in 1727. Like the Frankfort
edition of 1703 it contains 12 additional stories,
preceding No. 1 of the Basle edition. In Wilmers-
dorf there appeared another edition, which is a
reprint of the Amsterdam edition, and in Rödelheim, in 1753, the Frankfort edition was again
reprinted.

In later times abstracts of this book were
made under the title *Sippure ha-Pelaot*, which
were printed in Lemberg in 1851, and even as
late as 1909 in Lublin. The latter, which does
not indicate its immediate source, is nothing
else but a collection of a few stories taken from
the old *Ma'aseh Book*. Finally some of the
stories have become Yiddish Chap-Books.

A slight difference has, however, crept into
these various editions. If the book was to retain
its hold upon the reader, the older forms of the
language had to be modified. All the archaic
words had to be eliminated and the style slightly

---

* See, however, Appendix, p. 659.

altered so as to suit the changed form of the language. In fact it had to undergo the process of constant remodeling and renewing, which is a characteristic and outstanding feature of the genuine popular literature. It is in this literature that one realizes to what extent a new editor is often an author. No such respect is shown to the original as is expected of a modern editor; the editors treated the new edition as if it were their own production. They would occasionally omit and alter phrases, retaining only the substance.

To the student of German philology, and of the Judeo-German especially, a minute comparison of these various editions would yield a very remarkable result. But even so the book is not free from very old forms and quaint expressions. It throws a valuable light upon the language in the middle ages and, by the contents of these tales, it gives us an insight also into the spiritual longings of those times. The readers felt a deep satisfaction and a moral elevation in the examples set by the great men of old. They found in these stories the ideal of learning, the desire of becoming a master of the law, to be wise and courageous, to show examples of endurance and fortitude, of purity of action, and nobility of thought.

In 1612, Prof. Helvicus of Giessen printed in

that town a number of these tales from the *Ma'aseh Book*, in German transcript, omitting repetitions and shortening the dialogues. Eisenmenger borrowed from it the story of Amram. In modern times it became the source of some of the rhymed tales in Tendlau's collection, *Sagen und Legenden jüdischer Vorzeit*, Frankfort on Main, 1873; and Grünbaum in his *Jüdisch-Deutsche Chrestomathie*, Leipzig, 1882, pp. 385–459, published in Latin type a number of stories from the *Ma'aseh Book*, mostly from the Rödelheim edition. To these Reinhold Köhler added comparative notes, tracing parallels to a number of them in the other literatures of the world. Steinschneider's articles in *Serapeum*, 1864, 66ff. and 1866, 1ff. are very important. More recently there appeared a transliteration in German characters of all but four of the stories: *Allerlei Geschichten, Maasse-Buch*, bearbeitet von Bertha Pappenheim, Frankfort on Main, 1929.

The present translation is based on the Amsterdam edition of 1723, which is identical with that of 1701, and, with the exceptions noted above and some dialectal variations, with the edition of 1602. All these books are extremely rare, and very few complete copies of any of them are known. The Amsterdam edition forms an exception in the matter of completeness. The translation has been made to follow closely the Judeo-German text. It is almost literal in as much as it has been my desire to preserve as far as possible the quaintness of the original, the peculiarities of diction, the constant changes of tenses and moods, and all the peculiar characteristics which made this book one of foremost importance in the entire Judeo-German literature. Occasionally, though very rarely, I toned down some of the crudities inherent in popular texts. Our aesthetic standard differs somewhat from the outspokenness of the middle ages, but this change has been ventured by me on very rare occasions. In one instance the story is unquestionably incomplete. Evidently the author did not have the full story in the manuscript from which he took it. I have ventured to complete it from a Ms. in my possession.

The author indicates the sources very vaguely and sometimes erroneously, and these indications are practically restricted to the stories taken from the Talmud, i. e. about less than half. To the talmudic references I added the folios; and, as far as I have been able to trace them, I have also briefly indicated the immediate sources of the other stories. To some of them I have briefly added references to parallels in other literatures. I have limited myself to the briefest possible indications. It would have carried me far beyond the scope of this publication had I undertaken here a comparative study, or endeavored to give full parallels in the literature of the world to every story and incident found in this collection. But by references to my edition of the *Exempla* a complete parallel literature can be found. This is to be primarily a popular book, and with that aim in view I only wanted to make it a little more serviceable by pointing out briefly the sources whence these stories have been taken.

I wish to thank the Jewish Publication Society of America, which has honored me by the invitation to prepare this translation for its readers.

May it find in its new garb the same sympathetic reception among young and old, and above all among the womanhood of Israel, that has been accorded to the original for close upon three centuries.

## 1. A Scholar Who Died Young

Once upon a time there lived a scholar who did nothing all his life but study from morning to evening, and then died very young. His wife took his *tallit* and *tefillin* and went to the college to see the rabbis. She said to them: "It is written in the holy Torah, 'This is thy life and the length of thy days' (Deut. 30.20), i. e. the Torah is thy life and prolongs thy days. Now, my husband did nothing but study day and night. Why then did he die so young?" There was none in the college who could give her an answer. In sooth they did not know the reason why he died so young. Not long afterwards a scholar came to her on a visit, and she told him the same story. He asked her certain questions, to which she replied most indignantly that there could have been no grounds of suspicion in her husband's behavior. And yet, when pressed with questions she admitted that in his relations with her he had transgressed certain limits laid down by the Law. When the scholar heard this, he said: "Blessed be He who has taken him away so young, for he should have known that the

1

minutest prescriptions of the Law on such matters ought to have been observed by a man who
had devoted his life to the study of the Torah."*

## 2. MOSES RECEIVING THE LAW

Rabbi Joshua son of Levi said: After God,
blessed be He, had given the Law to Moses, and
Moses had come down from heaven, Satan said:
"Lord of the universe, where hast Thou put the
Torah? To whom hast Thou given it?" The
Lord replied, "I have given it to the Earth."
So Satan went to the Earth and said, "Where
hast thou put the Torah which the Lord, blessed
be He, has given thee?" The Earth replied:
" 'God understandeth the way thereof' (Job 28.
23). This means that the Lord, blessed be He,
knows everything. But I have not the Torah."
Then Satan went to the Sea and said, "Oh Sea,
where hast thou put the Torah which the Lord,
blessed be He, has given thee?" The Sea
replied, " 'The Torah is not with me' " (ibid.
v. 14). Then Satan went to the uttermost depth
of the earth and said, "Where hast thou put the
Torah which the Lord, blessed be He, has given

*In this translation some of the details have been omitted
or toned down for esthetic reasons.

thee?" The abyss of the earth replied, " 'It is not in me' " (ibid.). So Satan went all over the earth searching for the Torah, for the Lord had told him that He had given it to the earth. Then Satan went to the dead and the lost and asked them: "Where have you put the Torah which the Lord has given you?" And they replied, "Verily we have heard of it with our ears, but we know nothing more" (cf. Ps. 54.2). Then Satan came again before the Lord, blessed be He, and said, "Lord of the universe, I have searched the whole earth, but I have not found the Torah." Then the Lord said unto him, "Go to Moses, the son of Amram, to whom I have given it." Then Satan went to our master Moses and said, "Moses, where hast thou put the Torah which the Lord has given thee?" And Moses replied, "How dost thou come to ask me about the Torah? Who am I and what am I that the Lord should give me the Torah?" When the Lord, blessed be He, heard that Moses would not admit that he had received the Torah, He said, "Thou art a liar. Why dost thou deny that I have given thee the Torah?" And Moses replied, "Lord of the universe, the Torah is a desirable object, it filleth with joy him who is engaged in studying it. Thou rejoicest over it and studiest it Thyself every day. How then can I boast and

say that I have received the Torah? It is not
seemly for a man to boast of anything, even
though he has reason to do so. On the contrary,
it is better that he should be humble." And
the Lord said, "Since thou humblest thyself, and
dost not wish to claim the honor of having
received the Torah, it shall, as a reward, be
called by thy name." This is why it is written,
"Remember the Law of Moses, My servant, and
keep the Law of Moses" (Mal. 3.22).

### 3. The Angels Jealous of Moses

Rabbi Joshua, son of Levi, says that at the
time when Moses went up to heaven to receive
the Law, which the Lord, blessed be He, was
giving him, the angels said, "Lord of the universe, what is a mortal man doing here in the
heavens amongst us?" And the Lord replied,
"He has come to receive the Torah." Then the
angels said, "Wilt Thou hand over to man that
hidden jewel which Thou hast treasured up with
Thee during 974 generations, before Thou hadst
created the world? What is man whom Thou hast
created? 'Give Thy beauty to the heavens'
(Ps. 8.2). Leave the Torah here and do not give
it to man." Then God said, "Moses, answer the
angels concerning that which they have spoken

to Me." And Moses replied, "Lord of the universe, I would fain answer them, but I fear lest they burn me up with the breath of their mouths." Then God said, "Moses take hold of the throne of glory and answer their speech." And when our master Moses heard this, he began to speak, and said, "Lord of the universe, what is written in that Torah which Thou intendest to give to me? 'I am the Lord thy God who brought thee out of the land of Egypt' (Ex. 20.2). O angels, have you gone down into Egypt? Have you served Pharaoh? Then why should the Lord, blessed be He, give you the Torah? Again, what else is written in this Torah? Is it not written, 'Thou shalt have no other gods before Me' (ibid. v. 3)? Are you living among heathens that you should serve other gods? It is further written therein, 'Remember the Sabbath day, to keep it holy' (ibid. v. 8), which means, rest on that day. Are you working that you should have to be commanded to rest? Furthermore, it is written therein, 'Thou shalt not take a false oath' (cf. ibid. v. 7). Are you engaged in business that you should be commanded not to take a false oath? Furthermore, 'Honour thy father and thy mother' (ibid. v. 12). Have you a father and a mother that you should be commanded to honor them? 'Thou shalt not murder, thou shalt not

commit adultery, thou shalt not steal' (ibid.
v. 13).   Is there envy and hatred among you
that you should be commanded not to do these
things?  Of what good, therefore, is the Torah to
you?"  When the angels heard this, they became
friendly to Moses and every one of the angels
taught him something, even the angel of death.

### 4. ISAAC THE DEFENDER OF ISRAEL

Rabbi Samuel, son of Nahamani, said in the
name of Rabbi Johanan: What is the meaning
of the verse, "For Thou art our father; For
Abraham knoweth us not, and Israel doth not
acknowledge us"? (Is. 63.16). Thou Isaac, art our
father.  How so?  I will explain.  In later times
when Israel will commit sins, God will say to
Abraham, "Abraham, thy children have sinned."
And Abraham will reply, "Let them be blotted
out for the sake of Thy name," and will not pray
for forgiveness of the sins of Israel.  Then the
Lord, blessed be He, will say, "I will go to Jacob
and hear what he will say, for Jacob is sure to
have compassion on Israel, since he had much
trouble in his lifetime in bringing up his children."
So He will say to Jacob, "Thy children Israel
have sinned," and Jacob will reply, "Let them be
blotted out for the sake of Thy holy name," and

he also will not pray for the forgiveness of the sins of Israel. Then the Lord, blessed be He, will say, "Old men have no sense (this refers to Abraham, who is called an old man); and children have no counsel" (this refers to Jacob, who was the youngest of the patriarchs), meaning that God did not obtain from these two a satisfactory answer on behalf of Israel. Then the Lord will say, "I will go to Isaac and hear what he will reply." Then he will say, "Isaac, thy children have sinned." And Isaac will reply, "O Lord of the universe, are they only *my* children? Are they not also *Thy* children? Why then dost Thou call them *my* children? At the time when they received the Torah and said, 'We will do and obey' (Ex. 24.7), Thou didst call them, 'Israel, My son, My first born' (ibid. 4.22). But now, when they have sinned, Thou callest them *my* children and not *Thy* children. Moreover, how many are the days of man in which he can sin in this world? Threescore years and ten, and, if he live long, fourscore. Take off twenty years during which a man is not responsible for his actions, for a man under twenty is not commanded to fulfill all his duties. Take off, therefore, twenty years, and there remain only fifty. Then take off twenty-five years more, the time which one spends in sleeping and during which

one does not sin. Only twenty-five years remain.
Take off twelve and a half years which he spends
in praying and eating and in all the natural
functions, and there remain only twelve and a
half years. Now, if Thou art willing to take these
upon Thyself and forgive them, it is well. But
if Thou art not willing to take them upon
Thyself, then let us divide. Thou take half and
I will take half, and we shall thus free Israel
from their sins. But If Thou wishest me to
take them all upon myself, then remember that
I have offered myself entirely as a sacrifice to
Thee upon the altar, and I will take them over."
When the children of Israel heard all this, they
said, "Isaac, thou art our father." Then Isaac
replied, "O children of Israel, praise ye the Lord,
blessed be He, and point to Him with your eyes."
They then lifted up their eyes to Heaven and
said, "Thou art our Father, Thou hast redeemed
us from everlasting. Amen" (cf. Is. 63.16).

## 5. Why the Sabbath Meal Tastes So Good

Once upon a time the Emperor asked Rabbi
Joshua, the son of Hananiah, "Dear friend, tell
me, why does Sabbath food taste so pleasant and
so much better than the food you prepare during
the week?" Rabbi Joshua replied, "My Lord

Emperor, I will tell you the truth. We have a root called Sabbath which we put into our food and which makes it taste so pleasant." Then the Emperor said, "Friend, give me some of that root; I will put it into my food so that it may also have a good taste." Then Rabbi Joshua answered and said, "Lord Emperor, even if I were to give it to you it would not help you, for only he who observes the Sabbath can taste the root. For him who does not observe the Sabbath the root is tasteless. Therefore, Lord Emperor, I cannot give it to you." And so he put him off in regard to the Sabbath.

## 6. OBSERVANCE OF THE SABBATH REWARDED

Once upon a time there lived a man who was called Joseph Mokir Shabbat (he who honors the Sabbath), because he purchased whatever he could obtain in honor of the Sabbath. Nothing was too dear where the Sabbath was concerned. As soon as anything good was to be found at the market, he was sure to be there to buy it. No big fish was too dear for him to purchase if it was available. Now this Joseph had a very rich neighbor who always mocked and laughed at him, saying, "What good does it do you that you honor the Sabbath so much? You have not become richer through it, whereas I who do not honor the Sabbath am richer than you." But the good Joseph paid no heed to this and trusted to the Lord, blessed be He, to requite him. Now there were some astrologers in the town who said to the rich man, "Dear friend, what does it benefit you that you are so rich if you will not even obtain good fish for your money? We have read in the stars that your whole property will one day come into the hand of Joseph who, at any rate, enjoys a good meal for his money." When the rich man heard the words of the astrologers, he went and sold all his property and bought instead precious stones and pearls, of which he made a long string which he tied round his headgear, and then decided to leave for another country. Thus he thought to take away all the money which might go to Joseph. But when he was on the sea, there arose a heavy gale which nearly sank the ship. It blew his headgear from his head and carried it into the sea. A huge fish came along and swallowed it. Thus the rich man became very poor.

It so happened that one day, on a Friday, a large fish was caught and brought into the market. Many men bargained for it but found it too dear, and went away without buying it. And they said that no one would buy such a fish except Joseph Mokir Shabbat, for he alone bought big fish; none were ever too dear for him. In the meantime the good Joseph came to the market and wanted to buy his usual fish for the Sabbath. When he saw the big fish, he was very happy that he could obtain such a big and beautiful fish for the Sabbath. And he said to himself, "This fish will not be too dear for me even if I have to pay 100 florins for it." Then he asked the price and found it very high, but nevertheless he came to terms with the man and bought it, and with great joy he carried it home. When the fish was opened, the string of pearls which the rich man had lost was found inside. Thus was fulfilled the prophecy of the astrologers that the money of the rich man would belong to Joseph Mokir Shabbat. He rejoiced very much and became a rich man, for the string was worth a kingdom. There came an old man and said to Joseph, "To him who lends to the Sabbath, the Sabbath repays many times." That means, the Lord, blessed be He, rewards him who honors the Sabbath. Amen.

### 7. HONOR OF THE SABBATH REWARDED

Rabbi Hiyya told the following story: "Once upon a time I spent a night in Sepphoris at a butcher's. (Others say it was in Laodicea.)

They brought him a gold table, which was
carried by sixteen people, and sixteen silver
chains were hanging from the table. Upon the
table were many silver plates and silver spoons.
All the utensils on the table were made of pure
silver, and upon it were also many good dishes
of fine fruit. No sooner had they brought the
table before the master, than he began to praise
the Lord, blessed be He, saying, 'The earth and
all that is upon it belongs to God' (cf. Ps. 24.1).
And when they took the table away again, he
praised God and said, 'The heavens belong to the
Lord, and the earth He has given to the children
of man' (ib. 115.16). Then I asked him, 'How
have you become so rich, what good have you
done in your lifetime?' Then the master of the
house said, 'I will tell you. I was formerly a
butcher. Whenever I had a fit beast I said that
I would keep it for the Sabbath, so that I should
have a good piece of meat for the holy day.
And it is on account of this that the Lord,
blessed be He, has given me wealth, for I paid
honor to the Sabbath.' Then I said, 'Praised be
the Lord who has granted you all this wealth,
and may you be found worthy to remain a rich
man all your life.' "

## 8. Sabbath Observance Rewarded

Once upon a time it happened that a pious man (*ḥasid*) had a beautiful garden behind his house. One day he found that a gap was made in the wall of the garden and he wanted to mend it; but he remembered that it was the Sabbath and said, "If I repair the hole, I will have to break the Sabbath." Thinking thus he left it open, for he would not break the Sabbath. Then a miracle happened to him, for a tree grew exactly over the spot where the gap had been made, and thus it was filled. That tree was a berry bush. It was a very big tree and spread its branches very wide. It bore three kinds of fruit and supported the pious man and his family. This the Lord, blessed be He, did for him because he refrained from violating the Sabbath and did not repair the gap, but trusted that the Lord would protect the garden though the gap was not filled up. The moral is that if a man keeps the Sabbath properly, the Lord also watches over him.

## 9. Repent One Day before Thy Death

Rabbi Eliezer said, "Repent on the day before thy death." Thereupon his pupils asked, "How does one know on what day he will die?" And

Rabbi Eliezer replied, "If that be so, the more reason for every man to repent to-day, lest he die tomorrow. For no man is sure, even for one hour, of the time of his death." From this it follows that every man should always live in repentance. King Solomon also says: "Let thy garments be always white" (Eccl. 9.8). He means that the shroud should be always kept clean and ready, so that when the Lord, blessed be He, calls a man to die, he may be ready with repentance and good deeds. Concerning this Rabbi Johanan said, "This is to be compared with the parable of a king who invites his servants to a great feast, but does not tell them the day on which it will take place. The wise among them wash and dress in their best clothes and sit at the entrance of the palace before the king. For they know there is nothing wanting in the king's house to prevent the feast being ready at any time when the king should call them to dine. Therefore, they say, we must be prepared to appear before the king as soon as he sends for us. The foolish among the servants of the king go on with their work, thinking that such a feast cannot be quickly prepared since so many things are required, and that therefore they will have plenty of time to put on their clothes. Suddenly the king sends for his servants to come to the dinner, the feast being ready. The wise servants who have prepared themselves come at once to the king, dressed in their beautiful clothes. The fools, however, leave their work hurriedly and come in their dirty clothes before the king. Then the king rejoices with his wise servants, who have prepared themselves for the feast, although they did not know when the feast would take place, and is angry with the fools, who did not prepare themselves and have on their soiled clothes. "The wise among my servants," he says, "may come and sit at the table and eat and drink and be merry, but the fools must stand and look on while the others are eating and drinking, but must neither eat nor drink, because they did not prepare themselves." That is why King Solomon says, "Keep thyself wisely ready with thy white garments, so that when the Lord calls thee in death thou shalt be prepared with thy repentance, and do not act like the fools." He means thereby the wicked among the Israelites, who say, "Why should we repent and prepare ourselves with white garments?  Who knows when our death will take place?  We shall have time enough in which to repent and shall be able to cleanse ourselves and our garments."  But suddenly the Lord orders their death before they have repented, whereas the pious, who are ready with their repentance, can appear at once before the Lord, blessed be He, with their white garments. But these wicked ones appear only with their evil deeds. -Then the Lord rejoices with the pious, who appear before Him in a state of repentance and in white garments, and is angry with the wicked, who appear before Him with evil deeds, and He says, "You who have prepared yourselves may now partake of the feast which I am preparing for the pious. But you, the wicked ones, who have not prepared yourselves, shall not partake of the feast, but shall look on while the others eat and drink." That is why the rabbis say, "Repent one day before thy death," for no man is sure of the day of his death, and he should therefore repent to-day lest he die tomorrow, and repent again tomorrow lest he die the day after, and thus he will repent every day and will live a pious life, so that when he is called in death by the Lord, blessed be He, he is ready and prepared through good deeds to partake of the feast together with the other pious ones.

### 10. The Poor Widower Who Suckled His Infant with His Own Breasts

Once upon a time a man lost his wife, who left behind her a suckling baby. The man was so poor that he could not afford to hire a nurse for the child. But a miracle happened to him, and his breasts grew so large that he was able to feed his child like a nurse. Concerning this Rabbi Joseph said, "Come and see what a good man he must have been that the Lord, blessed be He, should have performed such a miracle for him." Abbaye said, "What a bad man he must have been that for his sake the order of creation had to be changed." Rabbi Judah said, "Come and see how many difficult tasks God must perform for man before He provides his food for him, seeing that God changed the order of creation for his sake and made it possible for him to suckle the child. For the Lord could have created food for the baby, and yet He performed a miracle so that the man himself could feed the child." For we find that God performs many miracles for the protection of man but does not create his food for him. For we do not find that the Lord, blessed be He, creates corn in the houses of the pious.

## 11. PIETY AND MODESTY

There was a man whose wife had no finger on her hand, but he had not noticed it until she died. Rabbi Joseph said, "What a modest woman she must have been if her husband did not notice in her lifetime the absence of her finger." Rabbi Ḥiyya then said to Rabbi Joseph, "Nay, this is no sign that the woman was specially modest, for every woman would take care to cover herself, much more so this one, but what great piety must the man have possessed if during her lifetime he never noticed anything of the sort."

## 12. The Humility of Hillel

Every man should be as meek as Hillel, and not quick to anger like Shammai. Once it came to pass that two men made a wager, the one saying that he would make Hillel angry and the other replying that it could not be done. The stake was 400 shillings. This happened on the eve of Sabbath when Hillel was washing his hair in honor of the day. The man who had laid the wager that he would make Hillel angry came to the door of Hillel's house and knocked, calling out, "Where is Hillel?" When Hillel heard it, he covered himself with his mantle and went to meet the man and said, "Dear son, what is your wish?" Then the man said, "Dear Rabbi, I want to ask a question." Then Hillel said, "My son, ask what you desire." Whereupon the man replied, "Dear Rabbi, why are the people of

Babylon round-headed?" Hillel replied, "My son, you have asked a difficult question. I will tell you. There are no wise men among the Babylonians, therefore they have heads in the shape of a ball." The man went away and said, "You have given a very proper answer to my question." A little while later he went again to Hillel's door and knocking, called out, "Where is Hillel?" The good Hillel again put on his mantle, went to meet him and said to him, "My son, what is your desire?" The man said, "Dear Rabbi, I wish to ask you a question." Hillel said, "My son, ask what you will." Then he said, "Dear Rabbi, why have the people of Tadmor (Palmyra) round eyes?" Hillel replied, "My son, you have asked a difficult question, I will tell you. They live in a sandy country and if they had eyes with two corners like ours, they could not remove the sand which the wind blows into their eyes and would lose their sight." Then the man said, "You have given me a very excellent answer to this question, also." And he went on his way. After a little while he came back again, thinking he would anger Hillel by calling him so often from the bath. Again he cried, "Where is Hillel, where is Hillel?" When Hillel heard that he was being called again, he put on his mantle and went out and said, "My son, what do you wish of me?" The man said, "Dear Rabbi, I want to ask you an important question." And Hillel replied, "Dear son, ask whatever question you like." Then he said, "Dear Rabbi, tell me why the Phrygians (Afriki) have broad feet?" Hillel replied, "You have asked me a difficult question. They live in moors and swamps; and they have broad soles on their feet so that they can walk about more easily, for if they had narrow feet they would sink in the swamps, but their broad feet enable them to walk better." Then the man said, "Dear Rabbi, I have still many more questions to ask, but I am afraid you will grow angry." Then the good Hillel put on his mantle and sitting down, said to the man, "My son, ask what you like, and I will answer as best I can." So he said, "Are you the Hillel whom they call the prince in Israel?" Hillel said, "Yes." Then the man said again, "May there not be many like you in Israel." Then Hillel said, "Why?" And the man replied, "I laid a wager of 400 shillings about you and you have caused me to lose them, as I could not make you angry." Then Hillel said to him, "My son, be warned in time and do not wager. Know that Hillel is well worth the 400 shillings which you have lost because of him; and you may wager another 100 florins, but you will not anger him." And the man went his way.

### 13. Hillel, Shammai, the Heathen and the Oral Law

Once upon a time a heathen came to Shammai and said to him, "How many Laws (*Torot*) have you, Jews?" and Shammai replied, "We have only two. One which has been given to us in writing and another which has been given to us by word of mouth." The heathen replied, "I believe in the written law and in what is recorded therein, but I do not believe in that which has been handed down as oral, nor in what is contained therein. Now accept me as a proselyte on condition that you teach me the written law." Then Shammai shouted at him and told him angrily to go away. The heathen went from Shammai to Hillel and asked him the same question as he had asked Shammai. Hillel accepted him as a proselyte and began to teach him. The first day he taught him *alef*, *bet*, *gimmel*, *dalet*. And the heathen repeated after Hillel exactly as he had told him. The next day Hillel taught him again and turned the names around and said, *dalet*, *gimmel*, *bet*, *alef*. Then the heathen said to Hillel, "Dear Rabbi, yesterday you taught me differently." Then Hillel said to him, "Just as you rely upon my word, so you must rely on the Law, which is also handed down by word of mouth, and on everything that is contained therein."

### 14. HILLEL, SHAMMAI AND THE HEATHEN WHO WANTED TO BE TAUGHT THE WHOLE TORAH WHILE STANDING ON ONE FOOT

Once upon a time a heathen came to Shammai and said to him, "I should like to become a Jew if you will teach me the whole of the Law whilst I am standing on one leg." When he heard this, Shammai took a measuring rod used by builders and drove him away with it. The heathen left Shammai and went to Hillel, and asked him whether he would accept him as a proselyte, and whether he would teach him the whole Torah while he was standing on one leg. Hillel accepted him and said, "Yes, I will teach you the whole Torah while you are standing on one leg." Then he said to the heathen, "Keep this commandment, 'Do not unto thy neighbor what thou wouldst not like to have done to thyself.' This is the fundamental principle of the law. All the

rest is a commentary upon it.   Now go and
study it." Thus Hillel taught him the whole
Torah while he was standing on one leg.

### 15. Hillel, Shammai and the Heathen Who Wanted to Become a High Priest

Once upon a time a heathen, passing behind
the *bet ha-midrash* (school), heard the children
being taught the verse of the Bible, "And these
are the garments which they shall make: a
breastplate, and an ephod . . ." (Ex. 28.4),
which the high priest is to put on when performing services in the temple, and so on with the
other vestments required for the high priest.
The heathen went into the *bet ha-midrash* and
asked the rabbi, "Who is to wear those garments
concerning which you have just taught your
children?"   The rabbi replied, "This refers to
the high priest of the Israelites when he is
performing the service before our God in the
temple."   Then the heathen bethought himself
and said, "I will also become a Jew, perchance
I shall also be able to serve in the temple and be
dressed in such glorious vestments as those worn
by the priest among the Jews."   So he went to
Shammai and said, "Make me a Jew so that I
may also become a high priest and be clothed in

such glorious garments as the high priest wears."
Shammai drove him away with the measuring
rod which he kept in his hand. Thereupon the
heathen left Shammai, went to Hillel, and spoke
to him as he had spoken to Shammai. Hillel
accepted him and said, "My son, you know
without doubt that no man is appointed a king
unless he has first been taught how to conduct
himself in his office. Now you desire to become a
high priest, but how can I make you one unless
you know first how a priest must conduct
himself? Go and learn all the rules of the priesthood and then come back to me, and I will
make you a high priest." So he went and studied
the laws pertaining to the high priest. When he
came to the verse in the Bible, "And the stranger
that draweth nigh shall be put to death" (Num.
1.51), he asked his teacher, "To whom does this
verse refer?" Hillel replied: "It refers to anyone
who is not born of the seed of Aaron. If such a
one draws near to the temple, he must die; and
even if he had been King David himself, peace be
upon him, he would have been put to death if
he had drawn near to the temple." When the
proselyte heard this, he thought: "Israel is called
a holy nation; God called them, 'My son, My
first born' (Ex. 4.22), yet no Israelite dare draw
near to the sanctuary, how much less an ordinary

heathen who has come only with his knapsack and his staff! He surely cannot become a priest." Then he went to Shammai again and said, "Why did you not tell me that the Bible forbids me to become a priest? I should then have known it myself and would not have desired it." Then he went to Hillel and said, "O Hillel, most modest of men, may the blessings of the Lord, blessed be He, rest upon your head because you have accepted me as a proselyte and have brought me under the wings of the Shekinah." Not long afterwards these three proselytes met and said, "The hot anger of Shammai nearly caused us to lose the bliss of the world to come, whilst the meekness of Hillel has caused us to win the glory of the other world."

## 16. THE STORY OF R. SIMEON BEN YOHAI

Rabbi Judah, Rabbi Jose and Rabbi Simeon, son of Yohai, were sitting together, and with them was a man called Judah, the son of the Proselytes (or Judah ben Gerim). Rabbi Judah commenced speaking and said, "How beautiful are the works made by the heathen! They build market places where one can buy cheaply. They build bridges over the water so that one may cross. They make bathhouses where one may wash and bathe." Rabbi Jose sat silent. Then Rabbi Simeon, son of Yohai, replied and said, "Whatever the heathen make they make for their own pleasure and comfort. They make market places and streets to put prostitutes there. They build bridges over the water for the purpose of levying toll. They make bath-houses to delight their bodies." Judah, son of the Proselytes, went home and related to his father and mother all that had been said. And the report of it spread until it reached the king. The king said, "I hear that Judah has praised our work, therefore he shall also be honored and exalted. Rabbi Jose, who sat silent, shall go into exile. Rabbi Simeon ben Yohai, who has reviled our work, shall be put to death." As soon as Rabbi Simeon heard of this, he took his son with him and hid in the *bet ha-midrash*, where his wife came every day and brought him stealthily bread to eat and water to drink. When Rabbi Simeon heard that men were searching for them and trying to capture them, he said to his son, "We cannot rely upon a woman's discretion, for she can easily be talked over. Or perhaps she may be tortured until she discloses our place of concealment." So they went together into the field and hid themselves in a cave so that no man knew what had become of them. And a miracle happened to them, for the Lord, blessed be He, caused a carob tree to grow up inside the cavern and a spring to appear so that they had enough to eat and drink. Then, taking off their clothes, they sat all day up to their necks in sand and studied the Torah. And when the time for prayer came, they put their clothes on and after having eaten, they again dug themselves into the sand and continued their study, so that their clothes should not wear away. Thus they spent twelve years in that cave. When the twelve years had come to an end, Elijah the prophet came and, standing at the mouth of the cavern, called out, "Rabbi Simeon ben Yohai and his son, be it known unto you that the king is dead and his decree has been annulled." When they heard this, they came out of the cave and saw the people ploughing the fields and sowing the seed. Said Rabbi Simeon to his son, "See, these people are forsaking the eternal world, losing the world to come, and are attending only to this world." And when they looked upon a man, he was immediately consumed by the fire of their eyes. Then a voice from heaven said, "If you came out of the cave to burn up the people and to destroy My world, you should have remained in your cave." Accordingly they returned to the cave and tarried there another

twelve months; "for," they said, "the punishment of the wicked in hell lasts twelve months.
Therefore we will spend another twelve months
in the cave."

When the twelve months had come to an end,
the voice was heard from heaven saying, "Come
out of the cave." They came out again, and
whenever his son Eleazar hurt the people, his
father healed them. Rabbi Simeon said to his
son Eleazar, "If only we two remain in this
world to study the Torah, that will be sufficient."
It was the eve of Sabbath when they left the
cave, and as they came out, they saw an old
man carrying two bunches of myrtles in his hand,
a sweet smelling herb having the perfume of
paradise. Rabbi Simeon asked the old man
what he intended to do with the myrtles, and
the old man replied, "I keep them in honor of the
Sabbath, because they smell so sweet." So Rabbi
Simeon said, "You have enough with one, why
do you need two?" The old man replied, "I
want them both, one in response to the commandment 'keep', and the other in response to
the commandment 'remember', the Sabbath."
Then Rabbi Simeon said to his son Eleazar,
"Behold and see how dear God's commands are
to His people Israel," and the son was pleased
in his mind.

When Rabbi Phinehas, son of Yair (a son-in-law of Rabbi Simeon), heard that his father-in-law, who had been absent from his home for thirteen years and whom everyone had believed (heaven forfend!) to be dead, was coming home, he went to meet him. He saw that his father-in-law's skin was shriveled up, because he had been sitting so long in the sand, and they went to the bath. When he saw him nude, Rabbi Phinehas began to weep and the tears ran down his face and he said, "Woe unto me that I see you in such a state." But Rabbi Simeon replied and said, "Happy are you that you can see me in this state. If you did not see me as I am, you would not find in me that which you now find." He meant to say that if he had not been sitting in the cave, he would never have learned so much of the Law.

Before Rabbi Simeon had gone away, Rabbi Phinehas would give twelve answers to every question that Rabbi Simeon asked, but now it was just the reverse—for every question that Rabbi Phinehas asked, Rabbi Simeon was able to give him twelve answers. All this he had learned while he was in the cave. One finds also in the Talmud what kind of a person Rabbi Simeon was. He was the author of that famous book called the *Zohar*.

## 17. KING DAVID AND THE ANGEL OF DEATH

King David asked the Lord, blessed be He, to tell him how long he would live. And the Lord, blessed be He, answered, "I never tell it to a human being, for I have taken an oath never to reveal it to any man." Then King David said, "Tell me at least on what day I am to die." Then the Lord, blessed be He, told him, "It will be on a Sabbath." King David again asked, "Let me die on a Sunday." Then the Lord, blessed be He, said, "No, for the rule of your son is to begin on a Sunday, and the kingdom of the one must not overlap that of the other even for one second." Then King David studied the whole day long every Sabbath so that the angel of death should not be able to touch him. On the Sabbath on which he was to die, the angel of death came and wanted to take his soul, but David was poring over a book without interrupting his study. Hence the angel of death could do nothing to him. Then the angel of death bethought himself, "How can I take his soul? For so long as he is engaged in study I cannot touch him." Now King David had a beautiful pleasure garden behind his house. So the angel of death went into the garden and shook the trees. King David wanted to see who was there amongst his trees. And as he went up a ladder, it broke under him and he stopped studying, whereupon the angel of death took his life, and he earned a seat in paradise.

### 18. THE MIRACLE OF THE PHYLACTERIES TURNING INTO DOVES' WINGS

Rabbi Yanai says, "He who wishes to put on the *tefillin* (phylacteries) must be physically clean and pure—as clean as Elisha, the Man of the Wings. Then the Gemara asks, "Why must he be so clean?" The answer is, because a man must be free from physical impurities whilst wearing the *tefillin*. Raba said, "A man must not sleep with his *tefillin* on." The Gemara asks further, "Why was Elisha called the Man of Wings?" The answer is: Once upon a time the king had forbidden the Jews to lay *tefillin*, and made a decree that if a Jew was seen with *tefillin* on his head he should have his head crushed. (In olden times they used to wear the *tefillin* all day long.) But Elisha paid no attention to the order and continued to wear his *tefillin*. One day one of the officers appointed to enforce this decree discovered him wearing them. Elisha ran away, and the officer ran after him. When he caught him, Elisha took off his *tefillin* and covered them with his hand. Then the officer asked him, "What have you in your hand?" And Elisha replied, "Oh, nothing; I have pigeon wings in my hand." "Show them to me," said the officer. Elisha opened his hand, and lo! there were the wings of a dove in his hand. This is why he was called the Man of the Wings.

But why did he say he had the wings of a dove in his hand? Why did he not mention another bird, such as the crow or the stork or any other bird? The answer is, because the Israelites have been compared to the dove. And why so? Because the wings protect her against all things and she uses her wings as a defence in a fight, not her mouth or any other member of her body. So are the Israelites. The commandments which they perform protect the Israelites from all trouble, and the nations cannot do them any harm. Therefore we should keep the commandments and no harm will befall us, as was the case with Elisha. For although the Government had forbidden the wearing of *tefillin* on pain of death, nevertheless he thought that since God, blessed be He, had given the commandment, he would keep it even if it cost him his life. This is why the miracle happened to him and the Lord rewarded him, so that the *tefillin* were changed in his hand

and Elisha was saved from death. We must therefore not neglect God even if we are threatened with death.

There is another interpretation. The wings of a dove protect her more than any other bird. For other birds when they get tired in their flight rest upon a rock or a tree, whilst the dove, when she grows tired, rests upon one wing and flies with the other, and then she flies with the first wing and rests on the second. And just as the wings protect the dove, so the commandments protect the children of Israel when they perform them.

## 19. THE REWARD OF TRUST

A man came down from Upper Galilee and hired himself out as a servant to a landowner in the south, and worked for him for three years. On the eve of the Day of Atonement the man said to his master, "Sir, give me my wages, for I wish to return to my home and support my wife and children." But the master said to him, "You ask me to give you money; I have no money." Then the man said, "If you have no money, give me corn. I will take it to my wife and children and feed them." Then the master said, "I have no corn to give you." And the man replied, "Then give me the vineyard or the field in lieu of wages." But the master replied, "I have neither field nor vineyard to give you." Then the man said, "Give me some cattle," but the master answered, "I have no cattle either." So the man said, "Give me some bedding or bedsteads," but the master said, "I have none." When the good man heard that his master had nothing to give him, he took his clothes in a bundle and put them on his back, and with an aching heart, he went on his way to his home.

When the holidays had passed, the master took the wages which the servant had earned, also three asses, which he loaded with as much as they could carry, one with food, one with good drink, and the third with good sweet fruit, and went up to his servant, and they sat down and ate and drank together. When they had eaten and drunk, the master gave the servant the wages which he had earned, and he gave him also as a gift everything which he had brought. Then the master asked him, "My dear servant, what did you think when you asked me for money and I said I had none? Did you suspect me of anything?" The servant replied, "I thought possibly some valuable merchandise had been offered you at a low price and you had spent all your money in buying it." Then the master asked, "What did you think of me when you asked me for corn and I said I had none to give you?" The servant replied, "I thought perhaps you had not yet tithed it." Again the master asked, "What did you think of me when you asked for my vineyard and field and I would not give them to you?" The servant replied, "I thought perhaps they did not belong to you,, and you could not part with them without permission." Then the master said, "When you asked for pillows and beds, and I refused to give them to you, did you suspect me?" The servant replied, "I thought you had devoted all your property to the sanctuary, and therefore it no longer belonged to you." Then the master took an oath by the Holy One and said, "It was just as you thought. I had devoted all my property to the sanctuary because of my son Hyrcanus who refused to study the Torah, and then I went to my colleagues in the south and they absolved me from my oath. And because you interpreted my actions in a kindly light, so may the Lord also look upon your works favorably and remember you always for good." Thus he praised him.

## 20. JUDGE YOUR FRIEND GENEROUSLY

Once upon a time a pious man ransomed a beautiful woman from the hands of the heathen, and when they came to the inn in the evening, he put the young woman to sleep at the foot of his bed. In the morning he went to the bath-house and took a bath, and then he went to teach his pupils. While he was teaching them he asked, "Did you suspect me of anything last night when you saw the young maiden lying at the foot of my bed?" They replied, "We did not suspect you of anything; we thought that you put her near you because you had among your pupils one whom you did not know, and you would not let her sleep in a separate room for fear that harm might come to her." Then the pious man asked, "Why did you think I went in the morning and took a bath?" "What else do you believe we could have thought," replied his pupils, "except that probably on the way you had touched something unclean which made it necessary for you to take a purifying bath?" Then he said, "I swear that it was exactly as you thought. And as you thought well of me and did not suspect me of anything wrong, so may the Lord, blessed be He, think well of you and of your work."

### 21. GIVE YOUR FRIEND THE BENEFIT OF THE DOUBT

Once upon a time it came to pass that the rabbis desired to obtain a favor from a heathen lady. She was a very important person and all the great men of Rome used to visit her. The rabbis discussed among themselves who should go on that errand. Then Rabbi Joshua said, "I will go." So Rabbi Joshua went there accompanied by his pupils. When they came within a distance of four cubits of the house of the lady, Rabbi Joshua took off his *tefillin* (phylacteries), entered the house, locked the door behind him, and would not allow his pupils to follow him. When he came out, he went to the bathhouse, took a bath, and then went to study with his pupils. He said to them, "Dear friends, did you suspect me of anything when you saw me taking off my *tefillin?*" The pupils replied, "What could we suspect you of? We thought you had taken off your *tefillin* because it is forbidden to take a holy object into an unclean place." Then he said, "Did you suspect me of anything when I locked the door in your face?" They replied, "We thought you had to discuss with her a matter which concerns the king, and you wanted to speak with her privately." "And when I took

the bath, did you think anything about it?" And
they replied, "We thought perhaps some of the
spittle of her mouth had fallen on your garments,
and it was therefore necessary for you to take
a bath." Then Rabbi Joshua replied, "I swear
that it was exactly as you thought. And as you
never suspected me of anything wrong, so may
the Lord, blessed be He, also look upon your
work with favor. Amen."

## 22. R. Joshua b. Hananiah and the Emperor's Daughter

Once upon a time the daughter of the Emperor
asked Rabbi Joshua, son of Hananiah, "Is it not
very strange that there is so much Torah
(learning) in you and you are so terribly ugly?
So much wisdom in such a contemptible vessel!"
Rabbi Joshua replied, "Prithee, where do you
keep your wine? In what kind of vessels?" And
she replied, "We keep our wine in simple earthenware vessels, because for many years past wine
has always been kept in earthen vessels." Rabbi
Joshua replied, "You are very rich people, you
ought to keep your wine in vessels of silver only,
the ordinary people keep it in earthen jars." So
she went and told the Emperor, who poured all
the wine into silver jars. Within a short time

the wine turned sour, and they reported to the Emperor that all his wine had turned into vinegar. Then the Emperor asked his daughter, "Who advised you to pour the wine into silver jars?" The princess replied, "Rabbi Joshua, son of Hananiah." So the Emperor sent for Rabbi Joshua and asked him, "Why did you give such advice to my daughter so that all my wine has turned to vinegar?" Rabbi Joshua replied, "As she spoke to me so I spoke to her. She said to me, what a pity such great learning is in such a contemptible vessel. So I said to her, 'Why do you keep wine in a cheap vessel?' I also said that as the Torah does not stay with a man of handsome appearance, so wine does not keep in a silver vessel." The Emperor said, "But there are many good looking men who possess learning." Then Rabbi Joshua replied, "If they were not so handsome they would be more learned still, for a man of handsome appearance is not a man of modesty, and therefore he forgets the Torah which he has learned."

## 23. THE BEAUTY OF R. JOHANAN

It came to pass when R. Eliezer was lying ill that R. Johanan came to visit him on his sick-bed. And he found R. Eliezer lying in a dark room. Then R. Johanan uncovered his arm, for he was a very handsome man, and the whole room was filled with light. R. Eliezer began to weep. R. Johanan said, "My dear Master, why do you weep? Surely not because you have not learned enough Torah? The amount is not of much importance, so long as one studies for the sake of Heaven. You weep perhaps because you are not rich. No man is privileged to have both gifts. One cannot be both rich and learned." R. Eliezer replied, "I weep for your beauty, which will one day be put under the earth." Then they both began to weep. R. Johanan said, "You no doubt are happy with your sufferings, for through them all your sins will be forgiven." R. Eliezer replied, "No, I do not like the suffering, nor the reward that follows upon it."

## 24. Let Your Fear of God Be as Great as Your Fear of Man

It happened that R. Johanan was lying ill and his pupils came to visit him. As soon as he saw them he wept, and his pupils said, "Dear Master, why do you weep, a man honored as you are, a master in the Torah?" R. Johanan replied, "My dear children, why should I not weep? If I were taken before a king of flesh and blood,

who is here today and gone tomorrow; whose
wrath, if he were angry with me, could not last
forever, because he could do no harm to me in
the world to come; who, even if he should put
me in fetters, could not keep me bound forever;
and even if he should put me to death, could
not keep me dead forever, for he could not take
my soul away; whom, moreover, it is possible
that by smooth words I might be able to appease
or induce to take a bribe and let me go—yet
for all that I should have reason to weep. How
much more reason is there for me to weep now
that I am to be brought before the King of
Kings, Blessed be He, and may His Holy Name
be blessed, who lives and rules forever; whose
wrath, if He were angry with me, would be an
everlasting wrath; who, if he kill me, would
put me to death forever; and who cannot be
appeased by kind words or bribes! And this is
not all. I see two ways before me, one leading to
*Gehinnom* (hell) and the other to *Gan 'Eden*
(paradise), and I do not know which way they
are going to lead me. Why, therefore, should I
not weep?" The pupils said, "Dear Master,
bless us." And R. Johanan replied, "May it be
the will of the Holy One, blessed be He, that
you should fear Him as much as you fear man."
The pupils said, "Should our fear of His Holy

Name not be greater than that of human beings? God forbid!" Then R. Johanan replied, "It would be enough if you feared the Holy One as much as you fear human beings; for if a man commits a sin, his first care is that no man should see him, but he is not concerned whether God sees him or not." Therefore he blessed them, wishing that they would fear God as much as they feared man.

### 25. Rab Huna and His Four Hundred Casks of Wine

R. Huna had four hundred vats of wine, and they all turned into vinegar. Then came to him Rab Ada, the nephew of Sala the Pious, and other sages. They said to R. Huna, "Examine your deeds and see whether you have committed any wrong, for no doubt the Lord is punishing you in this world so that you may not lose any of the reward in the world to come." R. Huna replied, "My dear friends, do you suspect me of having done anything wrong?" And they said, "Dear Master, do you believe that the Lord inflicts evil on His pious ones without cause?" Then R. Huna replied, "If there is anyone amongst you who knows anything against me, let him say it." Then they said, "We have been told that you have not paid the gardeners their wages." Then R. Huna said, "That would be stealing, but I am not guilty. I am ready to take an oath that I have paid them their wages."

Some say the vinegar turned back again into wine; others say that it remained vinegar, but the price of vinegar rose so high that it was sold at the price of wine.

## 26. The Prophet Elijah and R. Jose

There was a man called R. Jose. He said: "Once upon a time I walked across the country and I came to a ruined house. It was one of the houses ruined at the time of the destruction of Jerusalem. I went in and said my prayers. Thereupon the prophet Elijah of blessed memory came and stood at the door, waiting until I had finished. Then he came up to me, greeted me and said, 'Peace be unto you, master.' And I said to him, 'Peace unto you my master and teacher.' Then he said, 'Tell me, my son, why do you enter a house like this to say your prayer? You could have said your prayer while walking in the field. It is very dangerous to go into a ruined house.' So I replied, 'I feared that the people coming and going would have confused me if I had said my prayers in an open field.'

Then the prophet Elijah said, 'You should have said a short prayer on the way.' I have thus learned three lessons from the prophet: 1. That one must not enter into a ruin; 2. That one may say one's prayer while walking along the way; 3. That if one prays while walking across the country, one may say a short prayer.

"Then the prophet Elijah asked me again, 'Have you heard any voice in the ruin?' And I replied, 'I heard a voice like that of a dove saying, "Woe unto me that I have destroyed my house. Woe unto me that I have burnt my palace and that I have allowed my children to go into banishment among the other nations."' Then the prophet Elijah said, 'My son, as you live and as your head lives, know that it is not only at this time that this voice is heard, but every time that the Israelites say in their synagogues, "Amen, may His great name be blessed," The Lord shakes His head and says, "Happy the king whom they praise thus in His house; and woe unto the father who allows His children to be banished among the other nations and be dispersed among them; and woe unto the children who have been driven away from their father's table."' And having said this, the prophet Elijah went away."

## 27. How to See Demons

Aba Benjamin says, "If one could see all the evil spirits standing around us, no man would be able to bear it, for they are massed round us in rows like those of a vineyard. But if any one wishes to see them, let him take a black cat born of a black cat, which is a first born of a mother who was also a first born, and burn to ashes the skin in which it was born, and take a little of the ashes and put it into the eye and the rest into an iron pot, and seal it up in such wise that nothing can be taken away. Then he will be able to see the demons with his eyes; if, however, any part of the ashes is taken away, the demons may do him harm." R. Bibi son of Abbaye made the experiment once, but did not do it properly, and the demons did him harm. Thereupon the sages offered up prayers for him and he recovered his health and strength.

## 28. Bar Hadaya the Interpreter of Dreams

Bar Hadaya was an expert in interpreting dreams. When he was well paid he interpreted the dreams favorably, but when he was not well paid he interpreted them unfavorably. Abbaye and Raba each dreamt a dream. Abbaye paid him well for the interpretation of his dream, but Raba did not. Both had seen in their dream the verse, "Thine ox shall be slain before thine eyes" (Deut. 28.31). Bar Hadaya said to Raba, "You are going to lose your ox and will not be able to eat anything thereof because of your troubled mind." But to Abbaye he interpreted the same verse thus, "You will do excellent business, and you will slaughter an ox for a banquet. But you will not be able to eat thereof because you will be too busy. Wine, however, you will drink, to the full enjoyment of your heart." Then they said to him, "We both dreamt a dream that the gates of our houses fell in." He interpreted it very favorably to Abbaye, but to Raba he said, "Your wife will die." And so whenever they dreamt the same dream, he interpreted it favorably to Abbaye and unfavorably to Raba, because the one paid him well and the other never gave him anything.

Once upon a time, Raba and Bar Hadaya were traveling upon the seas. As he landed, a book fell out of the bosom of Bar Hadaya. Raba picked it up and began reading it, and he found written therein, "All dreams go according to the mouth," i. e. depend upon the interpretation. Then Raba turned to Bar Hadaya and said,

"You wicked man! Why have you always interpreted my dreams in an evil sense, whereas you always gave a good interpretation to Abbaye? I can well imagine that if I had given you money, you would have interpreted them favorably to me as you did to Abbaye. I am willing to forgive you everything except one thing which I cannot forgive you, namely your interpretation of one dream as signifying the death of my wife. May it be the will of God that you be delivered into the hands of a cruel king who will also have no mercy on you." Then Bar Hadaya said, "What am I to do now? We have been told that the curse of a learned man comes true even if the person cursed is innocent. How much more so in the present instance, where Raba had good reason to curse me! His curse will surely come true. I will take upon myself the penance of going into exile, for we have been told that if a man goes into exile, God forgives his sins." Accordingly, he departed from thence and traveled about as far as Rome. When he came to Rome, he sat down at the gate of one of the king's officers called *Tarzayana*, which means the guardian of the king's treasure. The latter dreamt that night that his finger was pricked by a needle. Coming out he met Bar Hadaya and told him his dream. Bar Hadaya said, "Have you money to pay? If so I will interpret it to you." The man refused to pay and Bar Hadaya declined to interpret his dream. The following night he dreamt that a worm was gnawing at two of his fingers, and he told it again to Bar Hadaya and asked him the meaning of it. Bar Hadaya again replied, "If you will pay me my fee, I will tell you what it means." Again he refused to pay, and Bar Hadaya again refused to give him any answer. The third night he dreamt that the worm had entered his hand. He told it again to Bar Hadaya, who asked him for a fee. He at last consented to pay and Bar Hadaya explained to him his dream. He told him that a moth had entered the clothes of the king which were in his keeping and had destroyed them.

When the king heard this he sent for the *Tarzayana* and ordered him to be killed for allowing his clothes to be destroyed. The *Tarzayana* said, "Why am I to be killed? Let that man be killed who knew of it and refused to tell me." So they fetched Bar Hadaya and upbraided him, saying, "Why did you not tell him of it till the third day, when you got your fee, and meanwhile the clothes were eaten by moths? You, therefore, deserve to be killed." They bent down two pines and tied Bar Hadaya's legs, one to each of the trees. Then they let the trees go and Bar Hadaya was torn to pieces, and thus the curse of Raba was fulfilled. Therefore no man should go about with a false heart, for in the end the truth will out and his deceit will not profit him, just as happened in the case of Bar Hadaya, who acted treacherously and came to a grievous end.

## 29. THE MARTYRDOM OF R. AKIBA

Once upon a time a decree was issued by the government forbidding the Jews to study the Torah. What did R. Akiba do? He gathered a large multitude of Israelites and sat down and preached to them. A certain Pappos, son of Judah, found him sitting and teaching. So Pappos said to him, "My dear Master, are you not afraid of the government which has forbidden the study of the Torah, and you dare to defy it by teaching the Torah in public?" Akiba replied, "Are you the Pappos who has the reputation of being a great sage, of whom everybody speaks? Verily you appear to be a great fool, as I gather from your speech. Let me tell you a parable of which you remind me. Once upon a time a fox went to the bank of a river and walked up and down along the shore.

He saw the fish swimming swiftly to and fro
in the water, for people were trying to catch
them and they were endeavoring to hide themselves in the water. So the fox asked, 'Why
are you running to and fro in the water?' The
fish replied, 'There are fishermen on the water
who are trying to catch us, and we are therefore
running to and fro, for we do not know how to
keep ourselves safely in the water.' The fox
replied, 'Come out of the water and follow me.
We shall live peacefully together and nobody
will be able to do you any harm.' The fox
thought he would first get the fish out of the
water and then he would eat them up. Then
the fish said to the fox, 'Are you the beast who
is thought to be the cleverest among the animals?
Surely you are a big fool, for if we cannot hide
ourselves from the people whilst in the water,
how much less shall we be able to hide ourselves
on dry land?' " And R. Akiba said to Pappos,
"You pretend to be a clever man, but you are
really a big fool. If I am afraid of the government
while studying the Torah, of which it is written,
'For that is thy life and the length of thy days'
(Deut. 30.20), how much more would that be the
case if I did not study the Torah?"

Not long afterwards Rabbi Akiba was cast
into prison, and shortly after Pappos was caught

too and put in the same prison with R. Akiba.
Said Pappos to R. Akiba, "Blessed are you,
R. Akiba, who have been caught because of your
study of the Torah, but woe unto me, Pappos,
for I have been cast into prison for my evil
deeds." When they brought out R. Akiba to
burn him to death it was the time for reciting the
*Shema'*. They were scraping his flesh with iron
combs, while he went on with his prayer,
accepting death for the sake of God and for the
love of Him. His pupils said to him, "Dear
Rabbi, you have prayed enough." Then Akiba
replied, "All my life I was troubled by the
words, 'And thou shalt love the Lord thy God
with all thy heart and with all thy soul' (Deut.
6.5), which means that even if people are tearing
your heart and taking your soul from you, you
must still love Him. And I thought, 'O God,
when will the time come when I shall be able to
fulfill this commandment?' And now when the
time has come for me to fulfill it, shall I stop in
my thanksgiving, and not complete the recital of
the whole *Shema'*?" And so he continued praying
and dwelt so long on the word *Eḥad* (One) that
his soul went out on that word. Then a voice
came from heaven saying, "Happy art thou,
Akiba, for thy soul went out on the word
*Eḥad*." Then the angels said to God, "Lord,

King of the universe, is this the reward for the
Torah, that R. Akiba should die such a miserable
death? It were much better if he had died by
Thy hand, he should then have died of old age
and not such a fearful death, at the hands of the
heathen." Then a voice again came from heaven
and said, "Happy art thou, Akiba, that thy soul
went out with the word *Eḥad.* Thou art worthy
of the bliss of the world to come, and ready to
enter into the light of Paradise." Amen. Selah.

## 30. THE DISHONEST BUTCHER

Once upon a time there lived a Jewish butcher
in Sepphoris who used to sell forbidden meat to
the Jews in lieu of proper *kasher* meat. Once on
the eve of the Sabbath he became dead drunk
and, going up to the roof of the house, fell down
and broke his neck and died, and the dogs came
and licked his blood. Then the people came to
R. Hanina and asked him whether they should
bury him or not, for the dogs were licking his
blood. R. Hanina replied, "In our Holy Torah
it is written: 'Ye shall not eat any flesh that is
torn of beasts in the field; ye shall cast it to
the dogs' (Ex. 22.30). Now this butcher has
deprived the dogs of their due, for he sold to
Jews the defiled (*terefah*) meat which belonged to

the dogs.   Now the dogs have come and are
eating their share of the butcher.   Leave the
wicked man, therefore, where he is, and bury
him not.  Let the dogs eat his flesh which he took
from them."

## 31. THE WIDOW AND THE GOLD PIECE

Once upon a time in a year of famine a man
gave to a poor widow a gold piece to take care of.
He had put the gold coin into a jar that was
full of flour.   The good woman took the flour,
made a cake and baked it and gave the cake to a
poor man, not knowing there was a gold piece
in it.   Not long afterwards, the man came and
asked for the gold piece which he had given into
her custody.   She replied, "If I have made any
use of your gold piece, may my child eat poison
and die."   The people tell that not long after that
one of the children of the woman died.   When
the sages heard of it, they said: "Behold, this
woman had taken a true oath, for she did not
know that there was a gold piece in the jar with
the flour, and yet the Lord, blessed be He,
punished her by taking one of her children.
How much more careful must one be not to
swear falsely!"   And God punished that woman
because she swore falsely in saying that she had

not had any benefit from the gold coin, whilst in fact she had derived benefit therefrom, for she saved in dough where the gold piece was lying. Therefore, good people, attend to the moral of this story. If every one of you swear true, many children God will give to you.

## 32. Crime and Punishment

Simeon ben Shetaḥ said, "The story I am about to tell is true, I swear. May I so live to see Zion rebuilt. I saw a man running after another into a deserted house in a field. And I ran after him, and saw a bloody sword in his hand from which blood was dripping, and the man whom he had pursued lay dead, still moving his hands and feet. Then I said to the murderer, 'You wicked man, who killed that person? It was either you or I. But what can I do? Your blood is not in my power, I cannot put you to death, since I am the only witness. For the Torah says, if there are two witnesses to testify that a man has killed his neighbor, he shall be put to death (Deut. 17.6), but as I am the only witness, it is not possible to have you put to death on the testimony of myself alone. But the Lord, blessed be He, who knows the inner thoughts of man, let Him punish the one who has done this evil deed.'"

The sages say that Simeon ben Shetaḥ had not
left that place before a snake came and stung
the murderer; and he fell dead on the very same
spot.   Now, my good people, see what this
story teaches, that the Lord, blessed be He,
never allows an injustice to be committed without punishing the evil doer.


### 33. RABBI AND THE EMPEROR ANTONINUS

Rabbi (Judah) had under his house a subterranean passage which led to the palace of the
Emperor Antoninus.  One could go under ground
from the palace to the house of Rabbi, and the
Emperor went daily in secret to study with
Rabbi.  Whenever he wanted to go, he used the
subterranean passage so that no one should see
him.   On every one of his trips he took two
servants with him, for he did not like to go alone,
and he killed one of them when he came to the
door of the house of Rabbi, and the other he put
to death when, on returning from the house of
Rabbi, he reached the door of his own house,
for he did not want anyone to know that he was
studying Torah.
One day he said, "Dear Rabbi, pray see to it
that there should be no one in your house when
I come to you to study."  One day on coming to

Rabbi, he found Rabbi Hanina ben Hama studying with Rabbi. The Emperor became very much frightened and said, "Rabbi, have I not told you that when I come no one should be with you? Why did you not obey my order? You have a visitor now though you know very well that this is the time when I come to study with you." Then Rabbi replied to the Emperor, "This is not a human being, but an angel." "If he is an angel," said the Emperor, "let him go out and tell the man who is sleeping by the door to come in." He meant that he should revive the dead man whom he had killed by the door and bring him in. Rabbi Hanina went out and found the man dead. So he thought to himself, "What shall I say to the Emperor? Shall I tell him the man is dead? But it is not proper to bring bad news. If I go away and let the dead man lie here without telling the Emperor anything, I am guilty of contempt of the Government." So R. Hanina prayed and the man came to life and went in to the Emperor. The Emperor was very much frightened and said, "I know that with your prayers you can bring the dead to life, as R. Hanina has done with this man, still I must insist that whenever I come to you there shall be no one here."

Every day the Emperor served Rabbi at table

with meat and drink and when Rabbi wanted to
go to bed, the Emperor bent down so that Rabbi
could mount on his back and get into his bed
more easily.    And the Emperor used to say,
"Step on my back so that you may get into
your bed."    But Rabbi said, "It is not proper
to show disrespect to the Emperor."    And the
Emperor replied, "I pray that I may be your
servant and your footstool in the world to come."
He also asked him, "Am I going to have a share
in the world to come, my dear Rabbi?"    And
Rabbi replied, "Yes."    Then the Emperor said,
"Is it not written that there shall not be any
remaining of the house of Esau"? (Ob. 1.18).
Rabbi replied, "This means only those who
act like Esau."    Then the Emperor said, "Does
it not say that all their kings and all their
princes and all their lords and all their dukes
shall be destroyed"? (Ezek. 32.29).    And Rabbi
replied, " 'Their kings', means some of their
kings, excepting Antoninus the son of Severus;
and 'their princes,' with the exception of Keti'a,
son of Shalom," who had also become a proselyte.
We have been told that Antoninus son of
Severus also became a proselyte before his death.

## 34. The Martyrdom of Keti'a

In the time of Keti'a, son of Shalom, there lived an Emperor who was a great enemy of the Jews. So he spoke to his counselors, of whom Keti'a was also one, "If a man is suffering of an old sore and there is much putrifying flesh growing, what is he to do? Should he cut out the foul flesh so as to be healed, or should he leave it alone and continue to suffer from the pain of the old sore?" This similitude the Emperor applied to the Jews, for he wanted to drive them out of his land. Then Keti'a said to the Emperor, "You can neither destroy the Jews, nor drive them away, for it is written, 'I have spread you abroad as the four winds of the heaven' (Zech. 2.10). The meaning is, as little as the world can exist without the winds, so little can it exist without the Jews, and you cannot drive them away. Moreover, if you destroy the Jews, you and your country will be known as the 'cut off' kingdom." The king replied, "You have answered me quite correctly, but whoever gains a victory over the king with his answer, as you have done, must be thrown into a pit of sand to be suffocated therein. And particularly since you have insulted me by saying that my kingdom will be called the 'cut off' kingdom, you deserve this judgment."

So they seized him and wanted to take him away and throw him into a house full of sand. A Roman princess saw him and said, "Woe to the ship that sails without toll!", meaning Keti'a who was allowing himself to be killed for the sake of the Jews. "You hope thereby to obtain a share in the world to come," she continued, "but you are not circumcised." On hearing this, some say, he performed the ceremony on himself and said, "I have paid my toll." When he was about to be cast into the sand pit, he exclaimed, "All my property I leave to R. Akiba and his colleagues." Then a voice came from heaven and said, "Keti'a, the son of Shalom, is prepared for the world to come." When Rabbi heard this, he began to weep and said, "Some people perform good deeds all their lifetime, and it is with great difficulty that they enter heavenly bliss, whilst others win paradise in one brief moment, like Keti'a, son of Shalom, who won a share in the world to come in one moment because he bequeathed all his property to R. Akiba and his colleagues."

### 35. The Wife of R. Hanina and the Miracles That Occurred to Her

The wife of R. Hanina had the habit of lighting her baking oven on the eve of Sabbath with twigs and herbs so as to make smoke in order that the people might think she was baking bread and cakes every Friday, for they were ashamed of their poverty. She had a wicked neighbor who said to herself, "I know that these people have nothing. How then can they bake anything?" So one Friday, while the wife of R. Hanina was lighting the oven, she knocked on her door and said, "Let me come in." When the pious woman heard her knocking on the door, she ran away and hid herself in the barn. The neighbor went in, and lo! a miracle happened! The oven was full of bread and the trough full of dough. So she called to the pious woman and said to her, "Come quickly and take the bread out of the oven, for it will be burned." The pious woman replied, "I am coming at once, I have just gone into the barn to get the shovel."

Some people say that she was accustomed to the occurrence of miracles. One day she said to her husband, R. Hanina, "How long are we going to suffer such poverty? Pray to Heaven that you may be given here a share of the future reward for the good deeds you have performed, so that we may not be so poor in this world." R. Hanina prayed, and a hand reached out from heaven and gave him a golden leg of a golden table, and he became very rich. That night the good woman was told in a dream that in heaven all the pious men would be sitting and eating at golden tables that had four legs, whilst she and her husband would have a table with only three legs. She told the dream to her husband. The good R. Hanina said, "What am I to do?" She replied, "Pray again and ask that the leg be taken back." So he prayed and the hand appeared and took the leg back again. We have been told that the taking back was even a greater miracle than the giving, for the rule is that gifts are bestowed from heaven, but nothing is ever taken back to heaven.

## 36. The Miracle of the Vinegar Which Burned like Oil

One Friday R. Hanina saw that his daughter looked very sad. So he asked her, "My dear daughter, why do you look so sad? What has happened?" She replied, "I wanted to kindle the Sabbath lamp and took what I thought was the oil jar and filled the lamp. I find, however, that I filled the lamp with vinegar from the vinegar jar." Then R. Hanina said, "My dear daughter, there is no reason for you to be sad, for He who commanded the oil to burn, can also order the vinegar to burn." We have been told that those lights kept on burning until the *Habdalah* candle was lit at the flame of this lamp, which was filled with vinegar.

### 37. The Goats Which Brought Bears on Their Horns

R. Hanina possessed many goats. One day the people came and said to him, "Your goats are causing us much damage in the field." R. Hanina replied, "If they really cause you loss, let bears come and devour them, but if you are doing them an injustice, then may it be the will of God that every goat should bring a bear on its horns at eventide." In the evening every goat came back carrying a bear on his horns. Thus it became evident that the goats had been falsely accused, as they had not caused any damage to the people.

The question is then raised in the Gemara: "Where did R. Hanina get those goats, since he was a very poor man, as you read in the stories above?" R. Phinehas said, "I will explain it to you. One day a man was carrying a basketful of hens before the house of R. Hanina and through an oversight left two hens at the door of R. Hanina. The wife of R. Hanina took them in, and the hens laid eggs. Then R. Hanina said to his wife, 'Preserve the eggs which the hens are laying, and do not use them, for the man to whom the hens belong may come back and ask for them, and we shall be able to give him the eggs along with the hens.' So the good woman gathered many eggs and the hens hatched them, and thus they had many chickens. Then they sold the eggs and the chickens which had come from the hens which the carrier had left, and bought goats with the money. Sometime afterwards, the hen carrier passed the house of R. Hanina and said to his companion, 'I passed this door sometime ago, carrying hens, and left two hens in front of the door and forgot to take them.' R. Hanina heard him and called him into his house and said to him, 'Can you give me a description of the hens which you left behind?' The carrier replied, 'Yes.' And gave him a description of the hens. Then R. Hanina gave him the goats which were the product of the hens, and these were the goats which had brought the bears on their horns from the field."

## 38. THE STORY OF ONKELOS THE PROSELYTE

Onkelos the son of Kalonika wanted to embrace Judaism. When the Emperor heard of it, he sent some persons to ask Onkelos to come to see him. As soon as they came to Onkelos, he told them so much about the Torah that they also became Jews. When the Emperor heard this, he sent some more people for him and told them not to have any conversation with Onkelos, but to bring him to the palace. As they came to him, they kept silent and took him away with them. Then he said, "I have something to say to you about worldly matters." And seeing a *mezuzah*, he took hold of it and began to smile. They asked him why he was smiling, and he replied, "Such is the way of the world, a servant carries the torch and keeps guard in front of the palace on the outside and protects his master against harm, whilst the king sits inside on his throne. But the Lord, blessed be He, is not so; He sits in front of the door and protects His beloved people Israel, who sit inside (therefore the *mezuzah* is fastened on the outside), as we say: 'May the Lord protect my going out and my coming in from now unto eternity' " (Ps. 121.8). When they heard this, they also became Jews. When the Emperor heard of it, he did not send any more persons after him, for he feared that his whole people might turn Jews and he would remain without a people.

## 39. Abba Umna the Venesector

There was once a man called Abba Umna. Every day he heard a voice from heaven. A similar voice came to Abbaye every Friday, whilst Raba heard the heavenly voice only once a year, on the eve of the Day of Atonement. Abbaye felt greatly hurt that the voice of heaven should come more often to Abba Umna than to him, for the people said to him, "Verily you do not perform so many good deeds as Abba Umna."

What were the good deeds performed by Abba Umna? He practiced bloodletting and had a separate operating room for men and for women. He also had a mantle with which he covered the women so that he should not see their bare bodies. He also had a box hanging on the wall into which everyone put his fee. He did this in order that no one might be put to shame, for it sometimes happened that people came to be bled who did not have money to pay. If they had been asked to pay, they would have been put to shame. So he used to say after the bleeding, "Put your fee into the box," so that he could

not see whether a person had put in any money
or not. And if anyone had no money, he could
pretend to have put money in, and was not put
to shame. And when a learned man came to be
bled, he refused to accept any fee; and when the
latter was about to leave, he put money in his
purse and said to him, "Go and buy something
good to eat that you may become strong and get
new blood."

At this time Abbaye sent two rabbis to Abba
Umna to find out whether he was equally pious
in other matters. When they came to him, he
gave them to eat and to drink and showed them
every honor appropriate to deserving men, and
when they retired, he put them in a comfortable
bed and covered them with many fine coverings.
The following morning they rose up very early
and departed, taking with them many of the
costly garments. When they came to the market
place, they met Abba Umna. So they went up to
him and said, "Dear friend, please tell us what
these garments are worth." He estimated them
at their true value. Then they said to him,
"Maybe they are worth more than the price you
put upon them." So he replied, "I will buy them
willingly for the price which I have put upon
them." Then they said to him, "Take these
garments, for they belong to you." And they

said further, "Dear friend, tell us, what did you imagine when you saw us taking away your clothes?" He replied, "I thought that you were collecting money for the ransom of captives and were ashamed to ask me for a contribution." Then they said, "Take your clothes back." But he replied, "No, I will not take them back, for I have already vowed them for a sacred cause."

Raba was grieved that the voice of heaven came more often to Abbaye than to him, for it came to Abbaye every Friday, whereas Raba heard it only on the day of the Eve of Atonement. Accordingly Raba was told in a dream, "You have no reason to grieve on that account, for it is quite sufficient for you that through your great merit you protect an entire city, therefore you need not grieve."

### 40. THE MAN WHO HAD NO PITY ON HIS SON AND DAUGHTER

Rabbi Jose son of Abin used to study with R. Jose of Yokreh. One day he left Jose of Yokreh and went to study in the school of Rabbi Ashi. Rabbi Ashi said to R. Jose son of Abin, "How is it that you come to my school to study? You used to attend the school of R. Jose of Yokreh. Why have you left him to come to me?" R. Jose son of Abin replied, "How can I show pity to a man who has no pity on his own son and daughter?"

What was the story about his son and daughter? One day R. Jose had many laborers working in his field, and it was his custom every day to bring their noon day meal for them into the field in person. One day he was late and could not bring their midday meal to his laborers. The latter were hungry and said to his son, "We should like to eat. It is noontime and your father has not yet come with the meal." They all sat together under a fig tree, but there was no fruit on the tree, as yet. And the son said to the tree, "Fig tree, bring out thy figs and let them grow ripe so that the laborers of my father may have something to eat." And there suddenly grew figs on the tree, and the workmen ate their fill of the figs that were growing on the tree. Not long after, the father appeared with the food which he had brought for the laborers, as was his custom. He said to the people, "Do not be angry with me for having come so late. An unexpected duty presented itself to me, and I was detained." And the laborers replied, "May God satisfy you as we are now satisfied." Then R. Jose asked, "How can you be satisfied when you had nothing to eat?" Then they told him the whole story about the figs that they had eaten. R. Jose was greatly frightened and said to his son, "O my son, you have troubled the Almighty to bring out figs from the tree before the proper time, therefore you shall also die before your time." Thus he cursed his son so that he had to die before his time.

What was the story about the daughter? I will tell you: R. Jose had a daughter whose beauty was beyond compare. One day R. Jose saw a young man making a hole in the wall of the garden, so that he might be able to look at his daughter. R. Jose had just come, and he said to the young man, "What is your purpose in making this hole in the wall?" The young man replied, "My dear Rabbi, if I am not worthy to have your daughter as a wife, at least let me look at her beauty." Then he said to her, "My daughter, your beauty causes trouble to the people, better return to earth, so that the people may not sin on your account." So he cursed her, showing no pity for his own daughter, and she died.

"Why then should I have pity on him?" said R. Jose, "and this is the reason why I refused to study with him any longer."

### 41. The Honest Ass of R. Jose

R. Jose had an ass which he let out for hire to those who wanted to ride upon him or to carry burdens, in order to earn some money. And when the ass came home in the evening, he brought the money along, for the people knew the habits of the animal. They tied the money round his neck when he finished his work, and if they put in too much or too little, the ass would not budge, for he was so pious that he would not take more than was due. One day a man hired the animal, hung his pay round his neck as usual, but had forgotten to take off a pair of shoes which were on the animal's back. The ass refused to go home, for he had noticed that there was something hanging from his back which did not belong to him. So he waited till the man took off the shoes, and then he went home. So pious was the ass of R. Jose of Yokreh.

### 42. The Charitable Eleazar of Bartota

Eleazar of Bartota was a very charitable man, and when the collectors who went round to gather money for charity saw him at a distance, they avoided him, for it was his custom when he saw the collectors soliciting alms to give them

all that he had. One day Eleazar went to the
market to buy a few more things which his
daughter needed for her wedding, for she was
engaged to be married. And as he was going
along, he saw the collectors of charity making
their rounds. As soon as they saw him, they tried
to hide. When he noticed this, he ran after them
and said, "I adjure you solemnly that you tell
me for what cause you are collecting." "We
are collecting," they said, "for the benefit of an
orphan boy and girl whom we desire to marry."
Then Eleazar swore by God that those orphans
had preference over his daughter, and took everything he had with him and gave it to the collectors, retaining only one shilling. With this
shilling he bought wheat, which he took home
and put in his corn-bin. When his wife came
home, she said to her daughter, "What has your
father brought home for you?" The daughter
replied, "Father put all that he had brought
into the corn-bin." The woman went up to see
what her husband had brought, but she could
not push the door open, for the corn-bin was full
of wheat. When she looked into the bin, she saw
that it was filled with wheat to the top. She told
her daughter, who ran quickly to her father to
the *bet ha-midrash*, and said to him, "O father
dear, just come home and see what your friend

the Lord, blessed be He, has done for you."
And she told him the whole story of the wheat.
Then he swore that it should all be devoted to a
sacred cause.   And he said, "You must not
benefit from it any more than the other poor
people."

R. Solomon in the Talmud asks, "Why did he
devote it to a public cause?"   And the answer
given is that this occurrence was a miracle, and
when a miracle happens to a person, it is deducted
from his reward in the other world.   Therefore
he would not enjoy it, and devoted it to charity.


### 43. THE MAN WITH THE BLACK SHOES

R. Berokah of Khuza lived in the market place
of a town called Laft.   The prophet Elijah often
used to visit him.   On such a visit, one day, the
prophet Elijah said to him, "Ask me a question."
He replied, "Dear Prophet, is there any one in
this multitude in the market place of whom you
know that he will have a share in the world to
come?"   Just then he saw a man dressed in black
shoes contrary to Jewish custom, and who,
moreover, had no *zizit* (fringes) in his garments.
Thereupon Elijah said to R. Berokah, "That
man there wearing black shoes is the one who
will have a share in the world to come."   So R.

Berokah ran after him and asked him, "Friend, what is your work?" The man replied, "I cannot tell you to-day, come tomorrow and I will tell you." The next day the man came back and R. Berokah said to him, "Friend, what is your occupation?" He replied, "I am the warden of the prison house. When a man is put in prison, I put him by himself, and when a woman is put in prison, I put her by herself, and I place my bed between them to separate them from one another, lest they, Heaven forfend! commit a sin. And if I have a Jewish woman in custody and see that the guards have an eye on her, I risk my life to protect her. Once upon a time a beautiful Jewish girl was put in the prison. She had already been betrothed but was not yet married, and the guards wanted to dishonor her. So I put lees of wine on her skirts and warned the guards not to touch her, or they would become leprous. They listened to me and let her alone." Then R. Berokah asked him, "Why do you wear black shoes against the Jewish custom? And why have you no *zizit* on your garments?" Then he replied, "I will tell you. I go very often to the king's palace and do not want to be known there as a Jew. And when I hear that they intend issuing a hostile decree against the Jews, I run quickly to the rabbis and ask them to pray to God to annul the decree. And I will also explain to you the reason why I did not tell you in the first place what my occupation was. It is because I had just heard that they intended issuing an evil decree, so I thought to myself, I will go at once and inform the rabbis so that they may have this decree annulled through their prayer. I would like to tell you more about my work, but I have no time."

Whilst they were talking, two brothers came along. "These two have also a share in the world to come," said the prophet Elijah. R. Berokah went to them also and asked them about their occupation. They replied, "We make people merry. When we see a person grieving, we make him forget his sorrow and become cheerful again. And when we see two people quarreling and in discord, we work so long until we make peace between them."

## 44. ILFA AND RABBI JOHANAN

Ilfa and R. Johanan were studying the Torah together, and they were so poor that they had no bread to eat. So they said to one another, "Let us go out into the world and engage in business, so that we may have bread to eat, and we will thus fulfill the verse: 'That there shall be no poor men in Israel' " (Deut. 15.4). So they went away to engage in business. After walking a while, they sat down near a stone wall in the middle of the field, which was very old and almost falling down. They were getting ready to eat, when two angels came down from heaven and placed themselves behind the wall. Thereupon R. Johanan heard them talking to one another and saying, "Let us throw the wall down upon the two rabbis and kill them, for they abandon the eternal world and desire to join the temporary world." The other angel replied, "No, we will not do it, for one of them is destined to be a great man in Israel and learned in the Torah. He must not die yet." This conversation was heard only by R. Johanan. Ilfa did not hear it. R. Johanan said to Ilfa, "Have you heard any one speaking behind the wall?" Ilfa replied, "No, I have not heard any one speak." Then R. Johanan thought, "Since I alone heard the conversation and Ilfa did not, I suppose that the angel meant me." Accordingly he said to Ilfa, "I will return and study the Torah again, even if I have to suffer greater privation than before. I will fulfill the verse, 'That the poor man shall never cease from the land' " (ib. 11). So R. Johanan returned to his home and studied and

became a great man in the Torah, so that the
people appointed him head of the college.

After a while Ilfa also returned home, but he
did not bring any money, nor had he learned any
Torah. Then the people said to Ilfa, "If you
had remained at home, you would have become
head of the college"; for Ilfa had been a better
student than R. Johanan. Ilfa replied: "Although I have been away, I still know more
than R. Johanan. Let any one come and ask
me a question from the Mishna." The people
came and asked him, and he answered all the
questions.


## 45. A RECIPE FOR LONG LIFE

The pupils of R. Ada son of Ahaba asked him,
"What have you done to live so long?" They
meant, "What good deeds have you done that
the Lord should have so prolonged your days?"
for he had reached a very great age. He replied,
"I have never been angry with my household. I
never preceded my superior. I never meditated
on the Torah in an unclean place, and never
walked four cubits without Torah and *tefillin*
(phylacteries). I never slept or dozed in the
*bet ha-midrash* (house of study). I never

rejoiced in the misfortune of my neighbor and never called a man by a nickname.  These are the good deeds which I have done."

## 46. THE GOOD DEEDS OF RAB HUNA

Raba asked Rafram son of Papa, "Friend, tell me, what good works did R. Huna perform?" He replied, "I do not remember him in his youth, but I remember him in his old age. Whenever a storm raged through the town he had himself carried in a golden chair through the streets and examined every wall in the town. When he found one weak, he ordered it to be taken down, for he feared lest the walls should fall in through the high wind and cause damage. If the wall belonged to a rich man, the owner had to rebuild it at his own cost, but if it belonged to a poor man who could not afford to have it rebuilt, R. Huna had it rebuilt at his own expense. Every Friday he sent his servant into the market place and bought all the vegetables which the market gardeners were not able to sell, and had them thrown into the water."

The question is raised in the Talmud, "Why did he not distribute them among the Jewish poor?" The answer is that if he had given them to the poor, they would have relied upon it and would never have bought vegetables for the Sabbath. A time might have come when the gardeners would have sold out all their fruit and vegetables, and the poor, relying on R. Huna, would not have been able to get any, and would have had nothing to eat, thus failing to do honor to the Sabbath. Why, then, did he not give them to the animals to eat? It would certainly have been preferable to having them thrown into the water. The reason was because he did not think it right to give to animals food fit for human beings, for it would have seemed as if he denied the blessing which God had vouchsafed to him. Therefore he threw them into the water, so that those who saw them floating in the water could draw them out and eat them. But why did he buy them at all? The reason was because he wanted the gardeners to come eagerly on Friday and bring their vegetables to the market. But if they had failed to sell all their vegetables, they might have refrained from bringing them on Friday and the people would have had nothing to eat, the Sabbath would not have been properly honored and the fault would have been his.

R. Huna furthermore used to hang up a jar with water in front of his gate, so that people should wash their hands in the morning, for there is always evil air resting on the hands, and it is a great danger to touch anything with unwashed hands. It is also dangerous to eat with hands unwashed.

When he sat down to his meals, he would open his door wide and say, "Whoever wishes to join me in my meal is welcome." When Raba heard this, he said, "I should like very much to imitate these good deeds, except in the matter of the meal. I could not say, 'whoever wishes to join me is welcome,' for there are very many poor people in my town, and if they all came down and joined me in my meal, they would soon eat me out of house and home. I could not therefore invite them."

## 47. Rabbi Meir and His Sister-in-Law

Once upon a time there lived a woman whose name was Beruriah. She was the wife of R. Meir and the daughter of R. Hanina, son of Teradyon, who is mentioned in the story of the destruction of the temple. This woman had a sister who had been taken captive by the heathen, and was placed in a brothel. We read elsewhere that she had been very proud, and that is why this punishment was decreed upon her; hence one should never be proud. Beruriah

said to her husband, R. Meir: "My dear husband,
I feel it is a great shame that my sister should
be in a brothel. See what you can do to get her
out." Then R. Meir took half a measure of gold
pieces and went to her in order to pay her ransom.
And he said to himself: "If she is still pure and
has not been defiled, I am sure a miracle will
happen to me and I shall be able to get her out,
otherwise I fear I shall not be able to redeem
her." So he traveled along until he reached the
town where his wife's sister was kept in the
brothel. Then R. Meir disguised himself as a
heathen noble and went into the brothel to
see the woman. And he said to her: "Give
yourself to me and I will pay you a high price."
She replied, "I am ill." Then he said: "I will
wait until you get well." And she replied:
"Why will you wait for me? There are many
other women here prettier than I." He thought
to himself: "I am sure this woman is pure."
So R. Meir went to the warden in charge and
said to him: "Let me take that woman with me."
The warden replied: "I dare not do such a thing
without an order from the king." So R. Meir
said: "Take these two measures of gold and if
the king should fine you, give him one measure
and keep the other for yourself." The warden
replied: "The king will find me guilty of a capital

crime and will condemn me to death." Then R. Meir said: "If they wish to harm you, say: 'God of R. Meir, save me!' and you will be saved." Then the warden replied, "How do I know that this charm will work?" R. Meir answered: "There are many wild dogs here. Throw a stone at them and they will run after you to bite you, then utter the words which I have told you and they will not touch you." He did as R. Meir had told him and the dogs wanted to bite him. Then he exclaimed: "May the God of R. Meir help me!" and all the dogs ran away.

Not long afterwards, the king heard that the warden had let the woman go free. So he ordered him to be put into prison and he was later taken out to have his head cut off. Immediately he exclaimed: "God of R. Meir, answer me!" And they could not touch him and had to let him go free. Then they asked him what he had said to escape from the punishment, and he told them the whole story about the woman. Then the king had an accurate likeness made of R. Meir, ordered copies of it posted on every gate throughout the city of Rome, and issued a proclamation in every street to the effect that if anyone saw a man in the likeness of that picture, he should at once arrest him and bring him to the king.

One day as R. Meir was going along the streets of Rome, the people saw him and ran after him in order to arrest him. So R. Meir entered a brothel. And the people said: "That cannot be R. Meir, for R. Meir would not go into a brothel." Others say he entered a cookshop where much food was standing on the hearth and, putting one finger into one of the boiling pots, he licked the other finger, so that people might think he had actually partaken of the food, and would then be convinced that it could not be R. Meir. Others again say that the prophet Elijah came to meet him disguised as a harlot, and embraced and kissed him in the street, so that the people said: "Surely that cannot be R. Meir, for he would not do such a thing."

When he saw that the king was pressing him hard and pursuing him, he left Rome and went to Babylon. There is another explanation of the reason why R. Meir went to settle in Babylon. But I do not care to tell it here. Whoever wishes to know more about it, may look up the commentary on the Talmud and there he will find the reason why R. Meir went to Babylon.

## 48. Rabban Gamaliel, the Emperor and His Daughter

The Emperor said to Rabban Gamaliel: "Your God is a thief, for it is written in the Torah: 'And the Lord God caused a deep sleep to fall upon Adam, and he slept; and he took a rib of his body and made a woman thereof'" (Gen. 2.21). Then the daughter of the Emperor said to Rabban Gamaliel, "I will answer my father in your stead." And she said to her father: "Father dear, give me a count or a prince who will assist me and avenge me on my enemies." Then the Emperor said: "Who has wronged you?" She replied: "Last night robbers entered my chamber, stole my silver ornaments and put gold ones in their place." When the Emperor heard it, he laughed and said: "I wish, my dear daughter, that such thieves would come to me every day." Then she replied: "Father dear, the same thing happened to Adam, the first man, for God took a rib from him and gave him instead a wife who cooks and washes for him and serves him in every way." The Emperor replied: "This is not what I meant. My question was, Why did God take the rib from Adam while he was asleep? Why did he not take it from him while he was awake?" Then the daughter said to the

Emperor, "Let them bring me a piece of raw meat." They brought her a piece of raw meat, and she took it and put it on hot ashes to broil it. When it was finished, she pulled it out and gave it to her father to eat without having previously washed it. The Emperor said, "I cannot eat it, the sight of it makes me sick; for I have seen it being baked in the ashes, and it is not yet fit to eat." Then she said, "My dear father, the same thing would have happened to Adam if he had seen God taking a rib out of his body and making a woman out of it. It would have been unpleasant to him also. That is the reason why God did not make the woman out of the rib while Adam was awake."

## 49. Rabbi Tanhum and the Den of Wild Beasts

The Emperor said to R. Tanhum: "Come, let us all become one people." And the Rabbi replied, "We, Jews, cannot be like you, for we are circumcised, but you can enter into the covenant of Abraham and become like us." The Emperor said: "Your reply is very good, but whoever contradicts the Emperor and refutes him is thrown into a pit of wild beasts to be devoured." For the kings of olden times had such pits wherein

they used to throw persons who had forfeited
their life. So they took R. Tanhum and cast him
into the pit. When he reached the bottom and
came among the wild beasts, they did not hurt
him. There was an infidel there, a man of no
belief, who is neither a Jew nor a Christian,
and he said: "No wonder the beasts do not
touch R. Tanhum, they are not hungry." So
they took R. Tanhum out and cast the infidel in.
He had scarcely touched the bottom when the
beasts devoured him completely without leaving
anything.

## 50. The Omnipresence of God

The Emperor said to R. Gamaliel: "You Jews
say that where ten of you are assembled together,
God is among you. How many gods there must
be in the world if a god is present with every
ten persons?" R. Gamaliel replied, "It is quite
true; wherever ten of our people are assembled,
God is among them, and yet there is no more
than one God in the universe. I will prove it to
you, and you will have to acknowledge it." R.
Gamaliel thereupon called one of the servants of
the king, and when the servant came in, he
struck him on the nape of the neck so that he
fell down. The servant said, "Why did you

strike me?" R. Gamaliel replied: "Because you allow the sun to shine into the king's palace." And the Emperor replied: "Why, the sun shines all over the world." Then R. Gamaliel said: "Consider this: the sun is only one of God's servants and yet it is all over the world. How much more so God who is Lord of the universe and the Creator of heaven and earth! Surely He is all over the world and with everyone." The Emperor was silenced, and said: "You answered correctly, and you are right."

## 51. RESURRECTION NOT IMPOSSIBLE

The Emperor said to R. Gamaliel: "You Jews maintain that the dead will come to life again, but they are only earth, and how can earth come to life?" Thereupon the daughter of the Emperor said to R. Gamaliel: "Do you be quiet, and I will answer my father." Then the daughter said to the Emperor: "Father dear, I want to ask you something. We have here in this town two potters, one makes his vessels out of water and one makes them out of clay. Which of the two is the greater master?" And the Emperor said: "What a question? Surely he who can make pots out of water is the greater workman." Then she replied: "Father dear, do you not think that he who can make pots out of water can make them still more easily out of clay?" And the Emperor replied: "I certainly think that he will make them much more easily out of clay than out of water." Then the daughter said: "Father dear, remember that God made man originally out of earth, which is like water, as it is easily dissolved in water. How much more easily can God remake him out of earth when he has been turned into earth?" And the Emperor agreed with her.

## 52. HONI HA-ME'AGGEL AND HIS PRAYER FOR RAIN

Once upon a time it came to pass that the month of Adar had passed and no rain had fallen. So the sages went to Honi, the Drawer of the Circle, and asked him to pray to God for rain. This Honi was a worthy man and he was as much at home before God as a house servant before a king. So much at home was he that he often prayed to God for rain. Or if there was anything else to be prayed for, he would bake a cake and stand in the middle of it—it was intended to symbolize a prison pit, in which he chastised himself, just as we find that the prophet Habakkuk, when he wanted to pray to God,

made a similar cake and stood in the midst of it
and prayed, chastising his body at the same time.
Honi, therefore, did the same and made a cake.
Then he began to pray and said: "Lord of the
universe, Thy people Israel are turning their
eyes toward me. Whenever they wish to obtain
something from Thee, they send to me and I
must pray for them before Thy holy name,
for they consider me as if I were Thy son and
Thou never refusest my request. I adjure Thee
by Thy holy and awe-inspiring name that Thou
shouldst hear me and grant rain for Thy people
Israel, and have mercy upon them lest they die
of starvation." Thereupon the rain began to fall
gently. The scholars who had come to him said:
"O Rabbi, we see indeed that it is beginning to
drizzle, but we shall starve after all, for the rain
is not of much help to us, and it seems to us that
the rain has come only in order to satisfy the
oath with which you adjured the Lord to send
rain." Honi replied: "No, I have asked of God
that He should send such a rain as to fill all the
wells and cisterns." Then the rain began to fall
fast and in large drops, each drop as big as the
bunghole of a barrel. The rabbis estimated that
each drop held a measure. Then the disciples
said again: "Dear Rabbi, we see the rain, but we
are afraid it will be our undoing, for it seems to

us the rain is coming down from heaven for the
sole purpose of destroying the world, for the rain
is falling too heavily." Then he said, "My dear
scholars, I asked of God only the rain of blessing
and goodwill." Then the rain began to fall
steadily like ordinary rain, and with such abund-
ance that all the people of Jerusalem had to leave
their houses and go up to the mountain of the
temple because of the rain. Then they said to
him again: "Dear Rabbi, as you prayed for
us that the rain should come, so pray now that
the rain should stop." Then he replied: "I have a
tradition from my teachers that a man should
pray for that which is for the good of the greatest
number. And I tell you this because the rain is a
blessing to the majority of the people. Nevertheless, bring me a heifer for a sacrifice of thanksgiving that I may offer it up to God whom I am
troubling so much, and I will pray to Him again."
So they brought him a heifer. He took it and,
placing it before God, put his hands upon it and
said: "Lord of the universe, Thy people Israel
whom Thou didst bring forth out of Egypt cannot bear either too many blessings or too many
troubles. If Thou art angry with them, they
cannot bear Thy anger, and if Thou bestowest
blessings upon them, they cannot bear it either.
Therefore may it be Thy will that the rain should

cease, so that there should be quiet in the world."
Immediately the wind began to blow, dispersing
the clouds, and the bright sun began to shine
again.    And the people went out to the fields
again and brought home various kinds of mush-
rooms, which had shot up in consequence of the
rain.    Then the people recognized that the rain
had been in truth a blessing, such as they had
asked through Honi, the Drawer of the Circle.

Then Simeon son of Shetah sent to Honi and
said to him: "If you were not such a worthy man,
we would have excommunicated you, because
you ventured to trouble the Lord so often and
have weakened His holy name.    But what shall
we do since the Lord, blessed be He, has fulfilled
your will?    You are before the Lord like a son
whose father does his will even though the son
has sinned. If the son says to the father, 'Father
dear, take me to a warm bath,' he takes him; and
then he says: 'Wash me with cold water,' and his
father washes him.    And then he says to the
father, 'Give me nuts, give me almonds, give me
fruit, give me pomegranates.'    And the father
gives him, though he has sinned against him.
Thus are you also before the Lord.    You have
troubled Him very often and sinned before Him,
and yet the Lord has fulfilled your wish.    To you

applies the verse, 'Thy father and thy mother shall be glad and she that bare thee shall rejoice' " (Prov. 23.25).

### 53. Honi ha-Me'aggel and His Seventy-Year-Long Sleep

R. Johanan said: "All his lifetime the pious Honi, the Circle Drawer, was worried over the verse in Psalm 126: 'Song of Degrees. When the Lord turned again the captivity of Zion we were like them that dream.' The meaning is that God regards the seventy years of the Babylonian exile as though they had been a dream and we had been asleep seventy years. But Honi said: 'Is there any man who can sleep seventy years in one stretch? It is not possible.' One day, as Honi was riding upon a she-ass through the field, he saw a man planting a carob tree. So he said to the man who was planting the tree: 'Friend, tell me, how long will it take before this tree which you are planting will grow up?' And the man replied: 'It will take seventy years before it can produce fruit.' Then he said to him: 'My dear son, are you sure that you are going to live seventy years and eat of the fruit of the tree?' And the man answered: 'My dear Rabbi, I found a carob tree when I came into the world,

one that had been planted by my father. Therefore I will also plant a carob tree for my son
after me.' Honi, the Circle Drawer, sat down and
ate some bread. Suddenly he became drowsy and
fell asleep. Then a rock grew up around him
and no one knew what had become of him.
And so he slept for seventy years. When he
woke up, he saw a man shaking the fruit from
the carob tree and picking it up to eat it. Honi
said to him: 'Are you the man who planted this
tree!' The man replied: 'No, I am not the man
who planted this tree, I am his grandson.' Then
Honi said: 'It seems that I have slept seventy
years.' Then he looked for his ass, and saw a
whole herd of young asses, for they had multi-
plied three or four times during the seventy
years that he had slept. Then Honi went
to his own home and said to the people there:
'Is the son of Honi, the Circle Drawer, still
living?' And the people replied: 'No, his son
is dead, but his grandson is still living.' Then
he said: 'I am Honi, the Circle Drawer.' But
the people did not believe him, for they thought
he had died long ago. Then Honi went to the
college and held a discourse. And he heard the
scholars say: 'This *halakah* sounds as if it had
been taught in the days of Honi, the Circle
Drawer.' For Honi, the Circle Drawer, was a

great scholar and whenever he came to the college he answered all the questions which were put to him. When he heard them speak thus, he said, 'I am Honi, the Circle Drawer.' But the rabbis did not believe him. They thought that he had died many years before, not knowing anything of his sleep. And they did not show him the respect that was due to him. Then he grew despondent and prayed to God that he might die, and shortly afterwards he died. In reference to this Raba said: 'This is the meaning of the proverb: When your associates cease to show you the honor that they gave you in the past, it is better to be dead; or, as the proverb runs: 'Either companionship or death.' "

### 54. R. Phinehas Son of Yair and the Miracles He Performed. Therein Also the Story of His Remarkable Ass

R. Phinehas the son of Yair went to ransom captives. On his way he came to a river called Ganai. R. Phinehas said: "Ganai, divide your waters in twain and let me pass through." And the river replied: "You are going to do the will of God and I also am doing the will of God. It is not certain whether you will succeed in ransoming the captives, but it is quite certain

that I am performing God's command, for I am
sure to reach the sea.    Therefore I will not
divide." Then R. Phinehas said: "If you refuse
to divide, I will decree that no water should ever
again flow into you." When the river heard this,
it divided, and he passed through dry-shod.
When he had crossed the river, there came a man
who carried wheat for Passover, which he was
taking to the mill to grind.    Then R. Phinehas
said again to the river: "Divide your water for
this man too, for he is also going to perform a
divine command for Passover." Thereupon the
river divided again for the man to cross.    There
went with him also an Arab merchant.    He had
met R. Phinehas on the way and they traveled
together as companions.    R. Phinehas said:
"Divide also for the sake of the Arab, so that
people should not say, 'Two companions traveled
together, and the one left the other behind.' "
Then the water divided again.

R. Jose said: "What a worthy man was this
Phinehas son of Yair!    He is even greater than
our teacher Moses, for when God divided the sea
in his time, He did it for the sake of all Israel and
the water divided only once, while in this case
there were no more than three people, yet the
water divided three times."

Going on his way, R. Phinehas came to an inn.

The innkeeper put barley in the crib for the ass, but the animal refused to eat. Thereupon the innkeeper winnowed the barley once more, for he thought that the ass refused to eat the barley because there was too much chaff, and he poured it again into the crib, but the ass again refused to eat. When the innkeeper saw this, he told Rabbi Phinehas that the ass refused to eat though the barley was quite clean. Then R. Phinehas said to the innkeeper: "Maybe the barley has not been tithed." The innkeeper then tithed the barley, and the animal ate it. R. Phinehas turned to the innkeeper and said to him: "Behold, this poor beast refuses to eat untithed barley, observing her Creator's command, while you give her barley that is not tithed."

When Rabbi heard that R. Phinehas had come, he went out to meet him and said to him: "I pray you, come and take a meal with me." R. Phinehas replied: "Yes, I will take a meal with you." The face of Rabbi flushed red for joy because R. Phinehas accepted his invitation. R. Phinehas then said to Rabbi: "Rabbi, you must think that I have taken an oath not to partake of the food of any Jew. It is true that I do not like to accept an invitation of an Israelite to eat with him, for this reason: Israelites are a holy people and there are some who are

eager to invite others to dine with them although
they cannot afford it. There are others who can
easily afford it, but are not eager to invite
people to dine with them. It is written: 'You
shall not eat with him who is not glad to see you
eat. Some invite people to dine with them, but
their heart is not in it' (Prov. 23.6). I know
that you can afford it and are hospitable, but I
cannot eat with you now, for I must hasten
on my way to perform a pious deed and cannot
tarry. But on my return I will eat with you."
When he came back he went to the house of
Rabbi and wanted to put his ass in Rabbi's
stable. But he saw that Rabbi had white mules
in his stables, which are dangerous animals. So
he said to himself: "How can I take a meal with
Rabbi when the angel of death is hovering over
his stable?"

When Rabbi heard that R. Phinehas had come,
he went out to meet him and took him into the
house and said to him: "I have heard what you
said, but let not this worry you, for I will sell
the mules." Then Rabbi Phinehas replied: "The
Bible says: 'Thou shalt not put a stumbling
block before the blind' " (Lev. 19.14). Then
Rabbi replied, "Very well, I will let them loose
in the field." R. Phinehas said: "They will do
more harm than before, because no one will take

care of them." Then Rabbi said: "I will lame
them so that they will not be able to kick."
Then R. Phinehas said: "That would be cruelty
to animals, which is forbidden." Then Rabbi
replied: "I will cut off their hoofs, which is not
painful." Then R. Phinehas replied: "It is
written: 'Thou shalt not destroy' (Deut. 20.19),
and to do that would also be a sin." Then Rabbi
asked him to have the meal with him as he had
promised on his last visit. Thereupon a miracle
happened. The Lord caused a mountain to grow
up between Rabbi and Rabbi Phinehas so that
they could not meet.

R. Hanina says: "There is no remedy for the
bite of a white mule." It is told of R. Phinehas
that from the day that he was able to think he
never uttered a blessing over a meal that was not
his own, for he would not profit from the property
of another, nay, he would not even partake of his
own father's food.

## 55. The Ass of R. Phinehas and His Extraordinary Traits

The ass of R. Phinehas ben Yair was stolen by
some robbers, who took it and led it into a
cavern and kept it there for three days. But the
ass would not eat anything, for it knew that they

had not tithed the corn. So the robbers said to one another: "What shall we do with this ass? It will die of hunger, for it refuses to eat. We had better thrust it out into the field. But if we do this, the people will find out where we are and will kill us. If, on the other hand, we keep the carcass in the cavern, it will decompose and make an evil smell in the cavern, which will cause illness." So they took counsel with one another and decided to let it go free. As soon as it was set free, the ass ran home quickly to its master, R. Phinehas, and when it came near the gate, the ass started braying aloud, as asses do. R. Phinehas, hearing the braying of the ass, said: "Open the gate for the poor beast and give it something to eat, for it has not tasted any food for three days."

R. Solomon says, R. Phinehas knew very well that his ass would not eat in any house except his own, and still less would it eat food among robbers. When they put barley before it, the ass still refused to eat. Then R. Phinehas asked: "Have you tithed it?" and the people replied: "No." But as soon as they separated the tithe, the ass ate up all the barley put before it until its appetite was satisfied.

## 56. R. Joshua ben Hananiah and the Roman Emperor

The Emperor said to R. Joshua son of Hananiah: "Your God is likened to a lion, as it is written: 'The lion hath roared, who will not fear!' (Amos 3.8). Hence your God has been compared to a lion. What sort of strength does this signify? A strong man can kill a lion." Then R. Joshua replied to the Emperor: "This does not mean an ordinary lion. The text means the lion of the forest of Ilai." Then the Emperor said: "I should like to see that lion." R. Joshua replied: "You cannot see it." Then the Emperor said: "You must show him to me whether you want to or not." Then R. Joshua began to pray and the lion came out of his den. When he was 400 miles away from the place where the Emperor was, he began to roar, as lions do. All the pregnant women, shaken by the terrible voice, miscarried, and the wall of Rome fell down. When he was 300 miles away, he began roaring again and the teeth of the people dropped out of their mouths and the Emperor fell from his throne through fear. Then the Emperor said to R. Joshua: "I asked you to pray that I might see the lion, now I ask you to pray that the lion may return to the lair whence he came, for if he should come still

nearer, he would destroy the whole world." Then
R. Joshua prayed, and the lion returned to his
resting place.

### 57. R. Joshua and the Emperor Who Wanted to See God

The Emperor said to R. Joshua: "I should like
to see your God." R. Joshua replied to the
Emperor: "You cannot see Him." The Emperor
said: "In sooth you must show Him to me."
Then R. Joshua took the Emperor with him into
the field. It was in the month of Tammuz
(July-August) when the sun is very hot, and he
said to the Emperor: "Now look up to the sky
and there you will see God." And he pointed to
the sun. The Emperor replied: "I cannot look
into the sun." Then R. Joshua said to the
Emperor: "Behold! This sun is only one of
God's servants and yet you cannot look at it,
how much less can you look at the Lord, blessed
be He, Himself!" When the Emperor heard his
reply, he was very much pleased.

### 58. R. Joshua and the Emperor Who Wanted to Prepare a Feast for God

The Emperor said to R. Joshua: "I should like
to prepare a banquet for your God that we may
partake of it together." Then R. Joshua replied

to the Emperor: "It is beyond your power, for God has many servants." Then the Emperor said: "I can do it." R. Joshua said: "Very well, go to the open field on the shore of the stream Rebita, and spread your banquet there." The Emperor worked six months during the summer and put up many chairs and tables covered with food, thinking that he had prepared everything properly. But there arose a mighty wind which carried all the tables and all the food into the stream. The Emperor again prepared a banquet during the six months of winter and set up many tables laden with excellent food. But then a heavy rain came down and flooded the country and carried the tables with the food into the stream. Then the Emperor said to R. Joshua: "What does it all mean? I have been preparing for a long while and no one has come to the banquet to partake of the meal, and yet it is all gone." Then R. Joshua replied: "The servants of God have eaten it all up." Then the Emperor replied: "If such is the case, all my efforts are in vain, and I had better give up the idea."

### 59. R. Joshua and the Emperor's Daughter Who Wanted God to Build a Palace for Her

The daughter of the Emperor said to R. Joshua: "Your God is a carpenter, as we find it written in your books: 'Who layeth the beams of His chambers in the waters' (Ps. 104.3). I should like Him to build me also a beautiful house, such as beseems an Emperor's daughter." R. Joshua replied: "Yes, we can easily bring it about." R. Joshua proceeded to pray very earnestly concerning her request. Suddenly she became leprous and was given a house in the market place of Rome to dwell therein, for it was the custom in Rome to give the leprous a house in the market place. So the daughter of the Emperor sat at the window of the house and spun flax. She sat at the window in order that the people might see her and pray for her recovery. One day R. Joshua passed the market place in front of the house as she sat there spinning the flax. And he said to her: "Has our God built you a pleasure palace?" And she said to him: "Dear friend, pray to God that He may take away that which He has given me." But Rabbi Joshua replied: "Our God always gives, but He never takes back."

## 60. Why It Is Forbidden to Throw Bread on the Ground

Every person should be careful not to throw bread upon the ground or to let it stay there, lest anyone should tread upon it. Abbaye remarked: "I had thought that the reason why people sweep the room after meals is in order that the room may be clean, but now I understand that it is for the purpose of preventing people from treading on the bread crumbs, for he who treads upon bread, may be reduced to extreme poverty. Once upon a time there was a man who was very hard pressed by the demon Nabil, who presides over bread, and who wanted to reduce him to poverty, thinking that he might leave bread on the ground to be trodden upon. One day the man took his meal upon the grass. Then the demon who presides over poverty thought: 'Now I will get the best of him, for he cannot pick up the bread crumbs from the grass, and is sure to tread upon them.' But no sooner had the man finished his meal than he took a rake and dug up the grass with the crumbs in it and threw the grass with the crumbs into the water. Then he heard a voice saying 'Woe unto me, this man has driven me away from his house where I have been living. I hoped to get the mastery over him, and now I must desist from him.' Therefore one should be careful not to drop bread on the ground or to leave it there." Nowadays we pay little regard, and many a good man has to suffer hard.

### 61. Why It Is Forbidden to Eat Vegetables before Untying the Bunch

Abbaye said: "I used to think that a man who eats from a parcel of vegetables tied up by the gardeners is considered to be a glutton and a drunkard, for he has no patience to wait until the bundle is loosened. (The gardeners are accustomed to tie together in one parcel onions, garlic and radishes.) But I was told afterwards that the reason is that such bundles can be used for witchcraft against anyone who is not forewarned. Therefore one should be careful to loosen the onions or the garlic or the radishes before he eats of them, for then no evil can happen to him."

## 62. The Roman Princess Foiled
### in Her Magic

Rab Hisda and Rabbah, the son of R. Huna, went on board a vessel. A Roman lady desired to travel with them, but they refused to take her along. So she cast a spell on the boat and it could not move from the harbor. The two rabbis then pronounced certain mystical names and the ship left the harbor. Thereupon the Roman lady said to the rabbis: "What can I do? My witchcraft does not avail against you, for none of you has eaten of a bundle, without cutting it open." Therefore friends, be careful of these three things so that no witchcraft may be practiced against you.

## 63. Rab Ashi, the Rain Pipe
### and the Demons

Abbaye said: I used to think that the reason one ought not to sit under a gutter is because the water might run down upon one; but that is not the reason, for I have learned that there is grave danger in sitting under a spout, for the evil spirits dwell under the rain spout. Once it happened that two poor men who earned their living by carrying baggage on a pole were carrying a barrel of wine. Wishing to take a rest, they

put down the barrel on the ground under a rain
pipe. Suddenly the barrel on the pole broke and
the wine ran out on the ground. So they went
to R. Ashi, who was then head of the college
(*yeshibah*). R. Ashi, knowing that this was the
work of evil spirits, uttered a spell, conjuring
the demon who had done the deed to present
himself before his court. The guilty demon
appeared before him. R. Ashi said to the demon:
"Tell me, why did you break the barrel of wine
of these poor people?" The demon replied:
"Because they put the barrel in my ear as I
was lying asleep." R. Ashi said: "Why did
you lie down in a spot where the people are
accustomed to walk? You must pay these men
for the wine, or they will bring a charge against
you." The demon said: "Dear Rabbi, set a time
and I will pay." The Rabbi set a time. When
the time came for him to pay those people, the
demon did not appear, but soon after the fixed
term had expired he came. So R. Ashi asked him:
"Why did you not come at the appointed time?"
The demon replied: "I will tell you the reason
why I did not come, because no demon has power
over anything that is counted, sealed or tied up.
A demon can only take of those things that are
neither sealed nor counted nor tied up. This is
the reason why I delayed payment."

## 64. THE POOR, THE RICH AND THE HANDSOME ON THE DAY OF JUDGMENT

The Rabbis taught, that on the day of judgment the rich and the poor will appear before the Lord, blessed be He, in the other world. They will say to the poor man: "Why did you not study the Torah while you were in the world below?" The poor man will reply: "O God, I was so sorely troubled with my poverty and anxious about my livelihood that I could not study." Then God will say to him: "Were you poorer than Hillel?" For it is told of the old Hillel that he earned one shilling a day, half of which he gave to the porter of the College (*bet ha-midrash*) and the other half he used to provide for himself, his wife and his children. Yet did he continue to study the Torah. One day he could not earn anything and the porter would not let him in, as he could not pay the entrance fee which everyone who went into the *bet ha-midrash* had to pay to the porter daily. So he went upon the roof and lay down upon the skylight in order to hear the teaching of Shemaya and Abtalion. It happened to be a Friday in winter, and a heavy snow fell upon him and covered him entirely. The following morning Shemaya said to Abtalion: "My dear brother, this house is always bright but to-day it is very dark. It must be a cloudy day." They looked up toward the skylight and saw the figure of a man lying across it. So they went up to the roof and found Hillel under three feet of snow. They removed the snow, placed him in a warm bath, anointed him and set him near the fire, for the people said: "A man like him is worthy of having the Sabbath broken for his sake." Thus a poor man has no excuse for neglecting the study of the Torah, for though a man be poor, he can very well study.

Then God turns to the rich man on the day of judgment and says: "Why did you not study the Torah?" The rich man says: "I had much wealth and was constantly busy with my affairs, and therefore I had no time to study the Torah." God replies to him: "You were surely not richer than Eleazar ben Harsom." For it is said of him that when his father died he left him a thousand cities on land and a thousand ships on the sea. And yet every day he put a pack on his back and traveled from place to place in order to study the Torah. One day, he was met by one of his servants who did not recognize him and said to him: "It is your turn to-day to do a day's work for your master R. Eleazar." So he said to him: "Please, let me go, I wish to study the Torah."

But the servant replied: "By the life of R. Eleazar ben Harsom, I will not let you go." Then R. Eleazar gave him all the money he had with him in order to be allowed to go, but did not make himself known, for he was eager to go and study the Torah. And during all the days of his life he never saw his father's property, cities or ships, but devoted all his time to the study of the Torah.

Then turning to the wicked man, God will say to him: "Why did you not study the Torah?" He will reply: "I was handsome and my passions troubled me and kept me from the study of the Torah." Then God will reply: "Were you exposed to greater temptation than the saintly Joseph? Every day the wife of Potiphar sent him beautiful garments to put on. Those he wore in the morning he did not wear in the evening, and the clothes he wore in the evening he did not wear in the morning, and fine clothes lead men into temptation. Once she said to him: 'Lie with me.' He said, 'No, I will not lie with you.' Then she said: 'If you refuse, I will have you put in prison.' And Joseph replied: ' "The Lord looseth the prisoners" ' (Ps. 146.7). Then she said to him: 'I will have your stature bent down.' He replied: ' "The Lord raiseth them that are bowed down" ' (ib. 8). Then she said:

'I will have your eyes put out.' He replied:
' "The Lord openeth the eyes of the blind"
(ib.). Therefore I refuse to listen to your wish,
the Lord will support me.' She gave him a
thousand talents of silver, but he refused, as is
said in the Bible: 'He hearkened not unto her,
to lie by her' " (Gen. 39.10). Thus the wicked
man has no answer either. And thus it is that
the old Hillel condemns the poor man, Eleazar
condemns the rich man, and the saintly Joseph
condemns the wicked man. Therefore everyone
shall take warning from the Torah and he will
not go to Gehenna.

### 65. RESH LAKISH AND THE CANNIBALS

Resh Lakish sold himself to the Ludites, a
tribe of cannibals, before he had studied the
Torah, for at that time he was still a robber by
profession. He took along a sack in which he had
a ball of lead, for he knew that the Ludites had
the following custom. On the day of a man's
execution the Ludites allowed him every wish
except to have his life spared. They did this in
order that he might forgive them for shedding his
blood. When the day of his death arrived, the
Ludites said to him: "Ask of us whatever you
like before your death and we will grant it,
except to spare your life." Resh Lakish replied:

"If I am to obtain from you the fulfillment of my wish, then I ask to be allowed to tie you up and to place you in a row, one next to the other, and then I will give you a stroke and a half with this sack. After that I will willingly forgive you for my murder." The Ludites granted his wish and allowed themselves to be tied up and placed one next to the other in a row. Then he gave them such violent blows that they fell down and died. As they died they gnashed their teeth, and he said: "Why are you mocking me? I owe you still another half stroke." And he gave each one another half blow and left them all dead and went on his way.

Whatever Resh Lakish earned he spent on eating and drinking. One day his daughter said to him: "Buy yourself a bed or a pillow to lie upon." He replied: "My abdomen is my bed and pillow." When he died, he left a small measure of saffrons, thus fulfilling the verse: "And leave their wealth to others" (Ps. 49.10).

## 66. Resh Lakish the Robber Converted to Judaism by Rabbi Johanan

R. Johanan was the most handsome man in the world. One day he felt very warm and went to bathe in the Jordan. A robber came along and,

seeing the man bathing in the Jordan, was
greatly astounded at his beauty. Thinking it
was a woman, he jumped into the water. This
robber was none other than Resh Lakish. R.
Johanan said to him: "How great your power
is for studying the Torah!" The robber replied:
"How beautiful you would be as a woman!"
Then R. Johanan said to him: "If you will study
the Torah, I will give you my sister, who is much
more beautiful than I am, as a wife." The robber
replied: "I am willing to study the Torah if you
will give me your sister as a wife." Then R.
Johanan said: "Jump out of the water again
upon the land and get me my clothes." But he
could not jump half as far as he did before.

R. Johanan knew that he was sincere in his
intention to give himself up to the study of the
Torah. So he made him a proselyte and taught
him the Torah and gave him his sister as a wife.
When a man has taken the yoke of the Torah
upon him, he cannot be as frivolous as he was
before. Resh Lakish studied until he became a
very great scholar, and was called R. Simeon the
son of Lakish, the promoter of learning in Israel.

One day there arose a dispute in the college
between R. Johanan and R. Simeon the son of
Lakish concerning a sword, a knife, a spear and a

sickle, as to when they become unclean, that is
to say, when they can be said to be finished.
R. Johanan maintained that as soon as they are
taken out of the fire they are finished.   R.
Simeon said they are not finished until they have
passed through water.   R. Johanan said: "Ah,
you robber, you know all about it, because it is
part of your trade, which robbers have to use."
R. Simeon son of Lakish replied: "What is the
good of studying all this Torah?   I am called
rabbi (master) now and was called rabbi (master)
before, for I was the chief of the robber band."
R. Johanan replied: "The difference is that with
your Torah you can obtain a share in the world
to come."   R. Johanan became angry and turned
his eyes upon R. Simeon son of Lakish so sternly
that he was taken seriously ill.

The wife of R. Simeon, seeing that her husband
was dying, went to her brother R. Johanan and
asked him to allow her husband to live that she
might not become a widow and her children poor
orphans.   But R. Johanan said: "Have no fear,
I will care for you and your children if your
husband should die."   And the good Resh Lakish
died.

R. Johanan was sorely grieved.   And the sages
said: "Who will go and comfort him?   We will
send R. Eleazar son of Pedat who will answer his

questions in place of R. Simeon ben Lakish."
When R. Eleazar began to study with him and
R. Johanan stated the law, he assented to everything that R. Johanan said, saying: "I have been
taught the same thing." R. Johanan said to him:
"How can you take the place of Resh Lakish?
Whenever I propounded the law he raised
twenty-four objections and followed them up
with twenty-four answers, and thus he sharpened
my mind, while you agree to everything I say,
remarking that you have been taught the same
thing. How then can I know whether mine is
the correct view?" Then R. Johanan rent his
garments and cried: "Where art thou, ben
Lakish? Where art thou ben Lakish?" And he
continued grieving for Resh Lakish until he lost
his mind. When the rabbis saw that R. Johanan
had become insane, they prayed for his death,
and then they buried him.

### 67. WHY NAKDIMON BEN GORION LOST HIS WEALTH

R. Johanan once left Jerusalem riding on an
ass and his pupils followed him. He saw a woman
picking out the grain from the dung of the
animals of the Arabs. When she beheld R.

Johanan, she tied her kerchief round her head and went up to him and said: "Rabbi, pray feed me." And R. Johanan said to her: "My dear daughter, who are you?" She replied: "I am the daughter of Nakdimon son of Gorion." Then he said: "My dear daughter, what has become of your father's wealth? He was a very rich man." Then she replied: "Dear Rabbi, there is a proverb in Jerusalem: 'Whoever wishes to salt his wealth so as to preserve it should give alms." (Others say: 'Whoever salts his wealth and does not give alms loses it in the end.') R. Johanan said: "Where is the wealth of your father-in-law?" And she replied: "The loss of the one brought about the loss of the other." And then she said: "Do you remember signing my *ketubah* (marriage contract) as one of the witnesses?" Then he turned to his pupils and said: "I well remember signing her marriage contract, and I read therein that the dowry was one thousand times one thousand gold florins, which she had from her father, besides the amount which she received from her father-in-law." Then R. Johanan wept and said: "Happy are ye, children of Israel, when you fulfill the will of God, for then there is no nation or tongue which can have power over you. But if you do not fulfill the will of God, you are delivered into the power of a low nation, nay, you are delivered into the power of their beasts."

The question is asked in the Gemara: "Is it true that Nakdimon ben Gorion did not give alms? Is there not a tradition that whenever he went from his house to the college, they spread under his feet silken garments for him to tread upon, and after he had passed the garments were divided among the poor?" Some say that he did this only for the sake of show and honor, but others say that he should have given more than he did, and that is why he lost all his wealth, as the proverb says: "According to the quantity which the camel eats is the size of the load that is put on his back," which means that if a man has much, he must also give much in charity. Nakdimon ben Gorion did not do this, therefore he became poor. R. Eliezer the son of Zadok said, "As surely as I should like to see the rebuilding of Zion, so sure am I that I have seen that woman in the town of Acco picking up the barley from between the horses' hoofs, so poor had she become."

### 68. THE ROMANCE OF RABBI AKIBA
### THE SHEPHERD

Before R. Akiba had become a learned man, he was a shepherd in the service of the rich Kalba Sabbu'a of Jerusalem. This rich man had a comely daughter, who noticed that the shepherd was very modest in all his actions. So she said to him: "If I betroth myself to you, will you go forth to study the Torah?" He replied: "Yes, with all my heart." And he was betrothed to her secretly so that the people knew nothing of it and, taking leave of his master, he gave up his work as a shepherd and went forth to study the Torah. When Kalba Sabbu'a learned that his daughter had become betrothed to the shepherd, he was very much vexed, for he could have given her in marriage to a more worthy man. So he sent his daughter out of his house and made a vow that she should not benefit from his property as long as he lived. The good man Akiba went forth to study and remained away twelve years. He then returned home and brought with him twelve thousand pupils. An old woman said to his wife: "You are like a widow, for your husband is living far away beyond the seas. You have not had much joy from him." She replied: "If my husband would listen to me, he would go away again to continue his studies for another twelve years." When Rabbi Akiba heard the words of his wife, he said to himself: "I see that she would be quite pleased if I went away again to study." So he went away again and continued his studies at another school, where he remained twelve years. At the end of that time, he came back and brought with him twelve thousand pupils more in addition to the other twelve thousand who had remained with him, making twenty-four thousand pupils.

When his wife heard that her husband was coming home, she went out to meet him, and the neighbors said to her: "We will lend you clothes so that you should not go to meet your husband in such shabby dress." But she replied: " 'A righteous man knoweth the soul of his beast' " (Prov. 12.10). She meant that her husband knew very well how she felt toward him even though she had no fine clothes on.

When she drew near, she fell at his feet and kissed them. His pupils wanted to push her aside. But R. Akiba said: "Do not push her away, for all my Torah and all your Torah is due to her. It was she who sent me forth to study the Torah." And he told his pupils the whole story, how it had come to pass.

When her father Kalba Sabbu'a heard that a great rabbi had come into the town, he said to himself: "I will go to him and ask him to absolve me from my vow." He did not know the rabbi was his son-in-law, but he felt compassion for his daughter. So he went to R. Akiba and told him that he had excluded his daughter from all benefit of his wealth, but was regretting it now. He had made the rash vow because it annoyed him very much to learn that she had allowed herself to become betrothed to a poor shepherd, who moreover was a very ignorant man. Then R. Akiba said: "If you had known that he was a great scholar, would you have made the vow?" He replied: "If he had known a single chapter or a single *halakah* (law), I would not have made that vow." Then R. Akiba said: "I am the shepherd who tended your flock, and it is your daughter who made me go forth to study and return with so many pupils." When Kalba Sabbu'a heard this, he fell at his feet and gave him half of his wealth.

The daughter of R. Akiba did the same thing to Ben Azzai as her mother had done to R. Akiba. She became betrothed to him on condition that he should go forth to study, as the popular proverb has it: "One sheep follows another;" as one sheep does so does the other; as the mother did, so did the daughter."

## 69. THE WIFE OF RABBI AKIBA DISINHERITED BY HER FATHER

When Kalba Sabbu'a heard that R. Akiba had married his daughter, he took an oath that she should not benefit from his wealth.  So they suffered great poverty and were obliged to sleep on straw all winter, for they had neither pillow nor mattresses.  Every morning she combed the straw out of her husband's hair.  So he said to her: "When I become rich I will give you a golden bodice embroidered with pearls," like the fine garments they used to wear at that time in Jerusalem.  One day the prophet Elijah came to their door in the guise of an ordinary person and cried: "Dear friends, give me a little straw, for my wife has been confined with a child and I am so poor that I have not even enough straw for her to lie upon.  I need not say that I have neither pillows nor covers."  The prophet Elijah said this in order to encourage them by making them believe that there were people in the world much poorer than they.  It was then that she told R. Akiba to go out again and study for another twelve years, as you have been told in the previous story.

When he came back he brought twelve thousand more pupils with him. Then she heard a wicked woman behind her house say: "Her father did right in denying her any benefit of his wealth, for this man is not of as good a family as Kalba Sabbu'a, and besides he allows her to lead the life of a widow whilst he is alive." When she heard this, she said: "If he would listen to me he would go away for twelve years more to study," which he did as you have been told in the previous story.

### 70. How Rabbi Akiba Became Rich

R. Akiba owed his wealth to six sources, which I will relate in order.

The first source of his wealth was his father-in-law Kalba Sabbu'a, who gave him half of his property.

The second was a wooden image of a roe (hart) which had been put at the prow of a ship like an ensign, for in olden times it was the custom to put the image of a carved roebuck or hart at the prow of the ship. The purpose of the symbol was that the ship should run as fast as a hart. It was made hollow within and all the money of the

ship was put therein. One day the sailors put
a large amount of money in the hollow of the
buck and left it on the shore, where R. Akiba
found it.

The third was a large piece of wood. One day
he gave four shillings to the sailors to bring him
something rare. They were not able to get
anything valuable, but finding on their way an
attractive piece of wood lying on the seashore,
they brought it to him on their return, saying to
him: "Be satisfied with this, for we could not
get anything else." R. Akiba took the wood and
was about to cut it up for fire wood when he
found that it was full of gold. A ship had gone
down, in whose mast the passengers had put all
their money, and the sea had cast the mast
upon the shore.

The fourth source of his wealth was a Roman
lady. At one time the Jews were in need of
money and they sent R. Akiba to borrow it
from the Roman lady. Accordingly R. Akiba
went to see her and asked her to lend him the
money. She fixed a time for the payment, and
said to R. Akiba: "Who will be your surety?"
R. Akiba replied: "Whoever you wish." Then
she said to R. Akiba: "You are the borrower, but
God and the sea shall stand surety for you." R.
Akiba consented. He took the money and went

away. When the time came for the payment of the money as agreed upon, R. Akiba was ill and could not repay it. Thereupon the lady went to the seashore and said: "Lord of the universe, it is known to Thy holy name that R. Akiba is ill and cannot repay the money, but Thou and the sea have become sureties, therefore I appeal now to my sureties." Whereupon the Lord caused the daughter of the Emperor to become insane, and she filled a chest with precious stones and gold, and threw it into the sea. The wind carried it towards the lady's house, which was built on the shore of the sea. She took it and carried it into her house and found herself well repaid.

When R. Akiba recovered, he took the money which he owed to the lady and came to her and said: "Be not angry with me for not paying at the agreed time, for I was ill, or I should have paid promptly." The lady replied: "My dear R. Akiba, I will tell you what happened. Seeing that you did not come at the appointed time, I appealed to the sureties, and they paid the debt, nay they gave me more than you owed me. You may therefore have the rest." Accordingly R. Akiba added the surplus to what he already had.

The fifth source of R. Akiba's wealth was the wife of Turnus Rufus. Turnus Rufus was a mighty ruler and viceroy to the king. He was

always disputing with R. Akiba before the
Emperor, and R. Akiba was always victorious.
This caused him vexation, and he felt disgraced
before the Emperor. One day Turnus Rufus
came home looking very sad, and his wife asked
him: "Why are you so sad to-day, sadder than
usual?" He told her how R. Akiba had put him
to shame before the Emperor several times when
he argued with him. "He always gets the better
of me," he said. Then his wife said to him: "I
know that the God of the Jews hates immorality.
Give me permission and I will bring him to his
fall. And he gave her permission. Being a most
beautiful woman, she dressed herself up in fine
clothes, came before R. Akiba and exposed her
leg. When R. Akiba saw her, he laughed and
wept and spat on the ground. "What do all
these three things which you have done mean?"
she said. "You laughed and you cried and you
spat." R. Akiba replied: "I will explain two
of them, but the third I will not tell you. I spat
because your origin is a drop of putrid seed; I
wept when I thought of such beauty rotting some
day under the ground."

But the reason why he laughed was that he
knew through the holy spirit of prophecy that
she would in the future embrace Judaism and

marry him. This he would not tell her. Then she said to him: "Dear Rabbi, tell me, can I repent?" And he said: "Yes." So she went and embraced Judaism and married R. Akiba and brought him a great deal of money as dowry, so that he became very rich.

The sixth source of his wealth was Keti'a, son of Shalom, who left all his property to R. Akiba and his pupils, as you have read in a previous story. When he was about to be killed he exclaimed: "I leave all my property to R. Akiba and his pupils."

### 71. How R. Gamda Became Rich

R. Gamda also gave four shillings to sailors that they should bring him something, but they found nothing except a monkey, which they brought to him. After a time the monkey escaped and hid himself in a hole under the earth, where he was found sitting upon a very rare pearl, which was worth much money. R. Gamda got a great deal of money for it. This was a reward for R. Gamda's great piety and saintliness.

## 72. Rabbi Tarfon and His Conscience

One day R. Tarfon who, as we are told in the
Mishna of Abot, was a very worthy man, passed
in front of a vineyard at the time of the ripening
of the figs and ate some of them.  In the vineyard
there was a guardian who watched over the figs,
for many had been stolen during the year and
he did not know who had taken them.  So now,
having caught R. Tarfon plucking a fig and
eating it, the guardian thought he was the thief.
So he thrust the good R. Tarfon into a sack with
the intention of throwing him into the water.
When he had brought him near the water and
was on the point of throwing him out of the sack,
he heard R. Tarfon exclaim: "Woe unto you,
R. Tarfon! for you are going to die."   When
the guardian heard that the man in the sack
was R. Tarfon, he put the sack on the ground
and ran away, whereupon R. Tarfon freed himself
from the sack.

Concerning this R. Abba said in the name of
R. Hananiah, son of Gamaliel, that ever since
that day R. Tarfon grieved all his life long over
the fact that he had used the Torah to save his
life.  For when the guardian heard that the man
in the sack was R. Tarfon, who was renowned
for his Torah, he let him go free for the sake of

his learning. It is not proper to save oneself through the merit of one's learning. We deduce this from the case of Belshazzar, by an argument a fortiori. He had made a profane use of the sacred vessels of the temple, and in consequence thereof his life was cut off. How much more so the man who makes profane use of the Torah, which is the holy of holies! He will surely lose his life. Therefore he grieved over it, especially as he could have induced the guardian to let him go by giving him money and there was no necessity of using the Torah, for R. Tarfon was a very wealthy man. Moreover we find a saying of his in the *Chapters of the Fathers* that no one should earn his living from the Torah, which means that no one should derive any benefit from his learning. This is why R. Tarfon grieved so much that he should have made use of the Torah to save his life from the watchman.

### 73. RABBI HANANIAH SURPRISES HIS WIFE

R. Hananiah, son of Hakinai, went to the marriage feast of R. Simeon, son of Yohai. When the ceremony was nearly at an end, R. Simeon said to R. Hananiah: "Friend, remain here until the feast is over, and I will journey with you for the purpose of study." R. Hananiah did not wait, but went on his way and remained twelve years in the college. When he returned home and entered his town, he found so much change in the conformation of the streets that he could not find his way to his own house and became quite confused. So he went and sat down at the riverside where the people came to draw water. And he heard one girl calling the other, "daughter of Hakinai." So he thought: "Surely this must be my daughter, I will follow her." And he followed her.

When he came to his house, he found his wife sifting the flour. When she lifted her eyes and saw her husband, she was so overjoyed that she fainted. Hananiah then said: "Lord of the universe, is this the reward of my poor wife who waited for me so long and suffered patiently all the while?" And he prayed for his wife until she came back to life. Therefore no man should enter his house suddenly, but should announce his arrival beforehand.

### 74. Rabbi Hama Returns Home after a Long Absence

R. Hama son of Bita also went to study for twelve years. When he returned home, he said: "I will not act like Hakinai, who entered his house without previous warning." So what did he do? He sat down at the entrance of the college and sent a message to his family, informing them that he had returned. Then his son R. Oshaya came and sat down beside him, but R. Hama did not recognize him. When R. Oshaya asked him a question in the *halakah*, R. Hama noticed that he was very clever in dialectics. So he said: "If I had stayed at home, I too might have had a clever son like this man." He meant that if he had stayed at home, he would have taught his son to become as clever as that man. Then he went home.

Soon afterwards, his son, R. Oshaya, came in. R. Hama rose to greet him. He thought that he had come to ask him another question of religious law, for he did not know that he was his son. Then the wife of R. Hama said: "It is not proper that the father should rise before his son." Then R. Hama said: "What is this that I hear? Is this my son? Blessed be the Lord who has granted me such a son, whilst I was away." And he applied to him the verse of the Bible: "And a threefold cord is not easily broken" (Eccl. 4.12), for R. Oshaya used to discuss also with his grandfather Bita, and if a man has grandchildren who study the Torah, then the Torah is permanently established and remains constantly with him.

## 75. RECIPE FOR LONG LIFE

The pupils of R. Johanan, son of Zakkai, asked their teacher: "Friend Johanan, tell us, how did you come to live so long?" They meant to say: "What meritorious deeds have obtained for you long life?" He replied: "I took care not to defile the neighborhood of the place of prayer, never called a man by his nickname, and have never omitted to sanctify the Sabbath over a cup of wine (*kiddush*). I had an old mother, and one day when I had no wine for the *kiddush*, she sold the veil from her head and bought wine and gave it to me so that I was able to say the *kiddush*."

We read in the Gemara that when his mother died, she left him four hundred ankers of wine; and when he died, he left three thousand vats.

## 76. A BLESSING COME TRUE

R. Huna was so poor that he used to make bundles of grass and sell them in order to obtain wine for the sanctification of the Sabbath (*kiddush*). One day Rab 'Anan met him and asked him what he was doing, saying to him: "What good is this grass that you are tying up in bundles?" R. Huna replied: "I had no wine for the past Sabbath, and pawned my Sabbath mantle and bought wine for the money. Now I wish to sell this grass and take my mantle out of pawn." Then Rab replied: "May it be the will of God that you shall be covered with silk clothes."

On the day when Rabbah, son of R. Huna, was married, R. Huna, who was a short man, lay down upon a bed and fell asleep, without anyone noticing him lying there. His daughters and his daughter-in-law came in, took off their silken garments and covered him up with them. They did not see him, and their deed was unintentional. R. Joseph had just come in and saw it. Then R. Johanan said to R. Huna: "Verily the blessing of Rab has come true, who blessed you that you should be covered with silken clothes." When Rab heard of it, he was very angry. R. Huna asked: "Why are you angry with me? Was it not your own blessing which has come true?" Then Rab said: "You should have replied: 'May you be blessed as you have blessed me.'"

## 77. THE PIETY OF RABBI AKIBA

R. Akiba was taken prisoner by the heathen and R. Joshua ha-Garsi ministered to him. Why was he called ha-Garsi? One explanation is that

Garsi was the name of his native town; another explanation is that he used to grind beans, the Hebrew name for beans being *garsi*. Every day he brought R. Akiba a measure of water to drink. Once the warden of the prison saw that R. Joshua brought him much water. So he asked him: "Why do you bring him so much water to-day? Do you want him to undermine the foundation of the prison?" Thus speaking, he poured out half of the water and gave him the other half. When R. Joshua brought the water to R. Akiba, the latter said to him: "Do you know that I am an old man and that my life depends on you?" He meant to say: "I have only that which you bring me. Why then have you been so late?" Then R. Joshua ha-Garsi told him of his experience with the warden. Then R. Akiba said: "Give me water enough to wash my hands." R. Joshua replied: "How can I give you enough water to wash your hands, when you have not enough water for drinking?" Then R. Akiba said: "What am I to do? He who eats with unwashed hands commits a capital sin. It is better to die of thirst than to go counter to the opinions of my colleagues and eat with unwashed hands."

It is said that he never took a morsel before he had water to wash his hands. When the sages heard of his conduct, namely that he would not eat with unwashed hands, they said: "If he acts in this manner now as an old man, how much more pious must he have been in his younger days! And if he observes this custom while in prison, how much more strict must he have been in his own home! As a young man he must have been very observant of the minutiae of the law." Therefore one should not neglect washing of the hands, but should follow the example of R. Akiba, peace be upon him.

## 78. The Miracle of R. Judah

The wife of R. Judah went to market and bought wool, which she spun and made a mantle thereof. Whenever she went to market she put on the mantle, and whenever R. Judah wanted to say his prayers, he also wrapped himself in the same mantle. Whenever he put it on, he said the following blessing: "Blessed art Thou O God, who causest me to be wrapped in a mantle," for they loved that mantle very much, having nothing else to put on. One day Rabbi Simeon, son of Gamaliel, who was head of the college, ordered a public fast. R. Judah did not come to the service. The other rabbis noticed it and said: "R. Judah is not here." Then they

said: "He has no mantle to put on." Thereupon
R. Simeon sent him a mantle, but he refused to
accept it. But he took up the rug upon which
he was sitting, and said to the man who brought
the mantle: "See how much money I have here!"
By a miracle there was actually a large quantity
of money under it. He said, however, that he
was not pleased with it.

### 79. Rule Not Thy Household with Fear

R. Abahu said: "A man should not cause his
household to be afraid of him, for many sins
are caused thereby." Once upon a time the cook
of R. Hananiah, son of Gamaliel, had lost the leg
of an ox, and she was so much afraid of her
master's anger when he should hear of it, that
she went to the stall, cut off the leg of a living
cow, cooked it and gave it to him to eat. But
R. Hananiah, who was a very pious man, had a
premonition that something was wrong before
he had eaten it, and thus escaped committing a
sin. And this is a lesson that a man should not
terrify the people in his house, for it may lead
to sin, as you have just read in this story.

## 80. Why Rabbi Akiba Laughed When His Companions Wept

Rabban Gamaliel, R. Eliezer son of Azariah, R. Joshua and R. Akiba were journeying together across the country. They heard a great noise in the Emperor's palace in Rome, although they were still 120 Sabbath leagues (*tehum*) away from it. Three of the rabbis began to weep, while R. Akiba began to laugh. They turned to R. Akiba and said: "Why do you laugh?" And he replied: "Why do you weep?" Then the three said: "Behold, these heathens are worshiping idols and yet they are living in peace and comfort, whilst we Jews have seen our sanctuary burned and we are lying under the heel of the heathen. Is there not reason for us to weep?" Then R. Akiba said: "For the very same reason do I laugh and rejoice, for I say to myself, If God is showing so much mercy to these people, how much more will He show unto us! This is why I laughed."

## 81. We Can Not Escape Our Fate

R. Johanan said: "The feet of a man stand surety for him, for they carry him to the spot where he is destined to die." There were once

two men from the land of Cush, one of whom
was called Elihoreph and the other Ahija son
of Shisha. They were both scribes of King
So omon, and he loved them very much. One
day King Solomon saw the angel of death looking
very sad. So he asked him: "Why are you so
sad?" The angel of death replied: "It is because
I am asked to take the souls of these two scribes
of yours, and I cannot do any harm to them here,
for they are not destined to die in this place."
When King Solomon heard this, he handed them
over to a demon who was to take them safely
to Luz, for Luz is a place where the people do
not die. But when the demon brought the two
men under the gate of Luz, the angel of death
was there waiting for them, and he killed them
there.

The next morning King Solomon saw the angel
of death and he was merry. The king asked him:
"Why are you so merry?" And he replied:
"Because you sent me the men to the very spot
where it was destined that they should die."
Then King Solomon said: "I see how true it is
that the feet of a man stand surety for him to
carry him to the place where he is to die." The
old Hillel said: "My feet carry me to the place
where I like to go." He meant to say, that the
feet carry one to the place where he is fated to die.

## 82. LEARN A TRADE AND TRUST IN GOD

R. Meir said: Every one should teach his son a clean and light trade, but he should always pray to God to whom belongs all the wealth and all the riches, for neither poverty nor wealth is dependent upon a man's profession, but upon Him alone who holds in His hands all the wealth of the world and who alone can send the blessing, as the verse says, "Mine is the silver and Mine the gold, saith the Lord of hosts" (Hag. 2.8). Therefore R. Simeon, the son of Eliezer, said: "I have never in all my life seen a roebuck carrying a heavy burden, nor have I seen a fox who kept a shop, and yet none of them die of hunger. All of these have been created in order to serve me, and I have been created to serve the Lord, blessed be He. Therefore I say, if these, who have been created to serve me are able to support themselves without trouble, how much more reasonable is it to expect that I, who have been created to serve the Lord, should be able to sustain myself without trouble! But why is this not the case? Because my deeds are evil, therefore my food is cut off because of my sins."

### 83. CHARITY DELIVERS FROM DEATH

Once upon a time there was a man named Benjamin the Pious, who was in charge of the distribution of the communal charity. One day in a year of famine a poor woman came to him and said: "Dear Rabbi, give me some food." Then he swore by God that there was no money in the charity box. The woman replied: "Dear Rabbi, if you refuse me food, then know by God that a poor woman and her seven children are sure to die of hunger." When Benjamin the Pious heard this, he gave her of his own.

Soon afterwards Benjamin the Pious fell very ill, and everyone believed he would die of his illness. Then the angels said to God: "Lord of the universe, You have said that he who feeds one Israelite is likened unto him who feeds the whole world, and this Benjamin the Pious fed a woman and her seven children, and kept them alive during the year of famine. Is it right that he should die so young?" When the Lord, blessed be He, heard the angels speak thus, He ordered the decree of death which had been pronounced against him to be torn up, and we are told that his life was prolonged twenty-two years. Therefore every man should dispense charity, as the verse has it, "Charity saveth from death" (Prov. 10.2).

## 84. In Praise of Charity

There once lived a king named Monobaz who, in a year of famine, gave away all his treasures and all the treasures of his forefathers to charity. This Monobaz was a descendant of Queen Helena of the family of the Hasmoneans. When he had given away all his treasures and those of his father, his brothers and the other members of his family came to him and spoke very angrily, saying: "Your forefathers had accumulated treasures and increased their wealth, but you have diminished it and have given it away uselessly." When he heard them speaking thus, he replied: "I have acted much better than my forefathers, and I will prove it in such a manner that you yourselves will agree with me. My parents accumulated wealth upon earth, but I have put my treasures in heaven, as we read in the Bible: 'Truth springeth out of the earth; and righteousness (charity) hath looked down from heaven' (Ps. 85.12). My parents have hid their treasures in a spot where they could be touched by human hands, but I have hidden my treasures in a place where no human hands can ever touch them, according to the verse: 'Righteousness (charity) and justice are the foundation of Thy Throne' (ib. 89.15). Mv parents hid their wealth in a spot where it could yield no fruit, but I have hidden mine in a place where it can yield fruit, according to the verse: 'Say ye of the righteous, that it shall be well with him; for they shall eat the fruit of their doings' (Is. 3.10). My parents treasured up their money, but I have treasured up my soul, as the verse says: 'He who preserves his life is wise' (Prov. 11.30). My parents treasured up their money for the benefit of others, but I have treasured it up for my own benefit, as is said in the verse: 'And for thee shall be the charity' (Deut. 24.13). My parents laid up their things in this world, but I have laid up my wealth in the world to come, as the Bible says: 'And thy righteousness (charity) shall go before thee,' in the next world, and the verse concludes: 'The glory of the Lord will gather thee in' (Is. 58.8). You have heard how uselessly I have given away my treasures." When his brothers heard this, they all agreed that he had acted very well and refrained from further opposition.

## 85. WHAT THERE IS IN A NAME. HEREIN ALSO OF WASHING THE HANDS AFTER A MEAL

R. Meir, R. Jose and R. Judah were journeying together across the country. R. Meir laid great stress upon the names of innkeepers, and whenever they came to one who had a peculiar name, R. Meir thought, "This man cannot be of much good," and would not entrust anything to his care, but when the host had a pleasant name, R. Meir thought he must be a pious man and gave him his purse to keep. But the other two companions paid no heed to this.

One day they came to an inn late on a Friday evening, and decided to remain there till after the Sabbath. After a while R. Meir asked the innkeeper what his name was. He replied: "My name is Kidor." Then R. Meir said to his companions: "I can see from his peculiar name that he is a wicked man, as the verse says: *Kidor tahapukot*, 'For they are a very froward generation'" (Deut. 32.20). R. Judah and R. Jose paid no attention to him, but gave their purses to the innkeeper to keep till after the Sabbath. Not so R. Meir, who went and buried his purse at the head of the grave of Kidor's father. In the night Kidor dreamt that if he dug up his father's grave, he would find a purse with money. In the morning the innkeeper came to R. Meir and told him his dream. R. Meir replied: "Dreams seen on the night of Friday have no significance." He told him this in order to drive the matter out of his mind so that he should not go to search for the purse. R. Meir himself went to the grave and kept watch the entire Sabbath day so that the purse might not be taken away. When night came, he took his purse and went his way.

On the Sunday morning, the two companions said to Kidor: "Dear host, give us our purses which we deposited with you till after the Sabbath." The innkeeper replied: "I know nothing of any purses that you deposited with me." Then R. Meir said to them: "Why did you not pay attention to his name?" They replied: "Why did you not warn us that he is a wicked man?" R. Meir replied: "I thought he might be a wicked man, but I was not sure of it."

Then the two men took the innkeeper into a wine shop and gave him wine to drink, thinking they might persuade him with kind treatment. As they were sitting there, they noticed on his beard lentils, which he had eaten before he left the house. So they went quietly away and came to the wife of the innkeeper and said to her: "Give us our purses which we gave your husband to keep for us till after the Sabbath. He sent us to get them from you, and the proof of it is that your husband had lentils for dinner." When the woman saw that they gave a correct sign, she gave them the purses. Having recovered their purses, they went their way.

When the innkeeper returned home, his wife told him that she had given the purses to the men, for they had brought a sign that he had eaten lentils. Then he fell upon his wife and beat her until he killed her. That was the reward which the good woman received from that wicked man.

This also agrees with what we find in the treatise *Hullin*, ch. *Kol ha-Basar*, fol. 106 a: "The non-observance of the washing of the hands before meals has been the cause of a Jew eating swine's flesh, while the neglect to wash the hands after meals has caused the loss of a human life." For if the innkeeper had washed his hands, he would also have washed his face and beard and removed the lentils. The rabbis would then have had no sign to give, and the poor woman would not have lost her life. Hence one should wash his hands after meals.

Now I will tell you how the neglect to wash the hands before meals caused a man to eat swine's flesh, as you shall hear.

## 86. OF WASHING THE HANDS BEFORE THE MEAL

There was once a Jewish innkeeper who, when Jewish guests came to him, gave them *kasher* meat, but when a non-Jew sat at his table, he gave him swine's flesh to eat. Once upon a time a Jew came in whom he did not know as a Jew, sat down at the table without washing his hands, and said to the host: "Give me a good piece of meat." Thinking he was a non-Jew, since he had not washed his hands, the host brought him a piece of pork. The Jew did not notice it, but thought it was a good piece of beef and ate it. After he had eaten his meal, he turned to the innkeeper and said: "Mr. Innkeeper, how much do I owe you?" The innkeeper said: "You owe me so and so much." The guest thought that the price was too high, and said to the host: "Do you charge so much for a piece of beef?" The host replied: "Swine's flesh is very expensive." Then the guest said: "But I am a Jew, why did you give me pork to eat?" Then the host said: "Why did you not wash your hands? Jews always wash their hands before eating, non-Jews do not. Therefore I took you for a non-Jew." So it happened that he was given swine's flesh to eat. Therefore one should always wash one's hands before and after meals.

## 87. EMPEROR ATONINUS BECOMES A PROSELYTE

The Emperor Antoninus asked R. Judah the Holy: "Friend, will you give me to eat of the flesh of the Leviathan in the world to come?" Rabbi replied: "Yes." Then the Emperor said: "But you would not let me eat of the paschal lamb." Rabbi replied: "What am I to do? It is written in the Bible that 'no uncircumcised person shall eat thereof'" (Ex. 12.48). When the Emperor heard this, he submitted to circumcision, and then came back to Rabbi and said: "Now I am a Jew." Rabbi said: "I must abide by your statement . . . ." R. Hezekiah and R. Abahu said: "When the proselytes will get together in the other world, the proselyte king Antoninus will occupy the highest place among them."

## 88. OF THE WICKED TAX GATHERER AND THE LEARNED RABBI WHOSE BODIES WERE INTERCHANGED AT THE FUNERAL. HEREIN ALSO OF RABBI SIMEON SON OF SHETAH AND THE WITCHES OF ASCALON

Once upon a time there lived a Jewish tax gatherer who was a wicked man. On the day of his death, there died also a very worthy and

pious scholar and the whole population of the
town came to attend the funeral of the scholar,
following the body to the cemetery. When both
bodies had been brought to the cemetery and
were about to be buried, enemies invaded the
grounds, and the people ran away in fear and
left the bodies as they were on the burial ground.
But there was a life-long pupil of the scholar
there who would not forsake the body of his
master, but sat down quietly by the coffin. The
next morning the people of the town returned
to bury the two bodies. But they mistook the
body of the tax gatherer for that of the scholar
and proceeded to bury him with great honor.
The young man who was sitting by the bed of
the master called out to the people and said:
"You are taking the wrong coffin, you are burying the body of the tax gatherer." But they
would not listen. The friends of the tax gatherer,
on the other hand, took the body of the scholar
and buried it in the grave prepared for the tax
gatherer. Whereupon the student was much
troubled in his mind, and asked himself what
kind of pious deed the tax gatherer had performed in his lifetime that he should have been
carried to his grave with so much honor. That
same night the master appeared to him in a
dream and said to him: "Dear son, do not grieve

on my account, come and I will show you my
place in paradise, and I will show you at the
same time the tax gatherer sitting in hell, his ear
serving as a socket for the hinges of the door as
it turns to and fro.   I will also explain to you
the reason why such shame has been put upon
me at my burial.   I once heard some one slandering a scholar and sat by quietly without protest-
ing, though I could have done so, therefore
have I been put to such shame.   I will also tell
you the good deed which the tax gatherer had
done, which won for him so much honor at his
burial.   Once upon a time he had prepared a
banquet for the governor of the town, but the
governor did not come.   So the tax gatherer
took the food and distributed it among the poor
of the town.   Therefore God paid him his reward
in this world."

Then the pupil asked his master: "How long
must the tax gatherer remain in hell and suffer
this terrible torture?"  The master replied: "Until
the death of Rabbi Simeon ben Shetah, who will
take his place."   Then the pupil said: "Why
should R. Simeon be so severely punished?  He
is such a worthy man."   The master replied:
"It is because R. Simeon ben Shetah allows the
witches in Ascalon, who are all Jewish, to live

and does not have them burned or condemned to death."

The next morning the pupil went to Rabbi Simeon ben Shetah and told him what he had heard from his master in the night. What did Rabbi Simeon do? He gathered together eighty strong youths on a rainy day and gave to each a big jar in which he had put a white garment, saying to them: "On your life, beware of the witches, for there are eighty of them. When you enter their abode, let everyone of you get hold of a witch and lift her up from the ground; she will then lose her power, otherwise we shall not be able to overcome them."

R. Simeon entered the house of the witches alone, having said to his pupils: "Remain outside until I give you the sign, then come in and do as I have instructed you." When he came into their house, the witches asked him: "Who are you?" He replied: "I am a magician and can perform as much witchcraft as you." They said to him: "What kind of witchcraft can you perform?" "I will bring in," he said, "eighty strong young men, each one wearing a dry mantle in spite of the rainy weather." "Let us see it," they said. He went to the door and quickly made a sign to his youths. They came in, having taken out their mantles from the jars and put them on. And as they went in, each one took one of the witches and lifted her from the ground, so that she could do no harm. Then they carried them out of the house and hanged them all on one tree.

When the relatives of the witches heard what had happened, they grew very angry and conceived a deep hatred against Rabbi Simeon because he had caused their relatives to lose their lives. A few days later two of them brought a capital charge against the son of R. Simeon, and he was condemned to death by stoning. Thereupon the son of R. Simeon ben Shetah said: "If I have committed the crime of which I stand accused, then may my death not atone for my sins; but if I am innocent, may my present death be an atonement for me and may you who are testifying against me die a violent death." The witnesses, knowing that they had borne false testimony, withdrew their accusation and explained that the reason why they had brought a false charge was because R. Simeon b. Shetah had put their relatives, the witches, to death. But nevertheless the sentence was not withdrawn and he was stoned to death, for the sentence had been passed and could not be recalled, the rule being that once a witness has given his testimony he cannot withdraw it. Thus

the son of R. Simeon ben Shetah was put to
death, though innocent, through false testimony.
May the Lord, blessed be He, avenge his blood
on them.

## 89. PRIDE GOES BEFORE A FALL

Issachar of the town of Barkai was a high
priest who paid much attention to his person
but did not pay sufficient respect to the sacrifice.
Whenever he brought the portions of the sacrifice
to the altar, he wrapped a silken handkerchief
around his hands so that they should not be
contaminated or soiled with the blood. I will
tell you now what his end was.

One day King Jannaeus and his wife were
having a discussion. The king said: "The flesh
of a young kid is better to eat than that of a
ewe lamb." The queen said: "No, the flesh of a
ewe lamb is better than that of a kid." So they
said: "Who can tell us? Let us ask Issachar, the
high priest; he knows, for he is constantly
engaged in sacrifice." They sent for him and
asked him which was the better. Whereupon
he replied: "Of course the flesh of a ewe is better,
for otherwise the kid would be used for the
*tamid* sacrifice." While he was speaking, he was
gesticulating with his hands as though he were

mocking the king. King Jannaeus said: "Since he mocks me with his gesticulations, I will have his right hand cut off." Issachar gave a huge bribe to the executioner and instead of the right, the left hand was cut off. When the king heard of it, he ordered the right hand to be cut off also, and thus Issachar lost both hands.

Then R. Joseph said: "Blessed be the Lord who punished the guilt of the man of Barkai in this world." And in the Talmud it is further explained that Issachar was mistaken, for both are equally good. The moral of the story is that no one should be arrogant when he reaches a high position, for God has everything in His hands to give and to take away. Therefore every man should cultivate modesty, and not be arrogant like Issachar of Barkai.

## 90. Abba Hilkiah

Abba Hilkiah was the grandson of Honi the Circle Drawer. Once upon a time there was a great drought, and the Jews were anxious for rain, so the rabbis sent to Hilkiah to ask him to pray for rain. When the two rabbis came to his house, they did not find him in, so they went out to the field to look for him. They found him in a vineyard, where he was removing the weeds to

prevent their further growth. They greeted him
with the words: "The Lord be with you," but
he did not even turn his face to them. When
it grew dark, he turned homewards, and the two
rabbis followed him. He carried the wood and
the spade, which he had used at his work, on
one shoulder and his mantle on the other. He
walked barefoot all the way, but when he came
to a river he put his shoes on. When he came
upon thorns in his way, he lifted up his clothes,
but when he was on the highway he did not lift
them up. When he came to his house, his wife
came out to meet him in her best clothes. He
let her go in first, then he went in, and after him
the two rabbis. When he sat down at the table,
he did not invite the rabbis to eat with him.
Then he cut a loaf of bread and gave one slice
to his eldest son and two slices to the youngest.
Then he whispered to his wife, saying: "I know
why the rabbis have come, they want me to
pray to God for rain. Come, let us go to the
roof and pray for rain. Maybe God will listen
to our prayer and grant us rain. We will then
be able to say that the rain did not come because
of our entreaties."

So they went up to the roof and Abba Hilkiah
stood in one corner and his wife stood in another
and they prayed. As they were praying, a rain

cloud came up from the corner where his wife was praying, and it began to rain. Then they both came down without saying what they had done, and Rabbi Hilkiah said to the two rabbis: "What is your wish and what has brought you here?" The two rabbis replied: "The sages sent us here to ask you to pray to God to send rain, for we are in great need of it." Abba Hilkiah said: "Blessed be the Lord that you do not require my prayer, for it is raining already." The rabbis replied: "We know very well that the rain has come for the sake of you two, but we should like you to explain your strange behavior on the road, which has made us wonder greatly." "Very well," he said, "I will explain it to you."

So they said to him: "When we greeted you the first time, why did you not pay any attention to us?" He replied: "I was hired to work by the day and could not spare the time to speak to you." Then they said: "Why did you carry the spade and the wood on one shoulder and the mantle on the other? Why did you not carry everything on one shoulder?" He replied: "The mantle is a borrowed one and was lent to me to wear, but not to carry things upon it." Then they said again: "Why did you carry the shoes in your hand all the way and when you had to cross the water you put them on?" "All along

the way," he said, "I could see what I was
stepping on, but I could not see in the water,
therefore I put my shoes on when I had to cross
the water." Then they said again: "Why did
you allow your clothes to hang down all along
the road, and when you came upon thorn bushes
you lifted them up? You should have let them
hang against the thorns to protect your body."
He replied: "The wounds of the body can be
healed, but the tears in the clothes cannot be
mended." Then they said: "Why did your wife
come out to meet you in her best clothes?" He
replied: "That I should pay no attention to
other women." Then they said: "Why did you
let her go into the house first, then you followed,
and we came in last?" He said: "Because I did
not know whether I could trust you, for it is not
wise to assume that a person is honorable, unless
one knows him to be such." Then they asked
him: "Why did you not ask us to share your
meal?" He replied: "I saw that there was not
enough bread for us all, and I did not want to
say one thing and mean another, for it is a
great sin to be insincere in one's speech." Then
they said to him: "Friend, why did you give to
the eldest son one slice and to the youngest two
slices of bread?" He replied: "The youngest boy
is all day at school with the teacher and does

not come home, whilst my eldest is always at home, and can eat whenever he likes; therefore I gave him one slice and the other two." Then they asked again: "Friend, why did the rain cloud come up from the corner where your wife was standing?" He replied: "Because my wife, being all day in the house, gives food to the poor, which is more useful to them than money, for if I give them money they must first buy the food before they can eat it. I will also give you another reason. We have bad neighbors, who are great rogues, and I pray for their death, but my wife prays that they should repent and turn away from their evil deeds."

## 91. THE MODESTY OF HANAN HA-NEHBA

Once upon a time there lived a man who was called Hanan the Hidden One, for he used to hide himself. He was the grandson of Honi the Circle Drawer on his mother's side. Whenever the Jews were in need of rain, the rabbis used to send young children to the house of the rabbi to ask him to pray for rain. When the children came to him, they took hold of his mantle and said to him: "Father, father, give us rain." Hanan began to  pray and said: "Lord of the universe, give rain for the sake of the little

children, for they cannot distinguish between a
father who gives rain and a father who does not
give rain, for they believe that it is I who give
them rain."

The reason why he was called the hidden is
that he used to hide in a privy place. Some say
he was very poor, and when he said his prayers,
he did so privily; others say that whenever he
gave anything to a poor man, he hid himself so
as not to put the poor man to shame, for it is
wrong to put a poor man to shame, as I will
tell you later on.

## 92. The Considerateness of Mar 'Ukba

Once upon a time there lived a man called
Mar 'Ukba, who had a very poor man as a
neighbor. Every morning, whenever Mar 'Ukba
went to the college, he put four shillings in the
socket of the door's hinges in the poor man's
house, so that when he opened the door to go
out, he found the four shillings. One day the
poor man thought to himself: "Who might that
man be who gives me four shillings every day?
I must find out who does it." On the day that
the poor man was on the watch, Mar 'Ukba was
late on his way to the college and his wife went
along with him. As he passed by the poor man's

house and wanted to put down the money, as was his custom, the poor man crouched down in order to find out who it was who, in the company of his wife, was leaving him money stealthily so as not to put him to shame. When they saw him, they ran away and hid themselves in a heated bake-oven so that the poor man should not catch sight of them. When they were in the heated oven, Mar 'Ukba said to his wife: "Oh! my knees are so hot." "Put your knee between my knees," the wife replied, "my knees are cold." Mar 'Ukba felt very angry that his knees should be hotter than those of his wife, but she said to him: "My dear husband, there is nothing strange in this, as I will explain to you. You give money to the poor and they must go to the trouble of buying bread or meat, but I am all day at home and give to the poor bread and meat and salt, which they like much better, as they do not have to run about to buy their food."

The sages ask in the Talmud: "Why did these good people run so great a risk by hiding in a heated oven?" R. Johanan explains: "They did it because they did not like to put the poor man to shame, for it is much better that one should hide in a burning limekiln than that one should put his neighbor to shame in public and cause

his face to blush." We learn this from the story
of Tamar, who preferred to be burned rather
than to expose the man who had been with her.

### 93. The Generosity of Mar 'Ukba

In the neighborhood of Mar 'Ukba there lived
a poor man.   Mar 'Ukba used to send him
every year, on the eve of the Day of Atonement,
four hundred florins.   Once he sent the four
hundred florins through his son, and when the
lad returned home, he said to his father: "The
poor man does not need your money, for when I
entered his house I found him drinking nothing
but the best old wine."   The pious man replied:
"I see that the poor man has a very refined
taste, and therefore must have more money
than I gave him."   And he sent him a larger sum
than before.

When the pious man was about to die, he said
to his children: "Bring me my list of charities."
And they found that he had spent on charity
seven thousand florins.   Then the pious man
said: "I have a long journey before me, and
have taken along so little provisions."   He meant
that he had not given enough charity, and so he
bequeathed half of his property for charitable
uses.   Then he said: "Now I have enough
provisions for my journey."

## 94. Nahum Ish Gamzo

Once upon a time there lived a man who was called Nahum Ish Gamzo. He was blind in both eyes, his two hands were cut off, he was lame on both legs, his body was full of sores and he lived in a tumbled down hut. The four legs of his bedstead stood in pails of water to prevent the ants from coming into his bed and biting him, since he could not protect himself against them.

One day his pupils, fearing that the house would fall in, wanted to carry him out in his bed first, and then the other pieces of furniture. But Nahum said to them: "My dear children, carry out the furniture first, and then carry me, for you may be assured that as long as I am in the house, it will not fall in." So they took out all the furniture, and after everything was out of the house, they carried him out on his bed. No sooner had they done so than the house fell in. Then his pupils asked him: "Dear Master, since you are such a pious man, how is it that so much evil has befallen you and that you are reduced to such poverty?" Nahum replied: "Dear children, I wished it on myself, and I will tell you how it all came to pass. Once I took a journey to visit my father-in-law, and had with me three asses well laden, one had good food, the other was laden with drink, and the third carried all kinds of good fruit. A poor man met me on the road and said: "Dear Rabbi, give me something to eat." I replied: "Dear man, wait a while until I unload the asses," and I began unloading, but before I had finished, the man had died on the road. I fell upon him and said: "The eyes which took no pity on yours, may they become blind; the hands which took no pity on yours, may they be cut off; and the feet which took no pity on yours, may they become lame." Not satisfied with this, I added: "May my body be full of sores." Then the pupils said to him: "Woe unto us, dear Master, that we should see you in such a plight!" Whereupon he replied: "Much more woe would have been unto me if you had not seen me in such a plight, for I hope that now the Lord will forgive my sin, as I am suffering so bitterly in this world."

Why was he called Nahum Ish Gamzo? It is because, whenever anything happened to him, good or evil, he said: *"Gam zo letobah,"* which means: "This is also for the best."

Once upon a time the Jews wished to send a gift to the Emperor, so they took counsel together whom they should send to present the gift, a man who would carry out the message to the best satisfaction. They decided to send

Nahum Ish Gamzo with the present, for miracles had often happened to him on his journeys. They sent a casketful of pearls and precious stones to present to the Emperor as a gift in the name of the whole of Israel. Nahum Ish Gamzo went on his journey and in the evening he reached an inn. There were many rogues at the inn, who rose in the night, stole the entire contents of the casket and filled it with earth, so that he should not notice that he had been robbed.

When Nahum got up in the morning and looked into the casket, he found that all the precious stones and pearls had been removed. So he said: "This is also for the best," went his way without further worry and presented the casket as it was to the Emperor, saying: "This is a present from the Jews, take it with good grace." For the Emperor knew that they were poor people. The Emperor took the casket and opened it to see how the Jews felt toward him. But when he opened it, he found that there was nothing in it but earth. Then the Emperor said: "The Jews are mocking me, they send me earth as a present, I will have them all put to death."

Suddenly Elijah the prophet appeared, disguised as one of the Emperor's counselors, and said: "My Lord the Emperor, do not shed

innocent blood, perchance this is some of the
earth which their forefathers used. For we find
that whenever Abraham their ancestor threw
this earth, it changed into swords, with which he
subdued his enemies. And when he threw it
upon an enemy it changed into arrows, as is
written: 'He makes his earth as swords and his
bow as stubble' (Is. 41.2). Perhaps this is of
the same earth, with which one can conquer
one's enemies." When the emperor heard this,
he said: "There is a province which has rebelled
against me, I will try this earth and see whether
I can subdue it." So he went to that city and
threw some of the earth into it. The earth
changed into swords, and he conquered the place.
The rest of the earth he placed into the treasury
and gave orders that the casket of Nahum should
be filled with precious stones and pearls. The
order was carried out, and Nahum was sent home
with honor and dignity.

On his way back, he came to the same inn
where his casket had been emptied. The thieves
asked him: "What did you bring the Emperor
as a present that he should have sent you back
with so much honor?" Nahum replied: "I
brought to the Emperor what I had taken with
me from here, and this is what brought me so
much honor." So the rogues took of the same

earth, brought it to the Emperor and said: "O Lord Emperor, we bring you of the same earth as the Jew brought. He obtained it from us." The Emperor tried it and found it to be the same as any other earth. Accordingly he gave orders that they should all be put to death. The Jews, however, fared very well, and may it go still better with us. Amen.

## 95. THE STORY OF ONKELOS THE PROSELYTE

Onkelos the proselyte was a son of Emperor Hadrian's sister. To him refers the verse in the Bible, which says: "He declareth His word unto Jacob, His statutes and His ordinances unto Israel. He hath not dealt so with any nation" (Ps. 147.19–20). I will explain to you the meaning of the verse.

Onkelos wanted to embrace Judaism and learn the Torah, but he stood in fear of his uncle the Emperor. So he went to the Emperor and said to him: "My dear uncle, I want to go out into the world to do business, and at the same time I want to learn a trade. I want to see the world and find out how the people earn their living. Here at home I am like a domestic calf, which knows nothing of the world." The Emperor replied: "What do you want to do? Do you want to become a merchant and make money? You had better remain at home. I will give you all my treasures, and you will have plenty of money without having to travel." But he replied: "Dear uncle, I wish to buy merchandise, and desire your advice in the matter of what to buy and what not to buy." The Emperor said: "If you have set your mind on buying goods, then buy those goods which are very low in the market and which no one wants to buy. The time will come when those goods will rise in price and you will make a very good profit."

So he departed and went to Palestine, where he studied Torah. Not long afterwards, R. Eliezer and R. Joshua saw him and said to one another: "Look at Onkelos, how ill he looks. He must have been studying the Torah, for he who studies the Torah becomes pale and weak." When he came up to the two rabbis, he asked them many questions, which they answered. Then he returned home to the Emperor. When the Emperor looked at him, he asked him: "My dear boy, why do you look so ill? You must have lost a great deal of money in your business, or else someone must have done you some harm." He replied: "No, who would dare to do me harm as long as you are alive? Everyone in the world is afraid of you." "Why then," said the Emperor,

"are you looking so badly?" He replied: "My
Lord, I will tell you why I am looking so ill.
I have been studying the Torah, and what is
more, I have had myself circumcised." The
Emperor said: "Who told you to do it?" Onkelos
replied: "I consulted you and followed your
advice." The Emperor said: "When did I
advise you to do this?" He replied: "I told you
that I wanted to go into the world to buy
merchandise, and you advised me to buy the
goods which were the lowest in the market, as
the time would come when they would rise in
price and I would make huge profits. Accordingly, I traveled throughout the world and I
found no nation on earth which was held in
lower esteem than the people of Israel. Surely
that is the people which in the future will be
very highly regarded, as we find the prophet
Isaiah (49.7) saying: 'To him who is despised
of men, to him who is abhorred of nations, to a
servant of rulers: kings shall see and arise,
princes and they shall prostrate themselves.'
Therefore I bought these goods, which are now
very low in the market, but will afterwards rise
very high. As you advised me so did I act."
The Emperor said: "But why did you adopt
Judaism and embrace the covenant of Abraham?"
He replied: "Because I wanted to study the

Torah." Then the Emperor said: "You could have studied the Torah without becoming a Jew." Onkelos replied: "I will give you an example. One does not entrust the guidance of a ship to a man unless he can put up the mast and turn it in the direction of the wind, in the proper way. In the same way, no one can study the Torah with the hope that it will remain with him permanently unless he embraces Judaism, as it is stated in the Bible: 'He declareth His word unto Jacob, His statutes and His ordinances unto Israel. He hath not dealt so with any nation' (Ps. 147.19–20). This means that God speaks and gives His Law and His statutes only to those who are circumcised as Jacob was, and not to the other nations who are not Jews. Therefore I was bound to embrace Judaism."

## 96. Nakdimon ben Gorion and the Twelve Wells of Water

Once upon a time when all Israel went up on a pilgrimage to Jerusalem, as they did three times a year, they had no water to drink because no rain had fallen for a long time. Now there was a rich man in Jerusalem called Nakdimon ben Gorion. Nakdimon went to the governor in Jerusalem and asked him to lend him twelve cisterns of water for the people to drink. "I will repay you," he said, "an equal amount of water in a given time; and if by the end of the appointed time I shall not have repaid you, I will pay you twelve talents of silver." The governor gave him the water.

The time arrived when Nakdimon promised to return the water, and it had not rained. Early in the morning the general sent to Nakdimon and asked him to fill his cisterns with water or to pay for it, as he had promised. Nakdimon replied: "The day is not yet over. Wait until the evening." The governor laughed and said: "If it has not rained all this time, do you expect it to rain in this short while?"

Full of joy and happiness, the governor went to the baths, thinking that he had won the money. At the same time Nakdimon went into the temple, and wrapping himself in the *Tallit* he prayed to God and said: "Lord of the universe, it is well known to Thy holy Name that I did this not for the sake of my own honor nor for the honor of my father, but for Thy honor, in order that the Israelites who came here on a pilgrimage should have water to drink." No sooner had he finished his prayer than God answered him. Heavy clouds covered the sky and the rain came down in such quantity that the cisterns were filled to overflowing. As the governor came out of the bath, he met Nakdimon coming out of the temple, and said to him: "I see that it is raining." Nakdimon replied: "You will have to pay *me*, for the cisterns are much fuller now than they were when you lent them to me." The governor replied: "I know full well that God has sent this heavy rain for your sake, nevertheless you owe me my money anyhow, for the sun has just set, and the time of the rain is mine, for it is night time." Nakdimon went back to the temple and, wrapping himself again in his *Tallit*, he prayed and said: "Lord of the universe, show that Thou hast friends in this world, and just as Thou hast performed a miracle for me by sending the rain, so perform another by causing the sun to reappear." Directly a wind arose, the clouds were scattered and the sun shone again.

When the governor saw it, he said: "If it were not that the sun is shining again, I should have a claim against you for the money."

Our sages tell us that the real name of Nakdimon was Buni, and that he was called Nakdimon, because the sun shone again on his behalf. We are further told that the sun stood still for the sake of three men, one was Nakdimon, the other was Joshua, for whom the sun stood still when he fought the kings before Gibeah, the third was our master Moses, when he defeated Amalek. Therefore, my dear friends, have faith in God, who does not forsake His pious ones who put their trust and hope in Him.

### 97. THE PRAYER OF R. HANINA BEN DOSA

Once upon a time the son of Rabban Gamaliel fell ill. So he sent two sages to Rabbi Hanina ben Dosa to pray that his son might recover from his illness. As soon as Hanina beheld the two men, he quickly ran up to the loft of the house and began praying that the fever might disappear, and as soon as he had finished he came down to them and said to them: "Return home, for he is better now and his fever has left him." They replied: "Who told you this? Are you a prophet?" R. Hanina replied: "I am neither a prophet nor the son of a prophet, but I have it as a tradition from my father's father that if a prayer runs smoothly, then it is a sign that it has been heard; my prayer just now ran smoothly without any hindrance, therefore I am sure that it has been heard."

They noted down the time when he had told them that the patient was better, and when they

returned to Rabban Gamaliel, they told him the
exact time when the turn for the better had set in
and showed him the note which they had taken.
R. Gamaliel swore by the Lord that this was the
very time when the fever had left the boy and
he asked for a drink.

### 98. The Efficacy of R. Hanina's Prayer

One day, as R. Hanina ben Dosa went to
R. Johanan ben Zakkai to study the Torah with
him, he found the son of R. Johanan very ill.
R. Johanan turned to R. Hanina ben Dosa and
said to him: "My son is very ill, pray for him
that his life may be saved." R. Hanina put his
head between the knees of the sick man and
prayed that he might live. Then R. Johanan
ben Zakkai said: "If I had even stuck my head
into the ground no one would have taken any
notice of it." Then his wife said to R. Johanan,
"Is R. Hanina a more worthy man than you?"
He replied, "I will tell you. R. Hanina is like a
servant, who enters the presence of the king
without asking special leave. Hanina ben Dosa
also appears before God without asking special
leave. But I am like a prince, who does not go
in and out as freely as the servant and therefore
his petition is less likely to be heard. Therefore

I asked him that he should pray for my dear son that his life may be spared. Although I could have prayed myself, nevertheless I asked him to pray."

## 99. TITHES MAKE RICH

The Bible says, "Give Me tithe in order that you may be able to give more tithes" (Deut. 14.22). This means that the more tithes a person gives the richer he becomes.

Once upon a time, there lived a man who was very wealthy. All his wealth was the result of the yield of a field which brought him a yearly income of a thousand measures of corn, of which he gave every year one hundred as tithe to the priest. And because he was so careful to give his tithe, the Lord caused his field to yield a thousand measures. When the time of his death drew near, he called his son, for he had only one son, and said to him, "My dear son, I am sick and may die. I leave you this field, which yields a harvest of one thousand measures of corn every year. Take care, my dear son, and give your tithe regularly. Be sure to give every year a hundred measures as tithe and the Lord will prosper the field for you as he has done for me." After these words the good man died.

The field yielded the son in that year the same amount of one thousand measures of corn as it had yielded for his father, and he gave one hundred measures as tithe just as his father had done before. The second year he again gave one hundred measures of corn. When he saw that the tithe which he had given away every year was so heavy, he bethought himself and said, "Next year I will not give so much, I will keep the tithe for myself," and he kept his word. The third year the yield of the field was only one hundred measures. And the man grieved very much over it and was very sorely troubled.

When his relatives saw that he grieved so much over the fact that his field brought him no more than one hundred measures, they came to him, dressed in fine garments and full of joy. When he saw them all dressed in beautiful white garments, he said to them: "I believe that you take pleasure in seeing my sad plight." They replied, "We are very much grieved over your sad plight and we grieve over the fact that you have not given the proper tithe as your father commanded you on his deathbed. Come, we will explain the matter to you. When you first came into possession of the field, you were the owner, and the Lord was the priest. And when you divided the one hundred measures among

His poor, you gave them to the priest, i.e. to God, to whom they were due, but now that you have refused to give the tithe, you have become the priest and the Lord the owner. He has, therefore, given you one hundred measures of corn and kept nine hundred for Himself." When the man heard this, he admitted that he was wrong.

This is what our sages mean when they say that if a man withholds the tithe and does not pay it up fully, the time will come when he will have one tenth of what he had before. Therefore, dear friends, give your tithe properly and the Lord will protect you also.

### 100. KEEP TROTH. THE STORY OF THE WELL AND THE WEASEL

R. Ami says: Come here, my dear son, and see what a wonderful thing it is for people to be truthful. If one makes a promise, he should keep it. This we learn from the story of the weasel and the well. The lesson that we learn is that if a man can put his trust in a weasel, how much more is it meet that he should put his trust in the Holy One, blessed be He!

One day a young damsel, dressed in fine clothes, went out of one town to go to another to visit her father and mother. She lost her way and came to a huge forest, where she wandered on until she came to a desert. She walked on and on till evening. The day had been very hot and by noon she had reached a deep well. But there was no bucket, only a rope hanging by the side of the well. She was so overcome by thirst that she took hold of the rope and let herself down to the level of the water at the bottom of the well. After having drunk her fill, she was not able to get up again, and thought to herself, "I shall surely die here," and began crying very bitterly and loudly.

As she was thus weeping and crying, a young man, having also lost his way, passed by. Hearing the cry, he followed it and came to the well. When he came near he looked into the well, but it was so deep that he could not see what was in it, so he called down, "Who is it that is crying there so bitterly?   Are you a human being or are you a demon?"   When the young damsel heard him, she was very glad that a human being had heard her voice, and she answered, "My dear man, I am a friend and a human being, and told him how she had gotten into the well." He replied, "If you will grant my request, I will help you."   The damsel said, "Yes."   Then he said to her, "Swear."   She swore that she would grant his request, and he

pulled her out. When she came up, he saw what
a beautiful maiden she was and what beautiful
clothes she had on. Then he said to her again,
"Now keep your promise, grant my request and
live with me." She replied, "My dear friend, tell
me of what nation you are." He replied, "I live
in that town yonder and am a *Cohen*." Then she
said, "I also come from that town and am a
Jewess and of good family." Then she said to
him: "My dear friend, you are a worthy man,
you come from a worthy family, from the priests
whom God Himself has chosen, and you want to
lie with me like an animal without a *ketubah*
and without *kiddushin!* I beg of you, do not do
this! but come with me to my father and tell him
the whole adventure that has befallen us. But
this I say to you that from now on I will consider
myself betrothed to you and will not marry any
other man but you." He replied, "But who shall
be witness that we are betrothed to each other?"
She said, "The little weasel which you see running along there and the well and the heavens
shall be our witnesses that neither of us shall
break his promise to the other." And with these
words they took leave of one another, each one
going his own way. The young man went to his
place and the damsel to hers. Before parting,

they said to each other: "We will meet again when it will be the will of the Lord."

The girl kept her oath a year or two and refused to marry anybody although many matches had been offered to her. She pretended to be out of her mind so that the *Shadkanim* should not come to her father to arrange a match for her. But she told no one her adventure and kept her oath. The young man, however, forgot his oath, married another woman and had a child by her. When the child was six months old, a weasel came and bit its throat, so that it died. She bore another child, which fell into a well and died. The mother wept bitterly and said: "If my children had died a natural death, I would not grieve so deeply, but seeing that my children have died in such an unusual manner, I am sure that it is on account of some sin which you or I have committed. My dear husband, think very carefully and tell me what you have done." Then he sighed and told her of the adventure which had befallen him with the damsel. Then she said, "I see now that it is the work of the Holy One, blessed be He, and we must part, for our children will all die. Go and fulfill the vow which you have sworn." And they gave each other a divorce.

Then he went to the town where the girl

lived, called on her father and asked him to give him his daughter to wife. The father replied: "How can I give her away in marriage, seeing that she is mad and subject to epileptic fits?" When the young man heard this, he understood the reason of her pretended madness. And he said to the father, "Give her to me and I will take upon myself to cure her of her illness." And he told him the whole adventure that had befallen her. When the father of the damsel heard it, he gave her to him as wife. And the girl was very happy, for she knew him as the man to whom she had been betrothed. They had many children who studied the Torah. To them the verse can be applied: "Mine eyes are upon the faithful of the land" (Ps. 101.6), i.e. God says: "My eyes look upon the faithful of the earth."

Concerning this R. Johanan says, "Whoever acts uprightly in this world, and keeps his promises, will also be judged righteous in the world to come, as it is said in the Bible, 'Truth springeth out of the earth; and righteousness hath looked down from the heavens' (Ps. 85.12). Therefore if one makes a promise, he must not think that there is no one present who will tell about it. There is always someone present, who has been sent by the Holy One, blessed be He."

## 101. The Evil of Pride

Our rabbis have taught: The *Pasuk* says, "A man should always be as soft as a reed, which is very soft, and not hard like a cedar, which is very hard and tall." This means that a man should not be proud but very meek.

A man by the name of Eleazar, son of Simeon, was coming one day from his teacher in Migdal Gedor. He was riding on an ass along the shore of the sea, feeling very happy and proud because he had studied so much Torah. As he was riding, he was met by a big dark man, who greeted him and said, "Peace unto you, O master." Rabbi Eleazar did not return the greeting and said to him, "Tell me, you wretch, are all the people of your town as black as you are?" The man replied, "I do not know, but go and say to the master who made me, 'Why have you made such a contemptible vessel'?" When the man replied to him so strangely, Eleazar realized that he had spoken improperly and that he had sinned against God. So he dismounted from his ass and fell down at the feet of the man and said, "My dear friend, forgive me for having spoken disrespectfully to you, I did not consider what I was saying." But the man replied, "I cannot forgive you until you go to the artisan who made me and ask him why he made such a black article?" And with these words he left him.

But R. Eleazar ben Simeon followed him into the town where he lived. There the people came out to meet R. Simeon, saying, "Peace unto you, O master and teacher." The black man turned to them and said, "Whom are you addressing as master and teacher?" The people replied, "The man who is following behind you!" Then the black man said, "If he be a master, may the like of him not multiply in Israel!" Then the people asked, "Why? What has he done to you?" And he told them all that had happened. Then the people said to the black man, "We beg you to forgive him if he has hurt you in any way, for he is a rare and worthy man in the knowledge of the Torah." He replied, "For your sakes I will forgive him, otherwise I would have insisted that he should go and ask the Master why He has made me so black. But in future let him be warned never to behave in such a manner again." Thereupon Rabbi Eleazar ben Simeon went to the *bet ha-midrash* and discoursed on the theme, "One should always be soft like a reed and not hard like a cedar." Rashi says that the

black man was none other than the prophet
Elijah, whose purpose was to punish him so that
he should not be proud of his knowledge of the
Torah.

## 102. RELY NOT UPON MIRACLES

Once upon a time there lived a man who was
called R. Huna. He lived in a tumble down
house, which had a large quantity of wine in it.
R. Ada, son of Ahabah, came into the house and
lectured on the *halakah* until everything had
been removed from the house. When he had
finished his lecture and everything had been
removed, he left the house, whereupon it tumbled
down. When R. Ada realized that a miracle had
happened for his sake, he was very much
troubled and said, "A person should not stay
in a dangerous place, thinking that a miracle
may happen to him, for it may be that the
miracle will not happen. And if a miracle should
happen, it will be deducted from the reward due
for his good deeds." For this reason he was very
angry with himself.

## 103. THE VALUE OF CHARITY

One night—it was the last night of *Rosh
Hashanah*—R. Johanan b. Zakkai dreamed that
his sister's son would lose seven hundred gold

florins. So he went to his sister's son and said.
"My dear friends, give me some money, for
there are people who are in need of alms." And
he arranged with his friends to collect money
from them from time to time during the year.
In this way he took from them during the year
money for charity up to seven hundred gold
florins, less ten (r. seventeen) florins which they
had not yet given him when the year came to an
end, namely, the year from the night of his
dream until the following New Year.

On the eve of the Day of Atonement of the
following year, there came an order from the
Emperor that they should immediately appear
before him. They were very much alarmed,
fearing that they would be heavily taxed. So
they went to their uncle, R. Johanan, and asked
him what to do. R. Johanan replied, "Fear not,
for you will not have to pay more than seventeen
gold florins." Then they said to him, "How do
you know?" He replied, "I have seen it in a
dream." When they came to the Emperor, he
imposed a fine of seventeen florins. They said
then to R. Johanan, "Dear uncle, since you knew
that we would lose seven (r. seventeen) florins,
why did you not tell us? We would have given
you the entire seven hundred gold florins the

first time for charity." R. Johanan replied, "I will tell you the reason. If I had asked you to give me as much as seven hundred florins in one sum, you would not have given it willingly and it would not have been a pious deed. As I came to you from time to time asking small amounts, you gave them to me with a willing heart; for unless one gives charity with a willing heart, it is not reckoned as a pious deed. On the contrary, it is considered like a sin."

Rabbi Joshua says concerning this that when a man turns away his eyes from charity and does not give alms to the poor, it is considered as if he were worshiping idols, for concerning charity it is said in the Torah, "Beware lest there be a wicked thought in thine heart, not to give charity" (Deut. 15.9), and in the same way wickedness is used in connection with the worship of idols, as it is said, "And there came out wicked men" (I Sam. 2.12). As the word wickedness here means that they were worshiping idols, so the word wicked used with reference to charity means that if one does not give charity, it is the same as if he worshiped idols.

## 104. Solomon and Ashmedai

When King Solomon was about to build the temple, he was forbidden to use iron in the building thereof. Not knowing how to break the stones, he sent for the sages and asked for their advice. The sages replied, "We will tell you. In the days of creation a worm was formed which is called *shamir*. This worm was used by our master Moses when he cut the stones for the breastplate. There is nothing in the world so hard but this worm cuts it in twain." Then King Solomon said, "But how can I get this worm?" The sages replied, "We will tell you how to get it. Capture a he-demon and a she-demon and torture them, and they will tell you how to get the *shamir*." The demons were brought before King Solomon and he asked them about the *shamir*. They replied, "We do not know, but Ashmedai the king of the demons— may God be with us!—he knows where the *shamir* is to be found." King Solomon replied, "I will torture you until you tell me where I can find Ashmedai." They replied, "We will tell you. Yonder in that mountain Ashmedai dug a deep pit, which is filled with water. It is covered with a stone called *tinra*, and the stone is sealed with the seal of Ashmedai. Every day he goes up to

heaven and studies in the heavenly college. Then
he comes down again, feeling very warm, and
drinks of the water, but he does not drink wine.
But before he begins to drink, he examines the
seal to make sure that no one has been there
and put wine into the well. When he is satisfied
that the seal has not been touched, he drinks his
fill, puts his seal again on the stone and goes
his way."

Then King Solomon sent for his counselor,
Benaiah son of Jehoiada, and gave him a chain,
on which the divine name was engraved, and a
packet of wool big enough to stop up a hole, and a
cask full of wine. The counselor journeyed until he
came to the well of Ashmedai, from which he
drank. Then Benaiah dug another well under
the ground, so that the water of the well could
drain itself into it, without breaking the seal.
Then he stopped up the hole with the wool. Then
he dug another well above the level of Ashmedai's
well and poured wine into it, and it emptied
itself into Ashmedai's well. The purpose was
that, as soon as he drank the wine, he should
fall asleep and could be bound. When he had
done all this, the counselor climbed up upon a
tree and hid himself, waiting for the return of
Ashmedai from heaven. As soon as Ashmedai
came down from heaven, he ran over to the well

and, seeing his seal, opened the well and wanted to drink. But as he smelled the wine, he refrained from drinking, for he said: "Whoever drinks wine loses his wit, therefore I will not drink." But he was so thirsty that he finally had to drink. And after he had drunk the wine, he felt heavy and laid himself down to sleep. As soon as he fell asleep, Benaiah came down from the tree and put the chain which had the divine name engraved upon it round his neck.

When Ashmedai awoke, he tried to break the chain in two. But the counselor said, "You cannot break the chain, for the name of God is written upon it." When he saw that, he went with him willingly. After they had walked some distance Ashmedai went up to a tree, rubbed against it, and it fell. Further along they came to the house of a widow. Ashmedai wanted to rub his back against the wall, but the widow came out and with words of flattery she begged him not to do it. As he tried to bend the other way, he broke a bone. Then Ashmedai quoted the verse: "A soft tongue breaketh the bone" (Prov. 25.15), which means that a man who allows himself to be flattered by fine words breaks a bone. They went further and met a blind man who had gone astray. Ashmedai led him into the right way. Then the counselor

asked him: "My dear man, why did you lead
the blind man into the right way?" Ashmedai
replied: "The blind man is very pious and they
proclaim in heaven that whosoever does him a
kindness will have a share in the world to come.
This is why I led him into the right way." As
they went further, they met a wedding party and
the people were making merry. Ashmedai began
to weep. The counselor asked him, "Why are
you weeping?" And he replied: "I weep because
I know that the groom will die tomorrow, and
the bride will have to wait thirteen years for
*halizah*." Then they came to a shoemaker's
house, and they heard a man saying: "Make me
a pair of shoes to last seven years." The shoemaker replied, "Very well, I will." Then
Ashmedai laughed and said, "He is ordering a
pair of shoes to last seven years, and I doubt
whether he will live seven days, not to speak of
seven years." They went on further and Ashmedai saw a drunken man who had lost his way.
So he took him by the hand and brought him
back to the right way. The counselor asked him:
"Why do you show him the right way?" Ashmedai replied: "They proclaim in heaven that he
is a very wicked man, therefore I showed him the
right way that he may obtain his reward in this
world." They went together further and he saw

a man digging for treasures and performing magic
in order to find where the treasures lay hidden.
Ashmedai laughed, and the counselor asked him
why he was laughing. Ashmedai replied, "How
can I help laughing when this fellow is digging for
treasures and performing magic, while the treasure with which Solomon will build the temple is
directly under him and he does not know it?
How then can he expect to find the other
places?"

When they reached the king's palace, King
Solomon kept him waiting three days before he
allowed him to appear before him. Then
Ashmedai asked, "Why does King Solomon not
allow me to appear before him?" They replied,
"The king is ill, having drunk too much."
Ashmedai said, "Give him a little more to drink."
The next day he again wished to appear before
the king, and he was told again, "The king is ill;
he has drunk and eaten too much." Then
Ashmedai said, "Let him take a purgative." The
third day he came before King Solomon. As he
entered, he took a yardstick and measured four
cubits in front of the king. The king asked him
what was the meaning of his act. Ashmedai
replied: "I will tell you. When you die you
will not have more than the space of four cubits,
and yet you have subdued the whole world and

are not satisfied until you have conquered me too." Then the king replied, "Do not fear, I do not desire anything of you except that you bring me the *shamir*. For I am about to build the temple and am not allowed to use any iron to break the stones. It can be done by means of the *shamir*, therefore I had you brought before me in order that you may help me get it." Then Ashmedai replied, "My Lord king, be it known unto you that I have no power over it. It is in the power of the ruler of the sea, and he does not entrust it to anyone except the wild cock (*hoopoo*), who must take an oath that he will restore it to him."

King Solomon then gave Benaiah a glass cover and ordered him to go and search for a nest of fledglings of the wild cock. Benaiah searched far and wide until he came to a mountain where no man lived. There he found a nest. So he took the glass and covered the fledglings with it. When the cock came and wanted to get to the young, he found them closed in. So he flew to the prince of the sea and took from him the *shamir*, which he laid on the glass, and the glass split in two. As he was about to fly away Benaiah frightened him, and he dropped the *shamir*. When Benaiah saw this, he picked up the *shamir* and went away. When the cock saw that he had lost the *shamir*, he strangled himself, because he could not keep his oath to the ruler of the sea to return the *shamir*.

When Solomon got possession of the *shamir*, he built the temple. When he had finished the building of the temple, he found himself one day alone in the chamber with Ashmedai. He said to him: "What can you, demons, do more than human beings?" Ashmedai replied, "Take off the chain with which you have bound me and give me the seal which you wear on your finger and I will show you many wonderful things." King Solomon removed the chain and gave him his seal. Thereupon Ashmedai put one leg on the earth and the other on the sky and swallowed King Solomon and threw him out a distance of four hundred miles. Then Ashmedai sat down on the king's throne and pretended to be King Solomon. It was then that King Solomon said, "What is left to man of all his work that he does in this world?" (Eccl. 1.3). And he went about begging at the doors for a piece of bread, repeating at the same time, "I, Koheleth, have been a king over Israel in Jerusalem" (ib. 1.12). And he walked so long until he came back to Jerusalem and appeared before the Sanhedrin. And all along, as he was traveling, he kept saying, "I am Koheleth, king over Israel in Jerusalem."

When the Sanhedrin heard that he was constantly repeating the same words, they said, "A madman does not always repeat the same words. Let us see if he is really the king or not." They called Benaiah and asked him whether he had been recently to see the king. He replied, "No." So they sent for the queen and asked her whether the king had been recently with her. She said, "Yes, he was with me last night." Then they asked her, "Did you notice his feet?" She said, "No, he has socks on his feet when he comes to stay with me." When the sages heard this, they understood that something was amiss, so they gave Solomon the chain with the name of God engraven on it, and the seal with the name of God engraved upon it, and led him to his throne. As soon as Ashmedai saw him, he flew away.

King Solomon then sat on the throne, but he was always in fear of Ashmedai. So he wrote charms over his bed, and at night he had guards to watch over him, as we find it in the verse of the Bible, that every night sixty men stood guard over Solomon (Cant. 3.7), for he was afraid of Ashmedai, may God be with us and protect us!

## 105. RABBI HANINA AND THE POISONOUS REPTILE

Once upon a time there was a reptile in the synagogue which bit the people and prevented their attending service. It was a kind of snake that was full of poison. The people complained to R. Hanina ben Dosa and begged him to pray for its removal. R. Hanina said: "Come with me and show me the hole where the snake is." The people took him and showed him the hole. Thereupon R. Hanina put his foot over the hole, covering it with his heel. The snake came out, bit him in the heel, and died as a result. R. Hanina took the snake on his shoulders and carried it to the college. Then he said: "You see, my dear children, it was not the snake that killed the people, it was their sins that killed them." Then he said again: "Woe unto the man who is met by this snake, and woe unto the snake if he is met by R. Hanina."

Rashi explains that the snake has a poison, and when it bites anyone, then whichever of the two reaches water first the other one dies. If the snake gets to the water first, the person must die, but if the person gets there first, the snake must die. But a miracle happened to

R. Hanina and a spring came out of his heel.
R. Hanina was therefore close to water before
the snake, and the snake had to die.

### 106. THE SAINTLY RAB AMRAM AND THE BEAUTIFUL WOMAN

Once upon a time women of Nehardea who
had been taken captive in battle were brought
into the house of a man called Rabbi Amram,
the Pious, in order that he might redeem them.
For it was the custom in olden times to redeem
captives. He put them all in the loft and
removed the ladder, so that no one should be
able (God forbid!) to go up and commit a sin
with them. Among them R. Amram noticed one
woman, as she passed by the opening, who was
very beautiful. The evil passion took possession
of R. Amram and so inflamed him with her
beauty that he longed to make her his own.
Thereupon he took a ladder, which ordinarily
required more than ten persons to carry it, and
carried it alone. For his passion was so strong
that he wanted to go up and lie with the woman.
When he had gone half way up the ladder, he
suddenly bethought of the great sin that he was
about to commit and began shouting: "Fire,
fire, in R. Amram's house!" When the scholars

came to put out the fire, they found none. Then R. Amram said: "I did this in order to put out the fire of evil passion." He told them what he had had in mind, for, he said, "It is better for me to be put to shame in this world than that I should (God forbid!) be put to shame in the world to come." Then he adjured the evil passion to depart from him, and the evil passion departed in the form of a pillar of fire. Then R. Amram said: "Behold, you are fire, and I am nothing but flesh and blood, and yet I have subdued you, and I am also better than you, evil passion, you Satan!"

One should therefore not allow oneself to be led astray by the *Yezer ha-Ra'* (evil passion), but should put him to shame.

### 107. WOMEN ARE FICKLE—BUT NOT ALL

The proverb says, women are weak-minded and can easily be persuaded. A story is told of a woman who had lost her husband, and she wept and cried bitterly, unable to forget her dear husband. She spent days and nights, weeping and crying over the grave of her husband. Not far from the cemetery there was a watchman who stood guard over the gallows to see that none of those hanged should be removed, under a penalty

of death from the king. One night the watchman
came to the woman and cajoled her so long until
he persuaded her to lie with him. While he was
with her a body was stolen from the gallows.
When he returned and saw what had happened,
he was sorely troubled for fear that he would be
hanged by order of the king for neglecting his
duty. So he went again to the woman and told
her of his troubles. The woman replied, "Do
not be frightened. Take the body of my husband
out of the grave and hang it on the gallows in the
place of the body that has been taken away."
So they went together, took the body out of the
grave and hanged it on the gallows.

You see, therefore, how the woman had
been weeping and crying so bitterly for her
husband, and yet she harbored within her the
evil passion and allowed herself to be persuaded
by the watchman. Hence the saying that women
are weak-minded or easily persuaded to do a
person's will even when they are in mourning.

But there are pious women also. For there
once was a woman who had seven children. One
died, and she mourned him very bitterly. People
said to her, "Do not weep so much, for if you
do, you may (Heaven forbid!) lose some more
children." But she would not desist and continued mourning until all her children died. And

finally she also died, through the great grief over
the loss of her children, and did not allow herself
to be persuaded as the other woman had done.

## 108. PELIMO AND SATAN

There once lived a pious man called Pelimo,
who used to say every day: "May an arrow stick
in the eye of Satan," and he cursed him always.
One day, on the eve of the Day of Atonement, Satan disguised himself as a poor man
and came to Pelimo's door and asked him for a
piece of bread. He said, "Dear friend, give me a
piece of bread for God's sake. On a holy day
like this, when everyone is sitting at home at his
table, I must eat my bread in the street."
Thereupon Pelimo took him into the house and
gave him a piece of bread. Then he said again,
"On such a holy day as this everyone sits at the
table while I must sit outside without a table
and eat by myself." Then Pelimo gave him a
seat at the table. As Satan was sitting at the
table, he assumed the appearance of a sick
person covered with running sores, and the
saliva flowed from his mouth. Then Pelimo said,
"Behave properly, why do you act in so disgust-
ing a manner?" But Satan replied: "Give me
also something to drink." Pelimo gave him a

cup of wine. But instead of drinking, he spat into the wine. He did this spitefully with the intention of insulting Pelimo for cursing him every day, as you have been told. When Pelimo saw that he had spat into the wine and had dropped the cup, he said to him: "Either drink properly or leave this place!" Then Satan fell backwards and pretended to be dead, and the rumor spread that Pelimo had killed a man in his house. Pelimo ran away and hid himself in a privy. When Satan saw how greatly Pelimo was troubled, he rose up again and said to Pelimo: "I am Satan. I disguised myself as a poor man in order to annoy you because you cursed me every day. Therefore curse me no more." Then Pelimo said: "What should I say then, thou Satan and *Yezer ha-Ra'*?" And Satan replied: "Pray to God that He may put away the *Yezer ha-Ra'* from you, so that he shall not make you stumble and commit sin, as King David did."

## 109. R. ZERA AND HIS FASTS

When R. Zera migrated from Babylon to Palestine, he fasted one hundred days, praying that he might forget the Gemara which he had learned in Babylon, so that he might learn the

Torah properly in Palestine from R. Johanan.
Then he fasted one hundred days more, praying
that R. Eliezer might not die before him, for
then the whole burden of communal work would
fall upon him, since R. Eliezer was the head of the
community. Then he fasted one hundred days
more, praying that he might be saved from the
punishment of Gehenna. Every thirty days he
tested himself by entering a burning limekiln, but
the fire did not touch him. Once the sages
expressed their envy of him in being safe from
the fire of Gehenna.

### 110. HEROD THE SLAVE OF THE HASMONEANS WHO BECAME KING AND R. JUDAH BEN BOTA

Once upon a time there lived a man called
Herod, who became king. Before he became
king, he was a slave of the Hasmoneans, and
among them there was a young girl whom Herod
loved. One day he heard a voice from heaven
saying, "Any slave that rebels this day against
his master will be fortunate." Thereupon Herod
killed all his masters except the young woman
with whom he was in love. He spared her, for
he wanted to marry her. What did the young
woman do? She said: "If anyone shall come and
say that he has won the king's daughter, having

put to death all the Hasmoneans except me, he shall not have me." And with these words she went up to the roof of the house, threw herself down and broke her neck. Then Herod said: "Who is there among you who interprets the verse: 'One from among thy brethren shalt thou set king over thee' (Deut. 17.15), as meaning from among thy brethren and not from a slave?" And the sages said that this was their interpretation. Whereupon he put them all to death with the exception of Judah son of Bota. Him he spared because he wanted to have his advice when he stood in need of it. But he had his eyes put out.

One day Herod was sitting in a chamber with Judah ben Bota, but the latter did not know who he was. And Herod said: "What a miserable slave Herod is! He has killed all the sages and murdered his masters." R. Judah replied: "What can I do?" Herod said: "Let us curse him." For he desired to find out what Judah ben Bota had in his mind. Then Baba replied, "The Bible says:'Curse not the king, no, not in thy thought'" (Eccl. 10.20). Herod rejoined: "But Herod is no king." Then Baba said: "Assume that he is no better than a rich man, who also must not be cursed, as we read in the verse: 'And curse not the rich in thy bed chamber'" (ibid.). Then

Herod revealed himself and said: "Had I known that you rabbis are so pious, I would not have killed them, but now that I have done it I fear me that God will not forgive the sin which I have committed. Now advise me what to do to obtain God's forgiveness." Then Baba replied: "I will advise you what to do. You have extinguished the light of the Torah, now go and rekindle it, for the sages are called the light of the Torah and you have put them all to death; therefore go and kindle it anew, i. e. go and build the temple, of which it is said in the Bible: 'And it shall be a light to all the nations' (Is. 2.2). Therefore go and build the temple." He took his advice and rebuilt the temple, as we are told in the Bible.

### 111. Be Not Too Sure of Thyself. Story of R. Meir

R. Meir used to scoff at people who committed sins, for he said: "Every man can subdue his evil inclinations so as not to commit sin." One time the *Yezer ha-Ra'* (evil inclination) tried to tempt him and, taking on the shape of a beautiful woman, stood on the opposite side of the river. When R. Meir beheld her, his passion flared up and he desired to possess her. But there was no bridge, nor was there a boat to ferry him across. So he took a small board and stood on it to ferry himself across, but before doing it he threw a rope across, which he fastened on the other side and held on to, so as not to fall. When he was half way across, his passion left him and he no longer desired the young woman. Then the *Yezer ha-Ra'* (evil spirit) said: "If it were not that they proclaim in heaven concerning you: 'Take care of R. Meir and his Torah,' I would throw you into the water and drown you."

### 112. BE NOT TOO SURE OF THYSELF. STORY OF R. AKIBA

R. Akiba also used to scoff at the people who committed sin. He also said, "Every man can easily subdue his evil passion." One day the *Yezer ha-Ra'* (evil inclination) took the shape of a beautiful woman and climbed to the top of a tall palm tree. When R. Akiba beheld her, he desired her and began to climb up. When he was half way up, his passion left him. The *Yezer ha-Ra'* then said to R. Akiba: "If it had not been announced in the heavens: 'Take care of R. Akiba and his Torah,' I would

have thrown you down from the tree so that
you would have broken your neck and died
instantly."

### 113. The Daughters of R. Nahman

The daughters of R. Nahman used to remove
the scum of the boiling broth with their bare
hands, and the people thought they were able to
do it because of their piety. R. Elos wondered,
saying to himself: "We find it written that a
pious man can be found among a thousand, but
among all women there is not a single one
(cf. Eccl. 7.28), yet we see that the daughters of
R. Nahman are pious women."

Once it happened that the daughters of R.
Nahman were taken captive by the Cutheans,
and among the captives was also R. Elos. There
was another prisoner among them also, who
understood all languages, even the language of
the birds. There came a crow, crying *Kra! Kra!*
as crows do. Then R. Elos asked: "What does
the crow say?" And the man who understood
their language replied: "The crow is speaking to
you and says, 'Elos, flee,' which means make
your escape, for it will go well with you." R.
Elos, replied: "I will pay no heed, for crows are
given to lying." Then came a dove and began

to coo. Elos asked: "What is the dove saying?"
And the man replied: "The dove also says:
'Elos, flee'." Then Elos said: "Doves do not tell
lies, for the community of Israel is compared to
the dove. A miracle will surely happen to me.
I wish to see at the same time whether the
daughters of R. Nahman, being prisoners in the
hands of the heathen, will persevere in their
piety. I will tell them that they should also
make their escape. Then I will know whether
they are pious. If they escape with me, it will
be proof of their piety, but if they prefer to
remain among the heathen, then unquestionably
they are not pious."

R. Elos went to look for them and found them
both together in a privy. Then he said to himself:
"All women tell each other their secrets in the
privy." Then he overheard them saying to one
another: "We do not wish to run away, for our
husbands are not with us and if the heathen wish
to possess us we will yield even though we have
husbands in Palestine. We will say that our
husbands are far away and will not redeem us."

When R. Elos heard this, he made his escape
together with the man who understood all
languages. R. Elos was lucky and came home
in safety across the water. But the other man
was caught and put to death. The daughters of

R. Nahman also returned and continued to remove the scum from the boiling broth with their bare hands as before. R. Elos concluded therefore that they did it by means of witchcraft. They had heard indeed of his flight, and R. Elos had heard their conversation in the privy, which showed what sort of modesty they possessed.

## 114 THE TWO FALSE PROPHETS

There were two brothers Ahab, son of Kolaiah, and Zedekiah, son of Maaseiah, who were very wicked men. Their home was in Jerusalem and when they were afterwards taken captive to Babylon with the other Jews, they continued their wicked actions as before. They pretended to be prophets and called on the daughters of Nebuchadnezzar. Ahab went to one daughter, and said to her: "I have been sent by the Lord my God to tell you to do the will of my friend Zedekiah and lie with him." Zedekiah went to the other daughter and spoke likewise to her, saying: "The Lord my God has sent me to you to tell you to do the bidding of my friend Ahab and lie with him." The two daughters of Nebuchadnezzar then went and told their father. The father replied: "When they come to you again tell them to ask me, for you must not do

anything without my permission." When they
came again to the daughters to carry out their
intention, the latter replied: "You must first go
and ask the consent of the king, for we dare not
do such things without leave from our father."
So they went to the king.

When they appeared before the king, he said:
"Are you the prophets whom God sent to my
daughters to lie with them?" They replied:
"The Lord God has sent us to your daughters to
give them the message that they should lie with
us so that the children they have by us may
also be prophets." The king replied: "God hates
unchastity and has Himself forbidden it in your
Torah. How, then, can I believe that God
should have given you a command of this kind?
I asked Hananiah, Mishael and Azariah, who
were also prophets, and they told me that God
has forbidden unchastity." These wicked men
replied: "We are prophets as much as they were,
God had not said this to them, He has said it to
us." The king replied: "I will tell you what I
will do. I will put you to the same test to which
I put Hananiah, Mishael and Azariah. I will
cast you into a burning furnace. If you come
out unscathed like them, I will believe that you
are true prophets and your wishes shall be
granted." The men replied: "Miracles do not

happen every day. Moreover, they were three
pious men, we are only two." The king replied:
"If that is your objection, then choose a third
pious man, whomsoever you like, as companion,
so that you may also be three, as Hananiah,
Mishael and Azariah were three." They said to
the king: "Give us Joshua, the High Priest, as
companion." For he was a very pious man,
and they thought that they would be saved by
his piety and would come out unscathed. The
king replied: "Let it be so," and gave orders to
heat the kiln.

The order was immediately carried out and the
two men, together with Joshua, the High Priest,
were cast into the furnace. The two false
prophets were at once burned to ashes, but
Joshua remained untouched, only his garments
were scorched. Then the king said to Joshua,
the High Priest: "I see that you are a worthy
man, but tell me why were your clothes scorched,
whilst those of Hananiah, Mishael and Azariah
were not even singed?" Joshua replied: "Each
one of those three men was a pious man, but I
was only one." Then the king said: "Abraham
was also one man and yet nothing happened to
him when he was cast into the fiery furnace."
Joshua, the High Priest, replied: "Abraham had
no wicked companions and the fire had no power

to burn, whereas I had two wicked men with me, therefore the fire had power to burn." This is the meaning of the proverb: "Two dry pieces of wood burn a third moist one." And the Bible also says: "The righteous is delivered out of trouble and the wicked cometh in his stead" (Prov. 11.8).

But still remains the question why were the clothes of Joshua scorched, seeing that he was a pious man? The answer is given in the Gemara: "The reason was because he had allowed his sons to wed women not fit for the priesthood and did not prevent them. Therefore were his clothes scorched."

### 115. THE MEN OF SODOM AND ELIEZER
### THE SERVANT OF ABRAHAM

The people of Sodom had the following custom. If a man struck another man's wife and caused her to miscarry and the husband demanded compensation, the guilty person would say: "Give me your wife and I will beget you another child." And the husband would give him his wife until she had another child.

Then they had another custom. If a man struck another and caused him to bleed, the person injured had to pay because he bled and blood-letting was good for his health.

They had still another custom. If one crossed a bridge he had to pay four florins, and if he waded across he had to pay eight florins. One day a washerman crossed the bridge and also waded through the water. The people of Sodom came to him and said: "Give us four florins for having crossed the bridge." Whereupon he replied: "I waded across." "If so," they replied, "pay us eight florins." The man refused to pay, and they fell upon him and beat him, causing a deep wound. They brought him before the judge, and the judge said: "Pay them for having caused you to bleed, and pay also the eight florins for having waded across the river."

One day Eliezer, the servant of Abraham, came to Sodom. They fell upon him and beat him and wounded him. Then they brought him before the judge, and he said: "Pay them for having bled you." Thereupon Eliezer fell upon the judge and beat and wounded him. Then they said: "What does this mean?" Eliezer replied: "The compensation which the judge has to pay me for bleeding him, you take from him to pay for the debt I owe you for having bled me, and I need not pay you anything out of my own pocket."

They had still another custom. If anyone invited a stranger to a meal, they came and stripped the host of his clothes. Once they were celebrating a wedding in the city, and Eliezer came in and sat down at the table. When he was asked who had invited him to the banquet, he pointed to a certain person and said, "This man has invited me." The latter quickly ran out, for he feared they would strip him of his clothes. They asked Eliezer again who had invited him and he pointed to another person, who also got up and ran out, for he was also afraid that they would take his clothes off. Then they asked him again, and he pointed to another one. And so they all ran out, for they feared that their clothes would be taken away, and Eliezer remained alone and enjoyed the feast.

They also had a custom in Sodom that when a stranger came, they put him into a certain bed. If he was too long for the bed, they cut his legs off down to the measure of the bed, and if he was too short, they stretched him until he fitted the measure of the bed. Eliezer, the servant of Abraham, came one day to Sodom and they said to him: "Lie down to sleep in this bed." He replied: "Ever since the death of my mistress Sarah, I have taken a vow never to sleep in a bed," for he feared they would either cut his legs off or stretch him.

They also had another custom. When a poor

man came to Sodom, everyone gave him a coin with the name of the giver written on it, but no one was allowed to sell him bread. The purpose was that he should die of hunger. And when he had died of hunger, they all came and each one took back the coin on which he had written his name. Once a young woman gave a poor man a piece of bread to save his life. When they heard of it, they took the young woman, stripped her naked, smeared her body with honey and put her on the roof. The bees came, ate the honey and stung her to death. This is the meaning of the verse in the Bible: "The cry of Sodom and Gomorrah is great" (Gen. 18.20). The word *rabbah* is the same as *ribah*, which means in Hebrew a "young woman," for it was the cry of the young woman that went up to God.

## 116. The Virtue of Visiting the Sick

Rabbi Akiba said, "When one visits a sick person one performs a good deed, as if he had saved a life in Israel." Once a pupil of Akiba fell ill and nobody visited him. Then R. Akiba came to see him, because he had been his pupil. When he came in, the pupil said: "Dear master, you have prolonged my life by coming to see me; so great has been to me the benefit of your visit."

Soon afterwards R. Akiba preached a sermon and
said: "If a man fails to pay a visit to the sick,
he is considered as one who has killed a person
in Israel." On the contrary, however, through
the visit of R. Akiba this pupil of his was restored
to health. Therefore, dear friends, it is indeed a
great and pious deed to visit the sick.

## 117. The Sincere Nazirite

Simeon the pious said: I have never in all my
life met a more genuine nazirite—one who was
more sincere in his motives—than a certain
young man. One day a fine, handsome young
man came into the land of the South. He had a
handsome countenance, beautiful eyes and golden
hair hanging down in wavy locks. One day he
had his hair cut off, which changed his appearance so much that he no longer looked the same
lad. So I said to the boy: "My son, why did you
have your hair cut off? What made you do it?"
And the lad replied: "I will tell you. I tended
my father's flocks, and once I led the sheep to
the well and, looking into the water, I saw the
reflection of my face. Then I thought: 'What a
fine young man I am, I will follow my own
pleasures, being so handsome.' Then I bethought
myself, 'What a great sin it is to bear oneself so

proudly and allow oneself to be led astray by the *Yezer ha-Ra'* (evil inclination).' And I said to the *Yezer ha-Ra'*: 'You wicked one, you are trying to make me sin, but I will not obey you. You are eager to lure me on so that I should lose my portion in the world to come, though man is only dust and the prey of worms. Therefore I have sworn by God that I would have my locks shorn, so that you may not be able to seduce me. For after that I am sure to lose my comeliness, and if a man is not handsome, the *Yezer ha-Ra'* does not lead him astray'."

When I had heard the lad's story, I rose from my seat and kissed him on the forehead, and said, "My son, may nazirites like you multiply in Israel, for you have taken the vow for the sake of Heaven and not from pride." Unfortunately we often find many people in our time, who do it for the sake of appearance rather than for the sake of Heaven.

## 118. The Adulterous Woman

We find in the Gemara that according to the measure which a man uses in this world, that is, as a person conducts himself in this world, well or ill, so does the Lord, blessed be He, requite him. We find an illustration of this in the *sotah*, i. e. the adulterous woman who turns away from her husband and misconducts herself with another man. As she does, so is it done to her.

A woman who wishes to commit adultery stands at the door that the people may see how fair she is, so that all men should desire her. And she is dealt with in the same manner. For when she is caught in the act of sinning, she is placed at the gate of the temple, which was called the gate of Nicanor, that everyone should see her shame. Moreover a prostitute covers her head with a white veil so that the people should be attracted to her. Therefore the priest proceeds correspondingly when he gives her the bitter waters to drink so that they should cause her to swell. He tears the veil from her head so that she should stand bareheaded before the public. Further, the prostitute paints her face to make it pretty, and correspondingly her face turns yellow when she drinks the bitter waters. She sprinkles her eyes with perfume that she may have a sweet odor; therefore her eyes protrude out of her head when she has drunk the bitter waters. She plaits her hair beautifully so that she may be attractively done up; therefore when the priest gives her the bitter waters to drink, her hair is undone. She beckons with her finger to make men come to her; therefore the nails of her fingers fall off when she has drunk the bitter water. She puts on a beautiful girdle and key (buckle)—for a beautiful girdle is an ornament to woman—therefore the priest takes a rope of hair and twists it round her breast, causing her great pain. When she lies with a man, she spreads her legs apart; therefore her feet drop. She supports the man on her belly; therefore when she drinks the water her belly swells. She feeds her lover with all manner of good food; therefore she must bring as a sacrifice food for a beast, namely, a measure of barley. She gives her lover the best wine that she can find to drink out of gold and silver goblets; therefore the priest gives her bitter water to drink out of an earthenware vessel. She allows no one to look on when she commits her sin; therefore God makes her face to turn yellow in the sight of all. Therefore, dear women, take this tale to heart and beware of falling a prey to sin, for retribution is bound to come.

## 119. The Testament of Rabbi

When Rabbi Judah died, he left in his will four commands to his children. In the first place, he forbade his children to dwell in a place called

Naza, for the people there were frivolous and nothing good could be learnt from them, but only evil. Secondly, he forbade them to sit on the bed of a Cuthean woman in her house. For it once happened to R. Papa that a Cuthean woman owed him some money and he went to her house frequently to ask for the payment of his debt. One day—it was a Sunday—the Cuthean woman took her son and strangled him and put him in her bed and covered him up so that no one should see him. R. Papa came as usual and asked for his money. The woman said to him: "Pray, take a seat on the bed while I go into the next room to fetch the money." R. Papa sat down on the bed. The woman went into the next chamber and tarried there a while. Then she came back, crying: "Woe, woe! you have killed my son!" When R. Papa heard this, he fled the country. Therefore, no one should sit on a bed in the house of a Cuthean woman. In the third place, he commanded that they should never try to evade the tax gatherer, for he might overtake them and take all their money away. The fourth command was that they should not stand in front of an ox when he returns from the meadow, for Satan sits between his horns. This is true especially in the month of Nisan and in the case of a black bull.

## 120. THE PIOUS MAN AND THE TWO SPIRITS

Once upon a time a pious man gave a poor man a shilling on the eve of the New Year in the name of God, for it was a year of great dearth. His wife became so angry with him that he was afraid to enter the house. So he went and laid himself down to sleep in the cemetery for fear of his wife. There he heard two damsels, who had recently died, speaking to one another: "Come, let us fly and listen from behind the heavenly curtain what the Lord has decreed for the coming year." The other replied: "I cannot rise, for I have been buried in a mat of reeds. You go and tell me what you have heard." So she went by herself, and when she returned, she said: "I heard that all grain that is sown before the middle of Marheshvan will be destroyed by hail." When the pious man heard this, he sowed his field in the second half of the month. The hail destroyed the corn in all the other fields but the corn of the pious man was not affected.

The next year, the pious man went again to the cemetery to overhear the talk of the damsels. And he heard one of them saying: "Come, let us go and learn what will happen in the world." But the other replied: "Have I not told you that

I cannot rise, for I am tied up in a mat of reeds? You go and tell me what you have heard." So she went alone, and when she returned, she said: "I have heard that all grain sown after the middle of Marḥeshvan will be destroyed by hail." When the pious man heard this, he sowed his seed in the first half of the month, and the hail destroyed all the grain sowed in the second half, but nothing happened to him, because he sowed his seed in the first half of the month. Then his wife said to him: "Dear husband, how is it that your corn has been spared whilst that of the rest of the world has been destroyed by the hail?" So he told her the whole story, of what had happened to him and what the damsels had said to one another, and that one of them had not been able to rise because she was buried in a mat of reeds.

Not long afterwards, it happened that the wife of the pious man and the mother of the girl who was buried in the mat of reeds quarreled, as women often do. And the wife of the pious man threw it up to the woman and said: "Come, I will show you your daughter buried in a mat of reeds."

The third year, the pious man went again to the cemetery in order to overhear the talk of the damsels. And he heard the one saying to the other: "Come, let us go and hear what will happen this year." And the other replied, "Say nothing about it, for our conversation has been overheard."

### 121. Ze'iri and the Dead Hostess

R. Ze'iri left a saddle-bag in the care of a woman to keep until he returned from the house of his teacher. When he returned from his teacher, he found that the woman had died. So he went to the cemetery to the grave of the woman and asked her what had become of the saddle-bag which he had left in her care. And she replied: "You ask me concerning the saddle-bag which you left in my charge until you returned from your teacher. I have taken good care of it. Therefore, go back to the house and you will find it in the hole where the bolt of the door enters." He went to the house to look for it and found it exactly in the spot where the woman had told him.

## 122. R. Gamaliel Deposed and R. Eleazar ben Azariah Appointed His Successor

A pupil once came to the *bet ha-midrash*, to R. Joshua, and said to him: "My dear master, tell me about the evening prayer. Is one obliged to say it or is it optional?" R. Joshua replied: "It is optional and not obligatory." The pupil left R. Joshua and went to Rabban Gamaliel, who was then the head of the college, and put to him the same question, whether the evening prayer is obligatory or optional. Rabban Gamaliel replied: "It is obligatory." Then the pupil said to Rabban Gamaliel: "But I have heard from R. Joshua that one is not obliged to say it if one does not wish to." Rabban Gamaliel said: "Wait until all the scholars come to the college, and I will hear their opinion." When they had all come, the pupil asked again: "Is the evening prayer obligatory or optional?" And Rabban Gamaliel said: "It is obligatory." And he said again: "If there is anyone here who differs from my decision, let him say so." Then R. Joshua said: "No, there is no one who differs from you." Then R. Gamaliel said: "How can you say that there is no one who differs from me? I have been informed in your name that you had decided that the recital of the evening prayer is not obligatory. You are therefore opposed to me. Therefore, go quickly and stand there and tell us whether you have said so or not." R. Joshua replied: "If I were alive and you were dead, I could deny it, for one can give the lie to the dead, but since we are both alive, how can I give you the lie?" Whereupon Rabban Gamaliel rose and delivered his lecture, while R. Joshua had to stand by silently and not take part in the discussion.

The interpreter of Rabban Gamaliel was a certain R. Huzpit, who continued lecturing until all the people became impatient and said to him: "Stop lecturing." Then they said: "How long will you continue to vex R. Joshua? Come, we will depose Rabban Gamaliel from his leadership. But whom shall we put in his place? Shall we put R. Joshua in his place? He is a quarrelsome person and will annoy Rabban Gamaliel even more than Rabban Gamaliel annoyed him. Shall we put R. Akiba in his place? He does not come of distinguished ancestry, and R. Gamaliel will humiliate him so keenly that he may die. We will put at the head of the college R. Eliezer son of Azariah. He is a scholar and a rich man and of noble descent, and he is able to answer any legal question put to him. And if there is a favor to be obtained from the government, he is in a position to pay for it. Moreover, he had worthy parents, and R. Gamaliel cannot do anything to hurt him, even if he wanted to give him the evil eye."

So the rabbis went to him and said: "It would be a great pleasure to us if you would be the head of our college." R. Eliezer replied: "I will consult my family." Then he went and asked his wife whether he should accept the post of head of the college. She replied: "You may fare as Rabban Gamaliel did and tomorrow you may be deposed." R. Eliezer said to his wife: "I will tell you a proverb. If one drinks out of a beautiful goblet and it gets broken the next day, it is not of much consequence. So even though I am head of the college only for one day and am deposed on the morrow, no great harm is done." She said: "But you are a young man, you have not one gray hair on your head, whereas the head of a college should be an old man, and you are only eighteen years old." Then a miracle happened and eighteen strands of gray hair grew on his head, so that the people thought he was an aged man, fully worthy of the position of the head of the college. This is why R. Eliezer said: "I am like a man of seventy."

Not long afterwards, Rabban Gamaliel and R. Joshua differed concerning a legal decision,

and the rabbis sided with R. Joshua. Then R.
Gamaliel said: "I will go and ask pardon of R.
Joshua." And when he entered the house of
R. Joshua, he saw that the walls were black.
Then Rabban Gamaliel said to him: "I see from
the blackness of your walls that you are
a charcoal-burner." R. Joshua replied to
Rabban Gamaliel: "Woe to the generation of
which you are a leader, for you know not how
they live." Then Rabban Gamaliel said: "Dear
master, I have spoken too harshly against you,
forgive me." But R. Joshua refused to forgive
him. Then R. Gamaliel said: "Forgive me for my
father's sake," and R. Joshua forgave him.


## 123. THE WIFE WHO COULD NOT UNDERSTAND THE LANGUAGE OF HER HUSBAND

A man had a wife who could not understand
his speech. For he had come from Babylon to
Palestine and married his wife in Palestine. One
day he said to her: "Cook lentils for us today."
So she cooked two lentils, for she thought that
when he said lentils, he meant two lentils. He
grew very angry. The next day he said to his
wife: "Cook a potful of lentils." Whereupon she
cooked a pot of lentils so full that one could not
add a single lentil, whereas all that he meant was

that she should cook a potful in the usual way. He grew more angry still. The third day he said to her: "Bring me two *bluzers*," which means two pumpkins, and she brought him two candlesticks, for she understood his words to have that meaning. Then he grew very angry and said to her: "Break the candlesticks on the *baba*, i.e. the door." So she took the candlesticks and struck R. Baba ben Bota on the head, for she understood her husband to mean that she should break the candlesticks over R. Baba's head. Baba ben Bota said to her: "My dear daughter, why do you strike me?" She replied: "My husband told me to strike Baba on the head with the candlesticks and I have done it." Baba ben Bota was just then presiding in the courts and administering justice. Then he said: "My daughter, you have done the will of your husband and followed his command, therefore may God grant you two sons who shall be like Baba ben Bota."

### 124. RABA, R. ZERA AND THE PURIM BANQUET

Raba and Rab Zera were feasting together at the Purim meal. And as they were very merry, Raba attacked R. Zera and killed him. In the morning, when he was sober, Raba felt great regret for having killed R. Zera, and he prayed so long until R. Zera came to life again. The next year on Purim day Raba came again to R. Zera and said: "Come, let us celebrate again and take the Purim meal together." R. Zera replied: "Miracles do not happen always that a person who dies should come back to life again."

### 125. THE DEATH OF RABBI AND HIS HOME VISITS ON FRIDAY NIGHTS

When Rabbi was dying, he called his children to him and said to them: "My dear children, I am lying on my deathbed and desire to make my will. Take care of your mother. Keep a light always burning on my table. Let the table be always set and the bed neatly covered with white sheets, for I will come back every Friday night to my house and pronounce the *kiddush*." And he did return.

One Friday evening, as he was sitting in his house, a neighbor came and knocked on the door, wishing to come in. The servant said: "No one is allowed to come in, for Rabbi is here." When Rabbi heard this, he disappeared and never came again on a Sabbath eve.

On the day of Rabbi's death a voice came from

heaven, saying: "All those attending the funeral of Rabbi will enter paradise." There was a fuller who used to come every day to Rabbi while he was ill to see how Rabbi was getting along. But on the day when Rabbi died, the fuller did not come. He had heard the voice say that all those present at the death of Rabbi would enter paradise and yet he had not been there. This grieved him so much that he mounted a ladder and threw himself down and died. Thereupon a voice came from heaven, saying: "The fuller will also enter paradise with Rabbi, although he was not present at the death of Rabbi."

While Rabbi was lying ill, R. Ḥiyya came to visit him. Seeing that Rabbi was weeping bitterly, R. Ḥiyya said: "Rabbi, why do you weep? Have we not been told that if a person is cheerful at the moment of death, it is a good sign, but if one dies weeping and in sadness, it is not a good sign for him?" Rabbi replied: "I weep because I shall not be able to study the Torah any longer and I shall no longer be able to fulfill the commandments."

On the day when Rabbi died, the sages decreed a public fast. They recited prayers and declared a ban, saying that whoever said Rabbi was dead, should be pierced with a sword. Thereupon Rabbi's maid went up to the loft and said:

"The sages who are below desire to keep Rabbi with them and the angels in heaven would like to have him with them. May it be the will of God that those below may prevail over those above, so that Rabbi may remain alive." But when the sages saw that Rabbi had to move his bowels frequently and they had to put his phylacteries off and on very often, for he had a malady of the bowels and defecation was very painful to him, they exclaimed: "May it be the will of God that those above may prevail over those below." Nevertheless the sages prayed that Rabbi should not die.

Suddenly the maid let a jar fall down the ladder. The noise startled the rabbis and they stopped studying. At that moment Rabbi died. Then the rabbis said: "Bar Kappara, go and see what Rabbi is doing." Bar Kappara went to see what Rabbi was doing and he found Rabbi dead. So he rent the back of his garment behind the door, for he dared not tell the rabbis. Then he said: "Those above and those below had a dispute and those above have won." Then the rabbis said: "How so? Is Rabbi dead?" For they understood his meaning. Bar Kappara said: "It is you who say it, not I," for he stood in fear of his life.

Now, when Rabbi was on the point of death,

he lifted up his ten fingers towards heaven and said: "Master of the universe, it is known before Thee that I have toiled with these ten fingers in the service of Thy Law, and all my life long I never enjoyed this world; not even as much as I have earned with my little finger did I enjoy in this world. May it be Thy will that I may find rest in the grave." And a voice came from heaven, saying: "Rabbi shall find rest in the grave and is prepared for the world to come."

### 126. TURNUS RUFUS AND R. AKIBA

Turnus Rufus, the wicked, once asked Rabbi Akiba, "Why is the day of Sabbath better than any other day, that you should honor it so highly?" R. Akiba replied: "Why are you better than any other man, that people should show you more respect than others?" Whereupon the wicked man replied: "It is the will of the Emperor that honor should be shown to me." Then R. Akiba rejoined: "It is the will of the Lord, blessed be He, that the Sabbath should be honored." Then the wicked man said: "How do you know that this is the right day, maybe it is another day which you do not think is the same? How do you know that this is the Sabbath day?" R. Akiba replied: "This can be proved from the river Sambation. For this river casts up stones all the six days of the week, so that one is not able to cross, but on the Sabbath it is quiet like any other body of water and rests, even as the Lord, blessed be He, Himself rests. But I can give you a still better proof from your own father's grave. Smoke issues from it during the six days of the week, for all those days he is punished in Gehenna, but on the Sabbath day there is no smoke, for on that day the wicked rest in Gehenna. Thus we can prove that the day we call Sabbath is the real Sabbath." Turnus Rufus replied: "You have insulted and offended me."

## 127. The Heathen Who Honored His Father

In Ascalon there lived a heathen called Dama son of Netina. One day the Israelites were in need of a precious stone for the ephod, which was worth 60,000 florins (or as some say, 80,000), and they had to go to Dama, who was a man of great wealth and had such a stone in his possession. When they came to him, they asked him whether he had such a stone. He replied: "Yes, but the key of my shop is under my father's pillow. He is asleep now and I must not wake him, for we are bound to honor father and mother." So the Israelites were obliged to go away. And although he could have made a large profit, yet he wished to honor his father and would not wake him. "Even though," he said, "my profit had been ever so much more. For I knew that I should not get so much for it in the future. Nevertheless the honor of my father is worth much more to me. And though I know that you must have it now and if I do not sell it to you this time you will get another, still I will not commit the sin of waking my father." Accordingly the Israelites went away and bought a stone elsewhere, and he suffered a loss of many thousand florins.

The following year the Lord gave him compensation in the shape of a red heifer, which used to be offered as a sacrifice in the temple. The Israelites had to have one, and they went to him again and wanted to buy it, for a red heifer that is red all over is very rare. Dama said: "I know full well that if I should ask all the money in the possession of the Israelites you would have to pay it to me, but I will not demand it. I will ask for it only the amount that you offered to pay me last year for the precious stone. Not wishing to wake my father, I lost 80,000 florins. This same amount I now request for the red

heifer which was born in my herd." The Israelites were, therefore, forced to pay him that
price.

When the rabbis heard this, they said: "If the
Lord rewards so bountifully him who performs a
pious deed, although he was not commanded to
do it, how much greater is the reward to him
who fulfills a commandment which is enjoined
upon him, for R. Hanina says: 'The reward of a
pious deed is greater when a man is commanded
to do it than when he is not, as was the case
with Dama son of Netina'."

Therefore, dear people, honor your father and
mother, and God will recompense you and
lengthen your life.

### 128. The Faithless Wife and Her Illegitimate Sons

A man once overheard his wife rebuking her
daughter for leading a loose life, and he heard
her say: "Do not practice prostitution publicly.
Do as I have done. I lived a loose life and have
had ten children, of which nine were bastards,
whom I had with other men, and only one was
the son of my husband. But my husband knew
nothing of it, as I carried on my amours secretly.
I advise you to do the same."

When the poor man heard all that his wife
had said, he was very much grieved, and yet
he did not dare to show knowledge of the fact
that his wife was an adulterous woman. He
grieved over it so much that he fell ill and was
about to die. He left a will, saying: "I bequeath
all my property to one only of my children."
But he did not say which one of his sons was to
be his heir. And so he died.

After his death each one of the children
claimed the whole property for himself, and they
came before R. Banaah, who was the head of the
college at that time, and asked him to decide
which of the sons was to be the heir. The rabbi
said: "It is a very difficult matter and I cannot
fathom it, nor am I a prophet that I should
know which of the sons your father had in mind.
But I will give you an advice. Go together to
your father's grave, and each take a stone in his
hand and knock with it upon your father's grave
and say: 'Dear father, tell us which is your real
son who is to be your sole heir'."

The rabbi gave them this advice, for he wanted
to put them to the test to see whether they
would perpetrate such insolence against their
father, for thereby he would be able to identify
the real heir. The one who would refuse to follow
his advice would be the true son. And so it

came to pass. They all went to the father's grave with stones in their hands, except one who refused to go. And he said to them: "What do you mean by putting such disgrace upon our dead father? I would not go to the grave even if I knew that I would lose every penny of my father's property." The rabbi concluded that he was the real son, and said: "This one shall inherit the whole property. He is the one whom your father had in mind."

It was through his wisdom that the rabbi was able to discover who the real son was. For a real child cannot bear to inflict so great a disgrace upon his father. But bastard children care nothing and are ready to inflict shame upon one even if he is in the grave.

## 129. MORDECAI AND HAMAN

When Haman brought the horse and the fine clothes to Mordecai, he said to him: "Put on these beautiful garments and mount the horse, for such is the desire of the king." And Mordecai replied: "No, I must first have my hair cut, for it is not proper to appear before the king with long hair." But Esther had given orders to all the barbers not to cut Mordecai's hair, so that Haman himself should be compelled to do it.

Haman fetched a pair of scissors from his house and began to cut Mordecai's hair, sighing deeply as he did so. Mordecai asked him why he was sighing. And he replied: "Why should I not sigh and grieve when I remember in what high esteem I was held by the king, more than all the other counselors, and now I must act as a bath attendant and cut the hair of a Jew!" And Mordecai replied: "O you wicked man, for twenty-two years you were a bath attendant in a village called Karsum, and now you pretend to play the great man."

After he had cut his hair, Haman clothed Mordecai in the royal robes. Then he said to Mordecai: "Mount the horse." Mordecai said: "My legs have grown so weak from fasting that I am not able to raise them so high." Thereupon Haman bent down and Mordecai stepped on Haman's back and thence on to the horse, and he rode along and mocked at Haman. And Haman said: "Mordecai, why do you laugh at me? Is it not written: 'Rejoice not when thine enemy falleth?' (Prov. 24.17), and you are rejoicing over me because I have sunk so low." Then Mordecai replied to Haman: "O you wicked man, the verse refers only to a Jewish enemy, but of a wicked man like you it is said: 'Thou shalt tread upon their high places'" (Deut. 33.29).

As they were riding along, Haman shouted before Mordecai: "Thus shall it be done to the man whom the king delighteth to honor" (Esth. 6.11). And as they passed the house of Haman, his daughter was standing at the top of the stairs and thinking: "The man who is riding on the horse is surely my father, whom the king is honoring in this manner, while he who is leading the horse is surely none other than Mordecai." And thereupon she quickly ran down the steps, took a pail full of dirt and emptied it on the head of Haman, thinking that it was Mordecai. Haman turned around to look, and she saw that it was her father. Thereupon she fell down the steps and broke her neck and died.

## 130. THE PIOUS MAN AND THE GOVERNOR

Once upon a time a pious man was walking across a field when the time for prayer arrived. So he stood still and began to pray. As he was praying, a governor came along riding on horseback and saluted him. But the pious man did not return the greeting and remained silent. The governor waited until he had finished his prayers, then he said to him: "You scoundrel, why did you not return my greeting when I saluted you? If I should cut your head off, who would say anything to me?" The pious man replied: "Pray, listen to my answer." And he began as follows: "Dear Sir, if you were standing before a human king of flesh and blood and speaking to him, and another man came along and addressed you, would you answer him?" The governor replied: "No, I would not answer him." Then the pious man continued: "And suppose you did answer him, what do you think would happen to you?" And the governor replied: "I would be afraid that the king might have my head cut off." The pious man replied: "Behold now, if standing before a king of flesh and blood who lives to-day and tomorrow he is dead, you would be afraid of having your head cut off, how much more should I have been afraid, standing as I was before a king who is called the King of Kings, who is not a being of flesh and blood, who lives forever and does not pass away! How, then, could I have answered your greeting? I had to fear that in His wrath He might have killed me." When the governor heard how well the pious man had answered, he was well pleased with him and said to him: "You have answered me very well." So the pious man returned home in peace. Therefore, every Jew should say his prayers with proper devotion, and no evil will happen to him.

### 131. THE BURNED POKER AND THE ANGEL OF DEATH

Once upon a time there lived a man called Dima son of Abbaye, who was on friendly terms with the angel of death. One day the angel of death said to his messenger: "Go and bring me a woman called Miriam, who is a women's hairdresser." The messenger misunderstood him and brought another Miriam, who was a children's hairdresser. Then the angel of death said to him: "I sent you to bring me the Miriam who dresses the hair of women and you brought me the Miriam who dresses the hair of children." The messenger replied: "Return her to me and I will bring her back to life." Said the angel of death to his servant: "How were you able to kill her, since the time for her death had not arrived?" And the messenger replied: "I will tell you. When I came to her, I found her sitting in front of the fire with the poker in her hand ready to rake the fire. She put the poker into the fire, and it was burnt, and with that her luck was also burnt, and I took her life." Then R. Dima asked: "But have you the power to do so?" And the angel of death replied: "Yes, do we not read in the book of Ecclesiastes: 'Some die without judgment'? (Prov. 13.23). That is, men die before their time. But I do not put them among the dead until the time arrives which has been fixed for their death. I keep them with me until I can put them among the dead."

Therefore women must be careful not to burn their pokers, for they burn their luck with it.

## 132. The Patient Teacher

Rabbi Pereda had a pupil who was very stupid, and whatever he taught him had to be repeated 400 times before he remembered it. One day Rabbi Pereda had repeated the lesson 400 times, when he was called away on some religious business and the pupil had not yet learned the lesson. Said R. Pereda to the pupil: "How is it that you know less now than at other times although I have repeated the lesson 400 times?" The pupil replied: "As you were called away, my mind was distracted and I paid no attention, for I was thinking, 'Now the teacher is going away'." Then R. Pereda said: "Now pay attention, I will repeat it again 400 times." And he repeated the lesson with him 400 times until he knew it. Then a voice came from heaven, saying: "Do you prefer to live 400 years more or to enter paradise at once with your generation?"

R. Pereda replied: "I prefer to be taken into paradise with my parents." Then the Lord, blessed be He, said: "Give the good man both, paradise and 400 more years of life."

Therefore, dear friends, be patient with your pupils.

### 133. THE PRENATAL INFLUENCE OF A MOTHER'S THOUGHTS

R. Johanan was in the habit of sitting at the door of the place whither the women used to repair for their ritual baths; for he said: "When the women come and take their ritual bath, they will look at me, and at night when they are with their husbands, they will think of me and they will have handsome children like me, who will be as studious as I am. For a great deal depends upon the thoughts of the woman when husband and wife lie together. If, God forbid! they have evil thoughts, the children do not turn out well, but if the thoughts of man and wife are good, the children turn out well." We have an example in the case of the wife of Elisha, the high priest, who gave birth to a child who became Rabbi Ishmael the high priest, and was one of the ten martyrs. The story is as follows.

Elisha was a very pious man, but his children

died as soon as they were born. One day his wife said to him: "How is it that other people have children and we have not?" Elisha replied: "I will tell you. The thing depends upon the state of mind of the women when they return from the bath, that is, whether they are modest and have good thoughts when they lie with their husbands. If a woman thinks of a learned man, the children are likely to turn out the same way." When the woman heard this, she said: "I will endeavor henceforth to concentrate my mind on good thoughts."

One day as she was returning home from the bath, a pig met her on the way. She went back and took another dip, for she was afraid she would be thinking of the pig the whole night. As she was going home again, an ass met her on the road and again she returned to the bath. The third time a leper met her on the way and she again returned to the bath. When the Lord saw how pure the woman was, He said to the angel Metatron: "Place yourself in her way when she comes out again from the bath, so that nothing may happen, for this night she will conceive a worthy man, who is to be a high priest before Me."

The angel came down and placed himself in her way, for she had taken the bath well nigh forty times that night. When she beheld the angel she was frightened, for he was as handsome as a king, and she thought it was her husband and wanted to return again to the bath. But the angel said to her: "You need not turn back, for I am the angel Metatron sent by the Lord, blessed be He, to tell you that He has seen the good thoughts which you had. Therefore I am to say to you that you will bear a son who will cause you joy." The good woman was frightened and came home with great joy, having her mind full of thoughts of the angel. That night she conceived and bore a son who became Ishmael, the high priest.

When the child was born, the angel Metatron came and took the child in his arms and he became its godfather. And he taught the child all that he knew, so that he knew everything that happened in the heavens above and the earth beneath, and he could ascend into heaven whenever he liked. That was the reward which the Lord gave her for her good and pious thoughts, for everything depends upon the thoughts entertained by husband and wife when they are together. The child takes after the thoughts of the mother at that time.

## 134. THE QUEEN WHO GAVE BIRTH TO A BLACK CHILD

Once upon a time there lived a very mighty king who had a beautiful wife, but they had no children. So they prayed earnestly to God to give them a son who would rule after their death. As they prayed, their request was granted and the queen conceived and bore a son, who was as black as a real moor. And the king felt very sad and in bad humor that his wife should have given birth to such a blackamoor, for they were both handsome people. Turning the matter over in his mind, he bethought himself: "I have a moor in my service, surely my wife had the child by him." He called his counselors together and desired to condemn the queen to death, for he began to hate her. The counselors were wise men, who were familiar with the science of nature. They considered the matter a while and then said to him: "O lord king, do not be in such haste to have the queen condemned to death, lest you shed innocent blood. You may condemn her to-day, and tomorrow you may regret having put her to death. We will tell you this. It may be the queen thought about the moor who is in your service; or maybe she saw the figure of a moor represented in the draperies hanging at the foot of your bed, and when she was with you she had her thoughts centered on the moor. For we find in books that the children resemble the thing which the mother has in her mind at the time of conception. We, therefore, counsel you to pause and look into the matter before you do anything." When the king heard this, he said: "This may very well be true, for there is the representation of a moor in the hangings around my bed, as it is customary for kings and princes to have images before their beds, and it is therefore likely that the queen may have thought of the moor while being with me." Then, without looking at her, he shrewdly asked the queen: "My dear, how is it that such handsome people as you and I should have a child as black as a moor?" The queen replied: "I will tell you how it happened. When we were together, I looked around and saw the picture of the moor in the hangings over our bed and I concentrated my thought upon it, and I think that this is why the child looks like a moor. For women easily wander in their thoughts and children resemble the thoughts of their mothers." When the king heard this, he recognized the truth in the advice of his counselors, and he loved the queen again and the child also.

Therefore women should have good thoughts and they will have good children. And this is what our sages mean when they say that he who thinks of committing a sin is worse than he who commits one with hands and feet. For the thoughts have their seat in the brain and the soul depends on the brain, hence he pollutes the soul; whereas he who commits a sin pollutes his body. Therefore R. Johanan used to sit at the door so that the women should look at him when they came from the bath. For the thoughts come from the brain, and the seed from which the child is formed also comes from the brain. Therefore women, when being with their husbands, should concentrate their thoughts on scholars, and their children will be influenced thereby. And this is the reason also why a woman should return to the bath if, on coming out, she meets anything, whatever it be, provided she desires to be pious and performs her ablutions properly, for anything that she meets makes an impression on her and she thinks about it at the time of coition and the child is affected thereby.

But there are two exceptions to this rule. The first is, if she meets a horse she need not return to the bath, for even if she should think of a horse, there would be no harm, for a horse is of a happy disposition, and therefore she may have a son whose heart will feel happy in the study of the Torah. The second is, if she meets a scholar she need not go back and repeat her ablution. On the contrary, she should think about him all the time. It is for this reason that our sages have made a rule that if one loses his wife he shall wait until three festivals have passed before marrying again. And the same thing applies to a widow. The reason is because a man continues to think of his first wife and this causes pain to the soul. During the first year after death, the soul, after ascending to heaven, comes down to the grave. This goes on for twelve months, but after the twelve months, the soul goes up to heaven and remains there. It is for this reason that a man should not marry before three festivals have passed; and the same thing applies to a woman, for it is a grievous trial to the soul of the dead. God's judgment also lasts twelve months. He requites everyone according to his deserts, and he who sins much must suffer much. You can therefore understand easily that much depends upon the state of the soul, and a great deal depends also upon the thoughts of man and wife when they are together. Follow, therefore, this rule and you will have

good and pious children, who will always shine
in the light of the Torah and will have a share
in this world and in the world to come. Amen.

### 135. THE EXCOMMUNICATION OF R. ELEAZAR BEN HYRCANUS

R. Eleazar, the son of Hyrcanus, had a dispute
with his colleagues. What he declared clean they
declared unclean, and would not agree with him.
R. Eliezer (sic) brought all the arguments that
there were, but they refused to give in. As there
was a carob tree nearby, R. Eliezer said: "If my
interpretation of the law is correct, let the
carob tree uproot itself and plant itself in another
place." A miracle happened, and the tree tore
itself with its roots from the place where it
stood and planted itself a hundred cubits away.
(Some say it was four hundred cubits.) It was
thus evident that R. Eliezer was right. But the
sages said: "We pay no attention to the tree,
and we will not accept your ruling." Then
R. Eliezer said: "If my interpretation of the
law is correct, let this stream reverse its course
and flow backwards as it is now flowing for-
wards." Again a miracle happened and the river
flowed backwards. It was again clear therefrom
that R. Eliezer was right, but they said again:

"We pay no heed to the course of the river."
Then R. Eliezer said again: "If my interpretation
of the law is correct, let the walls of the college
fall in and prove thereby which of us is right."
At these words the walls of the college began to
bend and were about to fall, when R. Joshua
cried out and said: "If the sages dispute among
themselves, what right have you to mix yourselves in their dispute?" Thereupon the walls
stood still and refused to fall in out of respect
for R. Joshua, who had rebuked them. But
neither would they right themselves again out of
respect for R. Eliezer. Then R. Eliezer said:
"If I am right, let a voice come from heaven
and decide between us." And a voice came from
heaven, saying: "Why do you dispute with R.
Eliezer? The law is as R. Eliezer says." Then
the sages said: "We pay no heed to the heavenly
voice, for the Lord, blessed be He, has written in
His Torah: 'Ye shall incline after the multitude'
(Ex. 23.2), which means that whenever an
individual is in disagreement with many, the
law is decided by the majority and not by the
individual. Therefore we will not yield."

Soon after, R. Nathan met the prophet Elijah
and said to him: "Pray, what did God do when
the sages were disputing?" The prophet replied:
"God looked on and smiled, and said: 'My

children have won a victory over Me'." (This is only a figure of speech.)

Then the sages put R. Eliezer in *herem* (excommunicated him). Then they said to one another: "Who shall go and announce to him that he has been excommunicated? For someone might tell him who is not worthy of the task." R. Akiba said: "I will go and inform him." R. Akiba dressed himself in black, like a man who is in mourning, and placed himself in front of R. Eliezer at a distance of four cubits. R. Eliezer said to him: "Dear Master, why are you dressed in black today?" And he replied: "Master, I believe your colleagues have excommunicated you and have cut themselves off from you." When R. Eliezer heard this, he took off his shoes, rent his garments, sat down on the ground and mourned, as if a corpse were lying before him, and wept bitterly.

At the time when they pronounced the excommunication, the world was smitten. One third suffered in its crop of olives, one third in its barley and the third part in its wheat, which was all destroyed. Some people say that even the dough in the hands of the women rotted away. Such an evil day was that in which R. Eliezer was excommunicated! Moreover, everything that R. Eliezer looked at on that day was

burned. The *Nasi* (prince) at that time was
Rabban Gamaliel, who took part in the excommunication. He was Rabbi Eliezer's brother-in-
law, being the brother of R. Eliezer's wife.

One day R. Eliezer was saying his prayers.
At that moment R. Gamaliel was traveling in a
ship on the sea. A strong wind arose, threatening
to upset the ship, and Rabban Gamaliel said,
"I believe, this evil has come upon me because
I have excommunicated R. Eliezer, the son of
Hyrcanus." Then he began to pray, and said:
"Lord of the universe, Thou knowest that I
have not done it for the sake of my own honor,
nor for the sake of my father's honor, but for
the sake of Thine honor, so that there may not
be disputes in Israel, one person disputing
against many." When he had finished his
earnest prayer, the wind ceased and the sea
became calm.

After this the wife of R. Eliezer would
not allow him to say the prayer known as
*taḥanun*. She was afraid it might cause the
death of her brother, Rabban Gamaliel, as had
almost happened on that occasion.

One day a poor man came to the door and
asked for a piece of bread. She went outside to
give him a piece of bread, and while she was
there, R. Eliezer fell upon his face and said the

prayer of *taḥanun*. When she returned and
found him praying, she said to him: "Alas and
woe unto me! Arise, for you have caused the death
of my brother." After a while a cry arose that
R. Eliezer had caused Rabban Gamaliel's death.
Then the people said to the wife of R. Eliezer:
"How did you know that your brother was
dead?" She replied: "I have it as a tradition
from my father, that all the gates of prayer are
closed except of the prayer of one who has been
unjustly excommunicated."

Therefore no man should stand up against the
whole community. R. Eliezer was a very worthy
man and won the approbation of God, and yet
he was excommunicated by the community. No
man should stand up against the whole community even if he thinks he is right. He should
be pious and bear in mind what such an attitude
may finally bring.


## 136. Torah the Best Merchandise

Once upon a time a ship carrying merchants
and merchandise sailed over the sea, and among
the passengers was a great scholar. The merchants began to converse about the wares which
they carried with them, and what they intended
to buy. Finally they asked the scholar what

merchandise he had, and he answered: "I carry all my goods with me." The merchants searched the whole ship for his wares, for they thought that he had precious stones, but they could find nothing. So they jeered at him and said that he had no merchandise at all. The scholar replied: "Why are you laughing at me? The goods which I carry are of greater value than any which you have in the ship's hold."

As they continued traveling on the high seas, they were attacked by pirates, who robbed them of all the merchandise which they had in the ship. When they landed, they found themselves quite poor and had nothing to eat or drink or any clothes to put on. The scholar, however, went into the town and entered the *bet hamidrash*. When the people heard what an important man he was, they at once brought him clothes and gave him a large amount of money. Moreover, the good people of the town followed him out of the city.

When the merchants saw the great honor which was shown to the Jew, they begged his pardon for having laughed at him, and asked him to request the townspeople to give them something to eat so that they might not die of hunger, for he had seen that they had been robbed of their property. And the scholar replied: "Did I not tell you that my merchandise was more valuable than yours? For you have lost your property, but mine is still with me. Furthermore, one who buys and sells does not always gain, sometimes he gains and sometimes he loses, and even when he gains he is not sure that the profit will remain with him, but the Torah remains forever, in this world and in the next. I was right, therefore, about the goods which I had with me."

### 137. TORAH MORE VALUABLE THAN WEALTH

R. Kisma says: "One day, when traveling abroad, I met a man who greeted me and I returned his greeting. Then he asked me: 'Dear rabbi, whence do you come?' I replied, 'I come from a town where there are only scholars and scribes.' Then the man said: 'Would to God that you would dwell in our city, and I would give you 100,000 florins and pearls and precious stones.' Then I replied: 'My dear son, if you would give me all the money and all the jewels that are in the whole world, I would not live in a place in which there is no Torah. I would live only where there is study of the Torah; for when a man dies, there goes with him neither gold nor silver nor precious stones, but the Torah accompanies him to the other world, as we find it written in the verse of the Bible (Prov. 6.22): "When thou goest into the other world, the Torah will guide thee and will follow thee even to thy grave, where she will keep guard over thee, and when thou wakest up, i. e. in the other world, the Torah will plead for thee before the Lord!" Therefore I ask not for money; as King David said in his book of Psalms. God said unto David: "Thy study of the Law is much dearer to Me than 100,000 florins" (Ps. 119.72). And God says further: "All the silver and all the gold are Mine, and I can make rich whomever I wish" ' (Hag. 2.8).

Therefore a person should always study the Torah and not run after silver or gold. For even when a person thinks he has much money, God can cause him to lose it in the twinkling of an eye. And when a person studies the Torah, God can make him rich, as we have learned from the two previous stories. Therefore every man should endeavor to increase his knowledge of the Torah and should trust and confide in God Almighty, who can always provide for him.

## 138. The Pious Man Who Was Protected by a Bear Because He Observed the Sabbath

Once upon a time three men were traveling abroad. It was on a Friday and it was getting late and the Sabbath was approaching. Said one to the other: "What shall we do? The road is infested with robbers, and many wild beasts are roaming about in this forest. It is much better to continue our journey and get out of this dangerous place so as to save our lives, rather than to keep the Sabbath and remain where we are, so that robbers and wild beasts may come and kill us." But there was one among them who said: "I will not move from here until the Sabbath is out, and I will not desecrate the Sabbath, for the Lord Himself has commanded that we should keep the Sabbath. Therefore I will not move hence, until the Sabbath is out, for I will not desecrate the Sabbath. The Lord, blessed be He, can protect me from all evil."

The two others went on and violated the Sabbath, but he remained where he was and refused to break the Sabbath. He put up his tent in the field, spread his table and observed the Sabbath. As he began to eat, there appeared a bear larger than any human being had ever seen before, and sat down in front of the pious man. When the pious man saw the bear, he gave him a piece of bread to eat, and the bear ate it. And the pious man had no fear of the bear. When he finished his meal, he said grace and lay down to sleep, and the bear lay down beside him and slept also. When the pious man awoke, he found the bear sleeping beside him and he was glad that the bear had done him no harm, and praised the Lord, blessed be He, who had protected him from the bear. In the morning the pious man said his prayers, spread his table and sat himself down to eat, and the bear ate with him, and in the afternoon he partook of the third meal. And when the Sabbath was out, he said the evening prayer and the *habdalah* and went on his way. And the bear accompanied him all through the night.

The same night robbers found the two other men in the forest and took away all their property. Just then the pious man came along with the bear, and when the bear saw the two men who had desecrated the Sabbath, he leaped upon them and tore them to pieces. When the pious man saw what the bear had done, he was frightened lest the bear should do the same to him. At the same moment the robbers came along and asked: "Who are you?" And he replied: "I am a Jew." He would not hide his Judaism, for he trusted that God who had protected him from the bear, would also protect him against the robbers. Then they said to him: "Whence do you come?" And he replied: "I come from the king's palace." Then they asked him: "Whence came this bear and who gave him to you?" The pious man replied: "The king gave him to me as a companion so that no one should harm me." Then one of the robbers said to the other: "The king must be very fond of this man to give him the bear as companion and protection." And another one said: "This man may betray us, seeing that we are robbers, and the king may cause us to be hanged. Let us give him all our money provided he keep silent." And they gave him all the money they had, so that he should not denounce them, and accompanied him to his house. And no sooner had the pious man reached his home, than the bear departed and went his way.

Therefore every man should observe the Sabbath and God will stand guard over him. He can protect you from robbers and wild beasts, as you have observed in this story. And no one should allow himself to be led astray.

### 139. The Story of Nanos Who Honored His Father and Mother

Once upon a time a man called R. Joshua dreamt that his companion in paradise was to be a certain Nanos, the son of Ish Kefar. When he woke up in the morning, he remembered his dream and journeyed from place to place in search of Nanos. When R. Joshua arrived at the place where Nanos lived, the elders of the town came out to meet him and paid him their respects and invited him and his pupils to eat and drink with them. R. Joshua replied: "I will neither eat nor drink before I have seen a certain Nanos, son of Ish Kefar, who is to be my companion in paradise. I wish to ascertain what virtuous deeds have made him worthy to become my companion in paradise. Then I will come and eat and drink with you." The elders said: "What concern have you with Nanos? He is not worthy even to stand beside you." R. Joshua replied: "Nevertheless, I am anxious to see him even though you hold him in such contempt." Then the people ran quickly to Nanos and told him to go to R. Joshua who desired to speak to him. Nanos laughed, for he did not believe them, and refused to go. Then the people returned and said to R. Joshua: "Nanos refuses to come; he thinks we are making fun of him." Then R. Joshua rose up with all his pupils and all the worthies of the town and went to the house of Nanos. When Nanos saw R. Joshua, he was very much frightened and went out to meet him, and falling at his feet, said to him: "What is the meaning of this, that a great and worthy sage who is likened to a king, should come and visit me in my house, seeing that I am a man of very low station?" Then R. Joshua said to him: "Friend, tell me what are your deeds in this world, for I came here to ask you this question." Nanos replied: "Dear Rabbi, I am, alas, a very poor man; I have nothing but a garden in which I work every day. I have an old father and an old mother, who are so old that they cannot move, and I take care of them, feed them and clothe them and carry them about when necessary. I support them from the proceeds of the garden." Then R. Joshua said: "Happy am I that I shall have a companion like you in paradise, for there is no deed more worthy than to honor father and mother, for which God grants long life, as we read in the Holy Scriptures: 'Honor thy father and thy mother that thy days may be long upon the land'" (Ex. 20.12).

## 140. THE PENITENCE OF R. MEIR

R. Meir lived in Babylon and visited Jerusalem every year. On his way he used to stop at an inn kept by a butcher named Judah. This Judah had a pious wife, who showed R. Meir great honor when he came to stay with them, for he was a worthy man, as we are also told about him in the Gemara. She looked after his food and drink, kept a separate bed for him and provided for all his wants.

Now it so happened that the good woman died and the butcher married another woman. And he instructed her that when R. Meir came, she should show him great honor, as his first wife had done. R. Meir came, as was his custom every year, and went to stay with the butcher, as he had done hitherto. But he found another woman there, whom he did not know. R. Meir asked where was the wife of the master of the house, and she answered: "She died some time ago and the butcher married me. But he instructed me to take good care of R. Meir when he came and to show him hospitality." And she was very pleased to do this, she said, even more so than his first wife had been.

When R. Meir heard that the first wife had died, he went out of the house and was very

much grieved over the death of his good hostess.
As he was standing outside the door, the butcher
came up and, seeing him, said: "Dear Rabbi,
why do you not come into the house as before?
Why do you stand outside the door? I have
instructed my wife to treat you well, as my first
wife did." Thereupon R. Meir entered the house
with him. The wife brought into the house
everything that she needed, prepared a meal for
R. Meir, gave him good wine to drink, and
showed him every respect.

R. Meir was a very handsome man and the
butcher's wife fell in love with him. But she did
not know how she could entice him to sin with
her. One night it happened that there was no one
in the house except herself and R. Meir, so she
prepared a good meal for him and showed him
great honor and drank with him until he became
drunk and did not know what he was doing.
Then she put him to sleep and lay down beside
him. But he did not know of her lying down
or her rising up. In the morning, when he
woke up, he said his prayers as usual. After
he had finished his prayer, the hostess set the
table and ate and drank with him and behaved
impudently in her conversation. R. Meir was
greatly astonished at the impudence of the
woman, was much embarrassed, and could not

bear to look at her.  Then the woman said:
"My dear Rabbi, why are you so much embarrassed now?  You slept with me the whole night
and were not embarrassed.  Why, then, so much
embarrassment now?"    When R. Meir heard
this, he was seized with a very great fear and
said: "Surely this is not true."  But the woman
described various marks which he had on his
body, and he had to believe her.   When he
found out that, alas! she had spoken the truth,
he began to cry bitterly and said: "Woe unto
me!  What have I done?   All my life I have
studied the Torah and performed the commandments.  Now all my labor is lost and I must
suffer in Gehenna."  Then he said, "I will go to
the head of the *Yeshibah* and tell him all the
sorrow that has befallen me, and whatever he
commands me to do in atonement for the sin,
I will willingly do."  And he went home in great
grief, rent his mantle and strewed earth upon
his head.

His family came to him and asked him what
had happened, and he told them all that had
befallen him.  Then they were seized with great
fear and asked him what he intended to do.
And he said: "I will go to the head of the
college (*Rosh Yeshibah*) and confess to him, and
whatever he orders me to do I will do."

His friends tried to dissuade him from doing it, seeing that he had not committed the sin willingly and knew nothing about it, the Lord would surely forgive him. He persisted, however, in his determination and went to the *Rosh Yeshibah*, told him what had happened and asked him to impose some penance upon him. The head of the *Yeshibah* replied: "Come tomorrow and I will find some penance for you." The next morning R. Meir came back, and the *Rosh Yeshibah* said: "I sought for a fitting penance and have found one. You deserve to be devoured by wild beasts." R. Meir said: "If that is the law, I willingly submit to it."

Then the *Rosh Yeshibah* ordered two strong men to take R. Meir into a forest infested with wild beasts and tie him to a tree, while they were to go up to the top of a very high tree and watch from there whether the wild beasts would devour R. Meir or not. Should the wild beasts eat him up, they should bring home the bones, so that the college might mourn for him, since he had taken upon himself the judgment of Heaven. The men took R. Meir into the forest, as the head of the *Yeshibah* had commanded, and tied him to a tree.

At midnight, a huge lion came roaring, sniffed at R. Meir and went his way. The two men

reported to the *Rosh Yeshibah* that the lion had
not touched him, whereupon the *Rosh Yeshibah*
ordered them to leave him there tied to the tree
a second night. The lion again appeared, turned
R. Meir around on the other side, and went
his way again. The men reported to the *Rosh
Yeshibah* again that the lion had come a second
time but had not touched him, whereupon the
*Rosh Yeshibah* ordered that he be tied again and
left in the forest a third night. The third night the
lion appeared, bit off a rib of R. Meir's body,
ate a piece of it no larger than the size of an
olive and left him lying on the ground. The two
men took R. Meir and brought him to the *Rosh
Yeshibah*, who took care of him until he was
healed of his wound. When he returned to his
own home, a voice came forth from heaven,
saying: "R. Meir, you are ready for the world
to come."

This is the meaning of the biblical verse: "A
bad woman is more bitter than death" (Eccl.
7.26). Observe what happened to R. Meir,
although he was quite innocent. How much
greater then must be the punishment of him who
commits a sin deliberately? Therefore everyone
should be on his guard lest any such thing, God
forbid! should befall him.

## 141. ALEXANDER OF MACEDON AND HIS DESIRE TO BE WORSHIPED AS A GOD

Alexander of Macedon was a mighty king who conquered the whole world. Having achieved such power, he ordered his servants to worship him as a god. The wise men among his servants said to him that he had no power over Jerusalem and the temple. Thereupon he went forth and conquered Jerusalem, and demanded that they too should worship him as a god. Three wise men were sitting before him. One of them said: "Will you rebel against your master in His own house? Go out of His house and I will worship you as a god. For His house is heaven and earth and you are therein. As long as you are therein I cannot worship you as a god." The second said: "You say that you are God? God created heaven and earth and you too. You are nothing." The third said: "Wait awhile, I have a message to send; after that I will worship you as a god." Alexander said: "What is it that you must do?" The wise man replied: "A ship of mine is now on the high seas and is about to sink." Thereupon the king said: "I will send my ships at once to rescue yours." The sage replied: "By the time your ship arrives, mine will have sunk. Do me the kindness and send a little wind to carry it forward." The king replied: "Where shall I get the wind?" The sage said: "If you cannot command the wind, you are not a god, for it is written: 'God created heaven and earth and the people upon it'" (cf. Is. 42.5).

The king went home and told his wife all that had happened to him, and asked her to worship him as a god. She replied: "I will do it gladly, but you have a deposit which has been entrusted to you. Give up the deposit and I will do your will and worship you as a God." Then the king asked: "What is the deposit?" His wife replied: "The soul which God gave you. Return it to the owner." The king said: "If I give back my soul, what can I do without a soul?" The wife replied: "If you have no power over yourself, how can you have power over others and be a god?" When the king heard this, he felt ashamed and gave up his evil intention.

## 142. R. Tarfon and His Old Mother

There was a certain R. Tarfon, whose mother was so old that she could not walk. So he carried her wherever she wanted to go, gave her at all times the best food and drink and took great pains to do everything possible for her with all his heart and soul. One day the sages came to visit the mother of R. Tarfon and asked her how she fared, whether her son was treating her well and whether she was in need of anything. She expressed her gratitude to her son and could not find enough words to praise him, and told them of the trouble and toil she was causing him. And the sages replied: "If he did a thousand times as much as he was doing, it would not be enough, for there is no limit to the honor due to father and mother, and one can never do too much."

Once the mother of R. Ishmael complained of her son and said: "He does not show me the respect which is my due." When the sages heard this, they hesitated to mention it to him, for he was a great and worthy scholar, and they could not understand how he could be wanting in respect to his mother. Then they asked the old mother what it was she was complaining of. And the mother said: "Dear friends, when he comes home from the college with the students, I want to wash his feet, but he will not allow it, and therein he fails to do my pleasure and does not show me the honor that is due." Then the sages said to R. Ishmael: "If it is the express wish of your mother and she looks upon it as an act of respect, you ought to allow her to wash your feet, for it does you honor at the same time."

## 143. R. HANINA AND THE FROG

There once lived a man in the Holy Land who was very close to the king. He was rich and pious and knew everything that was going to happen. He had a son called R. Hanina, who knew the whole Torah. When he grew old and was about to die, he sent for his son and gave him his testamentary message, that he should study the Torah day and night and perform the commandments and be good to the poor, for his father and his mother would die in one day, and the seven days of mourning would end on the eve of Passover. "You must not mourn too much," he said. "And when the seven days of mourning are over, you shall go to the market and buy whatever is offered for sale first, no matter how expensive it is. And if it should be a living thing that has to be taken care of, you shall bring it up with great care and love, for you will be amply repaid for your trouble." But he would not say what the thing would be. When he had finished giving his last instructions, he and his wife died the same day, as he had said.

R. Hanina did everything as his father had wished, and when the eve of Passover came he rose from the ground, the seven days of mourning being over, and went to the market place. There he met an old man who had a beautiful silver casket for sale. R. Hanina asked him: "What is the price of this silver casket?" The old man replied: "Eighty florins." R. Hanina offered sixty florins, but the old man replied: "I will not sell it for that price." In the end he paid the full price, although it was high, for he desired to fulfill his father's last wish.

The first *Seder* night he put the casket on the table. When he opened it, he found another casket inside, and inside this he found a frog merrily dancing and jumping about. He gave the frog food and drink, and by the end of Passover the frog had grown so big that the casket was too small for him. So R. Hanina made a small box for the frog and put him inside and fed him until the box also became too small. Then he built for him a small chamber, put the frog therein and kept him so well provided with food and drink that he consumed all that R. Hanina possessed.

R. Hanina did all this in order to fulfill his father's last wish. He was now so poor that he had nothing left. So he and his wife went into the chamber where the frog was and said to him: "Dear friend, we can no longer feed you, for we have spent everything we had on you." The frog began to speak and said: "My dear

R. Hanina, do not regret that you have brought
me up and nourished me. Ask of me whatever
you wish and I will give it to you." R. Hanina
said: "I do not desire anything of you except
that you should teach me the whole Torah."
The frog replied: "Very well, your wish shall be
fulfilled." And the frog taught him the whole
Torah and the seventy languages. He did it in
the following manner. He took a piece of paper,
wrote a few words upon it and gave it to R.
Hanina to swallow. In this way he learned the
whole Torah and the seventy languages. He
taught R. Hanina also the language of the beasts
and the birds. Then the frog said to the wife of R.
Hanina: "You have kept me well but I have not
yet repaid you. I will pay you now. I will
leave you now, but you must accompany me
until we reach the forest of Elani. There you
shall see what I will give you."

So they went with the frog until they reached
the forest, and when they got there the frog
uttered a loud cry, calling together all kinds of
beasts innumerable. Then the frog commanded
each one of them to bring as many precious
stones as they could carry, and also all kinds of
salutary roots and herbs for the woman, that she
might cure many ills therewith. He taught her
also how to use every one of them, and ordered

them all to be carried into the house of R. Hanina. And when the frog parted from them, he said: "May the Lord have mercy upon you for the trouble that you had on my account, without even asking me who I was. But I will tell you. I am the son of Adam, who begot me by Lilith during the hundred and thirty years that he was separated from Eve. God has given me the power to assume any shape or form I like." And with these words he took leave of R. Hanina and his wife and departed from them. They returned home and were very rich and held in high esteem by the king just as his father had been.

At that time the king of Israel, who was a very wicked man, had no wife. The elders of the people came to him and said that he ought to marry, for it was not proper for a king to live without a wife. They thought that if he had a wife he might become a better man. Then the king said: "Come back in eight days and I will give you a reply."

During those eight days, R. Hanina was studying the laws regarding birds and he discoursed about the subject with his pupils, when suddenly there appeared a black raven, who prayed to God to preserve R. Hanina from a great amount of trouble that he would have.

R. Hanina was greatly astonished on hearing this, for he understood the language of the raven. After a while another bird appeared, also cried aloud and prayed to God to save R. Hanina from the great amount of trouble that he would receive. R. Hanina knew what the birds were saying to one another, for the frog had taught him the language of the birds, as we have heard before.

When the eight days which the king had fixed had passed, the elders again came to the king and requested a reply concerning the matter of taking a wife. While they were talking to the king, a bird came, carrying a long hair in its beak. The hair was the color of gold, and the bird dropped it on the shoulder of the king. The king took the hair, examined it, and found that it was as long as he was tall. Then he said to the elders of Israel that he would marry no other woman except the one to whom that hair belonged, and he ordered them to find the woman and bring her to him, else he would, God forbid! have them all put to death. The elders became very much frightened, for they did not know where to find her.

Among the elders there were some who hated R. Hanina because he was held in great honor by the king. So they said to the king: "There is no man more capable of fulfilling the king's command than R. Hanina, who by his wisdom will surely find out where the queen lives." They gave this advice to the king because they did not believe that the queen could be found, and they reckoned that the king would then surely turn against R. Hanina. When the king heard what they said, he called R. Hanina and told him that he must go and look for the queen. R. Hanina could not refuse, for the king would have had him put to death immediately. The king offered to send a man to accompany him on his journey, but R. Hanina refused to take anyone with him.

So R. Hanina went home, took leave of his wife and children, and went on his journey, taking with him twelve florins and three loaves of bread. His pupils accompanied him as far as the outskirts of the town. There he ordered them to return home, and he went forth alone, walking knee-deep in the snow, until he became very tired and leaned against a tree for rest. Then he heard a raven crying that he had not anything to eat for three days. When he heard this, he gave the raven a piece of bread to eat and thus saved his life. The next day R. Hanina heard a dog howling bitterly and saying that he had not eaten anything for six days. R. Hanina gave the dog also a piece of bread and saved his life, but he had not a morsel left for himself.

On the third day as he came out of the forest, the sun was burning hot and he came to a beautiful green field, in which there grew all manner of sweet spices. He ate thereof and was revived. Then he came to a large brook, where he found fishermen fishing. They had just caught a large fish, which they were not able to pull out of the water. He came to their aid and they landed the fish. It was a beautiful large fish and R. Hanina bought it from them for twelve florins and threw it back into the water, giving the fish its freedom.

R. Hanina continued on his journey until he saw a town before him, which he entered. It was the very town in which the queen, whose hair had been brought to the king, lived. R. Hanina searched high and low for the queen until he found the place where she lived. As he came to the house in which she lived, the queen looked out of the window and saw R. Hanina standing before her house. She recognized that he was a wise man in all things and said to her counselors: "A worthy man is standing below, let him come before me." So they called him before the queen. When he appeared before her, he spoke to her in the proper manner, such as you can well imagine is fitting before a queen. He told her also how dire would be the fate of the Jews should she refuse to marry the king, for, God forbid! they would all lose their lives. The queen replied: "I fully understand your message and will go with you, for I am anxious to save the Jews. But I know that you are a very wise man. Therefore, I will ask you to do two things. If you carry them out, I will go with you. If not, I will not go. My first wish is that you bring me two jars of water, one with water from paradise and the other with water from hell. When you have done this, I will tell you what the other request is." She did this because she thought it would be impossible for him to carry out the first request. And in sooth, R. Hanina was very sad. She said to him: "I am well aware that the hair came from my head, for one day as I was washing my head in the garden a bird came and pulled out a hair; therefore, if you carry out my request I will go with you." What did R. Hanina do? He went out and stood before the door, sad and sorrowing, and prayed that he might get the water and save the Jews. For it would be sad if after having traveled so far and passed through so many dangers, he should accomplish nothing. As he was praying, the raven came, to whom he had given the

bread to eat because he had been without food
for three days. The raven called to R. Hanina
by name and said to him: "Dear Rabbi, do you
not know me? I am the bird whom you fed in
the forest with your own bread, which you gave
me to eat. I have heard you cry about the
water, therefore hang two jars on my wings and
I will fly and fetch the water for you, so that
you may save your people from the evil decree."
When R. Hanina heard these words, he was
overjoyed and tied the two jars properly to the
wings of the bird. The bird flew to Gehenna
and filled one of the jars, but the heat was so
great that his feathers were singed, so he flew
quickly to the river which flows out of paradise
and, bathing in it, his feathers became as white
as before and he was cured. Then he filled the
other jar and, with great joy, brought it to
R. Hanina, who took it immediately to the queen.
Then the queen said: "I will try the waters and
see whether they are as they should be." So
she took the jar with the water of hell and
poured it upon her hand, which became very
badly burned. Then she took quickly the water
of paradise and spread it over her hand, and it
was healed and became as well as before. She
knew then that the waters were genuine. Then
she said: "Now, I will make my other request.

I once traveled over the sea and dropped a beautiful gold ring with a precious stone into the water. If you can bring it back to me, I will go with you wherever you like." She thought it would be impossible to recover it. But the Lord, blessed be He, helped him again.

R. Hanina went out of the town sadly and came to the water and prayed again to God. Thereupon the big fish that he had saved from the fishermen came to the shore and said: "Dear Rabbi, I will give you whatever you desire." Then R. Hanina said: "I must have the ring which the queen once dropped into the sea." The good fish went straight to the Leviathan and told him how this pious man had once saved his life from a fisherman. "He is asking me for a ring which the queen had dropped into the sea; he is very anxious to have it, therefore I ask you to get the ring for R. Hanina." Then the Leviathan called the fish together and ordered them under threat of excommunication to produce the ring. Whereupon a fish came and threw up the ring. The big fish took the ring, brought it to R. Hanina and threw it up on the shore. At that moment a wild boar came and swallowed the ring. R. Hanina wept again and prayed to God. Thereupon the dog whom he had also fed in the wood appeared and said:

"Dear Rabbi, do you not know me? I am the dog to whom you gave your bread in the forest; I have now come to serve you in any way you desire." R. Hanina said: "You are very welcome at this moment. I lost a ring and a wild boar swallowed it." The dog ran after the boar and tore it in two pieces, and R. Hanina recovered the ring and returned with it to the queen. The queen was very much frightened, for she thought it was impossible that he should find it. And she said: "I promised that if you carried out my two requests I would go with you. And you have carried them out. Therefore I will keep my promise and go with you." And so she went to the king, accompanied by her counselors.

When the king saw her, he liked her very much and sent R. Hanina to invite people to the wedding. But when the sages saw that R. Hanina was again intimate in the house of the king, they waylaid him and killed him. When the queen heard of it, she was very much frightened and going quickly to the place where he lay, she said: "He is not dead." And she took the water of paradise and washed him with it, and he came back to life as if he had never been dead. The king and the sages wondered greatly at this revival and the king said: "I will not wed the queen unless she puts me to death first and then brings me back to life again." The queen replied: "Do not insist, I beg of you, for I can bring people back to life only if they are wholly righteous and God-fearing." But the king refused to listen and ordered one of his servants to kill him, whereupon the queen took the water of Gehenna and poured it over him, and he was burned up and turned into ashes and dust. Then she said: "My dear friends, you see if the king had been a really pious man he would have come to life. But I see very well that he was a very wicked man." When the sages saw that R. Hanina was a very wise and God-fearing man, they took counsel with one another and elected him king over Israel. And as his own wife had died, they gave him the queen as a wife and he judged Israel for many years. And thus he attained his purpose and obtained the queen as a wife.

### 144. THE OLD MAN AND THE SNAKE AND THE JUDGMENT OF SOLOMON

It came to pass in the time of King David, when his son Solomon was still a young lad, that an old man, walking along the road in winter time, found a half frozen snake in the road. The old man, bethinking himself of the command to take pity on all creatures, put the snake into his bosom to warm it. No sooner did the snake recover than it coiled itself round the man's body and squeezed him so hard that he nearly died. And the old man said to the snake, "Why do you harm me and try to kill me when I saved your life? If not for me you would have frozen to death." Continuing, the old man said: "Let us go before the court that they may decide whether you are treating me justly." The snake replied: "I am willing to do so, but to whom shall we go?" The old man replied: "To the very first thing we meet." So they walked together, and first they met an ox. The old man said to the ox: "Stand still and judge between us." And he related to him how he had saved the snake from death, and now the snake was doing all in its power to kill him. The snake replied: "I am acting properly, for it is written in Holy Scripture, 'I will put enmity between the man and the snake'" (cf. Gen. 3.15). The ox replied: "The snake is right in doing you harm, though you have treated it kindly, for such is the way of the world, that if one does good to another, he returns evil for good. My own master does the same. I work all day long in the field and benefit him a great deal, and yet in the evening he eats of the best and to me he gives

a little oats and straw. My master lies in a bed
and I must lie in the open yard on straw, where
the rain comes down upon me. This is the way
of the world, and therefore the snake is right in
wishing to kill you, although you have saved
its life." The old man was very much hurt
by these words. Farther on, they met an ass.
Addressing the ass, they said the same to it as
they had said to the ox. And the ass replied in
the same manner as the ox had done.

Then the old man came before King David
and complained of the snake. King David
replied: "The snake is right. Why did you not
carry out the word of the Scripture, which says:
'I will put enmity between you and the snake'?
Therefore I cannot help you. You did wrong in
warming the snake. You should have let it die,
for the snake is our enemy."

The old man left the king with tears in his
eyes, and as he walked on, he met young Solomon
in the field near a well. He had dropped a stick
into the well and was ordering the servants who
were with him to dig deeper below the source of
the well, so that the water should run into the
well and fill it, and thus carry the stick up, so
that he could reach it. When the old man saw
this, he said to himself: "He must be a clever
lad, I will put my case before him, maybe he

can protect me from the snake," and he told him
the story of what had befallen him with the
snake. Solomon replied: "Have you not been
before my father?" And the old man said:
"Yes, I have been there, but he said he could
not help me." Young Solomon said: "Let us go
to him again."

So they went together again before King
David, and the old man had a stick in his hand
upon which he leaned. When they appeared
before King David, Solomon said: "Why do you
not deliver judgment between this man and the
snake?" and King David replied: "I have no
judgment to declare. It serves him right. Why
did he not keep what is written in the Torah?"
Then Solomon said: "Dear father, give me leave
to pronounce judgment between the two." King
David replied: "Dear son, if you think you can
do so, go ahead without hesitation." Then
young Solomon, turning to the snake, said: "Why
do you do evil to a man who has done you
good?" And the snake replied: "The Lord,
blessed be He, has commanded me to bite the
heel of the man." Then Solomon said: "Do you
desire to observe the Torah and what is written
therein?" And the snake replied: "Yes, most
willingly." Then Solomon said: "If you desire
to do what is written in the Torah, then release

the man and stand on the ground beside
him, for it says in the Law that the two men
who have a quarrel with one another must stand
before the judge (cf. Deut. 19.17), therefore you
must also stand alongside of him." The snake
replied: "I am satisfied to do so;" and, uncoiling
itself from the man, he stood next to him. Then
Solomon said to the old man: "Now do to the
snake as it is written in the Law, for it is written
in the Torah that you should crush the snake's
head (cf. Gen. 3.15). Therefore do as is written
in the Torah, for the snake has promised to
accept the judgment of the Law." The good old
man had a stick in his hand which he used in
walking, for he was a very old man. So he
lifted the stick and smote the snake on the head
and killed it. And so the clever Solomon saved
the old man from the snake through his great
wisdom.

Therefore, no one should do good to a wicked
creature, as the old man did.

### 145. Joab's Capture of Rabbath the City of the Ammonites

It came to pass in the time of King David
that he sent his captain Joab son of Zeruyah, a
mighty man, to conquer the town of Rabbath of

the children of Ammon. Joab, with twelve
thousand chosen men of Israel, besieged the
town for six months. At the end of the six
months, all the officers of the Israelitish army
gathered themselves before Joab and said to
him: "We have been camping here for a long
time and have not accomplished anything, as we
have not been able to capture the town, and the
houses round about the city have been destroyed.
Why shall we stay here any longer?" Then he
asked the officers: "What is your intention?"
And they replied: "Our intention is to return
home, for we cannot accomplish anything by
staying any longer." Joab replied: "My dear
brethren, you must not think of going back
home without having accomplished our task, for
surely all the nations will mock at us and will
rise up against us. Listen to me and follow my
advice. Throw me into the city with this tree,
and continue your siege forty days longer. If by
then you do not see blood running out of the
town, then know that I am dead. Should you,
however, see blood flowing from the town, know
that I have killed most of the inhabitants. Then
storm the town bravely, for we shall win it
with the help of God. But I will not return to
the king with empty hands. I will either capture

the city or die before it." When the captains heard this, they were much pleased.

Then Joab took with him one thousand red gold florins and his good sword, and had himself cast into the town by means of a high tree. He fell upon his sword in front of a widow's house, and his sword broke in two pieces. The widow had a young married daughter, who found Joab lying in the courtyard. He was so weakened by the fall that he was almost dead. She carried him into the house and bathed him in water until he recovered consciousness. Then they asked him who he was and whence he had come. And Joab replied: "I am an Amalekite by birth. The Jews captured me and brought me before their captain, who ordered me to be thrown into the city. Therefore, I pray you, let me stay with you." Thereupon he took ten gold florins out of his purse and gave them to her to buy him good food.

Joab remained in the widow's house seven days. After seven days Joab wanted to visit the town and look around, but they would not let him go in his own clothes, but lent him other clothes. Then he went out and examined the town to see how strong it was, and he found therein no less than one hundred and forty market places, each one more beautiful than the other. He also examined all the gates, and came to the house of a sword-maker. Joab went in and said to him: "Can you make another sword like this one, which I have broken?" The sword-maker became frightened and astonished, and said: "I have never seen such a sword in all my life." Joab said: "Make me a sword like this, I will pay you well." So he made him a good sword. But Joab took it in his hand and broke it in two. And he did the same with three other swords, which he broke one after another. Then the smith made one the like of which had never been seen before, much better and stronger than the one which Joab had originally. Then Joab said to the smith: "Whom would you prefer to have me kill with this sword?" The smith replied: "The captain of the Jews." Then Joab said: "What is that thing behind you?" As the smith turned to look, Joab cut off his head. Then Joab said to the smith: "How do you feel?" For his head had not been completely severed. The smith replied: "I feel as if cold snow were pressing on my neck." Then Joab gave him another blow and sent the parts of the body flying in different directions. Then Joab went into a courtyard, in which there were five hundred strong men, well armed for battle. He killed them all and not one of them was left alive. Then sheathing his sword, he returned home. Soon there arose a cry in the town that five hundred men were found dead in the courtyard and no one knew who had killed them. And they said to one another: "No one else could have done this except Ashmedai." Joab's hostess asked him whether he had heard who had done it. And he said: "No, who would tell me?" Again he took ten gold florins out of his purse and gave them to the woman to buy him good food.

He remained in her house ten days longer and went out again into the market place, his sword in his hand, and killed 1500 men. His sword was so bloody that it stuck to his hand, and he could not loosen it. So he quickly ran home and said to the young woman: "Heat some water that I may loosen my hand from the sword." But she replied: "I should heat water for you, you who are eating and drinking with us and then killing the people of our city! I will not heat any water for you." When Joab heard that, he ripped her belly open and thrust his hand in and thus loosened his hand from the sword. Then he ran out of the house.

Outside he heard a proclamation to the effect that whosoever had a stranger in his house should deliver him up before the king. Joab met the crier and killed him on the spot, and whomever he met he put to death, until he came to the gate of the town, which he opened, causing the blood to flow out of the gate.

The Israelites had meanwhile been mourning for Joab, thinking he had died long since. But when they saw the blood running out of the gate, they all cried out with joy and with a loud voice: "Hear, O Israel!" When Joab heard this, he went to the top of a high tower and cried aloud the verse: "The Lord will not forsake His people Israel." Then he said: " 'The Lord, blessed be He, will fight for us, and ye shall hold your peace' (cf. Ex. 14.14). And now send a message quickly to King David, telling him to come, for we have conquered the whole town." Then Joab looked down and saw written on his right hand: "The Lord will answer thee from His sanctuary." Then David came and completed the whole psalm.

Then David said to Joab: "Have you killed all the Amalekites?" And Joab replied: "My lord, there is none left alive in the town except the king and a few of his people." They were brought before the king outside the town and he ordered them all to be put to death. And King David took the crown which weighed a talent of gold, besides many precious stones which were set therein, from the head of the king. Then he went into the town and burned all the idols. Then he took all the booty from the town and returned home in peace.

## 146. The Sinner Who Was Released from Hell through the Kaddish Prayer of His Son

It happened in the time of R. Akiba that a man committed a sin with a young woman on the Day of Atonement. The girl had been betrothed to another man and was soon to be married. When the people heard of it, they took the man out of the city and stoned him to death, for it was the same as if he had lain with a married woman. The woman became pregnant and a few weeks later gave birth to a male child. But the Jews refused to circumcise it, thinking that no good could come of the child since his father had done such a wicked act.

One day, as R. Akiba was walking across the country, he met a man carrying on his shoulders a heavy load of wood such as no ass or camel could carry. R. Akiba said: "I adjure you by the Holy Name to tell me whether you are man or demon or what kind of a creature you are." The man replied: "I was once a man and departed from this world. Now I am condemned to carry this load of wood daily, and I am burned therewith three times a day." R. Akiba asked him: "What sin had you committed?" The man replied that he had lain on the Day of Atonement with a virgin, who was betrothed to another man. And he added: "I have done more. I was overseer of the poor and I spared the rich by not taking from them as much as they should have given, whilst I exacted a heavier toll from the poor." R. Akiba asked him: "Have you heard whether there is any salvation for you?" The man replied: "Dear rabbi, do not detain me, for those who are put over me will be angry and then there will be no hope for me. I have heard, however, that if I had a son who would say *kaddish* for me, there would be hope for my salvation." R. Akiba asked him whether he had left a son, and he replied: "No, but when I died my wife was pregnant and I do not know whether she gave birth to a male child; but even if she gave birth to a son, the people would not allow him to study the Torah, for they hate me." Then R. Akiba asked him his name and the name of his wife and his town. He answered his questions and went his way. Then R. Akiba took it upon himself to go to that town and save the man if it were possible.

When he arrived in the city, the elders of the town came out to meet him and showed him great honor. Then R. Akiba asked: "Was there not once a man in this town whose name was so and so?" The people replied: "Yes, he was stoned to death a long time ago." Then he asked after the woman and they replied: "May her name be blotted out, she is no longer here, she ran away." Then he asked further: "Did he not leave a son?" And they replied: "Yes, but he has not yet been circumcised." Then R. Akiba rebuked them for refusing to circumcise the boy because his father was a bad man. "The child is not responsible," he said, "he may turn out a good man after all." Then R. Akiba sent for the boy and circumcised him and began to teach him the Torah, but it was in vain, he could not get the child to learn. Then R. Akiba fasted forty days and prayed to God on behalf of the child, and then he succeeded in teaching him the Torah. He taught him to say his prayers and the grace after meals and took him to the synagogue to recite the benediction *Bareku*, and the whole congregation responded.

Immediately the man was transferred from hell to paradise, and the same night he appeared to R. Akiba and said to him: "May the Lord reward you in this everlasting world, for you have delivered me from hell." R. Akiba replied: "The justice of God is everlasting, from generation to generation, therefore the Lord says: 'I have placed you in this world, therefore perform good deeds, study the Torah and observe the commandments, for one good deed leads to another and similarly one sin leads to another sin.'"

Therefore may every man be found worthy to leave behind children who will say the *kaddish* and thereby deliver him from hell and bring him into paradise, as happened to this man.

### 147. THE TORAH BRINGS FOOD FROM AFAR

R. Hanina married a wife who brought him a large dowry of gold and silver and precious stones, while he studied the Torah continually. All his menservants and maidservants waited upon him with respect and supplied him with food and drink of the best that could be had and served him at all times. After his meals he would say to his wife: "Do not imagine that I have eaten or drunk of anything that belongs to you or that you are supporting me. It is the Lord, blessed be He, who provides me for the sake of the Torah which I study and through the merit of my pupils." When his wife heard this, she grew very angry, but she did not show it. But women have long skirts and short minds. So one day she said to her servants: "What am I to do with my husband? I give him the best of food all the time, but it is no use, I never get any thanks for it, and he says continually that God gives it to him as a reward for his study of the Torah. I will see whether his Torah will give him anything to eat if I do not feed him." So saying, she took all the food she had in the house and had it carried away by her servants. That is why our sages said that it is good that a man should possess a handicraft in addition to the knowledge of the Torah, and one must also know the ways of the world, for the Torah without a craft cannot last.

As R. Hanina was sitting in the *bet ha-midrash* and studying, a ship sailing on the sea was in danger of foundering. The people in the ship cried: "O God, blessed be Thy name, Thou in whom R. Hanina believes, help us! If we are saved, we shall give to R. Hanina a tenth part of everything that we have in our ship." When R. Hanina heard this, he went to the *bet ha-midrash* and prayed for them. Before R. Hanina left the *bet ha-midrash*, the merchants who had been in the ship came and fell at his feet, saying: "Sir, come with us into the ship and take all that belongs to you." R. Hanina went with them, and they gave him the tenth part of everything that was in the ship, gold and silver and precious stones and food, and he had all of it carried to his house.

When he reached his house, he found no one there, nor did he know where they had gone. Then he understood that they had left the house because he had spoken against them concerning his food, having said that it was not his wife who provided for him, but the Lord, for the sake of the Torah which he studied. Then R. Hanina said to his pupils: "Go and hire menservants and maidservants and let them prepare a good meal." The pupils carried out his orders. Then he invited many learned men to his banquet to eat and drink with him, and they all came and made merry. When his wife heard of it, she returned home and fell at his feet and begged him to forgive her for having left the house. Then she said: "Blessed be the Almighty God, who has chosen you to study the Torah."

It is true, as the Torah says, that "from far does the Torah bring her food" (Prov. 31.14).

## 148. The Story of an Impoverished Man Whom Elijah Entrusted with Wealth for a Period of Seven Years

There was once a man who had lost all his wealth and became so poor that he had to work for others and tilled the ground for pay. One day, as he was working in the field, the prophet Elijah came to him and said to the poor man: "You shall have seven good years. When do you wish to have them, in your old age or now?" The poor man said: "You are a wizard, I have nothing wherewith to pay you." The next day the prophet Elijah came again and spoke to him in the same way as he had done the day before. The man replied in the same manner. For he believed that the man had spoken as he did with the intention of being paid. On the third day, he came again and said: "The Lord, blessed be He, says that you shall have seven prosperous years, therefore tell me when you desire to have them, now or in your old age?" The poor man replied: "Please let me go home and consult my wife."

So he went home and told his wife that the old man had come to him three or four days in succession and had told him that he would have seven prosperous years and asked him when he desired to have them. "Therefore, my dear wife, I have come to ask you when we should have them." The wife replied: "Let us take them now. Therefore go and ask that they be given to you at once." So the old man returned to the field and the prophet Elijah came and asked him when he desired to have the good years. He replied: "I like to have them now." Then the prophet Elijah said: "Go home and you will be satisfied. You will see God's blessing even before you enter your house."

The children of the man had meanwhile been rummaging in the dirt and found enough money to last them seven years. So they called the mother and showed her the treasure: and before her husband reached the house, the wife came to meet him and told him what had happened. Then they both praised God for the gift which He had bestowed upon them and felt very happy.

What did the pious woman do? She said to her husband: "God has been very merciful to us, and has given us enough to live for seven years. We will also show loving-kindness and give charity to the poor out of our money during the seven years. Perchance God will have mercy upon us and will grant us further blessing." They carried out their intention and were benevolent to other people. Every day, as she spent some money, she said to her youngest son: "My dear son, write down what we have spent of our money." And the son wrote it down.

When the end of the seven years drew near, the prophet Elijah came to the old man and said to him: "The time has come when I must take back what I have given you, I will therefore take the money away." The old man replied: "I will not give you the money without my wife's leave, as I refused to accept it except with her consent." So he went to his wife and said: "The old man has come and desires to have all the money that he has given us." So she said to him: "Go and say to the old man that if he can find other people more trustworthy than we are and wishes to take the money which has been left with us in trust and give it to those people, he can have it."

But God heard her words and saw the acts of charity which she had performed. Therefore He added more to the money which they had, in order to fulfill the words of Scripture: "And the work of charity is perfect" (Is. 32.17).

Therefore no man should rely on any wealth that he may possess, for the Lord can easily take it away from him. But He can also give it, as happened to this poor man. One should always rely on God, praised be His holy name. Amen.

### 149. R. JOSHUA BEN HANANIAH DISCOMFITED BY A WOMAN A YOUNG GIRL AND A SMALL BOY

R. Joshua son of Hananiah said: "I have never been defeated in an argument by anyone except a woman, a youth and a damsel. I once stayed in a house and the woman prepared lentils for my meal. (Some say it was beans.) The first day I ate the whole plateful and left nothing. The next day I also ate the whole plateful and left nothing. The third day the woman over-salted the lentils. I tasted the lentils and finding them salty, stopped eating. The woman said: 'Why do you not eat the lentils and why have you suddenly stopped eating'? I replied: 'I had a meal earlier in the day.' Then she said: 'Why, then, did you wash your hands and say the blessing if you had no desire to eat?' Then the woman said to me again: 'Dear Rabbi, why did you eat up all that was in the plate for the last two days? Do you not know that our sages tell us that nothing should be left in the pot, but one should leave some food in the dish for the manservant or the maidservant?' And thus the woman got the better of me. Thus far the story of the woman.

"The story of the damsel is as follows. One day I was walking along the highway, and there was a beaten path across the field, so I took that road. Then a girl said to me: 'Is this a highway across the sown field? Is there not a law that one should not walk across a sown field?' Then I said: 'My dear daughter, this is a beaten path.' Then the girl said to me: 'Yes, robbers and others like you made it.' Thus the girl also put me to shame, showing me that I was wrong.

"My third experience was with a young lad. One day as I was walking across a field, I saw a boy sitting at the crossing of two roads which led to the town. So I asked the boy: 'Which is the best road to town?' The boy replied: 'Dear Rabbi, this road is short and yet long, while the other is long and yet short.' So I took the road which was short and long. When I reached the outskirts of the town, I noticed that the town was surrounded by vineyards, which prevented my entering. So I had to go back to the boy. And I said to him: 'My dear boy, you told me this road was short.' The boy replied: 'My dear Rabbi, I told you that it was short and yet long. What I meant was that it was a short road to the town but that one could not enter the town by it, as one has to make a long detour by reason of the vineyards. The other road, however, is long, but it leads straight into the town.' When I heard the cleverness of the boy, I rose up and, kissing him on the forehead, said: 'Happy are you, O Israelites, that you have such clever boys in your midst'."

### 150. THE YEZER HA- RA' MOURNED BY THE RIGHTEOUS AND THE WICKED

Rabbi says: "In the future when the Messiah will come, all Israel will mourn. For whom will they mourn? There are various opinions among the sages concerning it. One says they will mourn for Messiah, the son of Joseph, who will be killed. Others say they will mourn for the *Yezer ha-Ra'* (evil inclination) which will be put to death. The Gemara comments as follows: He who says that the mourning will be for Messiah, the son of Joseph, has a plausible view, for it is written: 'And they shall mourn for him, as one mourneth for an only son' (Zech. 12.10), which means that the people should mourn for the Messiah, the son of Joseph, as one mourns for an only son. But the view of those who say that they will mourn for the *Yezer ha-Ra'* does not seem plausible. Why should one mourn for the *Yezer ha-Ra'*? On the contrary, one ought to rejoice over the death of the *Yezer-ha-Ra'*. However, the mourning can be explained in

accordance with the statement of R. Judah. He
said that when the Messiah will come, the Holy
One, blessed be He, will bring the *Yezer ha-Ra'*
before the righteous as well as the wicked, and
will slaughter him before their eyes. To the
righteous the *Yezer-ha-Ra'* will appear like a high
mountain, and to the wicked he will appear as
a small hair. The righteous will weep with great
joy, and the wicked will weep with great pain.
The wicked will cry: 'Woe unto us that we have
not been able to master the *Yezer ha-Ra'*, which
is as small as a hair.' And the Holy one, blessed
be He, will also wonder.''

Rab Ashi says, at first the *Yezer ha-Ra'* seems
like a delicate thread, but it gradually becomes
stronger until it is as strong as a rope. And why
does it get so strong? I will tell you. If you do
its will it leads you entirely astray and grows
strong within you, and if you give it a finger it
desires to take the whole hand. As the Gemara
says: ''There is a member in the human body
(meaning thereby the evil inclination), which the
more you satisfy the more hungry it becomes.
But if you do not do its will and do not satisfy
its hunger, it becomes tired of such a person and
ceases to lead him astray. But if you satisfy it
and do its will, it becomes more hungry in that

person, and the more he yields to it the more it leads him astray and refuses to let go."

Therefore every man should starve out the evil inclination and not do its will, for then it will desist and the person will have the privilege of sitting among the righteous, and the evil inclination will appear to him as a high mountain.

## 151. The Greater the Man the Stronger His Yezer ha-Ra'

Abbaye says: "The evil inclination is stronger in learned men than in other people," as I will explain. Abbaye says: "I once heard a man say to a woman, 'Tomorrow morning we will walk together through the field'." Thereupon Abbaye decided to follow them to make sure that they should (God forbid!) not commit a sin, and he followed them for three miles until they came to a meadow. There they parted, the woman going north and the man south. Then Abbaye heard the man say to the woman, "We have been out together a long time, it would be a pleasure if we could go out together again." And though they did not know that Abbaye was following them, neither of the two showed any intention of committing a sin. Thereupon Abbaye remarked: "If I had been in the company of that woman as that man was, I would not have been able to restrain myself from sin." Then he went and lay down in front of the house, absorbed in thoughts and very much worried. An old man came to him and taught him thus: "The greater a man is, the stronger is his evil inclination."

Rabbi Isaac says: "The evil inclination of a man grows stronger day by day, as the Bible says: 'Only evil continually' (Gen. 6.5), which means that the evil inclination becomes more furious daily and desires to put the person to death, as the Bible says: 'The wicked (*rasha'*) watcheth the righteous and seeketh to slay him' (Ps. 37.32), which means that the evil inclination, which is called *rasha'* (wicked), lies in wait against the righteous that he may take his life. If the Holy One, blessed be He, should not come to one's aid, one would not be able to withstand the evil inclination, as the Bible says: 'The Lord will not forsake him into his hand' (Ps. 37.33), meaning that the Holy One, blessed be He, does not leave anyone in the power of the evil inclination."

Rabbi Ishmael says: "If the evil inclination seeks to overpower you, go to the *bet ha-midrash*. For even though he be as hard as a stone, he must depart from you, for the evil inclination cannot remain with a man who studies and performs pious deeds." A woman should perform pious deeds, since she cannot study, and the evil inclination will leave her.

## 152. THE DIBBUK

An evil spirit had entered the body of a young man. Thereupon he was adjured to reveal his name or that of his wife. When they mentioned his wife, he began to scream and said that his wife was an 'agunah, which means that she had no right to marry, for he had lost his life at sea and the sages could not give her permission to remarry; that he had requested the sages to give her permission to marry again and had given them many indications that he had been lost at sea, but they did not know where his home had been and therefore said that they could not give her the permission. He was crying because she had become a harlot by reason of the fact that she could not obtain permission to marry.

The sages asked him why he could not rest in peace and what sins he had committed, to which he replied that he had committed adultery. When the sages asked him for the name of the woman with whom he had sinned, he refused to tell, as she has been dead a long time and it would do no one any good if he told. "I am in the position," he said, "of the man about whom the sages say that he who is guilty of adultery should have the four kinds of capital punishment inflicted upon him. But I have not been punished that way."

And while they were talking, the young man suddenly rose up and stood on his feet. The sages asked him: "Why have you risen up?" And the youth replied: "Because a great sage is coming in." And as they looked around, the sage entered, as the young man had said, and a company of young men followed him into the house to hear what was going on. Then the evil spirit said: "Why have you come in here to see me? There are among you some who have done the same as I and will suffer a similar fate." The youths became terribly frightened. Then the evil spirit said: "Why are you so astounded? That youth yonder who is standing among you dressed in white clothes, has committed sodomy, which is as bad as adultery." The youths became terrified and looked at one another. Thereupon the young man dressed in white clothes began screaming and said: "It is, alas, true, I am guilty." And another youth also confessed the same crime. Then one of the sages asked: "How did you know that they were guilty

of such a sin?" The evil spirit began to laugh
and said: "It is written: 'And in the hand of
every man is a seal,' meaning that every man
has written on his hand what deeds he has done."
Then they asked him: "How can you see their
hands, which are covered by their cloaks?" The
evil spirit again laughed and said: "I can see
everywhere." Then they asked him how he had
come to be in the young man. And he replied
that he had had no rest in the water, as the fish
ate his body. Then his soul departed from him
and entered a cow. The cow became insane, and
the gentile owner sold it to a Jew who killed it,
and as the youth was standing nearby, he flew
straight into him. Thereupon the sages exorcised
him and he left the youth and flew away.

## 153. The Observance of the Sabbath

The sages said with reference to Shammai
ha-Zaken (the old) that everything he ate was
kept in honor of the Sabbath. When he came
across a fine beast, he would say: "I will keep it
for the Sabbath." And when he saw a better one,
he would say: "I will slaughter the first one and
keep this for the Sabbath." Thus everything he
ate was in honor of the Sabbath.

Hillel ha-Zaken (the old) had a different
virtue. All his deeds were done for the sake of
Heaven. He always depended on God to provide
him with a fine beast for the Sabbath day. And
in general whenever he went to buy anything, he
always relied on God to provide for his want in
accordance with the verse: "Blessed be God who
provides for our needs every day" (Ps. 68.20).
We also learn that the School of Shammai say:
"On the morrow of the Sabbath for thy Sabbath,"
meaning that from the first of the week, i. e.
Sunday, one should begin buying for the Sabbath
day. And if one gets something better, he should
consume the first and keep the latter for the
Sabbath.

Furthermore, Rabbi Jose says in the name of
Rabbi Simeon son of Yohai, all the commandments which God gave to Israel He gave openly,
except the Sabbath, which he gave secretly to
Israel, as the Bible says: "Between Me and the
children of Israel it is for concealment" (Ex.
31.17). In other words, God says that the
Sabbath is a sign between Me and My children Israel for concealment, that is to say, it is
concealed from the other nations, except Israel
alone. Here the Gemara says: "If the Gentiles
do not know that we have the Sabbath, why
should they be punished to this day for not

keeping it?" The Gemara answers: "They know very well that we have the Sabbath and this is not a secret to them, therefore will they be punished. It is the reward of the Sabbath that is concealed from them."

Man has also one more soul on the Sabbath day than on a week day, and this can be easily observed in the fact that one is more care-free on the Sabbath than on any day of the week. Rabbi Simeon ben Lakish says: "The Holy One, blessed be He, gives man on Friday, on the eve of Sabbath, an additional soul, and at the termination of the Sabbath, the Holy One, blessed be He, takes it back again." The verse, "He rested and was refreshed (ibid.)," means that when one has completed the Sabbath rest, the second soul departs. And the reason why at the termination of the Sabbath we smell spices, is that we may regain our strength when the second soul leaves us. Therefore if one keeps the Sabbath properly, one is well rewarded and receives a second soul. But one should not do it for the purpose of being rewarded. For our sages say, "Be not as the servants who serve their master in order to obtain a reward." But man's relation to God should be like that of a servant who serves his master for love. When a man does a pious deed, he should not expect that the Holy One, blessed be He, will give him his reward in this world, but he should serve the Holy One, blessed be He, for love and the reward will come of itself. But if one does not keep the Sabbath properly, he does not receive the second soul and is unable to rest, as the Gemara says further: "On Friday evening, when a man comes out of the synagogue, two angels accompany him to his house. And when the angels find the candles lit and the table properly set, the good angel says: 'May it be the same the next Sabbath.' And the other angel, who forebodes evil, is obliged to say 'Amen,' against his will. On the other hand, if the candles are not burning and the table is not laid as it should be, the bad angel says, 'May it be the same the next Sabbath,' and the good angel is obliged, against his will, to say 'Amen.' "

Therefore a man should honor the Sabbath in the very best way he can, with good fish and good meat and good wine. And God will repay him more than double. Moreover he will also merit the second soul and be able to rest, as the Gemara says: "When one borrows for the Sabbath, the Sabbath repays," which means that if one spends a great deal for the Sabbath, the Sabbath will repay one, for the Holy One,

blessed be He, provides him amply so that he is
able to keep properly the following Sabbath also
and reach a good old age in peace.

### 154. The Wisdom of the Men of Jerusalem

Two Jews were once carried away into captivity from Mount Carmel, their captor going
behind them. Said one to the other: "In front
of us there has passed a camel blind in one eye
and carrying two casks, one containing wine and
the other oil. There are two men with the camel,
one a Jew and the other a Gentile." When the
captor heard this, he said: "You stiff-necked
Jews, how do you know all that?" "We will tell
you," they said. "The camel ate the grass on one
side of the road, which it could see, but it did
not eat the grass on the other side of the road
because it was blind in the other eye. As for
the second point, we can tell that it is carrying
two casks, one containing wine and the other oil,
because we can see the road is moist on both
sides, where the casks leaked. That which
dropped from one side sank into the earth,
showing that it was wine, while the drops on the
other side remained on the ground, hence we
know that it must be oil. In regard to the two
men who were along with the camel, we know

that one is a Jew and the other a Gentile,
because we can see that the Gentile performed
his necessities in the middle of the road, while the
Jew turned to the side of the road." The captor
hastened his pace, caught up with the camel, and
found that the facts were exactly as the two
captives had said. Such exceedingly wise people
were at this period in Jerusalem, who because of
their sins were taken into captivity.

### 155. THE FOUR MEN OF JERUSALEM AND THEIR GREAT WISDOM

Once upon a time four Jews coming from
Jerusalem stopped over night with a very rich
Jew. They were made very welcome by him
and he quickly ordered meat from a Jewish
butcher and wine from a Jewish wine dealer, and
they ate and drank together and their host was
happy with them. When they had finished eating
and drinking, he showed them the place where
they were going to sleep. Then he stood behind
the door to hear what they would talk about,
as he could easily tell that they were wise men,
because they came from Jerusalem. So he heard
one of them saying to his companion, "I am
lying in a bed which is neither in heaven nor on
the earth," for the bed was suspended by a rope

like a hammock, so that one could lie in it comfortably. And the rich man said to himself: "He has spoken the truth." Then his companion said, "The meat that we have eaten tasted like the flesh of a dog." The third one said: "The wine which we drank smelt of a corpse." The fourth one said: "Our host is a bastard and was not begotten by his mother's legal husband." Then the master of the house said: "What they said about the bed was true. I must therefore find out about the other things."

Early the next morning, he went to the butcher and said: "Will you please tell me what kind of meat you sent me with my servant yesterday?" The butcher answered: "What do you mean? I sent you good mutton." Then he said to him: "Where did you get the meat from?" To which he replied: "I will tell you. I had a sheep which bore a lamb, and died directly after. I also had a dog, who had pups. So I took the young ewe and put it with the bitch to be suckled. When you sent for meat and I had no other, I slaughtered the lamb and sent it to you." Then the master of the house said: "The other guest must also have spoken the truth. I must find out further." So he went to the wine dealer and said to him: "Will you please tell me what kind of wine you sent me yesterday?" The shopkeeper replied: "I sent you good wine." Then he asked further: "Where did you get it from?" The wine dealer replied: "I will tell you. When you sent for the wine, I had none except a single barrel, which I keep as a memorial. When my father died, I planted a vine over his grave, and I keep the wine which it produces in a separate cask in his memory. As I had no other wine, I sent you this wine out of respect for you." Then the man said to himself: "The third man has also spoken the truth. I will go to my mother and find out about myself." So he went to his mother and asked her: "Dear mother, who was my father? Whose son am I?" The mother replied: "Why do you ask? You are my son, begotten by your father." He said: "If you will not tell me the truth, you will surely die by my hand," and taking hold of a sword, he pointed it at her breast. She said: "My son, I will tell you the whole truth. I was not able to have any children with the man to whom I was married, and if he had died without leaving children, I would have lost all the property. So I went with another man, and he was your father. Thus I was able to keep the property." Then the master of the house thought: "The fourth man has also spoken the truth." Then he thought again: "If this be allowed to go on, the men

of Jerusalem will make us all to be bastards."
So the community bound itself by a solemn oath
of excommunication not to give shelter to any
men of Jerusalem. At the same time people
should learn not to be eavesdroppers. Had the
man not listened and overheard their conversation, he would not have heard all this from his
visitors.

## 156. R. Jose ben Kimha Redeems His Two Children from Captivity and Gets the Better of Their Captor

The two children of R. Jose son of Kimha
were carried away as captives from Jerusalem by
a cruel lord. Their father came to them and said:
"Dear children, take heart, I will ransom you,
but you must not do any wrong." R. Jose went
to the wicked master and said to him: "Sir, let
me ransom my children. I will give you 100
florins." The lord replied: "No, I will not do
it." R. Jose went away and, lifting up his eyes
to heaven, wept bitterly. Thereupon the angel
Michael came down from heaven and plagued
the master cruelly.

When his counselors saw the pain he was
suffering, they said to him: "Lord, have you
angered the pious man?" He replied: "Yes."

Then the counselors said: "That is why you are afflicted with pain. For he is a very holy man and Almighty God has listened to his complaint and is plaguing you sorely." So the master sent for R. Jose. As soon as R. Jose came before him, he had respite from his pain. Then the man said to R. Jose: "Give me the 100 florins and take your children home." But R. Jose said: "I have spent twenty florins and have only eighty left. Take these and give me my children." The man became very angry and said to his servants: "Tell him to leave me at once, or I will make him a prisoner like his two children." So R. Jose went out.

But no sooner had R. Jose left, than the pains recommenced. So he said to his counselors: "Tell R. Jose to come in again." And as soon as R. Jose came in, the pain again left him. The man then said to R. Jose: "Give me the eighty florins and take your children." But R. Jose replied: "I can only give you sixty." For he saw that the man was in great pain and was relieved only when he was there. Therefore R. Jose only desired to cause him more pain. The man then said: "Give me the sixty florins and take the children." Whereupon R. Jose said: "I will give you forty florins." Finally the man said: "Take your children without any money, for I see that

unless I satisfy you I shall not have peace."
Then R. Jose took an oath by God, saying:
"I will not go away from here until you have
repaid me the full amount for the time my
children have been kept prisoners by you and
have been unable to earn their living." They
figured out what the children would have earned
and R. Jose demanded to be paid that amount,
if the man desired to have relief from pain. The
man was therefore obliged to pay him eighty
florins as compensation, and allowed him to take
his children home in peace.

## 157. ELIJAH AND THE THREE SONS WHO WATCHED IN THE GARDEN

Once upon a time there lived a pious man who
had grown very old, and when the time for his
death approached, he called his three sons and
instructed them that they should never quarrel
with one another, for they might be led to
swearing and he had never sworn in his life.
Soon after that he died and left them a beautiful
spice garden, which he commanded them to
guard continually against thieves. The first
night, the eldest brother lay down in the garden
to watch. The Prophet Elijah came to him and
said: "My son, what is your wish? Do you prefer

to be a scholar, or a rich man or to marry a beautiful maiden?" He replied: "I should like to be a rich man." So the Prophet Elijah gave him a coin, and he became a rich man.

The following night, the second brother lay down in the garden. The Prophet Elijah came also to him and asked him the same question as to what he would like to have. He replied that he would like to study the whole Torah. So he gave him a book and he became a great scholar.

On the third night, the youngest son went into the garden. The Prophet Elijah came to him also and asked him what he would like to have. He said that he would like to have a beautiful wife. The Prophet Elijah then said: "You must go with me and I will give you a beautiful, pious wife." So they went away together. The first night they stopped at an inn, whose owner was a wicked man. In the night the Prophet Elijah heard the chickens and the geese talking to one another and saying: "The young man must be a great sinner if he is destined to marry the daughter of this wicked man. They are all worthless people and worshipers of idols." When the Prophet Elijah heard this, he understood what they said and went on his way.

The next night, as they stopped at another inn, they heard again the chickens and the geese talking to one another and saying: "The lad must be a great sinner if he is destined to take the master's daughter for a wife, for they are wicked people and worship idols." In the morning, they rose up early and went on their way.

The third night, they came to an inn, whose master had a beautiful daughter. In the night, the Prophet Elijah heard the chickens and the geese talking to one another and saying: "What a virtuous lad he must be if he is destined to get as a wife such a beautiful and pious girl. For all the people in this house are pious and righteous persons." Early in the morning the Prophet Elijah rose up and asked the master of the house to give his daughter to the young man as a wife. They were married and returned home in peace. God gave this wife to him because he had kept the last will of his father. Therefore he attained to a happy old age.*

---

* As told here in the *Ma'aseh Book*, this story is incomplete. I found a Hebrew version in an old Ms. of my collection, where it is continued as follows:—

After a time the Prophet Elijah came to visit the three brothers in order to see what use they had made of the gifts he had granted them. He disguised himself as a poor man and came to the first brother, who had gotten wealth. He was refused admittance and no assistance of any kind

was given to him.  The man had become a hard-hearted
miser.  Thereupon the Prophet Elijah made himself known
to the man and said to him: "Give me back the coin which
I gave you many years ago and which made you wealthy,
for you kept your wealth to yourself, you have not helped
the poor and have done no work of charity.  You are not
worthy of it." So he took back the coin, and the man lost all
that he possessed. Elijah then came to the second brother
in the guise of a scholar.  That man, however, had grown
so proud and arrogant that he treated every man with
contempt and boasted of his learning far beyond his
merits.  But he did not continue his study, nor did he have
a circle of students, and he treated the Prophet Elijah in
the same contemptuous manner as the rest.  So he revealed
himself to the man and said to him: "Have you forgotten
that all your learning comes from the book which I gave
you and not through any merit of yours?  You are no
longer worthy to keep it. Return it to me." The Prophet
Elijah then came to the house of the youngest brother.
He disguised himself as a poor man.  No sooner did the
wife of this man see the beggar than she called him in,
treated him hospitably and showed him all possible
kindness.  In the evening when her husband came home,
the Prophet Elijah told him who he was, took out the coin
and the book from his bosom and said to the man: "I give
you wealth and learning through the merits of your
good and pious wife. For you will know how to make the
proper use of both." Thus the choice of the young man
who had asked for a beautiful and pious wife proved to him
a real blessing.

I will now begin to write down the stories of Rabbi Samuel the Pious and of his son R. Judah the Pious of Regensburg and what happened in their times.

## 158. R. SAMUEL HASID POSING AS A PARCHMENT MAKER

Once upon a time there lived a great man called R. Jacob, who had heard a great deal about R. Samuel, the Pious, the father of R. Judah, the Pious, and desired very much to see him. One day R. Samuel went abroad to study and came to the very town in which R. Jacob lived. So he went to the house of R. Jacob to take up his lodgings there without making himself known, for he was afraid lest he would derive a special advantage on account of his great learning, and it is not permitted to derive profit from the Torah.

R. Jacob never spoke to him all the time that he was staying with him, for he thought that he was a simple fellow. Finally, however, R. Jacob said to him: "My dear friend, what is your name?" He replied: "Samuel." Then R. Jacob asked him: "Have you no surname?" He replied: "I am called Samuel Parchment Maker, after my trade." R. Jacob thought that he was in truth a parchment maker and showed him no more respect than any other guest.

When R. Samuel was leaving, R. Jacob and his pupils accompanied him for a short space, while R. Samuel went some distance ahead with one of R. Jacob's students. When R. Jacob had returned to the town, R. Samuel said to the young man: "Your master asked me yesterday what my name is and I told him that it was Samuel Parchment Maker. I gave myself that name because of my occupation, for I know thoroughly the whole Torah, which is written on parchment." With these words R. Samuel left the young man and went on his way.

When the student returned home, he told his master what the stranger had told him. Then R. Jacob said: "I am sure that he was R. Samuel the Pious and that he purposely refused to make himself known so that I should not show him any special honor, as in fact I did not. And turning to the young man, he said: "Let us hasten after him, perchance we may overtake him and bring him back with us, but assuredly you are not telling me a falsehood." The young man replied: "God forbid that I should tell you a falsehood." So R. Jacob hurried after Samuel, came up to him and entreated him so long that R. Samuel consented to come back with him. As soon as they had reached R. Jacob's house, they entered a room and stayed there ten days and ten nights and no man knew what they were doing. Then R. Samuel left R. Jacob, having been shown great honor. May the Lord, blessed be He, grant that we benefit by their merits through all ages.

### 159. R. Samuel Hasid Riding on a Lion

One day as he was traveling for the purpose of study, Rabbi Samuel the Pious came to the seashore and boarded a ship that had come to the harbor. As he was sailing, he heard a wild scream coming from the land. So he asked the boatman to return to the shore, which he did. R. Samuel went on shore and followed the noise until he beheld a savage lion pursued by an animal called *fandel* (leopard). The lion was very much afraid of the animal, which was spitting fire from its mouth and burning the animals that

it hit. The lion, not feeling himself safe anywhere, ran, roaring piteously all the time. When
the pious man saw this, he ran forth to protect
the lion from the *fandel*. No sooner did the
*fandel* behold the pious man than it ran away
and the lion was saved.

When the lion saw that the pious man had
saved him, he would not leave him and became
very friendly. Finally, the lion knelt down and
allowed R. Samuel to ride upon him. In this
way he rode on the lion until he came back to
the ship, which was waiting for him. Then he
boarded the ship again, while the lion remained
standing on the seashore, looking after him as
long as he could see the ship, like a human being
who sees his friend off and watches him depart
as long as he can see him.

One sees from this that if a man does good even
to a wild beast, no harm will come to him.


### 160. R. Samuel Hasid Amazes the Priests with His Wonderworking

One day three priests from foreign lands came
to see R. Samuel the Pious, for they had heard
that he was a very remarkable man. Informing
him that they were able to perform magic with
the aid of evil spirits, they said to him: "We have

heard much of your skill and wonderworking in all the countries through which we have passed. We, therefore, ask you to show us your clever tricks and we will show you our own, which are greater than yours. Do not refuse our request, for we have come specially to see you from very distant parts."

Now there lived at that time in another place a great man called R. Jacob, who had in his possession a book belonging to R. Samuel. So he said to the priests: "If you can conjure an evil spirit to carry a letter from me to R. Jacob, asking him to send me the book, I will believe you to be great masters of the art." The priests replied: "We have come here to honor you, therefore we will show you a greater wonder than this." Then they said to him: "Come, let us go out into the open country to a secret place and there you will see a very wonderful thing. One of us will draw a circle and the other companions will conjure his soul to leave his body, take the letter from your hand, carry it to R. Jacob, and bring you his answer together with your book, just as you have requested us to do. The man whose soul has left him, will not leave the spot for three days, but will remain lying still within the circle until the three days are over, and then the soul will return to the body,

which will become alive and healthy again."
So the pious man went with the priests to the
field, and they did exactly as they had promised.

As soon as the soul had left the body of the
priest, the remaining two said: "Let us return to
the town, for we have nothing further to do here.
On the third day, at noon, we will come back
when the soul will re-enter the body, after it has
fulfilled the errand which you asked us to do."
So they went back to the town, and on the third
day the two priests said to R. Samuel: "Now let
us go again to the field and there you will see
how the soul will reënter the body of our
companion." The pious man went with them to
the field, but by his art made it so that the soul,
when it came back, was not able to reënter the
dead body.

When the two priests saw that the corpse
would not rise again, but lay there like any other
corpse, they raised a great lamentation for their
companion and mourned bitterly for him. The
pious man then said: "If you will acknowledge
that I can do more than you, I will make the soul
enter the body again as before." So they both
fell at his feet and begged him in God's name to
bring their companion to life again. They were
glad, they said, to acknowledge that he was a
greater master than they. Then the pious man

conjured the evil spirit to cause the soul to reënter the body, and instantly the man stood up alive and gave the pious man the letter as well as the book which he had missed for a long time. The priests thanked the pious man and went their way, saying that his art was even greater than the reputation of it in foreign lands.

### 161. R. Samuel Hasid Uses the Name of God to Summon a Lion; Then He Does Penance

Once upon a time R. Samuel the Pious went to a mill to grind the Passover wheat for his father R. Kalonymos, and while he was in the mill grinding the wheat, there was a cloudburst and the waters rose so high that the asses could not carry the flour home without getting it wet and unfitting it for the use of Passover. R. Samuel was very much vexed and at first did not know what to do. Then he made use of the mystical name of God and there appeared a huge lion, bigger than a camel. He put the sack of flour on the back of the lion, sat down on the top, and thus rode through the water on the lion's back until he came home to his father's house.

When his father saw him coming home on the lion, he understood that his son must have used the sacred name. So he grew very angry and said to him: "You have committed a grave sin in having created the lion by means of the mystical name, and as a punishment for this great sin you will never have any children." R. Samuel was very much grieved, for he did not know that he had committed so grave a sin. Two days later he went to his father again and said to him: "Dear father, you say that I have committed a grave sin, I pray you to impose a penance upon me and I will gladly accept it." Then his father said to him: "Dear son, the penance which I ought to impose upon you would be far too heavy and you would not be able to carry it out." The son replied: "Dear father, I will do everything that you impose upon me." The father said: "My dear son, if you desire to receive atonement for the sin which you have committed, you must wander continuously for seven years, and must never stop more than one night in the same place, except on Sabbath and festivals. If you carry out this penance properly, I assure you that your sin will be forgiven, and you will have pious children." So he took the penance upon himself and wandered for seven years uninterruptedly, spending his time in study as an exile. Some say that he spent nine years as an exile so as to make up for the Sabbaths and festivals.

One day he came to the house of a widow and said to her: "Sell all that you have and buy corn, for there will be great scarcity next year, such as has not been within the memory of man." The poor woman followed the advice which the pious man gave her and, selling everything she possessed, she bought corn. When the people in the town saw that the poor widow was selling all her property and buying corn, they asked her why she did it, and she told them that she was doing it on the advice of the pious man who had been staying with her, for he had told her, she said, that next year there would be a great scarcity, such as had not been within the memory of man.

When the people heard these words of the poor widow, they sold all their possessions also and bought corn with the money. But it turned out that the next year was a very prosperous one, such as had not been known in many years, and corn was so cheap that the people lost much money in the corn that they had bought. The pious man grieved very much for having caused the people to lose their money. For he really thought that the year would be one of famine.

So he imposed upon himself two more years of
exile as an atonement for his sin. The following
year, however, a great famine was in the land
and the people suffered hunger. After that year
of famine there came a year of plenty.

When he had completed his penance, he returned home to his father and to his wife and
begat children. His wife gave birth to twin sons,
one of whom was called R. Eliezer and the other
R. Abraham, who became great masters of the
Law. Then he begat R. Judah the Pious. May
the Lord grant us the benefit of his merits.
Amen.

### 162. R. Samuel Hasid and the Rich Miser

Once upon a time R. Samuel, the Pious, came
to Cologne on the Rhine, begging alms, for he
owned very little. He went to the community of
Cologne and asked them to help him, as he was
in very bad circumstances and had a large
family. The community appointed two scholars
to go about and collect money from the rich
people in order to help R. Samuel the Pious.
In this way they collected seventy florins. While
they were thus engaged, the two rabbis came to
the house of a very rich man who was a great
miser, and asked him for a contribution. But he

grew very angry and, taking out a penny, threw it on the ground and told the two scholars to pick it up and give it to R. Samuel the Pious. The scholars were very much annoyed with him and left the penny on the ground. Then they went to R. Samuel and gave him the money which they had collected from among the members of the community. They told him also of the *Parnas* who had thrown the penny on the ground and asked them to pick it up, but that they had declined to do so. Then the pious man said to the two scholars: "My dear brothers, go and pick up the penny and give it to me; for since the Lord, blessed be He, has decreed that I must unfortunately depend upon the gifts of others, I must not reject anything, whether it be small or large." The two scholars went to the rich man and told him what the pious man had said. When the *Parnas* heard it, he was filled with deep regret for having done such a thing, and went to the pious man and asked him humbly for forgiveness. And at the same time he gave him a large sum of money, as was proper. The biblical verse says: "To a pious man his food comes from a distant land" (cf. Prov. 31.13).

### 163. R. Samuel Hasid Meets the Prophet Jeremiah in a Forest and Saves Three Wicked Men from Their Evil Ways

Once upon a time R. Samuel, the Pious, went forth to study at a *yeshibah*. When he was in the open country, three other Jews joined him and desired to travel the same way that he was going. They went along together until they came to a forest through which they had to pass. They went astray and walked the whole day without knowing where they were. As night approached, the pious man looked hither and thither to see if he could find a house. At last he saw one standing in the midst of the forest and, calling to his companions, said to them: "My dear friends, do not worry, for I have espied a house yonder. But by your life, beware that you do not go in, for I will go in first and see what kind of people live there." With these words he left his companions and went into the house.

When he entered the house, he saw a number of pots standing around the hearth, but there was no one in the house, so he wanted to return to call his companions. But as he was leaving the house, he met a very old man with a snow white beard. The old man greeted him and he returned the greeting. Then the old man said: "Stay with me over night, I will give you meat and drink." The pious man replied: "If I stay with you, where will my companions stay, who are wandering in the forest?" The old man said: "As for your companions who are wandering in the forest, you might very well let them go, for they deserve to be eaten up by wild beasts, for they are wicked people, bad in all their ways. Nevertheless, they shall benefit by your merit. Bid them come in to eat and drink, but be warned not to continue your journey in their company, lest some evil happen to you through them."

The pious man called his companions and invited them in. They spent the evening there, eating and drinking and making merry. After the meal, the old man took the pious man into a chamber and told him that he was the Prophet Jeremiah, and showed him many books which he had written. They consisted of lamentations, which he had composed in memory of the destruction of Jerusalem. "Every day," he said, "I go into this wild forest and weep for the destruction of Jerusalem." In the morning he took leave of the old man, who blessed him and showed him the right path through the forest. Otherwise they would have had to wander about

for a long time in the forest, for it was very large
and full of robbers and wild beasts. When they
left the old man, the pious man told his companions what the old man had said, namely that
they were wicked people and that it was through
his merit that they had been given shelter and
food in the old man's house. Otherwise the wild
beasts would have devoured them because of
their evil deeds.

When they heard these words and found that
their sins had become known, they wept before
the pious man and asked him to impose a penance
upon them for their sins, for they felt remorse
for the evil deeds which they had committed
and desired to do penance. So he imposed a
penance upon them and said to them: "If you
will perform properly the penance which I will
impose upon you, it will go well with you and I
have no doubt that you will enter paradise and
have a share in the world to come. But if you
will not perform properly the penance which I
impose upon you, you will not live to the end of
the year and you will have a miserable death."
They replied: "Master, whatever penance you
impose upon us we will do with our whole heart,
nay we will do more rather than less."

Thus they went together until they reached the
town whither he was going to study the Torah.

When they came to the town, they went into the synagogue and, standing in front of the Ark, they said to the assembled people: "Listen, friends, we are sinners and transgressors of the law. (And they confessed publicly all the sins which they had committed.) We have accepted the penance imposed upon us by this pious man, which we will carry out exactly as it was imposed upon us." And they did so.

One night a voice came to the pious man, saying: "Know that the Lord, blessed be He, has accepted the penance of the three men and they are assured of the bliss of the world to come." Next morning, the pious man went to the synagogue and preached on the subject that no man should despair of himself and say: "I have committed so many sins that I cannot expiate them. I will not do penitence, for it will be of no avail." Rather, let everyone take example from these three men, who had been very great sinners and had deserved to be eaten up by the wild beasts, as the old man had said, but as they properly fulfilled the penance which I had imposed upon them, they have been promised the bliss of the world to come, as if they had never sinned. Nay, they have become even more meritorious, for our sages tell us that even the most pious cannot occupy the place which is reserved for the penitent. And the reason is because a pious man has always lived a good and pure life, he has never had an evil thought nor done an evil deed. But the wicked, who have committed sins and then do penance, have to subdue their evil inclinations in order not to repeat the sin which they have done formerly.

The pious man continued his studies three years and then returned home in peace.

### 164. THE WICKED OFFICIAL WHO INSULTED R. SAMUEL HASID AND LATER REPENTED AND BECAME A JEW

Samuel the Pious once acted as *Hazzan* in Speyer on the Day of Atonement. There came into the synagogue a wicked man, who was the counselor of the duke. When he saw the pious man praying with so much devotion, he bethought himself and said to his companions in the synagogue: "I cannot allow him to go on, I must do some shameful thing to the reader, for he is praying very earnestly and is always lifting his eyes heavenward and praying to his God with great devotion." Thereupon the wicked man spat in the reader's face, hoping to confuse him in his prayer, but the pious man did not allow himself to be confused and continued praying. When

the wicked man saw that he could not confuse
the *Hasid*, he was filled with regret at having
spat in the pious man's face and said to his
servants: "I have done a great wrong in having
insulted the Jew so grievously, for I see that he
is a holy man and his singing is so sweet and
pleasant, I fear I have committed a great sin."
And he grieved much over what he had done.

The next day, after the Day of Atonement,
the wicked man went to the pious one and asked
him why he had been praying so devoutly the
day before. The pious man replied: "Why do
you ask me? You have offered me such an insult
as I have never experienced from any man before
in all my life, not to speak of your contemptuous
behavior generally in the synagogue yesterday,
and that too on such a holy day as we had.
For yesterday was the day which God Almighty
has appointed for us to spend wholly in the
synagogue, the day when God forgives our sins,
as is written in our holy Scriptures. I laughed
in my heart at your insults, for I have faith in my
Almighty God and know that He will forgive
our sins because of the insults which you have
offered me and the great misfortunes which we
suffer at your hands all the time and receive
without complaint. This is why I prayed with
such joy and devotion."

When the pious man had finished his long discourse, the wicked man was so astounded and frightened that he could not speak. Then he asked the pious man to forgive him, for he had acted thoughtlessly, and to pray to God for his sake to forgive him, saying that he would never do such a thing again as long as he lived, nay he would try all his life to deserve well of the Jews, be it in words or in deeds, and the pious man himself would feel it. The pious man listened to his words without answering, and the wicked man left.

On the third day the wicked man came back and pleaded more earnestly than before. He improved in his conduct from day to day and whatever he heard about the Jews in the house of the duke he interpreted in their favor. He pleaded so long and so earnestly that the pious man said to him: "Truly, you have committed a great sin in having insulted me as you have done, but seeing that the thing has caused you great regret and that you promise never to do any such thing again and to treat the Jews well, I will pray to God that He should forgive your sin, for nothing is better than the will not to do wrong."

Thus the pious man prayed to God, blessed be He, on behalf of the wicked man. Later on he

came to the pious man and embraced Judaism
and was known henceforth as the righteous
proselyte.  All his money he gave away in
charity to poor Jews.

## 165. R. Samuel Hasid through His Prayer Annuls an Evil Decree against the Jews of Speyer

R. Samuel was a very poor man.  One day he
said to his wife: "My dear wife, I see, alas, that
a great misfortune has been decreed upon the
community of Speyer.  Let us pray to God and
perchance we may avert the fated misfortune
through our prayer."  And he forbade her on
her life to say anything about it to anybody.
Then they fasted three days and three nights
and offered devout prayers, R. Samuel, the
Pious, standing in one corner and his wife in
another.  When the three days were over, the
pious man said to his wife: "Come, let us make
merry, for I see that the decree has been annulled
through the great loving-kindness of God." So he
took a young rooster and killed it and gave it to
her to cook.

In the meantime, one of his pupils entered and,
seeing that the rabbi had killed a rooster, he was
so astonished that he could not restrain himself

and said: "Master, how comes it that you are eating a fowl today? I know that this is not your custom, for unfortunately you cannot afford so much." When R. Samuel heard what the pupil had said, he said to him: "Dear son, be quiet, for if the people should hear that we are eating fowl, they would laugh at me." But the pupil would not desist. He was anxious to know why they were eating fowl then, seeing that they were not in the habit of doing it at any other time. And he pressed him so long until the rabbi had to tell him the truth. When the pupil heard it, he asked forgiveness for having insisted on the rabbi's telling him what had happened.

Thus the decree was averted through the prayers of the pious man and his wife by the help of the Almighty. May the Lord grant us at all times to enjoy the benefit of their merits. Amen.

### 166. R. Judah Hasid a Wild Youth Becomes a Great Scholar

R. Judah, the Pious, was eighteen years old before he had begun to study. He was a great ignoramus and a boor and did nothing else but shoot with his bow and arrow. One day, his father Samuel, the Pious, was explaining the *halakah* (law) in the *bet ha-midrash.* His pupils grew angry and said to him: "Dear master, all your ancestors were great scholars, like your father R. Kalonymos and your uncle (or father-in-law) R. Efraim, and yet you allow your son to go about shooting with his bow and arrow like an ordinary highwayman." R. Samuel replied: "You are right, and you will see that I shall henceforth train my boy differently."

When the pupils had gone home, he called his son Judah and said to him: "Dear son, I wish you would study the Torah, for I am ashamed of you." The son replied: "My dear father, I am perfectly willing to study if you would teach me as you teach the other young men." So R. Samuel took his son Judah with him to the *bet ha-midrash* and placed him by his side, while his other son R. Abraham he placed on the other side. Then R. Samuel pronounced the holy name and the whole *bet ha-midrash* was filled with a great light. Judah was overpowered by the light, covered his face with his mantle and fell to the ground, not being able to look into the light. R. Samuel then turned to his son Abraham and said to him: "This is a propitious hour for my son Judah. I know that you have been a great scholar all your life, but your brother

Judah will learn much more than you. He will know what is taking place in heaven above and what will happen on the earth below, and nothing will be hidden from him. He will not be as great a master in the Torah as you have always been, but he will achieve more than you."

R. Samuel the Pious began to teach his son Judah, and he knew immediately by heart everything he was taught. When the pupils assembled again to hear their master expound the *halakah*, Judah raised more questions than all the other pupils. They all looked surprised and said: "This young fellow has never studied in his life and yet he is asking more questions than all of us put together." When the lecture was finished, Judah went and fetched his bow and arrow and brought it to his father. R. Samuel took it and broke it before the students, saying at the same time: "My dear son Judah, until now your occupation was shooting with bow and arrow, but now your trade shall be the Torah." After that he devoted himself to study and became the famous R. Judah, the Pious, many of whose wonderful deeds you will now hear.

## 167. R. JUDAH HASID, THE MAYOR OF REGENSBURG AND THE BLEATING LAMB

One day R. Judah was walking along the street in Regensburg, when he met the mayor of the town, who was followed by a little lamb, calling *"me! me!"* as lambs do. The mayor said to R. Judah: "My dear Rabbi, you are the oldest rabbi among the Jews and profess to know all that happens in the heavens above and on the earth below, tell me, why is the lamb crying *'me! me'*? Surely you understand all languages." He said this in jest. The pious man replied: "I know very well what the lamb is saying, but it is not proper to tell." The mayor begged him insistently to tell him, but the rabbi refused, for he feared lest some harm might result. The mayor insisted that he should tell him, no matter who might be involved, and gave him his word of honor that no harm would come to him. Then the pious man said: "Dear sir, I will tell you. The lamb is crying so loudly to tell you that while you are walking about here, another man is lying with your wife in the house. To prove that this is true, go home quickly and you will still find them together." The mayor did not wait to be told a second time, and ran home as fast as he could and found them together, just as the pious rabbi had told him. So he sent for the pious man and said to him: "I thank you for having told me, you shall never have reason to regret it," and he gave him a generous present and became friendly to the Jews. But his wife was innocent, for the man had violently assaulted her, and he was punished by the mayor accordingly.

### 168. R. Amitai Who Was Born with the Word Emet Imprinted on His Forehead

In the days of R. Judah a child was born which had the word *emet* (truth) engraved upon its forehead. R. Judah took the child and brought it up carefully. Wherever he went he took the child with him, and the lad served him as a servant serves his master. R. Judah taught him, and he became a great scholar in the Torah and was called R. Amitai (from *emet*, the Hebrew word for truth, which was engraved upon his forehead and which signified that the child would become a great scholar). May the Lord convert all evil hearts to good. Amen.

### 169. THE STORY OF R. HANINA, THE SON-IN-LAW OF R. JUDAH HASID, AND HIS ADVENTURES IN THE FOREST

R. Judah, the Pious, wished to get his daughter married because he did not want her to engage any longer in money-lending and pawnbroking, for she was thereby putting herself into serious danger. So he said to his daughter: "I am going to find a husband for you." She replied: "Dear father, who will attend to the business of lending money and pawnbroking?" And he replied: "This is why I wish to find a husband for you who will attend to it." Whereupon she replied: "If you insist on giving me a husband, let him be a learned man, for it is written that to give one's daughter in marriage to an ignorant man is like tying her to a lion." The daughter desired a man upon whose wisdom she could depend, but the father was not concerned. The discussion went on until the father lost his temper and swore that she would have to marry. "My dear daughter," he said, "I have sworn that you must take a husband." The daughter replied: "If you have taken an oath, I will not break it. But, my dear father, if you insist on giving me a husband, let him be a scholar." The father replied: "I will go to the other pious man who lives here and ask his advice."

So he went to the other man and listened to his discourse on the laws. When he had finished his lecture and the pupils had retired to their rooms, R. Judah said to the other man: "Have you among the students of your *yeshibah* one who is a good scholar?" The Hasid replied: "I have two young men, who are both very good students. One is called R. Johanan and the other R. Hanina." R. Judah returned home and told his daughter that the other rabbi had two fine young men in his *yeshibah*, both good scholars, one called R. Johanan and the other R. Hanina, and that R. Hanina was a young man of unique merit. The daughter said: "Tell me, father, is he a good or a bad man?" The father replied: "No man knows that before his death." Then the daughter said: "I will take Hanina." The next day R. Judah went to the other rabbi and waited until the other pupils had returned home. Then he asked R. Hanina to wait, as he wanted to speak to him. Then the pious man said to R. Hanina: "Do you want to get married?" Hanina replied: "No, for I have not studied enough?" Then R. Judah said to him: "You must marry my daughter." R. Hanina replied: "No, my dear rabbi, I am not worthy to marry

your daughter." But R. Judah insisted that he
must marry her. Then R. Hanina said: "If you
insist, then I wish to make her a present and
betroth her to me, but I will not marry her until
I have studied more. When I, God willing,
come back from my studies, I will go through the
marriage ceremony." R. Judah repeated all this
to his daughter, who was very well pleased.
Accordingly they made the betrothal and fixed
the time of the wedding. The good R. Hanina
departed and the Lord, blessed be He, helped
him to meet a rabbi who knew the whole Torah.
R. Hanina was about a hundred miles away
from Regensburg and they heard nothing of him,
for he had gone so far away.

Now R. Judah and the other rabbi saw in a
dream that R. Hanina would not be able to come
back at the appointed time. The pious man wept
day and night and at last he told his daughter.
When she heard it from her father, she wept
more bitterly than the father, for she had not
wished to marry at all in the first place, but now
she found the time too long to wait. So the
father said: "My dear daughter, do not weep. If
he does not come on the Sunday before the time
fixed for the wedding, I will get you another
husband." In short, the day came and the

bridegroom did not appear. So they betrothed
her to another. But he was not worthy to go with
her under the wedding canopy. Therefore she
wept day and night and prayed to God that He
might bring back her bridegroom, R. Hanina.

R. Hanina remained ten years with his
teacher and became as great a scholar as the
rabbi himself. One day they had a discussion
about a certain word and R. Hanina found
therein the name of R. Judah. So he remembered
that he was to have married his daughter and,
looking up the date fixed for the marriage, he
found that the following Sunday was the day he
was expected to return. Having counted the
number of miles, he found he was more than a
hundred miles away from Regensburg. So R.
Hanina went to his rabbi, who was a prophet,
and told him the story. The latter said to him:
"If you do not arrive at the time fixed, your
bride will wed another man and the children will
be bastards (God forbid!) and it will all be your
fault." R. Hanina wept bitterly and said: "My
dear Rabbi, advise me what to do." The rabbi
said: "I will tell you what to do, I will send along
with you my best pupils; start tomorrow morning
at daybreak and it may be that the Lord, blessed
be He, will help you to reach home in time."

So he took fifty fine young men with him,

received a parting blessing from his teacher and departed with his young men in peace on a Friday morning. They journeyed until they reached a high mountain. R. Hanina rested a while at the foot of the mountain, while his companions went up. When they reached the top of the mountain, they felt very tired, lay down and fell asleep, while R. Hanina was lying asleep below. Towards evening one of them woke up and, awakening the others, called to R. Hanina, but there was no reply and they did not know what had become of him. Then they said: "Let us go on. It may be that we shall arrive in time and we will then join in the wedding festivities." Accordingly they went on.

After an hour had passed, R. Hanina woke up and, going up to the mountain, called for his companions, but they were not there. So he sat down and wept bitterly. He lifted up his hands over his head and prayed to God for help. Then he went on and thought that perhaps God would help him to reach Regensburg in time. Then he considered that it would be better to put up at an inn rather than break the Sabbath. But he saw before him a huge forest and he thought: "In this forest there surely are many robbers who would kill me, but it is better to lose my life than break the Sabbath." So he went on.

When he left the forest, it was three o'clock in
the afternoon. And as it was winter time, it was
near the time of the beginning of the Sabbath.
So he thought, "It will soon be Sabbath, therefore I will lie down under a tree and rest here."

Suddenly looking round, he saw a beautiful
house in front of him. He thought: "There are
surely robbers in this house, who will put me to
death, still it is better that I lose my life than
that I should break the Sabbath." And he
decided to stay in the house for the Sabbath.
As he opened the door and went in, he saw that
there were four rooms, one on each side. He
opened the room looking toward the east and
saw a beautiful bedstead therein, and into that
room opened three more rooms, one more beautiful than the other. Going into another room, he
found there also beautiful beds. The bedspreads
were of silk, the frame of the bed of pure silver,
and the posterns also of silver. In the innermost
chamber an old man was sitting on a beautiful
chair, holding the scroll of the Law in his hands.
Facing him there was another chair, on which
R. Hanina sat down, saying: "It is better that
I remain here and listen to words of learning
rather than break the Sabbath." The old man
had a long beard which almost touched the
ground.

As the Sabbath approached, an attendant came
in and said: "Is it time to call the people to
synagogue and to kindle the lights?" The old
man replied: "As you think fit." After a while,
the man came and brought some water and
washed his head in honor of the Sabbath, and
did likewise to R. Hanina. R. Hanina thought:
"The water is very fine, it smells of spices."
After he had washed them, the attendant went
away. After a while, he came back and summoned the people for service. Seven men came
in, the servant made the eighth, the old man
and R. Hanina completed the ten. The old man
rose up and said his prayers. The attendant
took R. Hanina and led him after the old man.
All the others knew where to go.

When they came to the synagogue, he saw
that it was all inlaid with precious stones and
everything was beautifully and tastefully arranged. The attendant took R. Hanina and
placed him next to the old man. When the old
man rose up and recited the prayers, R. Hanina
thought that he had never in his life heard a
more beautiful voice; it was finer than the sound
of the organ and the fife. He said the evening
prayer just as we do it. When they finished
prayer, R. Hanina looked round to see whether
there was an organ or pipes or a choir of singers

in the synagogue, but he saw nothing. The
reader sang alone, the others kept quiet. Sud-
denly he heard a voice saying: "O Lord, it is
known before Thee that I am desirous of doing
Thy will, but the evil inclination prevents me.
O Lord, may Thy loving-kindness warm up
toward me so that I may be able to fear Thee."
Then R. Hanina heard another voice saying:
"Do not grieve, for you will happily be in
Regensburg on Sunday in good time."

When they had finished prayers, the old man
took his seat again at the table, R. Hanina did
likewise, and they studied awhile, while the
others went up to heaven. The attendant put on
the table beautiful vessels of silver and gold.
Then he brought wine which had the aroma of
spices taken from paradise. It was the precious
wine known as the wine of Capri. When he had
laid the table, the attendant said to the old man,
"Come and wash your hands." And the old man
washed his hands. R. Hanina did likewise and
sat down at the table. Then the attendant
brought all kinds of delicious food, such as no
man had ever seen or heard of before. After
each course he brought a new kind of wine
better than the previous. After R. Hanina had
eaten and drunk, he thought of his bride but
he kept quiet and was thankful for all that had

happened to him, for it was assuredly much better than lying in the field. After they had finished their meal, the attendant took R. Hanina to his bedroom, in which there was a carbuncle which illuminated the room the whole night as if it were bright day. Then R. Hanina lay down upon a bed standing on four golden wheels. The pillows were studded with pearls, the sheets were of pure silk.

In the morning, R. Hanina rose up and again listened to the old man as he was studying, until the attendant called them to the synagogue. When they came to the synagogue, the reader rose up and began to pray. The previous night there were eight visitors, now there were sixteen, and they joined the reader in the services. Altogether there were twenty-two voices, which rose up to heaven. Then they took the scroll from the Ark and read the portion of the week. For the portion of Cohen they called up Aaron, the Priest, for the portion of Levi they called Moses our teacher, and then all the others, including R. Hanina. When they had finished the prayers, Aaron as well as the old man discoursed on the portion of the Torah. R. Hanina said nothing. Afterwards, the attendant called them to dinner and they had a very good meal. After the meal they went again to the synagogue and read the afternoon service. Then they ate the third meal, as prescribed, and discoursed on the Torah until the time came for evening service. The old man rose up and read the prayers. When he had finished, he gave R. Hanina the greeting of peace, to which R. Hanina responded, and then they read the *habdalah*. After *habdalah* they all suddenly disappeared except the attendant. He was about to leave also, when R. Hanina ran after him, caught hold of his mantle, and said to him: "Tell me, who were those men whom I have seen and who are you?" The man replied: "I am the Prophet Elijah, the reader who recited the prayers was our master Moses, and the others were Abraham, Isaac and Jacob and Aaron the Priest, while the old man was the Prophet Jeremiah." R. Hanina was very much frightened and let the attendant go. But the old man called R. Hanina again and said to him: "Come, let us study some more Torah." R. Hanina complied, and the old man taught him the whole of the Torah. He taught him also all the seventy languages.

When R. Hanina had mastered all his studies, the old man said to him: "Come, let us have some food together." After they had eaten, R. Hanina complained to the old man, telling

him of the plight he was in and said to him:
"Dear master, tell me what to do." The old
man said, "I know full well that unless you get
there tomorrow your bride will be wedded to
another man, therefore I will tell you what to do.
Rise up early tomorrow morning, go up the
mountain on the left, until you come to a wood.
There you will find the fifty students whom you
have lost and who will greatly rejoice at your
coming. Then a cloud will descend at your feet.
Step on it, together with your fifty friends, and
the cloud will rise in the air and bring you in a
little while to Regensburg."

So R. Hanina laid himself down to sleep, and
when the morning dawned, he rose up, received
a parting blessing from the old man and went on
his way, following the directions which the old
man had given him. When he came to the forest,
he found his young friends, who rejoiced mightily
at his return, greeted him and received his
greeting in return. After they had walked a
short distance, a cloud descended from heaven
and placed itself at their feet. They all mounted
it together and were carried very quickly to
Regensburg.

R. Judah was just then going out to perform
his natural functions—the privies were in those
days out in the fields—when he saw a cloud

approaching with many people on it. He sent
at once for the other pious man to come out and
see the cloud. The latter came out and saw the
wonderful sight, and they both watched it until
the cloud had descended on a high mountain
near the city of Regensburg. The two pious men
ran up to the mountain to see what kind of
people were in the cloud. As R. Hanina came out
of the cloud with his young friends, R. Judah
recognized his son-in-law, fell weeping upon his
neck and kissed him and bade him welcome.
The other rabbi did likewise and R. Hanina
returned their greetings. When they asked him
what he had learned, seeing that he had been
away so long, the young students replied: "He
knows the whole of the Torah as well as the
seventy languages, and moreover he is a prophet."
Thereupon R. Judah, the Pious, fell down at
his feet and kissed him, and when he rose up,
he sent for his daughter to come and meet her
bridegroom, R. Hanina, who had returned with
great splendor. The daughter quickly went up to
the mountain and fell down before R. Hanina
and kissed his feet, and wept for joy. Then
R. Judah took him into the town and performed
the marriage ceremony. They celebrated the
wedding feast on the mountain, eating and drinking seven whole days. All arrangements had

already been made for the daughter to marry
another man, if R. Hanina had not arrived that
day. Many people came and studied with R.
Hanina. May the Lord grant us the benefit of
their merit at all times. Amen. Selah.

### 170. The Man Who Was Punished for Shaving His Beard

In the time of R. Judah, the Pious, there
lived in Speyer a very wealthy man, who shaved
his beard with a razor in violation of the prohibition in our holy Torah. R. Judah, the Pious,
heard of it and rebuked him again and again and
forbade him to do it, but the rich man paid no
attention and said: "I am a sensitive person
and cannot bear to have a beard." Then the
pious man said to him: "If you do not take my
warning, then after your death demons (may
God protect us!) will come in the shape of large
cows and trample upon you. For it says in our
holy Law: 'Thou shalt not cut the corners of
thy beard nor destroy them'" (cf. Lev. 19.27).
The initial letters of the Hebrew words make
the word *parot* (cows).

When the time came for the rich man to die,
the elders of Speyer were sitting by his bedside,
and when he died, the people sat down to watch

the body, as is customary. R. Judah the Pious
came with a letter, on which were written holy
names and threw it upon the corpse. Thereupon
the dead body rose up and all the people ran
away in fright. The dead man began to cry and
tore the hair of his head for anguish and scratched
his face. The pious man asked him: "What ails
you that you are crying so bitterly and tearing
your hair?" He replied: "Woe unto me that I
did not listen to your words and refused to follow
your admonitions." Then R. Judah said: "What
did they do to your soul when it left your body?"
He replied: "When my soul left the body, there
came a demon in the shape of a large cow,
carrying a vessel filled with brimstone and pitch,
into which my soul was put so that I could not
get out? Then an angel came and took the vessel
with my soul in it from the demon and carried
it before the Lord, blessed be He, who created
all souls. Then I heard a voice in heaven saying
to me: 'Have you studied *Homesh* (Pentateuch)
or Gemara?' I replied: 'Yes.' Then I heard a
voice saying: 'Bring him a *Homesh*.' A *Homesh*
was brought and I was told to read. When I
opened the *Homesh*, I saw the very verse in
question: 'Thou shalt not cut the corners of
thine head,' which means, you must not cut off

the sidelocks. Then they said to me: 'What have you got to say for yourself? You have disobeyed the commandment!' I heard another voice, saying: 'Cast the soul of this man into the depths of hell.' As they were carrying my soul, I heard another voice saying: 'Hold the soul and do not take her into hell yet, for my son R. Judah, the Pious, is a little late',", which means that the Lord, blessed be He, knew that R. Judah, the Pious, would pray in his behalf to protect him from the punishment of hell. Then the rich man who had just died said to R. Judah, the Pious, "Dear friend, pray on my behalf that my soul may not go down into hell." R. Judah prayed, and he was saved from hell.

Therefore one should be careful not to commit a sin, for every sin that one commits has a special demon, who brings it before God as soon as the man dies, as you have just read in this story. The demon of this sin is called "cow", and the demon in charge of the sin of wearing *sha'atnez* (linen and wool mixed) is called Satan. Therefore every man should take care not to commit sins.

## 171. R. Judah Hasid Saves the Jews of Regensburg from the Charge of Murder

Story of what happened in Regensburg. Two builders worked in the house of a Jew in the Jewish street. During their work they noticed a large quantity of silver and gold in one of the rooms. Accordingly they plotted to get into the chamber while the Jews were absent in the synagogue and take everything away. And so they did. They entered the chamber and took many articles of silver and gold. Then one of the builders said to himself: "What do I want a partner for? I can do the job myself." So he took a hammer and when the other fellow was getting out of the hole, he knocked him on the head and he fell back into the chamber dead. Then he took all the silver and the gold from the dead man and ran away. All the while the Jews were in the synagogue.

When they returned home, the master of the house found the dead body in his house. They were very much frightened and wanted to remove the corpse outside the gate of the town, for they feared that a crowd might gather, as indeed happened. For the rumor spread in the Christian street that the Jews had murdered the Christian. Thereupon a large crowd of Christians came running into the Jewish street and were about to begin rioting. Then R. Judah the Pious came along and went straight to the mayor of the town and said to him: "Sir, what are you going to do? Will you allow so many people to be killed for the sake of one man, when you know well enough that we are not guilty? Two men were working in the house, and I can prove to you that one of them killed the other." Then the mayor said: "If you can prove what you say, no harm will befall any of you." And he gave orders that the people in the street should remain quiet. Then R. Judah said: "Close the gates, so that the murderer shall not be able to escape. This was immediately done. Then the pious man wrote a charm with holy names on it and placed it in the hands of the dead man. The dead man rose up, turned around and saw the murderer hiding behind another man. So he ran up to him and said: "You murderer, you killed me so that you should have the stolen property all to yourself. You struck me in the head with a hammer and I fell back into the chamber." The murderer was arrested, thrown into prison immediately, and condemned to death and executed. Then the pious man said to the mayor: "You see, if I had not stopped you, you would have shed much innocent blood." The mayor replied:"Quite true; therefore, my dear master, forgive me for such a thing. It shall not happen again. In the future I shall first try to find the true facts."

The man who had been killed had many rich friends, who offered a great deal of money to R. Judah and begged him to let the man live. But R. Judah had no such intention, for he said he was not allowed to do it. He took the charm away from the man who had been killed and he fell down again and lay dead like any other corpse. The mayor was very good to R. Judah after that.

### 172. R. Judah Hasid Detects the Thieves and Saves an Innocent Jew

In Regensburg there was a mighty duke who was a friend of the Jews, and whenever he went away he entrusted the keys of all his treasures to a Jew. (Some people say it was R. Ephraim and others say it was R. Samuel.) One day the duke went away and gave the keys to the rabbi so that he might take good care of his treasures, as he had done before. One night nine thieves broke into the duke's treasury and took away as much as they could carry. Some of the thieves lived in the city, and the others were burghers of the locality. In the morning, the

rabbi went to the treasury, as was his custom,
to see that everything was in order, and when he
entered the vault he found very little left, for
they had taken everything away. When he saw
this, he was seized with great fear, as one can
easily imagine, and went to R. Judah, the
Pious, and asked his advice as to what he
should do to recover the money, for when the
duke came home he might suspect him of the
theft and he might lose his life. And he cried
and wept most bitterly, as one can well imagine.
Then R. Judah, the Pious, said to him: "Come
with me." And he took him to the window and
said to him: "Look through the window and do
as I tell you." Rabbi Judah pronounced certain
mystical names of God and then asked the
rabbi: "What do you see now?" The window
was very high and one could see far out into
the country. The rabbi replied: "I see that the
room in which we are has been raised up very
high and I can see over all the roofs in the
town." Then the pious man said again: "What
do you see now?" The rabbi replied: "I see
the thieves carrying the stolen property in their
hands." Then the pious man said to him:
"Watch carefully and see where they put the
property." The rabbi replied: "I see that they
are trying to conceal the money under the

ground, but it seems to me they are taking it out again and behaving as if they did not know where to put it." Then the pious man said to the rabbi: "Do not lose sight of them, and see where they are taking the stolen property." Then the rabbi said: "Now they are taking the stolen property to a blacksmith's. Some of them have engaged the smith in conversation so that he should not see what the others are doing, while the others are burying the property in a stable and covering it with dung." Then the pious man said: "Have you seen exactly where they put the stolen property and do you know exactly where the house is? Observe the place carefully so that you may know how to get there. And now take heart, for they cannot carry the stolen things any farther, and do exactly as I tell you. When the duke comes home, fall at his feet and ask for grace. Then tell him what has happened."

The rabbi did as the pious man had ordered him. He waited until the duke returned home, then he fell at his feet and spoke to him as the pious man had ordered him. The duke said: "Rise and tell me of your trouble, I will be merciful." Then he told the duke all the circumstances of the theft. The duke asked him: "Can you tell me how many thieves there were and who they were and whence they came and whether there were among them citizens of our town?" The rabbi replied: "My gracious lord, I know them all very well and I also know where they have put the stolen property." The duke said: "My dear master, if you know where the stolen property is, take a sufficient number of my men with you, recover the property and put it in the place where it was before." The rabbi replied: "No, my dear sir, first have these men arrested and brought to trial. And if they confess the theft, let them receive the punishment they deserve, for if they are allowed to escape this time, they will do the same thing again tomorrow and you will never be safe from them, for they are mighty burghers of the town." The duke said: "My dear master, you are right, and we will punish the thieves as they deserve and no more. Tell me who they are." The rabbi named them one by one.

The duke sent for all the townspeople as well as the thieves. (For there were a few townspeople among the thieves, and they did not suspect the reason why the duke had sent for them, but if the duke had sent only for the thieves, the guilty townsmen would have suspected the reason and might have escaped.) When they had all come to the duke, he said to the rabbi: "Take as

many of my men as you need and bring the
money here secretly. I will detain the people
here without their suspecting anything and then
we will confront them with the facts of the
case." The rabbi took some of the duke's men
with him and brought back the stolen property
to the duke. Then the duke said to the people:
"Those scoundrels among you who have committed the theft stand together! for I know that
some of you are guilty of theft." The thieves
who were guilty did not know what to say, and
it became clear who they were. Then the duke
told the other townspeople to pronounce judgment upon the thieves, for they had sworn to be
faithful to him in all things and now they had
broken their solemn oath. The thieves had
broken into his vault and stolen the property.
"Moreover," he said, "they wanted me to accuse
my court Jew of the crime because I entrust him
with all my property." The thieves were
sentenced to be hanged on the gallows and the
sentence was carried out. But the Jew was
saved from death. And thus the verse of
Scripture is confirmed: "The pious man is saved
from evil and the wicked one takes his place"
(Prov. 11.8), as happened in this story.

## 173. R. Eliezer Son of R. Amnon Learns Mysteries from R. Judah Hasid and Travels from Regensburg to Mayence in a Brief While

In the town of Mayence there lived a very pious man, whose name is said to have been R. Amnon and who had a son R. Eliezer. When the father was about to die, he left a will forbidding his son to cross the river called Danube.

Now R. Eliezer had heard a great deal of R. Judah, the Pious, and was eager to go to see him in Regensburg and study with him, for he was also distantly related to him. So he crossed the Danube, contrary to his father's will, and came to Regensburg to visit the pious man. When the pious man saw him, he greeted him, and Eliezer returned the greeting. Then the pious man said to him: "I should really not have greeted you, for I see that you have disobeyed your father's will, but I greeted you out of respect for your father's memory." Eliezer was greatly frightened on hearing the words of the pious man.

R. Eliezer remained a long time with R. Judah, the Pious, and was very eager to learn from him the knowledge of the mystical science and many other great things, but the pious man kept putting him off and taught him nothing, although he was with him an entire term, and although he had gone on such a long journey and had been away from his house for such a long time, and yet he did not learn anything. The eve of Passover came and R. Eliezer felt very sad, for he thought: "At this season I ought to be at home and give *Seder* in my house, as beseems every respectable family man, whereas I am here, sitting at another man's table. I had hoped to be home for Passover, for I have been away from home now three seasons and my people do not know how I am." Thus thinking, he was very sad because he had been away so long and besides had learned nothing.

R. Judah, the Pious, saw that he was very sad and knew very well the reason thereof. But the treatment he accorded him was deliberate, as a punishment, namely, for his having disobeyed his father's will. Addressing R. Eliezer, he said to him: "I see that you are sad and I know the reason of your sadness and I know also that you would like to be at home now with your wife and children and give the *Seder*." R. Eliezer replied: "I would have liked it very much if it were possible by the will of God, but now it is impossible, for to-day is the eve of Passover and it is too late." The pious man said to him: "What will you give me if I bring you home to-day before the holy day begins?" Eliezer became sadder still and said to him: "Master, you are making fun of me!" The pious man said: "No, I am quite serious." Eliezer replied: "I would give anything I were asked, for I know of no greater joy than to be with my wife and child." The pious man replied: "It is getting late, we must go and bake *mazzot* and then I will see whether you can get home." Eliezer was greatly astonished at the words of the pious man.

R. Judah, the Pious, went to bake the *mazzot* and R. Eliezer helped him. And when they had taken the *mazzot* out of the oven, R. Judah said to R. Eliezer: "Take the special cakes for the blessings with you and put them in your bosom, for you must bring them home while they are still warm." R. Eliezer laughed with joy and made himself ready. R. Judah himself put the special cakes in R. Eliezer's bosom and went with him into the open country. R. Eliezer was still sad, for he had to go home now without having learned anything from R. Judah. R. Judah, the Pious, knew very well why R. Eliezer was so sad and he said to him: "I know what is troubling you now, you were eager to learn from me the knowledge of the mysteries." R. Eliezer replied: "Yes, that was the reason of my coming." Then the pious man replied: "In justice to your father's command, which you disobeyed, I should not teach you anything; still, in consideration of the fact that your father was related to me and was a pious man besides, I will teach you something."

Then R. Judah took the staff which he had in his hand and wrote some mystical names in the sand. Then he said: "My dear R. Eliezer, read what I have written here." As soon as he read it, he knew as much as the pious man himself. Then the pious man erased the writing and covered it with sand. Immediately R. Eliezer forgot everything that he had learned before. R. Judah, the Pious, did this three times, writing down the words and erasing them again. R. Eliezer grieved because he always forgot what he had learned. The fourth time R. Judah again wrote some words in the sand and told R. Eliezer to lick them up with his tongue. R. Eliezer did so, and as soon as he had swallowed the words with the sand, he knew as much as the pious man and never forgot it again.

Having acquired the mystic knowledge and

wisdom from the pious man, he took leave of him, having received his blessing, went away joyfully, feeling very happy, for he trusted the promise of the pious man that he would reach home before the beginning of the Passover. The pious man blessed him with the priestly benediction and pronounced so many mystic names that R. Eliezer soon saw Mayence, and in a short while found himself at home.

In the evening when the people went to the synagogue, they met R. Eliezer and greeted him. They asked him where he had spent the night, for it is not proper for a scholar to travel on the eve of Sabbath or on the eve of a festival. R. Eliezer replied: "At noon I was in Regensburg and I helped R. Judah, the Pious, to bake *mazzot*, and as a proof of my statement I have here in my bosom a *mizvah* (a special *mazzah*), still warm, which the pious man gave me to bring to my wife." He also delivered to the community a letter which R. Judah, the Pious, had written to them. His wife and child greatly rejoiced at his happy homecoming and at the great miracle which had happened to him.

## 174. The Bishop of Salzburg Who Came to Regensburg with the Intention of Killing R. Judah Hasid But Was Made to Change His Mind and Finally Became a Jew

In the days of R. Judah, the Pious, there was a governor in Salzburg who was a very wicked man. One day he said to his counselors, "I have heard that in Regensburg there lives a distinguished Jew, who is reputed to have knowledge and is highly respected by Jews and Christians. I cannot allow that a Jew shall have so much influence. I am going to Regensburg and will undertake to kill him with my own hand. I will not give anyone else the privilege, for the people believe him to be a holy man and say he can answer any question he is asked. He is also said to be a prophet. It is not right that such a Jew should be allowed to live and to have so much power. Therefore, my dear servants, be prepared whenever I call on you, for I cannot inflict a greater pain on the Jews than by killing their prophet, and I will show you that all his art is of no avail and that his God cannot save him from my hands."

Soon after, he went to Regensburg, accompanied by his servants, and he also had with him many judges and counts. As soon as he arrived in Regensburg he divided his men into two sections, saying that he would go into the city, into the Jewish street, to the house of the Jew, and put him to death. "For", he said, "I will go to him myself." The counselors said to him: "Dear sire and prince, we must obey your orders, but we have heard that he is a man of great skill, maybe you will not be able to conquer him, and he will kill us all. Therefore be careful that you do not fail or make a mistake." But the governor would not listen, and took a knife and put it in his boot to kill the Jew therewith. Then he said to his knights: "I am going to the Jew myself, but if you hear a noise, mount your horses so that we may escape and save ourselves from violence."

As soon as the governor had settled on his plan, R. Judah, the Pious, knew of it and said to his students: "Such and such a wicked man is coming and he has made up his mind to kill me, and he is on the way hither." Then he said to them: "When this wicked man comes into the *bet ha-midrash* and asks you who is your master, point to me. Nothing will happen to you, and you will see how I will disarm him." No sooner had he finished his speech, when the governor was at the door and came into the *bet ha-midrash* and asked who the master was. The students pointed to the pious man. As soon as the governor beheld R. Judah, his strength left him and he could not do anything to him. He greeted R. Judah, and the pious man returned the greeting. Then the governor changed his tune and said to him: "Dear master, I have heard much of your great art, that the like of you cannot be found anywhere on earth. Therefore, I have come to ask you to show me some of your wonderful deeds so that I may also be able to sing your praises before other princes and lords." The pious man replied: "Gladly, my gracious lord, but you must not take it amiss, I am only a poor Jew and cannot do much, but I will show you some of my clever performances, so that you may also be able to speak of me." And with these words he led him and his two counselors into a chamber. Then he said to him: "I will show you my cleverness. Look out of that window and you will see many clever and beautiful things." The wicked man put his head through the window, and R. Judah, by means of mystic names, made the window grow longer and narrower so that he could not get his head out again and was nearly strangled, while the two counselors whom he had brought with him stood still and dared not move. They saw their master's great suffering but could not prevent it.

Then the pious man said: "Ah, you scoundrels! you must all die. Do you think that because you are a free bishop you are going to kill me? Oh, no, you have made a mistake. God almighty has revealed to me your wicked heart and your infamy. I know full well that you have a knife in your boot with which you intended to kill me, but God Almighty has protected me from you and has placed you in a similar position. Now I cannot help you, you must die. Let your 200 men come, whom you have brought with you and let them save you from my hands. No, they cannot help you, you infamous rascal. What wrong have I ever done to you that you should come from Salzburg to Regensburg in order to kill me? But God has avenged Himself on you this day." The wicked man was much frightened and said: "Master of all masters, I pray you, be gracious to me this time, for I confess my guilt and beg for grace. Do not let me die such a shameful death. If God help me to return to my town and country, I will bring back the Jews whom I have expelled and will show them kindness all the days of my life, and I will treat all other Jews in the same way, in so far as it lies in my power, as you will see for yourself. Only let me go back in peace to my country."

When he had entreated the pious man a long

time, he replied to him and said: "Give me your hand and promise on your honor that you will keep the pledge which you have made concerning the Jews and will not break it, then I will show you favor, for I know very well that your 200 men have not been able to help you. I will now set you free and trust your word, for you are a mighty bishop and it behooves you to stand by your word and not to break the promise which you have given. You must be more careful of this than another, for you are a man of noble birth. But if you break your word and act treacherously to us, as you have done before, know that you will not be safe from me in your own house, for I can find you anywhere, even as I found you here." The governor swore to him on his honor, and the pious man could see that he intended to do good to the Jews as long as he lived. So he let him go free.

When the governor came back to his people, who were waiting for him, they asked him whether he had killed the pious man, and he told them all that had happened to him, and the people wondered greatly at the remarkable skill of the Jew. He went back home with his men, and as soon as he reached Salzburg, he sent for the poor Jews whom he had expelled and received them back and treated them well.

Finally he embraced Judaism and became a pious and righteous Jew. May God grant us the benefits of the merits of both. Amen.

### 175. R. JUDAH HASID ADVISES THE DUKE NOT TO JOIN KING PHILIP OF ROME IN WAR

In the time of R. Judah, the Pious, there lived a mighty duke who in all things followed the advice of R. Judah. One day a Roman king called Philippus came to the duke and asked him to join him in war and to give him his help. The duke replied: "I must first go to see my Jew, and find out whether he will advise me to go with you or not. For the Jew knows whether we shall be successful or not." The duke sent for the pious man and told him of the king's request that he join him in war. "Therefore," he said, "I ask for your advice whether I should go or not." The pious man replied: "I warn your gracious lordship on your life not to go. For if you do, be assured that your gracious lordship will not return alive, for they will all be killed in the war." The duke went back to the king and told him that he could not go with him because his wise Jew had advised him against it and had told him that if he went with the king they would both be killed. "Therefore,"

he said, "I beg your royal majesty not to take
it amiss if I do not go with you this time, for I
follow the advice of my Jew in all matters."
The king said: "Do you pay attention to the
words of a false Jew? How can he know what
our fortunes will be in the war? I will go alone.
And as for your false Jew, in whom you put so
much faith, if God help me to return home to
my land I will fight you, and if God help me to
conquer you I will have that false Jew of yours
hanged by his feet, and this will be the outcome
of his wisdom." And with these words he
departed. When he had gone, the duke repeated
the king's words to the pious Jew. The pious
man replied: "By all means let him go to war.
He said that when he returned from the war he
would fight you, and when he had conquered
you, he would kill me. I will forgive him if he
kills me when he returns from the war."

Not long after, the news came that the king
of Rome with all his army had been killed in the
war. The duke sent for the pious man and read
the tidings to him. The pious man replied: "I
knew full well that he would never return alive.
And if you had gone with him, you would have
shared the same fate." The pious man thanked
God, Blessed be He, and said: "Blessed be the
Lord, who frustrates the evil intentions of the

wicked." The duke kissed the pious man and said: "Happy are you, for you are a wonderful people, and God reveals to you the things that are to be." And he held the pious man in higher esteem than ever.

## 176. R. Judah Hasid Saves the Son of a Rich Man from Becoming Baptized

Once upon a time there lived a rich man, who had a son. He brought him to R. Judah the Pious to study under him, and begged the pious man to take special care of the young lad. The pious man said to him: "Bring the lad to me, for I wish to see him first." The rich man brought the lad to the pious man who, as soon as he saw him, said: "I will not take your son whether you pay much or little. Take your boy home and do not bring him back for a whole year. When the year has passed bring him to me again and I will study the Torah with him and do my best for him." The rich man said: "Dear rabbi, why will you not take my son this year?" The pious man did not reply. But the rich man continued asking until the pious man allowed himself to be persuaded. He took the rich man into a chamber and said to him: "I will tell you the reason why I refuse to take your son this

year. In the course of this year, there will be a
day when your son will have an evil moment
and will conceive a desire to be converted to
Christianity. Therefore if you wish to save your
son from apostacy, keep him in your house a
whole year until that day has passed, and then
bring him to me. I know for certain that I can
make a great scholar out of him and a pious Jew
to boot." Then the rich man said: "Dear
Rabbi, can't you advise me how I can
prevent that misfortune?" The pious man
replied: "I will advise you. Build an underground chamber for your son, deep in the
ground and far from your house and the high
road, so that he can hear and see nothing that is
going on outside, and get the young man a
teacher to study with him. Put the two together
in the vault and lock them in so that they cannot
get out, and send them food and drink. Observe
carefully what I am telling you until the evil
day has passed, and then you may let him go
wherever he likes."

The rich man departed very sad, as one can
well imagine, took his son home and followed the
instructions of the *Hasid* to the letter. He built
an underground chamber, employed a teacher
for his son, put them both in the vault and sent
them food and drink. He also hired a servant

to attend them and made a strong lock in the door so that the son could not get out. Thus the teacher and the young lad remained together until the day arrived which the pious man had foretold. On that day the rabbi began his lessons with the lad as usual. The lad said: "I do not want to study to-day, and I regret very much that I allowed myself to be persuaded to come into this chamber and that I have studied so much." And he acted with great impertinence and spoke many strange words, which cannot be recounted here. The teacher said: "My dear son, what has come over you that you act this day as you have never acted before?" The young lad replied with great effrontery: "I want to go away and become a Christian." When the teacher heard these strange words from the lad, he refused to remain with him any longer and contrived to get out of the vault and locked the door behind him.

The boy began to cry and tried to get out of the chamber into the street, and uttered blasphemous words against the Lord, blessed be His holy name for ever and ever, and denied God and continued saying: "Let me out, for I want to join the Church." And the teacher as well as the father and mother stood outside the chamber and heard the impudent words of the young man.

This lasted for a whole hour. Finally, the father,
mother and teacher entered the chamber and
asked the lad why he was acting so strangely
and whether he was in want of anything. But
the lad would not listen to anything they said,
but cried out all the while: "Bring the priest, for
I want to join the Church. If I were outside,
no one could keep me back. I would kill everyone
who came near me and tried to prevent me from
joining the Church." And he acted like a
madman. When the father and mother saw that
there was no improvement in the lad and that
he tried to make his way out by force, they
thrust him back into the vault, tied him hand
and foot and let him lie there the whole day and
the whole night, while they went out of the vault
and locked the door.

The next morning, the father went into the
vault again and found the young man lying quite
still. Then the lad asked his father to loosen the
bands, saying they need not have any further
anxiety about him, for the evil day had passed.
He wept bitterly because of what he had done,
and desired to repent and ask God's forgiveness.
And he said to his father: "Take me to R.
Judah, the Pious." For he was again eager to
study. So they brought him to R. Judah, the
Pious, where he did great penance, as beseems a

pious Jew, and studied day and night and became a great scholar in the Law. And his friends rejoiced in him greatly. May God grant us joy, too.

### 177. R. JUDAH HASID DETAINS A YOUNG MAN UNTIL THE IMPULSE TO BECOME BAPTIZED PASSES

One day R. Judah, sitting at the window, saw a young lad running quickly along the road. So he said to his students: "Run after that young man and hold him by his mantle until I call you." They ran after him and called him, but he would not listen. They overtook him and held him by his mantle and asked him why he was running, what was his object, and why he did not answer when they called him? The young man replied: "What right have you to ask me why I am running?" They said: "Never mind, we want to know and we have a reason for asking." But the young man refused to tell them and was trying to run away. But the students would not let him go and kept him so long until they were about to get into a fight.

When the pious man saw it, he called to one of his young men and said: "Go and tell them to stop their fighting and bring the lad here," which

they did. When they came to the pious man, he
said to the lad: "Why were you running so fast?
What necessity was there for you to run?" The
boy began to cry and said: "Rabbi, I must
confess my sin. I had the intention of committing
a wrong, but I was prevented by your pupils.
They kept me back this time, and now the evil
hour has passed. Therefore my dear rabbi,
impose a penance upon me fitting a thing of this
sort, so that I may atone for my sins." The
pious man imposed a penance, which he carried
out most faithfully and became a very pious
man. Then the students said: "Blessed be God
who grants a portion of His wisdom to those
who fear Him."

### 178. R. JUDAH HASID AND THE APOSTATE

Once upon a time there lived a renegade,
who was a very wicked man and had caused the
death of many Jews by his wicked conduct,
which he pursued for many years. One day
he came to R. Judah, the Pious, and asked him
to impose a penance upon him, for he regretted
very much the sins he had committed. And he
recited to him the grave sins which he had
done from the day he had become a renegade. When R. Judah heard the terrible deeds

that he had perpetrated, he refused to give him penance. "For," he said, "your sins are too great." The pious man was just then whittling a stick, and he said to the renegade: "You have as much chance for atonement as this stick has of becoming green again and sprouting leaves. I cannot therefore give you any penance." The renegade went away and said: "Since the pious man refuses to give me penance, I will continue my evil way and do worse things than before."

Soon after the apostate had left, the pious man saw that the stick had turned green and was growing green leaves. He was greatly astonished and remembered the words which he had spoken to the renegade and said: "The renegade may still have atonement, for the stick has become green again." He sent at once for the apostate and said to him: "I refused to give you penance, saying that you had as much chance of atonement as this stick has of becoming green and sprouting leaves. Now this stick has turned green and is growing leaves. Now, tell me, what good deed have you done to deserve such a miracle? I will give you heavy penance and if you carry it out properly, you will obtain forgiveness and atonement." The Apostate said: "I must confess my sins. Dear Rabbi, I will tell you. Ever since I became a renegade, I have never done any

good to a Jew; on the contrary, I have always
done them evil, except once. I came to a town
in which there were many Jews, whom the
Christians hated and wanted to get rid of, but
did not know how. So they invented a false
accusation. They took a dead child and threw it
into a Jew's house and said that the Jews had
killed it. All the citizens of the town gathered
together, prepared to attack the Jews and put
all of them to death. Now among the counselors
there was a noble man, who was friendly to the
Jews, and he said to the people who had gathered
together: 'Be not in a hurry to shed innocent
blood. Let us first inquire into the root of the
matter, viz. whether they require our blood. I
will tell you how we can find out. There is a
baptized Jew among us, who surely knows. If
he says that they do require our blood, then
unquestionably the Jews must have killed that
boy. But if he says that they do not require
blood, then assuredly they are innocent. Why
then should you shed innocent blood?' Then the
townspeople sent for me and made me swear that
I would tell them the truth, whether the Jews
make use of blood or not, for such and such a
thing had happened to the boy. Then I said to
them under oath that they were wronging the
Jews in this matter, and I gave them many

reasons why such an accusation must be false.
In the first place, the Jews are not allowed to eat
meat unless the animal has been killed and the
blood entirely removed. Then they have to keep
the meat for an hour in salt; then they must
rinse it over and over again so as to remove all
the traces of blood, for it is written in their Law
that they must not eat blood. How then could
they use human blood? Then the townspeople
said, 'If that is the case, no harm shall befall
the Jews,' and the impending evil was averted.
But if I had said yes, they would have all lost
their lives. This is the best deed that I have
done in my life." The pious man said: "That
was a very good deed." Then he gave him
penance, which he carried out and became again
a good and pious Jew.

## 179. The Proud Prince Who Unwittingly Gave His Daughter in Marriage to a Demon

In the time of R. Judah, the Pious, there
lived a lord of noble birth and of royal blood,
who was very rich and owned precious stones of
inestimable value. Now this lord had an only
daughter, whom he would not allow anyone to
marry unless he was as rich as himself, for he

believed there was no one in the world as rich
as he was. One day a demon (may God protect
us!), in the guise of a handsome young man of
royal carriage, bearing beautiful objects of precious stones and pearls such as had never been
seen before and a great deal of money, more
than one could count, came to the lord and said
to him: "Gracious sir, I have heard that you have
an only daughter, whom you will not allow
anyone to marry unless he is as rich as you are
and of equally noble lineage." The lord said to
him: "It is true." The demon said: "Then give
her to me, for I am as rich as you are and of
equally noble birth. And if you do not believe
me, come with me and I will show you all kinds
of precious stones and pearls and rich garments
and silver and gold, such as you have never seen
in all the days of your life."

The lord went with the demon to his inn and
he showed him in his chamber everything that
he had mentioned. Then he said to the lord: "All
this is nothing. When I marry your daughter
and bring her home, then she will see what wealth
is, for I am a king mightier than any king now
living upon earth. However, I think that you can
see my status for yourself. I do not believe there
is another man in the world who has as much
wealth as I have shown you, not to speak of

what I have at home. You can also see from my appearance that I am a king's son. Therefore, if you are willing to give me your daughter as a wife, let me know."

Then the lord asked him: "Whence do you come, my dear sir? What is the name of your kingdom and in what country is it situated?" To make a long story short, the demon was too clever for the lord and persuaded him to give him his daughter as a wife. Then the lord made a proclamation throughout his land that he was going to give his daughter away in marriage and invited all the people to the wedding. He made a brilliant wedding. There was great joy and dancing and fencing and tournaments, as befits a wedding of this kind.

When the wedding was over, the demon said to the lord: "My dear father-in-law, I desire to go to my country with my wife. I ask you, therefore, to give me leave, for I have promised my people that I will not remain away long." The lord asked his son-in-law to remain with him a little longer, but he would not consent, saying he was afraid that he would suffer great harm if he remained away any longer. When the lord saw that his son-in-law's decision was final, he ordered many of his friends to accompany them on horseback and many went on foot.

The lord had an old musician, who played the harp and other instruments. He also went along with the demon, for he wanted to see his country. Thus they all left together, the nobles and the people and a great army. The lord and his lady also went with them, accompanying them a short distance. At last they took leave of one another with great weeping and crying. The lord returned home, and the demon with his wife and the people continued on their journey.

Having traveled three days, they saw a beautiful city in front of them. The demon said to the people: "Turn back, for I cannot allow you to enter the city." But the people begged him earnestly to allow them to go with them into the city. So the demon replied: "I will grant you that pleasure, for you have shown so much loyalty in coming with me into a strange country, and I will afterwards allow you to return home in peace. If you had not been so faithful, I would have done you harm." Then he told them that he was a demon and that the father had brought it upon himself through his own sin in refusing to give his daughter to anyone as a wife. When the people heard it, they were very much frightened and the young woman also was so scared that she fell down in a dead faint, for she thought that her life was forfeit, since she must go with him though she would have much preferred to go back home with her people, but it was not possible. Then the demon told the people to return home. But they replied: "How can we tell such a thing to our master when we come home? Moreover, he will not believe us. Give us a true sign, which we can show to our master." The demon replied: "This is a true sign: It took you three days to come here with me and now it will take you full three weeks to get home. This will convince your master that you have been led by a demon." So they had to take leave of the demon and departed with great weeping and lamentation. After three weeks, they reached their home and told the lord what had happened to them on their journey and that his son-in-law was a demon. The parents mourned bitterly, as one can well imagine, at having made so unfortunate a marriage for their daughter, and they both died of sorrow and grief.

Now the old musician followed his young mistress into the town, which was solely inhabited by demons (may God protect us!). The demon lived in the town with his wife three years. In the fourth year, the demon said to her: "My wife, you must come with me, for your time has come to die." So she had to go with him, and the old musician went along with them. The demon brought his wife to the gate of hell, where he handed over his pretty wife to the devils, who destroy human beings and are called in Hebrew *mal'ake habbalah*.  They took the young woman into hell, and the demon returned to his city to the other demons.  The old musician looked into hell and saw there another musician whom he had known before, for they had been companions.  So he said to him: "My dear fellow, tell me, what are you doing in hell?" The other replied: "Can you not see that I am playing on the harp?"  And he added: "Take care on your life that you do not go to the woman with whom you came here, for the moment you go to her you must remain here. She has been handed over to the devils, therefore do not go to her."  Then the musician who was standing outside said to the one that was inside: "Tell me, how is it that you are not burnt, seeing that you are in hell?  I thought that everyone who went to hell was burnt. You must have done some good deed, which has saved you from being burned."  The musician replied: "I do not remember having done any good deed in my life except that I have played at Jewish weddings and made the people merry.  I am now being rewarded for that service." Then the musician who was standing outside thought to himself: "If a non-Jew who has merely played at Jewish weddings and made the people merry is saved from burning in hell, how would it be if one became a Jew himself? I believe that such a man would not enter hell at all." So he said to him: "My dear friend, tell me how to find my way home, and give me a sign that I have spoken to you, so that if God grant me the good fortune to come among people again, I might tell them that you have spoken to me and they will believe me." Then the other said to him: "Stretch out your hand and touch me with your little finger and you will see great wonders." He touched him, and the finger took fire and burned and he could not put it out. Then he showed him the right way home. He went away, but his finger was burning all the time. After a while he lost a whole limb. He found the right way and wherever he came he asked for Jews. At last he came to a town where many Jews dwelt, and he asked them to accept him as a proselyte. They replied: "Go to R. Judah, the Pious, he will convert you." So he left them, intending to go to Regensburg to see the pious man.

When he was three miles from Regensburg, R. Judah, the Pious, saw in a prophetic vision that so and so was coming to see him. Then he said to his students: "I smell the fire of hell. A Gentile is coming, who will ask for me. Tell him I am not at home and he cannot see me. Then ask him what he wants. If he says that he wishes to become a Jew, convert him to our faith so that the evil smell of hell may leave him." The musician came to the students in Regensburg and told them that he wanted to become a Jew and asked where the master was. They replied that he was not at home and that he could not see him. Then he said: "I would like to embrace Judaism." The pupils then received him into the faith in a chamber which the pious man had designated. From that moment on the fire of hell that burned his limbs was extinguished and the smell disappeared. Then the pious man came and found the musician sitting in the chamber. So he asked him what his business was and whence he had come with the fire of hell on him. Then he told him the whole story of the lord and his daughter. Then the pious man taught him and he became a pious Jew.

## 180. Story of the Child at Whose Circumcision R. Judah Hasid Refused to Rise from His Seat

It happened in the time of R. Judah, the Pious, that a child was born in the city of Regensburg, where R. Judah lived. When the child was brought into the synagogue for circumcision and the people said *Baruk ha-ba*,* the whole congregation rose up, as is customary, but R. Judah remained sitting. Everyone said *Baruk ha-ba*, while R. Judah kept quiet, for he did not see the Prophet Elijah come in, as he usually does. All the people wondered and asked him why he was so disrespectful to the child. The pious man replied: "Because I did not see the Prophet Elijah come in with the child, nor did he sit in the chair which had been prepared for him. He must have believed that no good would come of the child." He also said to some persons: "Look through that window yonder and you will see the Prophet Elijah, in the guise of an old man with a long snow-white beard, sitting and praying."

*"Blessed be he that cometh!" These words are addressed to the Prophet Elijah, who always comes with the child. And this is the reason also for the custom of putting a second chair. [This explanation is in the original text, and has here been made a note.]

Then the people asked R. Judah to tell them why it was that the Prophet Elijah had not taken his seat on the chair, as was his custom. He replied: "I will tell you. An evil moment will come over the child in the future, and he will have a desire to apostatize from Judaism. That is the reason why the Prophet Elijah does not wish to sit by him." This is the same child about which you read above in number 177.

### 181. R. Judah Hasid Makes a Dumb Child Speak

In the time of R. Judah, the Pious, a child was born dumb and remained so until he was grown up. The mother had heard a great deal about R. Judah, the Pious, of Regensburg, so she went to him and told him of her trouble, viz. that she had a grown-up child that was unable to speak, and asked him what she should do. The pious man replied: "Take the child and carry it in the direction of Landshut (this was a small place not far from Regensburg). On the way thither you will come to a village called Gomla. There accost the first man you meet and say to him: 'I have a dumb child. What am I to do to make it speak?' And whatever he tells you to do, do it."

The woman did as she was told by the pious man, and when she came to the village she met a Christian, whom she asked what she should do to make her child speak. The Christian replied with great malice: "Throw him into the fire." The woman said to him: "Go to the devil as an atonement for me and my child!" For she did not believe that the child would be cured that way. She went again to the pious man and told him what had happened to her. The pious man replied: "You were wrong in not doing what the Christian told you to do. You did not have to burn the child. All that you had to do was to put the child on a hot board on the hearth, cover it with a trough, let it lie there a while and then take it up again, and the child would have recovered its speech. Therefore go again to the same village and ask the first man you meet, as I told you before, and do whatever the man tells you."

So the good woman went again to the village and met a Gentile again and said to him: "Dear friend, what shall I do to make my child learn to speak?" The Gentile replied maliciously: "Throw him into the water," meaning the river Isar. Now the woman had a Christian servant with her. So she said to her: "I will support the child so that he should not drown." The servant

did as her mistress had told her and threw the
child into the water, and as the mother caught
him in her lap the child began screaming: "*Shu!
Shu! Shu!* I am so cold." From that moment
the child was able to speak like anyone else.
The pious man taught him afterward, and he
became a great scholar.

### 182. R. JUDAH HASID AND R. JUDAH BEN
### SHENEOR OF SPEYER

There lived in Speyer a great man called R.
Judah son of Sheneor. One day he went to
Regensburg and came to R. Judah, the Pious,
on the eve of Passover. And when R. Judah
gave the *Seder* on the first night, he was full of
joy. When the pious man of Speyer saw how
happy R. Judah was, he waited until the *Seder*
was over and then jumped up from the table
with great joy. When R. Judah, the Pious,
asked him why he was so joyful, he danced and
clapped his hands with glee. Again R. Judah
asked him why he was so happy and he replied:
"I am happy because I see that you are happy."
Then R. Judah, the Pious, said: "I will tell you
why I am so happy. The Prophet Elijah was
with us when we made the *Seder*." Then the
*Hasid* of Speyer said: "Woe unto me that I

was not worthy to see the Prophet Elijah."
R. Judah, the Pious, replied: "He was sitting
nearer to you than to me." The *Hasid* of Speyer
still felt disappointed until R. Judah, the Pious,
said to him: "You are assured of a share in the
world to come and you need not be afraid
of suffering *hibbut ha-keber* (punishment after
death)." R. Judah, the Pious, added further:
"There are three best men in the world and you
are one of them." May God grant us the benefit
of their merits. Amen.

### 183. THE DEATH OF R. JUDAH HASID AND THE FALLEN TOWER OF REGENSBURG

In the time of R. Judah the Pious, there lived
in Regensburg a gatekeeper who was a very
wicked man. When a Jew died, the body had
to be carried through that gate. And as it was
being carried, he showed his malice by tolling
the bell. When R. Judah, the Pious, became ill
and was about to die, he sent for the Jews of the
community and said to them: "Dear friends, here
I lie in the power of God and am about to die.
I will give you a sign whereby you will know
that I shall have a share in the world to come.
The sign is this. When you carry my body to
the gate over which that wicked man is living,

he will begin to toll the bell, as usual. Directly
the gate will fall down and you will not be able
to carry me out that way. When that happens,
you will know that I shall enter paradise."

When the pious man died and they proceeded
to carry the body through the gate, the wicked
porter became aware of it and began tolling the
bell. Immediately the gate fell in, killing the
gatekeeper, and they could not carry the body
through.

If you do not believe this story go to Regensburg and you will see for yourself, and will hear
why the gate cannot be rebuilt. It has been
rebuilt many times, but no sooner was it erected
than it fell down again and would not stand.


### 184. RASHI AND THE DUKE OF LORRAINE

The following story happened in the days of
Rashi. The word Rashi is composed of the initial
Letters of Rabbi Shelomoh Isaac. Rashi was by
birth a Frenchman, but he lived in Worms,
where he had a college, which also contained an
ark. For he used the college also as a synagogue,
which is called to this very day the Synagogue of
Rashi. Special prayers were read there on the
eve of New Moon and the students conducted

services there every *Simhat Torah.* All this was
done in honor of Rashi.

One day, the duke of Lorraine, whose name
was Godfrey of Bouillon, came with a large army
on his way to Jerusalem to fight the Turks. He
had heard a great deal of the wisdom of Rashi
and was told that he was regarded as a wise man
by Jew and Gentile. Nay, he was looked upon
as a prophet, which, indeed, he was. So the duke
sent for Rashi, to ask his advice. But Rashi
refused to go. When the duke heard that Rashi
refused to come, he felt very angry that a Jew
should disobey his command, and with his army
he went to Worms to the house of Rashi. He
found all the doors open, the books lying open on
the table, but he saw no one in the house. The
duke called out in a loud voice, "Solomon,
Solomon, where are you?" Rashi replied: "What
does your lordship want?" The duke asked
again: "Solomon, where are you?" and Rashi
replied: "Here I am, my lord." And as often
as the duke called him, Rashi gave answer, but
the duke saw no one. The duke was greatly
astonished and went out of the house. Then one
of Rashi's students passed and the duke asked
him: "Does Rashi live here?" and the pupil
replied: "Yes, he is my master." Then the duke
said: "Tell your master to come to me. I swear

by my head that no harm will come to him."
When Rashi heard it, he came to the duke and
fell at his feet. But the duke raised him up and
said: "I have seen your cleverness. Now I will
tell you why I have come to see you. I wish to
ask your opinion with regard to a very great
undertaking upon which I have decided. I have
collected a large army of infantry and cavalry
and I intend to capture Jerusalem, for I am sure
that with the help of God I shall defeat the
Turks so thoroughly that they will not be able
to fight any longer. Now I wish to hear your
advice. Speak freely, do not be afraid whether
you foretell success or failure. Whatever your
advice may be I will follow it, for I know that
you are half a prophet and can foretell truly how
one will fare in war. Therefore I beg of you to
tell me truthfully whether I shall be victorious
or not." Rashi replied in a few words: "My lord,
I will tell you the truth. At first you will be very
successful and will capture Jerusalem and reign
therein for three days. On the fourth day, the
Saracens will gather again and drive you out and
you will have to flee. Most of your army will be
killed and those who survive will die on the way,
and you will come back to the city with three
men and one horse's head. Now you may do as
you please, but you have heard my opinion."

When the duke heard the words of Rashi, he felt very sad and said to Rashi: "It may be that you are speaking the truth and that I will have the experience you describe, but I promise you that if I return with four men, I will give your flesh to the dogs and will kill all the Jews in my country." And the duke departed with his army. All that Rashi had foretold came to pass, and he returned to Worms with three men and three horses, the duke himself and his horse making four. Meanwhile four years had passed, for the war had lasted all that time.

When he approached Worms he remembered that Rashi had foretold that he would return with three horses, whereas he was coming back with four. His mind was full of evil thoughts and he planned to put Rashi to death. For he had promised that if he came back with four horses, he would give Rashi's flesh to the dogs. But the Lord, blessed be He, frustrates the thoughts of the wicked. For as the duke was about to enter the gate of Worms, a beam with iron spikes (such as are commonly used at the gates and are lowered in front in time of war) fell by itself and knocked off the head of the fourth horse, and the rider had to remain outside. So the duke came to Worms with three men only and not four. The duke became very much

frightened and admitted that Rashi had proph-
esied correctly that he would not enter the town
with four horses.

Before going to his own house the duke wanted
to go to the house of Rashi to bow down and
kneel before him and to thank him for his prophecy.  But when he came to the house of Rashi,
he found him lying dead in the coffin and about
to be buried.  When the duke heard of Rashi's
death, he mourned him deeply, as such a man
should be mourned.  May the Lord grant us
and the whole of Israel to enjoy the benefits of
his merits.  Amen.


### 185. Ritual Murder Charge in Constanti-nople and the Acquittal of the Jews through the Sleeplessness of the Sultan

The following is the story of what happened in
Constantinople.  The Turks told the king that
the Jews had killed a Turk and wanted to bring
misfortune upon them, as has, unfortunately,
often happened before that false accusations had
been brought against the Jews and many of them
lost their lives.  So the king sent for the Jews, and
when they came, he said to them:  "Can you
interpret for me the verse in the book of Psalms:
'The guardian of Israel neither slumbereth nor

sleepeth?' " (Ps. 121.4). They replied: "It means that He who guards us from all evil neither slumbers nor sleeps." The king said: "You are wrong. The meaning is that God who is the guardian of Israel, does not allow others to sleep so that He may protect His people Israel against the Gentiles and others." And he went on to say: "Last night I could not sleep, so I got up from my bed and looked out of the window. The moon shone so brightly that one could see clearly down the street. Then I saw two men carrying a dead body on their shoulders. Immediately I sent two of my servants to see where they were carrying the dead body, and they reported that they had seen them throw the body into the house of a Jew. Now they are accusing the Jews of having murdered a Gentile and are eager to take revenge. Now if I had been asleep and had not seen the incident myself, I would have put the Jews to death and shed innocent blood. But God, the guardian of Israel, did not allow me to sleep so that I might see the deed myself. Therefore nothing shall happen to you."

The king then punished the murderers, who had thrown the dead body into the Jew's home and the Jews were saved this time from the people. May the Lord, blessed be He, protect us in the future also from all evil. Amen. Selah.

## 186. STORY OF THE HUMILITY OF A RICH MAN

One day R. Akiba was in the synagogue and was holding in his hand a very precious pearl, worth a great deal of money. At the same time there was in the synagogue a man so poorly clad that people thought he was not able to spend a florin. He sat among the poor people in the synagogue and every one thought he was a very poor man. But when he saw the beautiful pearl in the hand of R. Akiba, he asked him whether he desired to sell it and invited R. Akiba to accompany him home. R. Akiba allowed himself to be persuaded and accompanied the shabbily dressed man to his house, his students following him. When they reached the house, servants came out to meet him and placed him on a golden chair. Then they washed and bathed him. And the man paid R. Akiba the price of the pearl and then gave orders that he and his students should be shown great honor. A table was set and R. Akiba and his students ate and made merry.

When they had finished, R. Akiba said to the man: "My dear friend, since God has been so good to you and has granted you so much honor and wealth, why do you wear tattered garments and why are you so humble and sit among the poor people in the synagogue?" The man replied: "My dear Rabbi, I will tell you. The Bible says: 'Man is like unto vanity, and his days are like a shadow that passeth away' (Ps. 144.4). Man is like that, to-day he is alive, tomorrow he is dead. If a man be rich to-day, tomorrow he may be poor, for the wheel of fortune is always turning. Therefore I thought it would be better for me to sit among the poor and not to boast of my wealth. If I should insist on my dignity and take a front seat, and then (God forbid!) I should be punished and become poor, I would have to move to a back seat. But now I remain where I am. Besides, my dear Rabbi, why should I be proud of my money? Have we not all one God, praised be He, who has created us all? Why, then, should one man think himself better than his neighbor? Moreover, God hates the proud man and hell is open before him. Moreover, when I sit among the poor, I can hear what they lack in their homes."

When R. Akiba heard the words of the man, he was greatly pleased and said: "You are different from the generality of men. Nowadays, when a man has money, he is very proud and therefore he often loses it."

Therefore, ye people, learn the moral of this

tale.   Even if one has a great deal of money, he should not be haughty in his demeanor to others, but should take an example from this man who, although he was very rich, was very modest and did much good to the poor.

This story is taken from the Midrash.

### 187. The Rich Merchant of Jerusalem Who Died in a Strange Land Leaving His Fortune There and the Manner in Which His Wise Son Recovered the Same

A wealthy merchant of Jerusalem took a great deal of merchandise with him over sea, for he was engaged in foreign trade, which took him overseas.  And he also took a great deal of money with him.  In the course of his travels, he spent one night in a certain house, intending to continue his journey on the next day.  But he was suddenly taken very ill and could not proceed any further, and was forced to lie down on the bed, from which he was not able to rise again. When he knew that he was about to die, he gave his host all the money he had with him to take care of and instructed him to keep the money until a person came who would show three clever devices.  To him should the money be given. He could not give him any other sign by which he might know his heirs. Then the merchant from Jerusalem made his confession of faith and died in a strange country among strange people, and was buried there in an honorable manner. The master of the house kept the money a long time and no one came to claim it.

When the wife of the merchant of Jerusalem saw that her husband did not return home, she became anxious and said to her son: "My dear son, what shall we do? Your father went over seas with a great deal of wealth and has been away many years. I fear that he must have died and that the money has gone into strange hands, unless he was drowned in the sea, for your father was not in the habit of remaining away so long. Therefore, my dear son, it is my wish that you go to distant lands and make inquiries until you find out where your father died. If he died in the house of a Jew, you will get your money back." The son followed the advice of his mother, took leave of her and went over sea, and traveled from city to city, until he came to the city where his father died.

Now there was a custom in that city that no stranger should be allowed to stay over night. When the son had come near the town, the people living outside told him of this rule. Then the son thought: "I must devise some clever trick

in order to get into the city." So he asked
the people who lived outside: "Is it not true
that a man of Jerusalem died here many years
ago and left a great deal of money?" They
said: "Yes", and gave him the name of the man
with whom the money had been left.

When he reached the gate of the town, he saw
a man who had a bundle of wood for sale, so he
bought the wood from the poor man on condition
that he should carry it to the house of so and so,
and he named the man in whose house his father
had died. The poor man carried the wood, and
the heir from Jerusalem followed him. When he
brought the wood to the house, the master of
the house said: "What do I want with the wood?
I did not buy it." The poor man replied: "He
who bought the wood is following me." The
master of the house thought: "This is no accident," and took the wood, and greeted the heir
from Jerusalem. This was one example of cleverness. And the master of the house suspected that
he might be the heir of the man who had died
some years before.

"Now", said he, "I must test him further, and
if everything turns out as the father declared in
his will, I will not withhold the money from him."
He ordered a good meal to be prepared for the
evening and the first course which was brought

to the table consisted of five young pigeons. Desiring to test him, the master placed the five pigeons before the young man and said to him: "My young friend, do us the honor and divide the pigeons among us so that each of us should get an equal portion." The heir replied: "My dear sir, I do not deserve the honor, for I am a stranger." But the master of the house pressed him so long that he took the pigeons and divided them. Now the host had two sons and two daughters. Accordingly, the heir gave one pigeon to the host and his wife. One pigeon he gave to the two sons, and a third to the daughters, while he kept two pigeons for himself. The master of the house was very angry and thought to himself: "Surely this is no accident. There must be a clever reason for it. I will test him again." For he could not understand why the guest should keep two pigeons for himself and give only one pigeon each to the two other couples.

The next night they made another meal, and this time they prepared only one chicken. The master took the chicken, set it again in front of the young man and said to him: "My dear guest, divide this chicken among us. You divided the pigeons very well yesterday and I am pleased with you." But the young man refused. The

master, however, urged him so insistently that
he took the chicken and divided it. He gave the
master the head of the chicken. To the wife
he gave the inside of the chicken; to the two sons,
the two legs, to the two daughters he gave the
two wings, while he kept the body of the chicken
for himself. The master was again greatly
astonished that he should have kept the whole
body of the chicken for himself, and said to him:
"My dear man, what do you mean by keeping
the largest part of the pigeons and the chicken
for yourself?" The guest replied: "My dear sir,
I will explain it to you. You told me to divide
the pigeons equally and that is what I have done.
You and your wife are two, add one pigeon and
that makes three. Your two sons and one pigeon
also make three, and your two daughters and
one pigeon again make three, and I and two
pigeons also make three. Hence all the parts are
equal." When the master heard this, he thought:
"This is also very clever, and we have two
instances so far."

"As to the chicken," continued the young man,
"the division is as follows. I placed the head of
the chicken before you as a sign that you are the
highest authority in the house, as the head is the
highest part of the chicken. I gave your wife
the inside as an allusion to the fact that she

bears the children in her womb. I gave your two sons the two legs, that is the two thighs upon which the chicken stands, to indicate that the sons are the support of the house and maintain their father and mother, staying at home to give it stability. I gave the two wings to your daughters, because the daughters will marry and must fly out of the house, as the chicken flies far with its wings. I kept the body of the chicken for myself because the chicken without head, legs and wings looks like a ship, alluding to the fact that I have come in a ship and intend going back in a ship. And now I will tell you what my business is that has brought me here." And he told him the story.

Then the master of the house thought: "This surely is the heir whom the father meant when he spoke of three examples of cleverness. The first was in the purchase of the wood, the second in the division of the pigeon, and the third in the division of the chicken." And he wondered greatly at the dead man and the will he had made concerning this person. Then he said to him: "My dear man, I see from your wisdom that you are the rightful heir. Come and I will give into your hands all your father's money." And so he did, for he was a pious Jew. (In our time such a thing would not have happened.) And he added: "I have heard much about the wise men of Jerusalem and now I see it for myself."

In former times when a visitor came from Jerusalem, he was offered a chair to sit down and people listened to his wisdom, but nowadays, unfortunately, things have greatly changed. One can find many stories of their wisdom in the book *Ekah Rabbati*, and anyone who desires to read the book will find all the stories there.

### 188. The Jewish Child Who Was Stolen by a Servant and Later Became Pope

R. Simeon the Great, who lived in Mayence on the Rhine, had three large mirrors in his house in which he saw all that had happened and all that was going to happen. He also had at the head of his couch a spring, whose waters issued from his grave in the cemetery. R. Simeon had a young son named Elhanan. One day the *Sabbath Goyah* came in, as usual, on the Sabbath, to light a fire in the stove, and when she left she took the child with her. The servant who was in the house, did not take any special notice, thinking that the woman would bring the child back, and the other people of the house had gone to the synagogue. The Christian woman took the child and had him baptized. She thought that she had thereby offered up a sacrifice to God, for in olden times they attached great importance to the baptism of Jewish children. When R. Simeon the Great returned home the maid was not in, for she had gone after the woman but could not find her, so he found neither the maid nor the child. Suddenly the maid appeared, crying bitterly. When R. Simeon asked her why she was crying, she replied: "My dear rabbi, alas, the *Sabbath Goyah* took the child away and I do not know where she has gone." They searched everywhere, but could not find him. The child had completely disappeared. The father and the mother mourned bitterly for the child, as one can well imagine. R. Simeon fasted day and night, but the Lord concealed from him the place where the child had gone.

The child passed from hand to hand until he fell into the hands of the priests, who brought him up, and he became a great scholar, for he had the intellect of his father, R. Simeon the Great. The lad went from one university to another until he came to Rome. There he learned all languages, and became a cardinal in Rome. His fame spread far and wide, his praises were sung everywhere, he was very much respected and he was handsome besides. Then the Pope died, and the young man, being very bright and master of many

languages, became Pope. He remembered, however, that he had been a Jew and that he was a
son of R. Simeon the Great of Mayence. Yet
he remained among the Christians, as one may
well imagine, considering that it went well with
him and that he was held in high esteem.

One day he said: "I must make an effort to
bring my father from Mayence to Rome." So he
wrote a letter to the bishop of Mayence—for
as he was Pope all bishops were subject to his
commands—and ordered him to forbid the Jews
to keep their Sabbath or to circumcise their sons
and to forbid the Jewish women to take their
ritual baths. He thought that the Jews would
send his father R. Simeon to him to ask for a
revocation of the decree, and so it was.

When the letter of the Pope reached the
bishop, the latter immediately informed the Jews
of the decree. And when the Jews made urgent
representations to the bishop, he showed them
the letter of the Pope and said that he could not
help them, but if they wished to present their
case they must go to Rome and see the Pope.

The poor Jews, finding themselves in this
terrible position, did penance and prayed and
gave charity. Finally they decided to send
R. Simeon the Great and two other rabbis to
Rome to intercede with the Pope, in the hope

that God would perform a miracle for them.
In the meantime they circumcised their children
secretly, for they had obtained permission from
the bishop to do it in secret. Then the rabbis
journeyed to Rome to see the Pope. As soon as
they arrived, they informed the Jews there of
their arrival and explained the situation to them.
When they heard of it, they wondered greatly,
for they said that within the memory of man
they had never had a Pope who was kinder to
the Jews than this one. He could not live
without Jews. He often had Jews visiting him
secretly and occasionally played chess with them.
Moreover, they had not heard anything about
the decree and could not believe that it came
from the Pope. The bishop himself, they
thought, was responsible for it. But R. Simeon
showed them the letter of the Pope with his seal
on it, and they were convinced and said: "This
must be a punishment for some great sin of
which you Jews in Germany are guilty. Then
the Jews in Rome also did penance and prayed
and gave alms, and the *Parnasim* of the Roman
community went to the cardinal, with whom
they were on friendly terms, and asked him to
intercede in their behalf. The cardinal replied:
"This letter was written by the Pope's own hand
and addressed to the bishop of Mayence. I am

afraid I cannot do much for you." Nevertheless he promised to do all that he could and
told them to prepare a petition, and he would
see that it got into the hands of the Pope, and
would do his best to help them.

The Jews prepared a petition and gave it to
the Pope. When the Pope saw the petition, he
knew what the situation was and ordered the
Jews to appear before him in person. R. Simeon
came to the chief cardinal, who presented them
to the Pope, saying: "These are the Jews from
Mayence, who are anxious to see you and speak
to you." The Pope replied: "Let the oldest of
them appear before me." R. Simeon the Great
was the oldest among them and his appearance
was like that of an angel of the Lord. As soon as
he entered the room, he fell upon his knees. The
Pope was playing chess with one of the cardinals.
When the Pope saw R. Simeon, he was very
much frightened and told him to rise and take
a seat, until he had finished the game. He knew
his father, but the father did not recognize him.
When the game was finished, the Pope asked R.
Simeon what he wished. R. Simeon replied amid
tears and was about to fall down again on his
knees before the Pope, but the Pope would not
allow it. He said: "I have now heard your
petition, but strange reports have reached me

from Mayence, which caused me to give the order in question." Then the Pope began a talmudic discussion with R. Simeon and almost vanquished R. Simeon in the dispute. The latter was greatly astonished to find such a great intellect among the Christians. They spent almost a half day together, and then the Pope said to him: "My learned man, I see that you are a great scholar, otherwise the Jews would not have sent you as their advocate. Now I have Jews who come every day to play chess with me. Will you not also play a game with me? You will not lose anything by it."

Now R. Simeon was an adept at chess. There was none like him in the whole world, and yet the Pope checkmated him. The rabbi was greatly astonished, and they began to talk again about religion, and R. Simeon was astonished at the keen mind of the Pope. Finally, after further complaint and entreaty by R. Simeon, the Pope sent all the cardinals away and fell on his neck with tears in his eyes and said: "My dear old father, do you not know me?" The father replied: "How should I know your royal grace?" The Pope said: "My dear old father, did you not lose a son once?" When R. Simeon heard this, he was greatly frightened and said, "Yes." The Pope replied: "I am your son

Elhanan, whom you lost through the fault of the
*Sabbath Goyah.* What sin of yours was responsible
for it or what the reason was I do not know, I
think it was the will of God. I issued the decree
in question for the purpose of bringing you to
me, as has actually happened. Now I wish to
return to my faith, therefore I will annul the
decree." And he gave him letters to the bishop of
Mayence, revoking the decree. Then the son
said to his father: "Can you advise me how I
can atone for my sin?" The father replied:
"You need not worry, it was against your will,
for you were only a child when you were taken
away from me." Then the Pope said: "My dear
father, all the time that I lived among Gentiles
I knew that I had been born a Jew and yet,
as you see, the good circumstances in which I
was kept me from returning to my faith. Do
you think I shall be forgiven for that?" (R.
Simeon could tell from the way in which he
played chess that he was of Jewish descent.)
Then the son said to his father again: "Return
home, in the name of the God of Israel, and take
the letter to the bishop and say nothing further
about me. I will be with you in Mayence soon.
But before I return to my faith, I wish to leave

behind me as a memorial something that will benefit the Jews."

R. Simeon went to the Jews of Rome and showed them the letter by which the decree was annulled, and they rejoiced greatly. R. Simeon and his companions then went home and brought the letter to the bishop, and they all rejoiced. R. Simeon told his wife of his adventure and that the Pope was their own son. When she heard this she wept bitterly, but R. Simeon said to her: "Do not grieve, we will soon have our son with us." The Pope then wrote a book against the faith, locked it in a vault and gave orders that every candidate for the papacy should read the book. It would take too long to tell what is written in that book.

Soon after, taking much wealth with him, he went to Mayence and became a good Jew again. In Rome they did not know what had happened to the Pope. R. Simeon commemorated this story in a poem recited on the second day of the New Year which begins: "Elhanan my son." Therefore do not think that this is mere fiction, nay, it really happened as is described here. Some say that R. Simeon knew his son by a move he made in chess. He had taught him that move while he was still young, and he made that move on the day when they were playing

together. He knew then that he was his son.
May the Lord forgive us our sins through the
merits of R. Simeon. Amen. Selah.

### 189. GOD MAKES THE RICH POOR AND THE POOR RICH

Once upon a time there lived a man who
scoffed at the idea of giving indiscriminate
charity, for he said: "No man takes alms unless
he has given up every hope of success in this
world. A man of this sort is obliged to take
charity." One day as he was going along the
road, he saw a poor man in tattered garments
lying on the rubbish heap. Then he thought:
"This man has lost every hope in the world.
He requires charity." And he turned to the man
on the rubbish heap and said: "Here is a florin,
for I see that you are in need of it and that your
hope is cut off in this world." The poor man
replied: "Your hope is cut off, not mine." Then
the rich man said: "Why do you curse me when
I wish to do you good?" The poor man replied:
"Do you not know what is written: 'The Lord
casteth down the high and the proud and raiseth
up the humble?' Because you see me lying on
the rubbish heap, you think that my hope is cut
off. Do you not know what is written: 'He

raiseth up the poor from the dust and the needy
He lifteth from the rubbish heap?' " (Ps. 113.7).
Then the rich man said: "Tell me, then, who
are they whose hope is cut off in this world and
who require charity?" The poor man replied:
"The dead. They have no more hope in this
world." Then the rich man said: "If that is so,
then I will give charity to those who lie in the
cemetery." [The rich man committed a sin when
he told the poor man that he had no more hope
left in this world.] And the rich man went to the
cemetery and buried one hundred florins in a
grave, saying: "Behold, you dead man, I have
given you a hundred florins, keep them, for you
have no more hope in this world and are in need
of charity." Then he went his way.

Many years later, God Almighty remembered
the poor man who lay on the rubbish heap and he
became the richest man in the town, while the
rich man became so poor that he had no bread to
eat. Then he remembered the hundred florins
that he had buried in the cemetery, and thought:
"They will be useful to me now in my need. I will
go and dig them up." So he went to the cemetery
and was about to begin digging. But the people
of the town saw him and, thinking that he
intended to rob the dead of their shrouds, had
him arrested and brought before the mayor of

the town, who was none else than the poor man who had lain on the rubbish heap. For God had exalted him and, when the mayor of the town had died, he was appointed in his place. The people accused the erstwhile rich man of having tried to steal the shrouds of the dead.

As soon as the mayor saw the rich man, he knew him and spoke very severely to him. The man replied: "God forbid that I should have had such a thought in my mind!" And he told him the whole story, how the poor man had cursed him and that he had hidden away a hundred florins in the cemetery, which he was now trying to recover. The mayor said to him: "Do you not know me?" And he replied: "How should I know you?" The mayor said: "I am the poor man who lay on the rubbish heap and to whom you said that his hope was cut off in this world. Now God has exalted me and I am the mayor of the town." And he rose from his seat and embraced him and kissed him, and ordered the money to be dug up and returned to him. Then the mayor said: "You see, friend, no one should rely on his money. But since you had the intention of giving alms, you shall remain with me in my house all the days of your life, you shall eat at my table and sleep in my bed."

Therefore, ye people, consider what this story

teaches. Even though a man be despised and held in contempt, God can make him rich very quickly; and though a man rejoice in his wealth, God Almighty can quickly make him poor. Therefore take this story to heart that ye be preserved from poverty.

### 190. THE PIOUS MAN WHO WAS TEMPTED BY A DEMON LIVING IN A TREE

Once upon a time there lived a pious man who had a beautiful field, in which grew a beautiful tree. The heathen worshiped the tree and brought much money as gifts, but they destroyed everything which the pious man planted in the field. And the pious man said to his wife: "How is it that our field is so damaged, although we fertilize it most diligently?"

One day the pious man was taking a walk over his field, when he saw the heathen playing and dancing round the tree. The pious man said: "Now I understand why my field is damaged." And he went straight home and took an axe to cut down the tree. When he told his wife what he was going to do, she said: "Since you have seen this, cut the tree down so that we may not lose all our grain." The pious man took the axe and was about to cut the tree down, when

the tree said to him (it was a demon who spoke):
"Dear friend, let me remain and you will have
three florins every morning." The pious man
thought: "Three florins a day are not bad, I will
let the tree stand." And he went home joyfully,
thinking that it was a gift from God. When he
came home, he told his wife what had happened
to him and what the tree had said to him. She
was very well pleased, too, and they both
rejoiced at such a great find. Every morning the
pious man went to his field and found the three
florins. So he said: "Now they can destroy my
corn if they like." But he did not know that
the heathen were worshiping his tree as an idol.
The pious man became immensely wealthy and
acquired many menservants and maidservants,
and houses and cattle and barns.

Not long afterwards, however, all his children
died. He grieved very much and thought: "O
Lord, what sin have I committed that all my
children should die?" For he believed himself to
be very pious, as he really was, save for the sin
about the tree, which he committed unwittingly,
not knowing that it was an idol.

One day, as the pious man was walking over
his field, he saw the heathen throwing money at
the tree. Then he knew that the tree was
worshiped as an idol and understood that this

was the sin which had caused the death of his children. Then he said: "O God, Thou hast punished me severely by the death of my children. I will cut down the tree, even if it should promise me a thousand florins." And with these words the pious man went home, took an axe, ran quickly and began to cut it down. The tree again said: "Dear man, why do you cut me down when you find so much money in me every day?" But the pious man continued cutting, and the tree said: "Dear man, let me stand and you will find ten florins every day." The pious man replied: "I will not let you stand if you give me a thousand florins every day." When the demon saw that the pious man had no pity on him and would not let the tree stand, he flew out of the tree.

Then the pious man went to the Sanhedrin and asked them what he should do with the money he had received from the idol. They told him to take all the money that he had received from the tree and give it back to the tree. The pious man did so. He returned all the money to the tree and buried it under the tree. Then he tilled the ground and sowed the seed and the field yielded him that year one hundred measures of corn. Thus God gave him enough and he became rich again. Still he had committed a sin and had lost his children as a punishment.

Therefore, my dear friends, do not let yourselves be led astray by idol worship, even if it should fill your purses, for it causes one's destruction. The Lord, blessed be He can make a man rich if he deserves it.

## 191. Trust Not in Magic

Once upon a time there lived a Jew who was led astray by a wizard. The Jew was lame and could not walk. One day he was told that there lived, in a certain town, a man who by means of an ointment enabled the lame to walk, the blind to see and healed all the sick. So he said he would also like to go to that town so that he might be cured. Now the man who healed the people was a demon, may God protect us from them! The Jew went to that city, and when he arrived there, he saw a man walking about in the night and healing the sick. The demon came up to him also and asked him what he wanted. He replied: "I am a Jew and have heard that you heal all the sick and make all the lame walk, therefore I have come to you that you may cure my lameness also." The man said: "Do you know who I am?  I am a demon and have assumed the form of a physician to lead all the people astray who follow sorcery, in order to destroy them. Now your time has come to be cured of your lameness, but since you allowed yourself to be led astray by sorcerers, the Lord has decreed that you should remain lame all your life."

Therefore one should beware of being led astray by sorcerers and should believe in God, blessed be His name.

## 192. THE DECREE AGAINST CIRCUMCISION AND THE BIRTH OF RABBI JUDAH HA-NASI

Once upon a time the government forbade the Jews to circumcise their children. At that time a son was born to R. Simeon son of Gamaliel. This son came to be known as Rabbenu ha-Kadosh (our holy master). R. Simeon said: "Circumcision is a divine command and we must keep it. It is one of the great commandments, for our forefather Abraham sanctified the name of God the first time by means of it. Now the king has forbidden us to keep this commandment. Shall we neglect the divine commandment and obey the commandment of the wicked king? To do so would be to transgress the commandment of circumcision. It is better, therefore, that we

should obey the commandment of circumcision
which God Himself gave to Abraham our father,
and reject the command of the king even though
it may cost me my life." And the father went and
circumcised his son, as God had commanded.

In that town there was a prefect, appointed to
see that the Jews should not circumcise their
children; and if anyone had his son circumcised,
the father and the child should be sent to the
king to be killed. Now the prefect had heard
that R. Simeon son of Gamaliel had circumcised
his son, so he sent for R. Simeon and said to him:
"You know that it is forbidden to circumcise
children and yet you transgressed the command
of the king and circumcised your child yourself."
R. Simeon replied: "It is better that I should
obey the command of God Almighty, who
created heaven and earth, than that I should
disobey it and keep the command of the king,
who is only flesh and blood." The prefect said:
"You have spoken right and I think as you do.
I know that you are a pious Jew and I would
gladly give you the benefit of my mercy, since
you are the greatest man among the Jews. But
what can I do, seeing that the king has forbidden
circumcision under a severe penalty and it has
become known among the people of the town?
I fear therefore that if I let you go I shall be

betrayed to the king and may lose my life. I cannot therefore let you go." Then R. Simeon said: "What do you intend to do with me?" The prefect replied: "I must send you and the child to the king and leave it to him to do with you whatever he wishes." R. Simeon said: "I am quite satisfied." Then the prefect gave orders that he should send the mother with the child to the king, for the child could not be without the mother. So the mother and the child started off on their journey.

In the evening they came to an inn, and it so happened luckily, by the will of God, that the mistress of the inn had given birth to a male child. The name of the child was Antoninus son of Severus. When the wife of R. Simeon came to the hostess with her child, she asked her where she was going and what she was going to do with the child. "For," she said, "I see that you are still suffering from your confinement." She told her the whole story, that she had to go to the king because she had had her son circumcised, and she was very much afraid that she would lose her life. Then the mistress of the inn said: "Listen to me, I will give you good advice. Take my child, which is not circumcised, and carry it to the king, and leave your child with me until you return from the king. You will be able to

show that the child is not circumcised and thus
save your life." The woman was well pleased
with this advice and followed it.

She took the innkeeper's child with her, leaving
her own child in the inn, and went to the king's
palace. The prefect was there also, and he went
before the king and told him that he had sent to
him a woman and a child which had been
circumcised, and that the mother and child had
arrived. Let the king do what he pleased, for
they had disobeyed his orders. The good woman
was sent before the king, and when she appeared
before him, he asked her: "Tell me, why did you
disobey my command? You must now lose your
life." The good woman fell down at the king's
feet and said: "Most gracious king, the report is
not true. Examine my child, and if it is as you
have been told, then I have forfeited my life,
but the prefect is an enemy of the Jews and he
can find some more evil stories to tell about us."
They took off the swaddling clothes and found
that the child was not circumcised. The king
became angry with the prefect for making false
charges. But the prefect said: "My lord the
king, this child was circumcised. Ask your
servants who have seen it done. Some miracle
must have happened." The counselors then said:
"My lord the king, we are sure that the child has

been circumcised, but the Jews have such a faithful God that when they pray to Him with their full heart, He does their will, as is written in their books: 'Who is a God like our God, when we call upon Him?'" (cf. Deut. 4.7). Then the king said: "If God performs such wonders for them, what use is it for me to give such orders?" Accordingly he revoked his decree throughout his dominions, and ordered the prefect to be punished, which was done, although he was innocent.

The king sent the woman home in peace, and she came safely to the inn with the child. The mistress of the inn said: "In as much as God has performed such a miracle for you with the aid of my child and yours, they shall both of them (God preserve them!), when they grow up, be intimate friends as long as they live." They both grew up and became great men, the one was the patriarch, Rabbenu ha-Kadosh (our holy rabbi) and the other was Antoninus, also a very worthy man and deserving a share in the world to come. They were friends all their lives, as you have read above in one of these stories. May God prolong our life. Amen.

### 193. Three Pious Jews Go through Fire Unscathed and Save the Rest of the Community from Harm

Once upon a time a ship full of Jews from the captivity of Jerusalem came to a certain place. The bishop sent for them and asked them: "Of what nation are you?" They replied: "We are Jews." Then he said: "If you are Jews, I will put you to the same test as Hananiah, Mishael, and Azariah, who were thrown into a burning furnace. If you are protected as they were and will come out unscathed, I will believe that you are true Jews." The Jews replied: "Give us three days, and we will pray to our God to protect us as He protected Hananiah, Mishael and Azariah." The bishop granted their request. They fasted three days and three nights, and on each morning everyone had to tell what he had dreamt during the night.

When the third day arrived, an old man, extremely God-fearing, came forward and said: "I dreamed that a biblical verse was recited to me, which contained the word *ki* (if) twice, and the word *lo* (not) three times. But I do not know what the verse meant, nor do I know where the verse is found in the Bible." Now there was another old man among them, who was a great scholar, and he said: "The dream which you saw indicates that the verse will be of great help and that the Lord will have mercy upon us. The verse is found in Isaiah, chapter 43, verse 2: 'If (ki) thou passest through the water I am with thee; and through the rivers, they will not (lo) sweep thee away, and if (ki) thou walkest through fire it will not (lo) burn thee, and the flame will not (lo) singe thee.' You will surely be the one who will go through the fire and will be protected, because you had the dream. The verse was announced in heaven concerning you."

On the third day the bishop ordered a great fire to be made, sent for the Jews and said to them: "The time for which you asked has elapsed and you must now go into the fire. We will see whether your God will protect you as He protected Hananiah, Mishael and Azariah." That day was a Christian holiday and a great concourse of people had assembled to witness the event. The old man, who had seen the dream, and two others went into the fire voluntarily and unsolicited. Thereupon the fire divided itself into three parts, and the three men passed through unharmed and came out. When the bishop saw that they remained unscathed, he said: "I have never in all my life seen such a nation as the Jews. As soon as they call upon

their God, He hears them." So they all praised
God and said: "Blessed be the Lord for ever and
ever." The three men composed the prayer
beginning with the words: "And He is merciful,"*
which is recited on Mondays and Thursdays,
for those are the days on which the heavenly
tribunal sits in judgment. Therefore everyone
should trust in God, who never forsakes us in
time of trouble.

## 194. THE MAN WHO OBEYED HIS FATHER'S LAST WILL; HOW HE FELL INTO THE WATER AND WAS FINALLY REWARDED

Once upon a time there lived a pious man who
had an only son. When he felt his death approaching, he said to his son: "I am in the hands
of God and my time has come to die. I wish
that you should go to the water every day after
my death and cast a loaf of bread to the fish,
for I know that in time you will be repaid."
The son promised his father, with tears in his
eyes, and said: "My dear father, I hope you will
not die yet, but whatever you ask me to do I
will, with the help of God, carry out, however

* This legend of the origin of the supplicatory prayer
beginning with *Vehu Rahum* is found in *Sefer Asufoth*,
ed. Gaster.

difficult it may be, exactly as you have commanded me." And the pious man died and was deeply mourned, for he was truly a pious man. After the seven days of mourning were over, the son went to the water every day and cast a loaf of bread into it, as his dear father had willed.

There was one fish in the water that always caught the loaf which the lad threw in, and whenever one of the small fish came to catch it, the big one drove it away. He soon grew very large, having eaten all the fresh bread which the lad had thrown into the water. When the little fish saw that they could not get any of the bread, they went to the Leviathan, who is the king of the fish, as we find in the books, and complained to him and said: "O lord king, if you will look on quietly and not interefere, this fish will grow as big as you are. Therefore see that you prevent the fish eating all the bread." When the king heard this, he said to the fish: "Go and dig a pit where the man goes to throw the bread into the water, and ask the big fish to help you. And when the man falls into the pit, bring him to me."

The little fish rejoiced in the thought that the big fish would no longer get the bread. So they went and told the big fish what the king had

ordered them to do and that he must help them
to capture the man. The fish grew very sad,
for he lived on that bread. But he had to obey,
for it was the order of the king. So they dug a
pit in the place where the man stood. When
the lad came to throw the bread in as usual, he
fell into the water, and the big fish came and
swallowed him up and brought him to the king,
and spat him out. No sooner had the fish spat
him out than the king swallowed him up. Then
the man began to complain bitterly of the
suffering he had to endure on account of his
father's will. Then the king spoke to him and
said: "Tell me, what was your purpose in coming
every day and throwing bread into the water?"
The man replied: "My lord king, I am obeying
my father's last wish." And he told him that his
father had instructed him that he should cast a
loaf of bread every day into the water, and that
he would finally be rewarded. But he could not
understand, he said, what sin he had committed
that he should have fallen into the water.

When the king heard this from the man, he
said to him: "Since you have kept your father's
last wish so faithfully, I will teach you the
seventy languages as your reward." The king
taught him seventy languages and then spat
him out on dry land again. He felt so weak and

sleepy that he lay down and fell asleep. Two black crows, a father and a son, were sitting in a tree, and the son said to the father: "I would like to peck out the eyes of the man who is lying there," for the crow believed that he was dead. The other crow said: "Do not go near him, for he pretends to be asleep, but he will catch you and kill you." The son said to the father: "I will risk it."

Now the man had learned all the languages while he had been in the water, and he understood what the crows were saying to one another. The crow sat down on the man's face and was about to peck at his eyes when the man caught it and wanted to kill it. Then the other crow cried out: "It serves you right. I told you not to go near the man, but you would not listen." And then turning to the man, the crow said: "My dear man, let my son go free and I will show you a treasure full of money, and you will become very wealthy and happy." The man replied: "If you will show it to me, I will let your son go." Then the crow said: "Go to that tree yonder and dig underneath and you will become rich and happy." The man went and dug under the tree and found a treasure so rich that it could not be counted. So he let the crow go free. Then the man said: "Now that God

has given me such a great treasure, I will build
a house for myself." He built himself a house
and bought land and menservants and maidservants, and was immensely rich. This was
granted to him by the Lord as a reward for
having observed his father's will.

Therefore, my dear friends, take to heart the
moral of this story. Obey your fathers' wishes
and it will go well with you, as it did with
that man, and to this let us say Amen.

## 195. THE BRIDE WHO SAVED HER HUSBAND FROM THE ANGEL OF DEATH AND OBTAINED A REPRIEVE OF SEVEN YEARS

Once upon a time there lived a man called
R. Reuben. He was a very good and learned
man. He studied day and night and the Lord
received his prayers with favor, for whenever
great danger threatened the people, he averted it
by his devout prayer. He had an only son who
was a very fine lad. One day the angel of death
came to R. Reuben and said: "I have been sent
by the Lord, blessed be He, to tell you that the
time for your son's death has come." He replied:
"What God does no man can prevent, but I pray
you, let me first marry my son, and then you can
do what you have been commanded, but I wish

first to have the joy of leading my son under the wedding canopy." The angel of death replied: "Your wish is granted to marry your son first." The father went home in sorrow, betrothed his son and fixed the wedding to take place in four weeks. The people wondered at his having fixed the marriage to take place so soon.

Then he sent his son to invite a few people to the wedding ceremony. On his way the son met the Prophet Elijah, who said: "My dear son, where are you going?" He replied: "I am going to invite people to my wedding." The Prophet Elijah said: "Do you not know that you are to die before your wedding and that the Lord wishes to take your soul away, for the time of your death has arrived?" The bridegroom replied: "If that is the will of the Lord, I will submit to it willingly, for I am no better than our fathers Abraham, Isaac and Jacob, who also died." The Prophet Elijah said: "I will give you good advice which you should follow. When the time comes for the blessing and the people are seated round the table, sit down with them, but do not eat or drink, and keep your eyes downcast. A man will come with uncovered head and disheveled hair, and his garments will be torn. As soon as you see him enter the room, get up from the table, go and bow down before him, bid him welcome and invite him to sit at the head of the table among the distinguished guests. And if he refuses to sit at the head of the table, then sit down next to him and show him great honor. Take care to fulfill my instructions." The young man promised to follow his advice and the Prophet Elijah went his way.

The young man invited the people to his wedding and behaved as if nothing had happened. He then returned home to his father and said to him: "I have carried out all your instructions." The father made all the preparations for the wedding, and both father and son behaved as if nothing had happened. People came to the blessing, and sat round the table eating and drinking. The bridegroom sat with them, looking very sad, but no one knew the cause of his sadness. After they had been eating a while, there came into the room a man in tattered garments and bareheaded, looking like a poor man. It was the angel of death, who had disguised himself as a poor man, as the Prophet Elijah had foretold the young man. As soon as the bridegroom saw him, he at once knew who he was. Accordingly he rose from his seat, went up to the old man, took him by the hand and said: "Come with me and sit at the head of the table." The old man refused. So the bridegroom took the shabby old man by the hand, placed him by his own side at the table and brought all kinds of good food, which the old man pretended to eat. The bridegroom did exactly as the Prophet Elijah had told him. The people who were sitting at the table were greatly surprised at the honor the bridegroom paid to the poor man. The bridegroom, on the other hand, was so frightened that he could scarcely speak.

Then the poor man said to the bridegroom: "My dear son, I wish to ask you a question. If you are building a house and are in need of straw to mix with the clay, whence do you get the straw?" The young man replied: "I go to the man in the barn and buy the straw from him, for he makes the straw." Then the old man said: "But suppose after you have made use of the straw, the man came from the barn and asked to have the straw back, what would you do?" The bridegroom replied: "I would pay him for the straw, or I would give him other straw instead." The old man continued: "But suppose the man insisted on having his own straw and refused to accept any other, what would you do?" The young man replied: "I would break up the clay and take out the straw and give it back to him." Then the old man said: "The Lord, blessed be He, is the master of the barn. The straw is the soul of man, and I am the angel of death. The Lord is asking for the straw which He gave you and refuses to accept any other straw. Therefore I am here to take your soul."

When the people heard this, they were all very much frightened, but the young man recovered from his fright and said to him: "If it is the will of God that I should die, then pray allow me first to see my father and my mother and my dear bride, and bid them farewell, then I shall willingly die." The angel of death said: "Very well, go." The young man went to his father and mother and to the bride and took leave of them amid great weeping. The father began to pray. Meanwhile the bridegroom went to the bride to bid her farewell, and she said to him: "Who is it that wants to take your soul?" The bridegroom replied: "The angel of death is here and wants to take my life." And he kissed her and wept. Then the bride said: "Stay here, and I will go to the angel of death." She went to him and said: "Are you the man who wants to take my bridegroom's soul?" He replied: "Yes, I am the man." Then the bride said: "Then I ask you to go back to God and say to Him: 'Is it not written in the Holy Law that a man who takes a wife shall be free for a whole year to rejoice with the wife he has taken'

(Deut. 24.5), and now will the Lord, blessed be He, violate His own law?" When the angel of death heard this, he felt pity for them and went before the Lord and begged for his life, and the other angels joined in the prayer, and the father also prayed fervently. The Lord took pity on him and prolonged his life seven years, corresponding to the seven days of the wedding festivity. This is the meaning of the verse: "The Lord does the will of them who fear Him and call on Him with their whole heart" (Ps. 145.19). God saves them from all pain.

### 196. Story of the Avaricious Woman

Once upon a time there lived a very rich man, who always took pleasure in giving charity and did much good to the poor. But he had a bad-tempered wife, who never gave anyone to eat or to drink. The man possessed three treasures filled with wealth. He had one treasure of gold, from which he gave alms to the scholars. The second was filled with silver, from which he gave to widows and orphans. The third was filled with small coins, from which he gave charity to the poor. He gave to every man as much as he needed.

One day the rich man was not at home, and

the poor came and begged for alms. When they heard that the man was not at home, they would not enter the house and remained standing outside before the door. When the wife saw the poor people standing before the door, she wanted to give them alms as her husband was wont to do. She went to the treasure of gold, but found it full of frogs. Then she went to the treasure of silver, and found it full of mice. And she went to the treasure of small coins and found it full of fleas and lice. She began to weep and was ashamed to go back to the poor, for she had nothing to give them. So she remained inside, waiting for her husband to return.

When he came home and found the poor people standing in front of the door, he was annoyed with them for not having gone into the house. When he entered the house, he found his wife weeping and crying, and she said to him: "I want a divorce, for I see that you did not give me the right keys of the treasures, but you gave me the keys of the frogs and the mice and the fleas and the lice." The man replied: "I swear by God that you have the right keys to all my treasures, but I do not know what has happened to you. Give me the keys and I will see for myself." When he opened the treasures, he found them just as he had left them and gave

to the poor, as was his custom. This is the meaning of the verse: "Thou shalt not eat bread with
a man who grudges the food and is not glad to
see you eat" (Prov. 23.1 ff.). The Bible also says:
"Blessed be the man with a good eye, for he
gives of his bread to the poor" (Prov. 22.9).

Therefore everyone should give of his bread to
the poor with love and kindness, then it is
acceptable to God. One should not wait until
the poor come to him and are put to shame. It
is the duty of the rich man to investigate and
find out the needs of the poor, especially for
Sabbaths and festivals, for the Sabbaths and the
festivals were instituted for the purpose of giving
pleasure to the poor.

## 197. STORY OF THE FAITHLESS WIFE

In the time of king Solomon a handsome
young man went from Tiberias to a city called
Beth-ther to study the Torah. The daughter of a
well-to-do man in Beth-ther saw the young man,
and said to her father: "My dear father, please
give me this young man as a husband." The
father ran after the young man and said to him:
"If you are willing to marry, I will give you my
daughter as a wife." The young man replied at
once: "Yes." The young man went home with

the father, married the daughter, took her home
and lived happily with her a whole year.

At the end of the year, his wife said to him:
"My dear husband, let us go to my father and
mother and see how they are getting along."
When he heard this, he took two horses and
put his wife on one, and the other he loaded
with good fruit and all kinds of good food and
drink. Then they went away in peace. On the
road they met armed robbers. When the wife
saw the robbers, she became enamored of one of
them. The robbers took them both prisoners
and tied the husband to a tree with strong ropes,
while they took the woman and disported themselves with her. Then the robbers ate and drank
together, while the poor man was all the while
tied to the tree and looked on at what was
happening. After they had eaten and drunk,
they all lay down to sleep, having put the wine
barrels under their heads. While they were
asleep a snake came and drank from the barrels
and dropped poison into them. The poor man
saw the miracle. Soon after, one robber after
another woke up and drank out of his barrel.
No sooner had he drunk than each one fell down
dead, until they all died.

When the husband saw this wonder, he
thanked and praised God, who had protected

him. Then he turned to his wife and said: "My dear wife, loosen me from the tree and take the ropes off my body." She replied: "I fear you will kill me if I free you." The husband swore that he would not harm her. Then she went to the robber to see if he was dead, and she found he was as dead as a log. Then she freed her husband and they went to her father's house. When the father heard that the daughter had come with her husband, he was very glad and made merry with food and drink. Then the son-in-law said: "I can neither eat nor drink until I have told you all that has happened to us on the journey." And he told his father-in-law how his wife had behaved with the robber. As soon as the father heard this, he killed his daughter. Therefore did king Solomon say: "A faithful woman I have not found" (Eccl. 7.28).

## 198. THE THREE BROTHERS WHO WENT TO KING SOLOMON TO LEARN WISDOM

Once upon a time three brothers traveled together for the purpose of study and came to King Solomon. King Solomon said: "Stay here and serve me, and I will teach you wisdom." King Solomon appointed them as his chamberlains, and they remained with him thirteen years. When the thirteen years were over, one said to the other: "What have we done? We have left our homes and our families and have not seen them for thirteen years. We came here to study the Torah, but all we did was to serve the king and we learned nothing. Let us take leave of the king and go back home."

One day they appeared before King Solomon and said to him: "Lord king, we have now been with you and have served you thirteen years, and we do not know whether our families are alive or dead. We believe we have been long enough here and have learned nothing. Therefore grant us leave to return home and see how our people are getting along." King Solomon called the official who was in charge of his treasures, and ordered him to bring three hundred florins. Then he said: "Make your choice. Do you prefer that I teach each of you three wise things or that I give each of you one hundred florins?" They took counsel together and decided to take the money. They took the money, bade him farewell and went away.

When they were four miles distant from Jerusalem, the youngest said to the others: "What have we done? Did we come here to learn or to make money? We came here to learn and now

we allowed ourselves to be led astray by the
*yezer ha-ra'* and have taken a hundred florins
each instead. Therefore take my advice, let us
go back, return the money and learn wisdom.
For money disappears, but wisdom remains."
The other two said: "You may return the money
and learn wisdom, but we will not exchange
words for money."

The youngest brother went back to the king
and said: "My lord king, I did not come for the
sake of money. Therefore I beg of you, take
back the money and teach me instead three
words of wisdom." When king Solomon heard
this, he began to teach him the Torah and said to
him: "My son, when you are traveling, take care
to be ready to start with the morning star, and
in the evening endeavor to reach an inn before
it is dark. This is the first word of wisdom.
When you come to a brook that has risen, do
not cross it, but wait until the waters have
subsided. This is the second word of wisdom.
Do not confide a secret to any woman, not even
your own wife. This is the third word of wisdom." After he had learned these wise maxims,
he took leave of the king, mounted his horse and
rode fast so as to overtake his brothers. When
he had caught up with them, they asked him
what wisdom he had learned, and jeered at him.

He replied: "I learned what I learned, don't ask me."

They traveled together until evening, when they came to a very beautiful town. The youngest brother said: "This is a good place to spend the night. We can find everything here, water and wood and fodder for the horses. If you will take my advice, we will stop here overnight, and tomorrow, as soon as the morning star rises, we will start on our journey again." But the others replied: "You are a fool. You gave away your money to learn wisdom. Your advice is foolish. We can still push on for another mile before night comes, and you advise us to stay here over night!" But the youngest replied: "You can do as you please, I will remain here until tomorrow morning." So the other two went on while the youngest brother remained behind. He cut some wood, lit a fire, and made himself a tent to sleep in. His horse he put to graze until it became dark. Then he brought the horse into the tent and gave him oats to eat. Then, having taken some food, he lay down and slept peacefully all through the night.

His brothers, who had continued their journey till it grew very dark, could not find a place where the horses could graze nor could they find any wood for a fire. During the night snow fell, and they died of cold. But the youngest did not suffer at all, for he had provided against everything. Early in the morning he got ready, mounted his horse, and hastened after his brothers, but when he found them they were both dead. When he saw this, he dismounted and fell upon them and wept and cried. Then he buried them, took their money and went his way. When the sun rose the snow melted and all the brooks overflowed, so that he could not cross with his horse. So he dismounted and waited until the waters had subsided.

While he was sitting there, he saw the servants of King Solomon coming with two beasts heavily laden with gold. The servants said to him: "Why do you not cross over?" He replied: "The brook has risen so high that I prefer to wait until it subsides." The servants began to go across to the other side, but when they came to the middle of the brook, the current was so strong that it carried them along and they were all drowned. The young man waited until the brook had subsided. Then he found all the gold that the servants had brought with them, crossed the brook and arrived home in peace. Thus the two wise maxims which King Solomon had taught him helped him to acquire much money.

When the wives of his brothers saw that their

husbands had not returned, they asked him why they had not come home with him, and he replied: "Your husbands remained with King Solomon to learn more wisdom." Then he bought fields and vineyards, menservants and maidservants, flocks and herds and built himself beautiful houses. One day his wife asked him where he had gotten all his wealth. He became very angry and struck her, and said: "What business have you to ask me?" But she nagged him all the time and said: "I see that you do not love me, because you will not tell me. Please tell me, where did you get that money?" And she nagged him so long (as women will do) that he allowed himself to be persuaded and told her all that had happened to him with his brothers and the king's servants. Herein he did not follow the third wise maxim of the king, and this might have brought him into great trouble, as you will soon hear.

One day he quarreled with his wife and struck her. She commenced to weep and said: "Is it not enough that you killed your two brothers and the king's servants, that you want to kill me, too?" When the other two women heard that their husbands were dead and that the youngest brother had killed them, they went to King Solomon and brought an accusation against their brother-in-law. When King Solomon heard this, he gave orders that he should be brought before him. But the youngest brother asked to be allowed to go himself before the king, for he wanted to speak to him. So he was presented before the king. When he appeared before the king, he fell upon his knees and said: "My lord, may the king live for ever. I am one of the three brothers who served you thirteen years in order to learn wisdom, and I am the youngest of the three, who brought back the money to the king to learn wise maxims instead, and these very maxims have saved me from all evil. But I did not observe the third one and revealed my secret to my wife. She has now denounced me and brought me into this trouble." As soon as the king heard this, he recognized him and said: "Rise up and fear nothing. Though you have taken the property of your brothers and of my servants, it is nothing, for it is all yours. The wisdom which you have bought from me has saved you from death and from the hand of your wife. Return, therefore, to your home in peace, and rejoice with your wife." This is the reason why King Solomon said: "It is better to obtain wisdom than to obtain the finest gold" (cf. Prov. 8.19). Nevertheless, do not reveal your secret to your wife.

### 199. The Woman Who Hid Her Gold in a Jar of Honey and the Clever Way in Which King David Enabled Her to Recover It from the Dishonest Man to Whom She Had Entrusted It

It came to pass in the days of King Saul that there lived an old man who had a very beautiful wife, who was immensely wealthy. When the old man died, his wife mourned for him a long time. As she was a very beautiful woman, the governor of the province cast his eye upon her and wanted to take her by force, but she was a very pious woman and would not dishonor her husband in the grave. Therefore she was very much afraid. Accordingly, she took half her money, put it into a jar and placed some honey on the top so that no one could see what was underneath. Then in the presence of witnesses, she put the jar in the care of a man whom she knew well and who had been a relative of her late husband. Then she left the country in order to get away from the governor. Not long afterwards, the governor died, and when the good woman heard of his death, she came back to her town.

Now the man with whom she had left her money, while celebrating the wedding of his son, needed some honey. As he went to take some from the jar, he found that there was money under the honey. So he took out all the money and filled the jar with honey. When the good woman came to him and asked for the jar which she had placed in his care, the man said: "Bring the witnesses who were present at the time and I will give you the jar." She brought her two witnesses and the man gave her the jar. When she reached home and examined the jar in order to see if her money was still there, she found that the jar was full of honey and that the money had been taken out. So she started crying and wailing and summoned the man before the judge of the town. The judge said: "Did you have witnesses when you gave him the jar with gold?" She replied: "My lord, my witnesses know only that the jar was full of honey." Whereupon the judge replied: "How can I help you, then? You must go before King Saul, and let him help you." So she went to King Saul and brought her charge against the man. King Saul called the Sanhedrin together, and they said likewise: "Dear daughter, did you have witnesses when you gave him a jar of gold to take care of?" The woman replied: "I had no witnesses for the gold, for I did it as a stratagem in order that the governor should not know that I had so much wealth, otherwise he would have taken it by force." Then the Sanhedrin said: "Dear daughter, we cannot pass judgment in Israel unless we have the testimony of witnesses, for we cannot tell what a man thinks in his heart."

The woman went away with a sad heart, crying and weeping. On her way home she met King David, who was still a young lad, taking care of the sheep and playing with his companions. When he heard the woman crying, he asked her why she was crying so bitterly, and she told him all that had happened to her and that she had had the man up before the king and before the Sanhedrin, but that they had not decided in her favor. "Therefore," she said, "I would ask you to help me to get my property, and to decide the case." David said: "Go to King Saul and ask him to give me permission, and I will prove that you are in the right, and will give a true judgment." She ran at once to the king and said to him: "My lord king, I have found a young lad who will decide the case in such a way that everyone will be able to see who is right." The king replied: "My daughter, if you know such a person, bring him to me." Then she brought the young lad before King Saul. And the king said to David: "Are you the one who says he can decide this case justly?" David replied: "My lord king, with your leave I am confident that I will, with the help of God, be able to decide the case." And the king replied: "Well, then, go with this woman and help her, for she is crying very bitterly and there is none to help her."

David went with the woman to her house and said to her: "Let me see the jar which you gave into the man's keeping." She brought out the jar and David said to her: "Are you sure that this is the right jar?" She answered: "Yes, sir, this is the jar, I know it well." Then, turning to the man with whom the woman had deposited the jar, he said to him: "Is this the jar which this woman gave you?" The man replied: "Yes, I had no other jar." Then David said: "Bring me an empty jar." She brought him an empty jar, and he emptied the contents of the full jar into the empty one. Then he took the jar which had contained the honey and, in the sight of all the people, broke it up into small pieces. He examined the pieces and found two gold pieces sticking to the fragments. Then David said to the assembled people: "You see that she spoke the truth." And he said to the man: "Fetch all the money which you took out of this jar and give it back to the woman, for it is clear that you took the money from the jar." When the assembled multitude heard the judgment,

King Saul wondered at it and all knew that the
spirit of prophecy rested on David, since he was
able to know all this. May the Lord grant us
the benefit of their merits and send us the
Messiah. Amen. Selah.

### 200. BAR SEBAR AND R. SHEFIFON. HOW THEIR LIVES WERE PROLONGED 200 YEARS

Once upon a time there lived a man who was
called Bar Sebar. In the same town there lived
an orphan who had become betrothed to a
young maiden, but they were so poor that they
were engaged for seven years and were not able
to marry. Then Ben Sebar took the bridegroom,
much silver and gold and all sorts of good food,
and went with him on a fifteen days' journey
until they came to the city where the bride lived.
There he brought the bride and groom together
and celebrated the wedding, which lasted seven
days.

When the pious man was on his journey home,
he came to a very high mountain upon which
grew the most luscious fruit in the whole world.
But everyone who passed by was bound to die,
for the place was full of all kinds of poisonous
worms and reptiles, and the moment they
smelled a human being they killed him. And

there was also a large dragon there. The good
man, Ben Sebar, walked over the dragon, thinking it was a goat. As he passed the dragon, he
met a man of very unprepossessing appearance,
who was the angel of death, and who asked him
who he was. He replied: "My right name is
Ben Sebar." Then the angel of death asked him:
"Whence do you come and where are you
going?" Ben Sebar replied: "I come from a
town fifteen days journey from here, I went
there with a poor orphan to give him a wife, I
celebrated the wedding at my own cost and gave
him much silver and gold besides." Then the
angel of death said to him: "Do you know that
I have come to take your soul? For the time of
your death has arrived." When Ben Sebar heard
the words of the angel of death, he lifted up his
hands to heaven and began to pray: "Lord of
the universe, it is written in Thy holy Torah
that anyone who is engaged in a pious act is
free from harm. I have traveled many miles to
perform a good deed and have spent much
money in alms before I arrived here. Will all
the good that I have done be of no avail to me
now, and am I to die miserably on the road?
I wish I were at least home with my people so
that I might make my will and instruct them
how to behave after my death!" Thereupon a

voice came from heaven and said: "Ben Sebar, you still have fifteen days to live. You still have time to go home to your family and make a will, instructing them how to conduct themselves after your death."

When he heard this, he greatly rejoiced and continued his way until he came into a big town. In the gateway he met a man and asked him whether there were any learned men in the city. The man replied: "Yes, there are many scholars here and the head of the *Yeshibah* is a very excellent man. His name is R. Shefifon of Laish. (Some say his name was Ben Laish.) He has many thousands of pupils, who study under him." Then Ben Sebar said: "My dear son, take me to his house." The man took him to the chamber of R. Shefifon. When Ben Sebar came to R. Shefifon, Ben Sebar's face shone like the moon; and when R. Shefifon saw this, he and his pupils rose up and welcomed him and invited him to sit down. After they had been sitting awhile, the face of Ben Sebar became very pale. When R. Shefifon saw this, he asked Ben Sebar what was ailing him, and whether he wanted some food or drink or something else. Then Ben Sebar told the rabbi his adventure with the angel of death. The rabbi said: "Sit down next to me and do not worry, for I assure you that you will not die." Then Ben Sebar said: "How can you assure me? Is it not written that no money or wealth is of any avail?" R. Shefifon replied: "Fear not, you will not die this time, for I will save you from death." Then Ben Sebar sat down by the rabbi, and together they studied the Torah for fourteen days and nights without interruption.

Now it happened one Friday that it grew dark in the presence of R. Shefifon. Then the pupils said: "Rabbi, how is it that it has grown dark so soon?" R. Shefifon said to his pupils: "Go outside and see if it is dark there also." They came back and said: "Nowhere is it so dark as here in the *bet ha-midrash*." So the rabbi began to pray, for he understood that it was an evil omen for Ben Sebar. Then came the angel of death and revealed himself to R. Shefifon, and said to him: "Deliver up the deposit which you have, for the time has come for Ben Sebar to die." R. Shefifon adjured the angel of death to go away. The angel of death went up to the Lord and said: "Lord of the universe, R. Shefifon refuses to deliver Ben Sebar to me so that I might take his soul." Then the Lord said to the angel of death: "Go to R. Shefifon again and tell him to give you the soul of Ben Sebar, or he will have to die in

Ben Sebar's place. Ask him if his own life is not dearer to him than that of Ben Sebar." So the angel of death went down again and delivered the message from God. R. Shefifon replied: "No, my life is not dearer to me than the life of Ben Sebar. Therefore go to God and tell Him that if He desires to kill the one, he should kill the other too, for we have taken an oath that we would not part from one another." The angel of death went up to God and repeated to Him the words of R. Shefifon.

As soon as the angel of death had departed, R. Shefifon rose up and prayed devoutly until his prayer was heard by the Lord, blessed be He, and accepted. Then a voice came from heaven and said: "I decreed that Ben Sebar should die, but the prayers of these two righteous men overrule My command. And because of their charity I must prolong their lives." And the Lord prolonged the lives of R. Shefifon and Ben Sebar 200 years each. As long as these two men lived, there was no famine in the land, no child died before its father, and no woman gave premature birth. But after their death famine came into the land. Then there arose a rabbi called R. Tanhuma, who ordered a fast and did much penance and prayed to God: "Almighty God, we are the children of Abraham Thy

friend, of Isaac Thy chosen one, of Jacob, the
perfect and the pious." And he prayed so long
until his prayer was heard also and the famine
ceased.

### 201. MAIMONIDES AND R. MEIR OF GERMANY

Once upon a time there lived a rabbi called
Moses Maimuni, who was a mighty master in the
Torah, as can be seen from the works which he
composed, such as the one called Maimuni, and
many other books. He was also a very great
physician. Then he composed a new book, of
which no one in those days could understand
much, because it was so difficult. He lived in
Spain, but there were many rabbis there who did
not agree with him and considered him a heretic,
i. e. an unbeliever, a man who is neither a Jew
nor a Christian, and who interprets the Law
according to his own opinion and not in accordance with the interpretation of our sages.

Now the rabbis of Spain wrote to Germany
that R. Moses Maimuni deserved excommunication, for he had no true faith in God. When the
rabbis of Germany received these letters from
Spain, they came together and said: "It is
unbelievable that a man like R. Moses should be
a heretic, in spite of what the rabbis of Spain

have written, for he has been a pious Jew all his life." Accordingly, the German rabbis agreed that it would be best to send a German Jew to R. Maimuni in Spain, to examine the contents of R. Maimuni's book, in order to get at the root of the matter and determine what kind of man he was. So they went to one named R. Meir and told him all about Maimuni and showed him the letters received from Spain, and said: "We ask you to go to see him, for you will soon be able to see whether he is a heretic or not." For R. Meir was also a great master in the Torah and half a prophet.

R. Meir took an attendant with him and started for Spain. When he was a half mile from the city where Maimuni lived, R. Meir and his servant sat down near a cool spring and drank and then continued their journey. But R. Meir forgot a book at the spring, one that he had been studying on his journey. When they came into the city, R. Meir asked for the house of R. Moses and was directed there. When he knocked at the door, a servant looked out of the window and said to R. Meir: "You cannot come in now, for the master is at table and cannot receive anyone. Pray, wait until he has finished." R. Meir said to the servant: "I know that your master is now at table, and as a sign

I tell you that he is eating eggs." When the servant heard this, he went to his master and said to him: "A man knocked at the door and when I told him that you were at dinner, he replied that he knew it, and as a sign said that you were eating eggs." Then R. Moses said to the servant: "Go and tell him he has spoken the truth, and as a sign from me tell him that he left his book at the spring."

R. Meir searched for his book and could not find it. Then he remembered that he had read it at the spring. So he said to himself: "I see that he knows more than I." R. Meir and his attendant went quickly to the spring and found the book in the ditch where he had been reading it. So he took the book and came back to the city. Then he went to R. Moses' house and again knocked at the door, for it was getting dark. He was admitted at once, as it was time for the evening meal. The servant brought food to the table, which looked like human hands. R. Meir refused to touch it, saying that he felt unwell and would prefer not to eat anything. Then R. Moses asked him if he would like to drink something, and he called the other servant and said: "Peter, go and draw a jug of wine from the same cask as before." R. Meir thought: "What! Shall Peter bring me wine? He is a

Gentile, and the wine will be forbidden to drink."
When Peter brought the wine, R. Moses asked
R. Meir to drink of the wine, since he had not
eaten anything.   R. Meir said: "I do not care
to drink.  I do not feel very well.  I am tired and
have walked too much.  I would rather go to
bed."  Then R. Moses said to the third servant:
"Get up early tomorrow morning and strike
down the ox so that we may have fresh meat
for our honored guest, for he does not feel well."
When R. Meir heard all this, he thought that it
was all true that the rabbis of Spain had written
about R. Moses, for he had very bad habits,
and acted in a very queer manner.

On the morrow, when R. Meir got up, R.
Moses took him into his chamber and said to
him: "My dear R. Meir, I know very well why
you came to me from Germany, and I also know
who sent you, and I also know the suspicion in
which I am held, but I want to tell you that no
man should suspect another unless he is quite
sure that the facts are true.  I know very well
why you refused to eat and drink with me.  You
refused to eat because the food resembled human
hands.  Now let me tell you, it was a vegetable
which looked like a human hand."   And R.
Moses showed him the vegetable, for he was a
great physician and knew what vegetables were

good to eat. "I will also tell you," he said, "why you refused to drink the wine. It was because I called my servant Peter and you thought he was a Gentile and would pollute the wine. His real name is Peter, but he is as pious a Jew as you can find and is named after a distinguished sage." And he showed him in the Gemara a sage who was called R. Peter. "And as for the fresh meat which you refused to eat, because I ordered the ox to be struck down instead of being slaughtered, I will explain that to you also. The ox was found alive inside the cow after she had been slaughtered. Therefore he does not require slaughtering, nor a benediction when killed, for the blessing pronounced over the dam is sufficient." And he explained to him many other points in the Law and complained to him of the hostility of his colleagues, who persecuted him because they could not understand the book which he had written. And he taught R. Meir the book, called Maimuni, which is full of novel things, and from which one can see to this very day what a great man he was. In the Introduction he gives the whole chain of tradition, and from the time of Moses to his own time there has never been another Moses.

When R. Meir heard all this from R. Moses, he begged his forgiveness, which R. Moses granted,

and R. Meir departed and vindicated the name
of R. Moses and perpetuated his fame. But
his colleagues who suspected him of heresy, were
plagued in their body, as it is written: "He who
suspects the innocent suffers in his body."
Therefore one should beware of suspecting others
and he will live in peace.


202. STORY OF R. JOSE HA-GELILI; HOW HE
DIVORCED HIS FIRST WIFE BECAUSE OF HER
AVARICE; HOW SHE WAS PUNISHED; HOW HE
MARRIED AGAIN; HOW HE DIED AND VISITED
HIS HOME ON FRIDAY EVENINGS AND FESTIVALS
TO PRONOUNCE THE KIDDUSH

Once upon a time there lived a great rabbi,
called R. Jose the Galilean, who had an ill-
tempered wife, more bitter than death. She
insulted her husband in public and gave vent to
her malice. One day the rabbis said to R. Jose:
"Why don't you divorce your wife? How can
you stand continual insults? She never says a
kind word to you and is unworthy of being your
wife." But R. Jose replied: "No, I will not do
that, for she is of a good family."
One day R. Jose and R. Eliezer lectured in the
college and then R. Jose said to R. Eliezer:
"Come home and dine with me." R. Eliezer

accepted the invitation. When the wife of R. Jose saw that he brought R. Eliezer with him, she quickly removed from the fire the meat she had been cooking and put a pot of lentils there instead. R. Jose asked his wife: "Have you prepared anything good to eat? I have brought a noble guest with me?" She replied: "I have nothing but a pot of lentils on the fire." R. Jose went to the fire to see whether she had told the truth, and found the pot full of young pigeons. Then he said to his wife: "Why did you tell me that you had put lentils on the fire? The pot is full of pigeons." The wife replied: "Upon my word, I put nothing but lentils on the fire." Then R. Jose said: "I see that God has done a miracle for us." And they ate the young pigeons.

When they had finished, R. Eliezer said to R. Jose: "Divorce your wife, for she is not worthy of you." He replied: "I cannot divorce her, for she brought me a rich dowry and I cannot repay it." Then R. Eliezer said: "We will raise the amount among ourselves and you will repay her dowry." R. Jose allowed himself to be persuaded, gave his wife a bill of divorce, and the rabbis raised the amount of the dowry among them. Then R. Jose married another woman, who was very modest, and who held him in great honor, as was proper, and they lived together happily. His former wife also married again, this time a governor of the town, and a rich man.

Not long after, the governor became poor and lost his sight. He had to go begging at the houses of the rich and his wife led him from door to door. The governor knew all the streets of the town in spite of his blindness. And he noticed that when they passed the street in which R. Jose lived, his wife would not lead him through it. So he said to her: "Why do you always turn away when you come to this street and never lead me to the house of R. Jose? I have heard that he is a very charitable man." But the poor woman was ashamed to look him in the face, and excused herself by saying that she would not do it again. But she did it again and again. At last the blind man struck her and forced her to bring him to R. Jose's house. The poor woman cried bitterly and was compelled to do her husband's will. R. Jose heard her cry and, looking out of the window, saw that it was his former wife, whom he had divorced. He took pity on her and gave her a generous gift, placed both of them in a house next to his own and supported them as long as they lived. Thus he fulfilled the verse:

"Thou shalt not hide thyself from thine own flesh" (Is. 58.7).

The second wife whom R. Jose married had the following custom. Every Friday night when he came from synagogue, she met him with a cup of wine in her hand, and he had to sit down at the table at once and make *kiddush*, so that he should have no opportunity to get angry with the household. This she did also on the eve of every festival.

When the time came for R. Jose to die, the angel of death came to him in the shape of a human being. R. Jose was studying. R. Jose said to him: "What is your business and who are you?" The angel of death replied: "I have been sent by the Lord, blessed be He, to take your soul, for your time has come to die." Then R. Jose said to him: "I know full well that you can do nothing to me so long as I am studying." So the angel of death went back to God and said to Him: "Lord of the universe, Thou has sent me to take the soul of R. Jose the Galilean, but I cannot do anything to him, for he is continually studying the Holy Law." Then the Lord said to him: "Take off the clothes you have on and put on your inexorable garments, which you wear when you take people's

souls and go to R. Jose again." Then the angel
of death did as the Lord commanded him

Our sages tell us that the angel of death
reaches from heaven to earth and that he is full
of eyes from head to foot. When the angel of
death came to R. Jose again, he found him again
studying. When R. Jose beheld him, he was
seized with fear, for he knew that it was the
angel of death. Then he fell at his feet and said to
him: "Wait a while, for I wish to tell my wife
that you are here, as I know who you are. But
I am not afraid of you. For it is written in the
Torah: 'He who studies the Torah purchases
life'." The angel of death replied: "But it also
says: 'Thy first father sinned and thine inter-
cessors have transgressed against Me'" (Is. 43.28).
When R. Jose heard this verse, he felt very
weak and said: "I am ready to die, for I am
not better than my forefathers." Then the angel
of death said to R. Jose: "Go and tell your wife,
and leave a will for your children, instructing
them how to behave after your death." R. Jose
went to his wife and said: "My good, pious wife,
you must now prepare to earn your own living,
for I shall not be able to support you any longer
in this world." When the wife heard this, she
said to him: "My dearest husband, why do you
speak like this all of a sudden? You never spoke

like this before." R. Jose replied: "My beloved
wife, I am now forced to do so because I have to
go away from you on a long journey." When
the woman heard these words of her husband,
she began to weep and would not be comforted.
When R. Jose saw how bitterly she was lamenting, he said to her: "My dear wife, it cannot be
otherwise, but this I will do for you after my
death. On the eve of every Sabbath and festival
I will come to you and will say the *kiddush*, as I
have done during my life." Thereupon his soul
departed and he was buried, and the sages
mourned him deeply.

On the next Friday evening, when it was
time to say *kiddush*, R. Jose the Galilean came
and said the *kiddush* for his wife, and as soon as
he had finished he disappeared, without touching
a morsel of food or drink. He did this a long time.
One Friday evening, as R. Jose was sitting with
his wife and saying the blessing, some people
passed by the window and heard a man saying
the benediction in her house. So they said:
"The woman is concealing a strange man in her
house, who is saying *kiddush* for her." On the
morrow the story was told in the synagogue and
it reached the ears of the sages. When they
heard it, they said: "We cannot overlook a thing
like this, it would not be right." They sent for

the woman and told her what people were saying
about her and asked her to defend herself. Then
the woman replied: "It is a lie. No strange man
has been in my house to say the *kiddush* for me."
But the sages said: "How can you deny it when
two trustworthy men have heard it?" When the
good woman saw that she could not deny it, she
told the rabbis the whole story, how her husband
R. Jose came on the eve of every Sabbath and
festival and said the benediction for her. But
the rabbis would not believe her. So she said:
"Wait until Friday night, and you will see for
yourselves." And the good woman was very sad,
because people suspected her of harboring a
strange man. When the eve of Sabbath arrived,
her husband R. Jose came as usual and found his
wife very sad. Moreover, she had not cooked
anything for the Sabbath. So he asked her why
she was more sad on this Friday night than at
any other time. She told him all that had
happened. He replied: "Do not grieve or be
sad, for I will answer for you myself and they
will have to believe me." So he went with his
wife before the rabbis. And when they saw him,
they were frightened, and fell upon their faces.
Then he said: "Witnesses, stand on your feet,
and declare what you have seen and heard. I
am the man who made *kiddush* for her on the

eve of Sabbath and festival. I am R. Jose the Galilean, and you want to give my wife a bad name. May God judge between her and you." They all kept silent and no one could answer for great fear. R. Jose said: "As you do not reply, I will not pursue the matter further, but from this time onwards you will no longer see me or my wife in this world." With these words they went away, the woman still very sad. She died not long afterwards. May the Lord grant us the benefits of their merits and send us the Messiah. Amen. Selah.

### 203. ABRAHAM THE CARPENTER OF JERUSALEM AND THE MONEY BURIED UNDER A TREE

Once upon a time there was a rich man, who lived near Jerusalem. One day a Gentile came to him with an article of value and wanted to borrow money on it. So he told his wife to go up into the chamber, to open the chest and fetch the money. The good woman went upstairs. But as she opened the chest and wanted to take the money, she heard a voice saying: "Do not touch the money, it is not yours." She was very much frightened, went down and told her husband what had happened to her, and told him to go and fetch the money himself. The man went upstairs to fetch the money, and the voice said again: "Do not touch the money, it is not yours" When the man heard it, he also became very much frightened. Then he recovered himself and said: "If the money is not mine, tell me to whom it belongs." And the voice answered: "If you wish to know, then I tell you that this money belongs to Abraham the carpenter of Jerusalem." Then the good man thought: "If the money does not belong to me, I do not want to have it." And he took all the money and the gold and the silver and the articles of value and the ornaments which he had, cut a hole in the tree which was standing in his garden and put it all in. Then he left, accepting with resignation this misfortune which God had inflicted upon him.

Not long afterwards, there was a great flood, which carried away many houses and trees, including the tree in which all the money had been concealed. A fisherman came along in his boat and, seeing the tree floating on the water, he thought: "That is a very fine tree and very useful for a carpenter. I know a Jewish man in Jerusalem, who is called Abraham the carpenter. I will take it to him and he will pay me well for it." When the fisherman took his fish to Jerusalem on Friday, Abraham the carpenter came to buy fish for the Sabbath. The fisherman said to him:

"Abraham, I have a fine log at home, which I took out of the water. I am sure it will be useful to you and you can make many pretty articles out of it." Abraham went home with the fisherman, saw the log, was well pleased with it and had it taken to his house. When he split the tree apart, he found all the rich treasure which the good man had put in. R. Abraham rejoiced greatly at the wonderful luck which God had granted him.

Not long afterwards, it came to pass that the good man who had put the money in the tree became very poor and had to go about the country begging for alms. One day he said to his wife: "My dear wife, let us go to Jerusalem and see if our money has reached its destination, as the voice said." So they went to Jerusalem, to the house of Abraham the carpenter, pretending that they knew nothing. When they arrived there one Friday, Abraham was busy making a toy for his son. It is customary to put beautiful silver cups on the table, and when these good people saw their own vessels standing on the table, they began to weep. When Abraham's wife saw these poor people crying, she asked them why they were crying, but they would not tell her. Then the good woman said: "Surely, you do not weep for nothing," and she pressed them so long until they told her the whole story, viz. that all those beautiful vessels had belonged to them, and they told her about the money and the voice and about the tree trunk that had been carried away by the waters. And they asked them if it was all true. "For", they said, "we see all the ornaments and the beautiful things in your possession, as the voice had said." When the woman heard this, she said: "My dear friends, spend your Sabbath in joy. If these things belonged to you, we will give them back to you, for we have, thank God, enough without taking yours." But the poor people replied: "No, we cannot accept it. For if the money had been destined for us, the voice from heaven would not have spoken as it did. We see that the money is intended for you, and we will have none of it. We must have sinned before the Lord." And then they kept silent. The wife told the story to Abraham. Then they made a beautiful cake to give the poor people on their journey. They prepared it with good spices, and put inside, so that no one should know, four hundred gold florins. For Abraham thought: "We will give them this cake to take with them on their journey, and when they open it, they will find the four hundred florins." On Sunday morning they were preparing to leave and bade farewell to Abraham and his wife with tears in their eyes. Abraham wanted to give them money, but they refused. Finally, they gave them the cake and said to them: "Take the cake with you on your journey, it will be useful to you. When you are hungry, break it and refresh your heart." The poor woman did not wish to take the cake either, but Abraham and his wife begged them so hard that they finally accepted it and went away.

On the way they came to a town where they had to pay toll, but they had no money. So they said to the toll-keeper: "We have no money, take this cake for your toll." The man said: "This cake comes at the right moment. I will give it as a present to Abraham the carpenter of Jerusalem on the occasion of his son's wedding, and I will be made welcome there." The toll-keeper took the cake and allowed them to go away in peace. Then he took the cake to Jerusalem and presented it to Abraham, who thus got the cake back with the money. This is the meaning of the verse: "Mine is the silver and Mine is the gold, saith the Lord of hosts" (Hag. 2.8).

The man and the woman died in poverty, because they had never given alms. Therefore God punished them. Therefore he who desires to preserve his money against taint should give much to the poor. Then his wealth will remain. But the converse is also true. If a person does not preserve his money against taint and does not give charity, his wealth will not remain with him, but will pass away with him, as happened to these two people. May God grant us better luck. Amen. Selah.

### 204. The Treacherous Brother

Once upon a time there lived a man who traveled to foreign countries to do business there. He left his wife in the care of his brother and asked him to see that no harm should befall his dear wife and that she should not suffer any want; for he knew that she was a good and pious woman, and he had full confidence in his brother. The brother promised to do his best by her, as became a brother-in-law.

The man went on his travels and the brother took the wife into his own house and gave her a separate room. He visited his sister-in-law frequently and saw to it that she was in want of nothing. She was a very beautiful and attractive woman. One day he cast his eyes upon her and, going into her chamber, said to her: "My dear sister-in-law, do my will, and I will do everything that you desire." The woman replied: "It is forbidden me to do such a thing, for any woman who gives up her chastity and lies with another man, denies the Lord as well as her good husband. Why should I do such a thing? Moreover, you know that we shall both lose our share in the world to come if we do such an evil thing. And how dare you propose such a thing to me, knowing as you do that your brother has entrusted me to your protection and care? How can you find it in your heart to do such a thing? I am especially forbidden to you, because your brother is still living. And it is written in the Holy Torah that whoever loves the wife of his neighbor is smitten with leprosy and punished in hell." The brother-in-law yielded to her dissuasions for the time being and continued to visit her daily to see that she was not in want of anything.

One day he sent his servant out to fetch water and in the meantime went to his sister-in-law, intending to take her by force. The woman began to scream, but there was no one to hear her, as there was no one in the house. Nevertheless, she fought him with so much force that he was not able to carry out his will and had to leave her. He went to the market and bribed two men to testify that they had seen her with

a young man while her husband was away. The
two false witnesses appeared before the court and
testified that they had seen her commit adultery
with a young man. The court sent for the woman
and told her of the charge of adultery, while the
two false witnesses made their statement to her
face. The good woman replied: "It is all false
and the truth will come out." And she told the
court of her experience with her brother-in-law.
The witnesses replied: "We have nothing to do
with your brother-in-law, we only state what we
have seen." The poor woman was condemned
to be stoned to death, which is the punishment
in such a case. She was taken out to the stone-
heap and stoned to death, being buried under a
great heap of stones. The poor woman lay under
the stones for three days.

On the third day a man passed by who came
from a foreign country, accompanied by his
son, whom he was taking to Jerusalem for the
purpose of study. They stopped near the stone-
heap and, seeing that it was very late and they
could not reach a town in time, they spent the
night near the stone-heap. They did not know,
however, that someone was lying buried underneath. In the night they heard a voice moaning:
"Woe unto me, I was stoned for no cause. It was
a false charge and I am innocent and not

deserving of death." When the stranger heard this, he rose up and removed the stones in order to see who was lying underneath and speaking in such a manner. He kept removing the stones until he found the woman, who was still alive. Then he said: "My dear woman, why were you stoned?" She told him all that had happened to her and how two witnesses had given false testimony against her. Then she asked the man where he was going with the young lad, and the man replied that he was taking him to Jerusalem to study. Then the woman said: "If you take me home with you, I will teach your son the whole of the Torah." The man replied: "If you know the Torah I will take you home with me." She replied: "Yes, I know the Torah well." So the man returned home with the woman, with the help of the God of Israel. When he arrived home, he built for her a separate house, 2000 cubits from the town, where she could live undisturbed, and he also hired a servant to bring her food.

One day the servant cast his eyes upon the woman, conceived a passion for her and asked her to lie with him. The good woman refused to listen to him and said to him: "God forbid that I should do such a thing! I am a married woman and, with the help of God, my husband may soon

return." The servant became very angry, took a
sword and threatened to kill her. The lad tried
to shield her from the blow, and the servant split
his head in two and killed him. When the
servant saw what he had done, he ran into a wild
forest and a lion came and tore him to pieces
and ate him up. God sent the lion to punish him
for the grievous sin which he had committed.

When the good woman saw that the lad had
lost his life for her sake, she ran away too,
although she was innocent, for she did not want
to see the terrible weeping and mourning of the
parents of the young boy. She came to the
seashore and was captured by pirates, who took
her on board and departed. But the Lord sent a
mighty storm upon the sea and the ship was in
danger of foundering. The sailors cried aloud,
and said: "Let us cast lots to find out on whose
account God is angry with us, and we will throw
the guilty one into the sea, for we see that ours
is the only ship that has stormy weather. The
other ships have favorable winds and sunshine,
while we have bad weather. It must be for
some sin on our part that we are suffering."
They cast lots among themselves and the lot
fell upon the good woman, so they said to her:
"What have you done to deserve God's anger?
For we fear that we shall all be drowned on your

account." The good woman replied: "I am a Jewess, and believe in the Lord God, who has created heaven and earth." And she told the sailors her adventures from beginning to end. Then all the people who were on the ship had great pity on her and refrained from casting her to the waves, and they lifted up their hands to heaven and prayed to God to protect them from the evil deed of casting the good woman into the sea. God heard their prayer and calmed the sea. Thereupon they made for the shore, put the woman down in a beautiful field, and continued their journey.

The good woman never lost her trust in God who had protected her, and took up her abode near the seashore. She built herself a small hut, and God caused many herbs to grow on her land, which were good for many illnesses and kept her from starving. God granted her mercy and knowledge and she knew the virtues of the various herbs and what they were good for. She was also able to cure all those who suffered from boils and leprosy and all other diseases, all through the virtue of the herbs. She acquired a great name as a physician in distant lands. Many people who suffered from disease came to her to be cured, and she cured everyone, with the help of God. She became very wealthy and acquired many menservants and maidservants, horses, cows, oxen and sheep.

Now, while the woman underwent these unfortunate experiences that you have read about, her husband came home and brought rich merchandise from distant lands, and hoped to find his dear wife at home, kept in the honorable care of his brother. He asked his brother where his wife was and why he did not see her. The brother replied: "She is where the other harlots are. She rebelled against the will of God and committed sin with a young man. Two witnesses saw the act and she was condemned to be stoned." When the husband heard this story, he began to mourn for his dear wife, for he did not expect such a deed from her, and said: "Say what you will, I do not believe it. She was a good and virtuous woman. But what can I do when there are two witnesses who say that they have seen the act?" And the man grieved deeply for many months. But the Lord, who never allows wrong to remain unpunished, caused the brother and the two false witnesses to be smitten with leprosy, because of the great sin they had committed against the woman. After they had suffered a long time, they said to one another: "We have heard that in a certain place, by the shore of the sea, there lives a Jewish woman who can cure leprosy.   Let us also go to her and maybe she will be able to cure us." So they all decided to go.

Then the good man, whose wife had been stoned to death, said: "I cannot bear to stay at home, I will come with you, perhaps I will be able to forget my pain." So all four went together to see the woman. As soon as they came, the good woman knew them all, but she acted as though she did not know them, and asked the men: "Where do you come from and what has brought you hither?" And they replied: "We have come here because we have heard that you are a skillful healer and that you can heal all lepers. We beg of you, therefore, to heal us also and we will give you gold and silver in plenty if you can cure us of leprosy." The woman replied: "I see very well that you are leprous, but I see also that God has punished you with leprosy for good cause. I see that you are sinners. Therefore I cannot help you unless you first confess to me the sins which you have committed, for God does not punish a man with leprosy unless he has committed a great sin." So they told her some of their sins. But she replied: "These are not the real ones, God does not punish such trivial sins with leprosy. If you will not tell me the real truth, I cannot help

you and you might as well return home." She
wanted her husband to hear from them the
infamy which they had committed. And so it
came to pass.

When the men saw that she would not help
them unless they told her the truth about their
sins, they related to her how they had treated a
certain woman, never thinking that she was that
woman. And thus in the presence of the husband,
they admitted that they had borne false witness
against his wife and that through them the
woman had been stoned to death. When the
woman heard these confessions from the sinners,
she said: "You have done wrong, and I swear by
God the Almighty that I will not help you.
There is no cure in the world for you. God is
not like man that He should lie, and He Himself
said to Moses: 'Thou shalt not slander the sons
of thy people' (Lev. 19.16), and furthermore, it is
written in the Torah: 'Thou shalt not stand by
the blood of thy neighbor' (ibid.). For slander
leads to murder. You wicked men, I am the
woman whom you slandered and against whom
you have brought false witness. Through you I
have been stoned unjustly, but the Almighty,
praised be His Holy Name, protected me with
His great mercy, for He knows the secrets of all
hearts, and all hidden things at last come to

light.    You wicked men must remain lepers until the end of your days, and must carry your sin to the other world."

When the husband heard these words, he thanked God for having restored his good wife to him, and said: "I refused to believe the charges brought against you, although I had to admit them since these false witnesses alleged that they had seen you." They jeered at the false witnesses, who had to remain lepers all the days of their life. The husband remained with his wife and they were rich and happy.

As to the man whose son had been killed for her sake, God granted him another son, who studied much and became a great scholar, for the Lord had mercy upon him. Therefore, dear people, see how great is the sin of slander and the evil tongue. For on account of their false testimony they became leprous and could not be healed as long as they lived. Whoever fears God should keep his tongue from false testimony, as is written: "He who keeps his tongue and his mouth, preserves his body from pain, and obtains everlasting joy" (Prov. 21.23). This is true, I swear, be it man or maid.

## 205. LULIANUS AND PAPPOS

Once upon a time there lived a king who had an only daughter. One day she was found dead in the field, and the king falsely accused the Jews of having killed her, for he was a very wicked man and wanted to kill all the Jews, although he knew that the accusation was false. Accordingly he gave orders to kill all the Jews in the city. When the Jews heard of the danger that threatened them, they came together and took counsel how to avert the danger by interceding with the authorities. They promised the nobles rich gifts, but in vain.

Now there were two brothers, good and pious men, named Lulianus and Pappos who, after a secret consultation, decided to take the guilt upon themselves in order to save the rest of the Jews from death. So they went secretly to the king and said to him: "My lord king, do not punish the rest of the Jews, for they are innocent; we alone have done the deed, but we did not do it deliberately. We were traveling along the road, when we were attacked and defended ourselves and she was killed in the fight, but we had no intention of killing her." And they pleaded with the king so long that he was convinced. But they had only done this for the purpose of saving the rest of the Jews. Then the king sent for the executioner to kill the two brothers, although they were innocent. The king addressed them and said: "If you are of the people of Hananiah, Mishael and Azariah, let God save you from my hand as He saved them from the hand of Nebuchadnezzar." They replied: "My lord king, in the first place we are not so virtuous as they were that God should perform such a miracle for us; secondly, you are not so mighty a king as Nebuchadnezzar was. We deserve death and God has chosen you as the executioner in order that He may avenge our blood on you. Otherwise God might have sent lions or bears or other wild animals against us, and had no need of delivering us into your hands, but God did this in order to avenge our blood on you." The king paid no heed to their words and killed them in a cruel manner. But when he was on his way home, two counts, who were his enemies, fell upon him and killed him, and thus God requited him at once.

Our sages say that neither penitents nor the most pious men occupy a place in the future world as prominent as those two brothers, who saved so many people from death and submitted to such terrible tortures.

### 206. THE WOMAN WITH CHILD WHO WITHSTOOD THE DESIRE TO EAT ON THE DAY OF ATONEMENT. SHE BECAME THE MOTHER OF R. JOHANAN, A GREAT SAGE

Once upon a time a pregnant woman felt a strong desire to eat on the Day of Atonement, for she had had a hard confinement. The people asked R. Tarfon what they should do, and he replied: "Whisper in her ear that to-day is the Day of Atonement, and see whether she will listen to you." So they went to the woman and whispered in her ear: "To-day is the Day of Atonement," as R. Tarfon had told them to do. As soon as she heard it, she lost her desire to eat and felt satisfied. Then R. Tarfon applied to her the verse: "Before I created thee in the womb I have known thee" (Jer. 1.5). And when the time came, she gave birth to a male child, who became afterwards the famous R. Johanan, so often mentioned in the Talmud as a great sage.

207. THE WOMAN WITH CHILD WHO YIELDED TO
HER DESIRE TO EAT ON THE DAY OF ATONE-
MENT. SHE BECAME THE MOTHER OF SHABBATAI
OZAR PERI A WICKED MAN

In the time of R. Hanina it also happened that
a woman desired to eat on the Day of Atonement.
The people went to R. Hanina and asked him
whether they should allow her to eat or not.
R. Hanina replied: "Whisper in her ear that
to-day is the Day of Atonement and see if she
will be satisfied." The people followed R.
Hanina's advice and whispered in her ear: "This
is the Day of Atonement and one is not allowed
to eat." But she did not listen and insisted on
eating. Then R. Hanina applied to her the verse:
"The wicked estranged themselves from the
womb" (Ps. 58.4). And when the time came she
gave birth to a son named Shabbatai Ozar Peri,
who grew up to be a wicked man.

208. STORY OF THE KING'S SON WHO TRAVELED
WITH THE MASTER OF THE HORSE TO LEARN THE
WAYS OF THE WORLD

Once upon a time there was a king who had
an only son, whom he never sent abroad to
learn the ways of the world, as other princes do.
He loved him so much that he was afraid to let

him go out of his sight, and the boy was therefore
like a home-raised calf, a glutton and a drunkard.
One day visitors from distant lands came to see
the king, and as they were sitting at table, they
asked the king why his son was not at the table
with them, for they would like to see him also.
The king replied: "My dear friends, there is
nothing to see in my son. He has never been
away from me and has never learned courtly
manners. Therefore I do not like to have him
sit at my table when I have guests." But the
nobles insisted that they would like to see him,
and the king asked him to come to the table.
When he sat down he ate and drank like an
animal. The nobles saw what kind of a creature
he was and soon became tired of him, though
they did not show it. But the king noticed
that they looked upon his son with contempt
and he thought: "What will I make out of
my son?" Then he remembered that he had
a very clever Master of the Horse in his service
and he decided to give him plenty of money
and send him with his son to see the world.
So he sent for the Master of the Horse and
said to him: "My faithful servant, I want you
to travel with my son so that he may see the
world. I will give you plenty of money, so that
my son may see the world and learn manners."

The Master of the Horse could not refuse the king and promised to do his best. The king accordingly ordered two horses to be saddled, gave them plenty of money and sent them forth.

They came to a town in which there was a king and stopped at the house of one of his counselors. When the counselor heard that two distinguished visitors had come to his house, he called on them and bade them welcome and asked whence they had come. They replied: "We come from Pomerania." Whereupon the counselor went to the king and informed him that two noblemen from Pomerania had come to his house. Accordingly the king ordered him to bring them in the evening to dinner. In the evening the nobleman brought his two visitors to the king's court and they sat down at the royal table.

Now it is the custom to place in front of each guest a plateful of bread, and when he has eaten, the plate is taken away, and whatever is left is given to the poor. But as soon as the bread was placed on the plate of the prince he seized it and ate it all up. The Master of the Horse was very much embarrassed and all those who sat at the table looked at the prince, not knowing what to think. The Master of the Horse then pulled his purse out of the bag, took some gold crowns out of it and threw them to the poor. The nobles

thought that the prince had purposely eaten all
the bread in order to give money instead. After
this the prince allowed himself to be taught by
the Master of the Horse not to be such a glutton
as before.

They continued their journey until they came
to a castle inhabited by another king, who
invited them to eat with him. And as they were
all seated and making merry, the king addressed
them and said: "My beloved guests, assembled
here together, I would like to make a request
that each one of you relate an adventure, so as
to while away the time, as is the custom among
kings and princes that each one briefly tells an
adventure." When the Master of the Horse
heard this, he thought to himself: "How will the
young prince be able to relate his adventures?
He knows nothing of the world, for he has never
been away from home." So he thought of a way
out. He took the young prince aside and said
to him: "Now, listen to me. Everyone is going
to tell one of his adventures. What will you tell?
You know nothing, since you never traveled.
Listen to me, and I will tell you how to get out
of the difficulty. Go back to your seat, and
when the nobles drink your health, I will do
so, too. Then say to me: 'My dear Master of the
Horse, do you want to make me more drunk

than I am? I have drunk enough.' Then drop
your head on your arm and pretend you have
fallen asleep. Then they will let you sleep and
you will escape the duty of relating your adventure." The prince went back to the table,
and as they were sitting, the nobles drank his
health and tried to make him drunk. When
the Master of the Horse raised his cup and drank
his health, the young prince said: "My dear
friend, I am full as it is, and you want me to
drink more." But he responded to the toast,
and as soon as he had drunk it, his head dropped
on his arms and he pretended to fall asleep. The
nobles were annoyed on seeing him sleep and
said: "Let us wake him up." But the Master
of the Horse said: "Let him alone, he is full.
We will tell our adventures another time." And
thus the prince escaped. On the morrow they
continued their journey and came to a town in
which there was a mill for the polishing of precious stones. There was a count in the town, who
had beautiful daughters, the like of which could
not be found anywhere in the world. As soon as
the prince saw them, he fell in love with them
and would have liked to marry one of them, but
the count refused to give him any one of them.

Now it so happened that at that time the
annual fair took place near the castle, and many

merchants came with their wares. Among them
was one who had three beautiful carbuncles for
sale. The prince wanted to get the carbuncles,
but he did not know how, as he did not have
enough money with him to pay the price. So
he ordered himself a fool's costume of many
colors and said to the Master of the Horse:
"Watch me get the carbuncles. You see I have
a fool's costume over my royal garments. Now
watch and you will see. I will take the three
stones in my hand and bargain with him. Then
I will quickly conclude the bargain and he will
try to take the stones away from me. Then
you come to my help, and ask the man if I did
not buy the carbuncles in an honest deal. And
say to him also: 'Whom do you think you are
dealing with, a fool or a serious merchant? See
what kind of a bird you have in your trap'."
Then the prince, in his fool's costume, went up to
the merchant, took the three carbuncles in his
hand, and said: "How much do you want for
these three fire stones?" The merchant, thinking
he was a fool, replied: "One hundred florins."
The prince said: "That is too much, let me
have them for ten florins." The merchant replied: "Let me have your money quick and the
stones will be yours." The prince paid him the
ten florins at once and wanted to take the three

carbuncles with him, but the merchant would not let him go and said: "You, there! I did not mean that seriously, I would not have offered it to you for that price if I had been serious. The stones are worth a kingdom." Then the prince took off his fool's costume and stood like a prince. Then he said to the merchant: "Do you see now who I am and to whom you have sold your stones? You must let me have them, for I bought them from you in an honest deal, or I shall take other measures which you will not like." At that moment the Master of the Horse came up, accompanied by many followers whom he had brought from the castle, and said: "What are you shouting at my master for?" And attempted to pull him away from the merchant. The people who stood by said: "Let him alone. We want to see if they can be brought to an equitable agreement." The Master of the Horse consented. When the other nobles heard what had happened, they said: "The prince bought the stones in a fair deal and should insist on his rights." The matter was brought before the court and it was decided that the prince had bought the stones legally, nevertheless he should pay the merchant two thousand florins more, so that his loss should not be so great. When the poor merchant heard this, he wept and cried and would not be satisfied.

But the judges said: "Has not the prince done enough? He was not bound to give you anything. Therefore take your money and away with you!" The prince rejoiced very much and was rich and happy, whilst the merchant was sad.

The prince then considered what he could do to obtain one of the daughters of the count as his wife. He went away for a while with the Master of the Horse, but soon afterwards he returned to the castle where the count lived with his daughters and was assigned a separate chamber to sleep in. And he kept the three carbuncles in his chamber to light up the room. One day when he was out walking with the Master of the Horse, the daughters of the count went to his chamber and saw the beautiful stones and liked them very much. When the prince and his companion returned home, they noticed at once that some one had been in their chamber, but they behaved as if they knew nothing. Then the three daughters came to the prince and said to him: "My lord king, if you give each of us one of your stones, we will play the woman's game with you one hour, as a return for the gifts." The prince agreed to the bargain to play one hour with each one. But the eldest one went to the man in the clock tower and said to him: "Ring the bell twice quickly one after the other, for I am

going to play the woman's game with the prince
for an hour. Therefore when you see me get into
his bed, strike the next hour immediately. Also
take notice, and if he gives me a spurious gift,
strike the bell, and I shall have earned my
money." Then she went in to the prince's
chamber. The man in the tower was able to see
her get into bed and play the woman's game
with the prince. Then he noticed that the prince
wanted to give her a spurious gift, and he struck
the bell at once. Then the young woman said:
"I have earned my share. The hour is over, for
the clock has struck. Now give me my carbuncle." And he gave it to her. Then she ran
to her sisters and told them how she had earned
her stone. They made the same arrangement
with the man in the tower as the oldest had done,
and the second sister got the stone in the same
manner. But when the youngest tried to get out
of bed on the stroke of the bell, the prince took
hold of her and gave her a false gift as mentioned
above, and then he gave her the stone also. Then
she went to her sisters and told them what had
happened. The others replied: "It does not
matter, though you should have done what we
did."

The prince went to the other two sisters
and said: "Lie with me or give me back my

carbuncle." They thought it was a fair bargain and lay with him. When he had done his will with them, he said: "Give me back my stones or I will tell your father." Fearing their father, they gave him back all the three stones. To make a long story short, the youngest daughter became pregnant and her face grew pale, as one can easily imagine. Her father noticed it and said to her: "My dear daughter, what ails you? Why are you so pale? You were the prettiest of my daughters." Then she told her father all that had happened. But he replied: "Though you are pregnant by him, I will not give you to him as a wife." When the youngest daughter heard from her father that he would not marry her to the prince, she felt very sad, and went to the prince and told him what her father had said and that it was breaking her heart, as she loved him dearly. The prince also grew sad, for he loved her very much and did not know how to win her. So he went to the Master of the Horse and complained to him about it. He replied: "I will advise you how to get her. Take one of your carbuncles and make a scratch on it, so small that it shall not be visible. Then go to the count and say to him: 'My dear count, may I ask you to do me a great favor and have a hole made in this carbuncle in your mill.' I know they will ruin it. Then you can value your stone as high as you like, the count will not be able to pay it and he will have to do whatever you wish." The prince took the carbuncle to the count and made his request, as the Master of the Horse had advised him. The count sent the stone to the mill and gave strict orders that no other hole should be bored in the stone than the one for which the young prince had asked, or the stone would be ruined. The master of the mill took the stone and promised to do the best he could, for he was sure he could do the work perfectly. The master gave it to the workmen to bore the hole in such a manner that no other hole should be made. The master of the mill went for a walk in the fields, and when the workmen tried to bore the hole in the stone, it broke in two. When the workmen saw what had happened they all ran away from the mill, for they knew that they could not pay for it with all the money they owned. The count sent his servant to fetch the stone from the mill, and he found no one there.

Meanwhile the master came home, and the servant asked him for the stone, saying that the count wanted it. The master saw no one in the mill and looking for the stone, he found it broken in two. He gave the pieces to the count's

servant and ran away, for he could not pay for it.
The servant brought the pieces to the count.
When the count saw the broken carbuncle he
became very much frightened, for he did not
know what he could say to the prince. Meanwhile the prince came and asked to see whether
the stone had been bored properly. And the
count said: "Illustrious king, I cannot conceal
from you what has happened. Your stone broke
in two." And the count began to cry and tear
his hair, saying: "I do not know how I can pay
you for the stone." The prince said to the count:
"Be not so despondent, there is still a remedy.
Give me your youngest daughter as a wife and
I will forgive you the broken stone." The count
was very much pleased that he could repay him
with his youngest daughter. So he gave his
daughter to him as a wife and they made a
very happy wedding feast, and as usual everyone
related his adventures at the table. Then the
prince told his first adventure: "One day I went
over the field and I met three white doves, one
of them of pure white. I shot an arrow at one,
but could not hit her; then I shot an arrow at
the second and missed her too, then I shot at
the third and hit her between the wings so that
her belly swelled up." And the other counts

understood what he meant and laughed and made merry. Thus the prince won the youngest daughter and lived happily with her.

### 209. THE PIOUS COW WHICH REFUSED TO WORK ON THE SABBATH AND THE EXAMPLE SHE SET

Once upon a time there lived a pious man, who supported himself by means of a cow which he owned. They ploughed together the whole week and on the Sabbath they rested, in accordance with the command of the Lord, blessed be He: "On the Sabbath thou shalt rest, and thy maidservants and thy menservants and thy beasts" (Ex. 20.10).

Now it came to pass that the pious man grew very poor and was compelled to sell his cow to a Gentile, warranting her to be without blemish. The man worked his field with her all the days of the week without discovering any defect. But when the Sabbath came, he took her to the field as usual, but the cow lay down and refused to work, for she had not been accustomed to work on the Sabbath when she was with the Jew, and had rested on that day. The man beat the poor animal very hard, but she would not budge, lay down on the ground and would not get up. When the man saw that

the cow had a defect, he went to the Jew and
said to him: "You warranted the cow without
defect and now she refuses to work, and when I
strike her she lies down on the ground. Give me
back my money." The poor man was very much
upset, for he had spent the money. Then it
occurred to him that perhaps the cow still
remembered the Sabbath and he asked the man:
"Does she always refuse to work?" The man
replied: "She works very well all week, but on
the Sabbath she refuses to work." When the
Sabbath came again, the pious man went with
the Gentile to the field and found the cow lying
on the ground. The man struck her, but she
would not rise. Then the pious man addressed
the cow and said to her: "As long as you were
in my service you were obliged to rest on the
Sabbath, for so the Lord God commanded us.
But since you are no longer with me but are
employed by a Gentile, you are not obliged
to rest on the Sabbath, for the Gentile does not
keep the Sabbath. Rise, therefore, and do your
work so that I may have no further trouble from
your master." When the cow heard this, she
arose and went to work. When the Gentile saw
this, he was greatly astonished and asked the
Jew what he had whispered to the cow, so that
he might do the same, should the cow again

refuse to work. So he told him what he had whispered to the cow. When the Gentile heard this, he began to weep and said: "See, this animal is anxious to keep the Sabbath as commanded by God. How much more should a human being be anxious to observe it!" Thereupon he, together with his whole household, embraced Judaism and became a very pious Jew. He assumed the name R. Hanina and became the rabbi of a town.

## 210. R. JEHIEL OF PARIS, THE LEARNED BISHOP AND THE TWO DEMONS

Once upon a time there lived in the city of Paris, in the country of France, a good and pious man by the name of R. Jehiel. He was, besides, a great cabalist, astronomer and philosopher, as you will learn further from his deeds, and he studied day and night. In the city of Paris there also lived a priest, provost of the cathedral, who was a great scholar and a devout believer, and with whom R. Jehiel was very friendly.

One night, as Rabbi Jehiel was studying as usual, he heard a pitiful cry at the back of the house. Not knowing what it was, he became very much frightened and began to recite the *Shema'* until the cry ceased. Reading, he fell asleep, and when the cry was repeated, he did not hear it.

Now I will tell you what the cry was. Two demons (may God protect us!) came into the garden, and one asked the other why he had come to the home of the pious man rather than to some other place. The other demon replied that he had heard from the angels that there was no rabbi in the world more distinguished by his good deeds than R. Jehiel. "And it is true," he said, "for there you can see him poring over his book and studying. The whole world depends on his merits." The other demon said: "I come from hell, where I heard about the priest, who is so strong in his faith that no man can move him, any more than the rabbi can be moved from his." These words seemed to the other demon like a depreciation of the rabbi, and the two demons finally entered into a wager, staking their lives on the result. One demon was on the side of the rabbi, and he wagered that he would convert the priest to Judaism. The other demon was on the side of the priest, and he wagered that he would cause the Jew to abandon his faith. The wager was that whoever won should cut the throat of the other. Accordingly, one demon went to the rabbi and said to him: "I was sent by the Lord to tell you that you should give up

Judaism." He spoke so suavely and persuasively that he thought he would succeed. The pious man grew frightened and immediately realized that he must be a demon. He therefore jeered at him and adjured him to depart. The following night the demon came again, this time in the shape of an old man, and pretended to be the Prophet Elijah. Again he spoke smooth words in the hope of succeeding in his attempt, but in vain. When the demon saw that the rabbi refused to listen to him, he came again on the third night, this time in the shape of a beautiful woman, but he accomplished nothing. When the pious man saw that the demon would not desist, he feared that he had committed sins, or such things would not have happened to him. So he fasted and gave alms to the poor and did penance, so that all the world wondered at his piety.

When the demon beheld his great piety and penance and saw that the time limit had expired and he had accomplished nothing, he ceased troubling him and went to the other demon and related his experience with the rabbi.

The other demon was very glad that his life was now safe and said: "Now I will go and see what I can do with the priest." And he went to him, dressed in costly garments. The priest was sitting in a room filled with candles, and many

servants were sitting with him, as is the custom
with dignitaries of the Church. The demon
addressed him and said: "Listen to me, Provost,
the Lord sent me to tell you that you have been
a Christian long enough. From now on you must
become a Jew and enter into the covenant of
Abraham. Otherwise you will perish for ever
and ever and will go to hell." And he took the
priest and carried him to hell and showed him
the people there, and among them were his
father and mother and all the friends he had
known during their lifetime. When the priest
saw this, he cried out and said to the demon:
"Take me away quickly and I will do everything
you ask." Then the demon carried him to
paradise, where he saw the pious men, each one
more glorious than the other, and he knew many
among them, to whom he said: "Happy are you
that you have been found worthy to enjoy this
dignity and happiness." Then he saw some
empty seats and asked the demon to whom they
belonged. And the demon replied: "They are
reserved for some pious men who are still alive.
If, therefore, you embrace Judaism and accept
the covenant of Abraham, you will also enter
paradise." The priest replied: "If I were sure
that I would be among the pious and share
everlasting life with them, I would embrace

Judaism." The demon replied: "I assure you that you will." Then the priest promised the demon he would embrace Judaism, and the demon brought him home. After a time the demons met again in the court of R. Jehiel the Pious to hear the result of the wager. One demon said: "I have succeeded in persuading the priest to become a Jew." The other replied: "You have not won yet, for I do not believe that the priest will embrace Judaism." The following night, the priest took all the jewels and money that he could carry with him, went to the house of R. Jehiel and asked to be admitted. But the rabbi was afraid of a false charge, because the priest came at night time, and the rabbi said that he would not open the door to him in the night. The priest assured him that there was nothing to fear and begged to be admitted. R. Jehiel let him in, and the priest told him of all that had happened and asked him to help him to get away in order to embrace Judaism. R. Jehiel performed the ceremony himself and taught him the Torah.

That same night, as they were sitting together, R. Jehiel heard a voice pronouncing the blessing used on the occasion of slaughtering animals. They both went out to see and found the two demons, one of whom was about to slaughter the other. R. Jehiel asked them what they were doing, and they replied: "We are the two demons who made a wager as to which of us would succeed in converting either of you, and the arrangement was that the victor should slaughter the other. I won the wager, for I have persuaded the priest to forsake his faith, but he could not convert you, therefore I am going to slaughter him." When the pious man heard this, he thanked God for having protected him from the wiles of Satan. The proselyte rejoiced because he had become a Jew and thanked God likewise. But R. Jehiel would not allow the demon to kill his associate in his garden and told him to go to the field and slaughter him there.

R. Jehiel assigned two Jews to accompany the proselyte to the Holy Land, where he lived as a very pious Jew. He married and begat children. In time he married his children into good families, and left a good name behind him at his death. And the rabbi remained always a truly pious man.

## 211. R. Jehiel of Paris and the King

R. Jehiel, who was a great sage and a cabalist, had a lamp in his study which he lighted every Friday and which burned the whole week without oil. Soon everybody knew of this remarkable

phenomenon, and the king sent for R. Jehiel
and asked him whether the story he had heard
about the lamp was true. The rabbi denied the
story, because he was modest and did not want
to boast. Moreover, he was afraid that he would
be regarded as a magician. The king said
nothing, pretending to be satisfied, but he had in
mind to go and see for himself whether the story
was true or not. He consulted his advisers and
decided to go on a certain Wednesday night and
find out the truth.

Now the people of Paris were hostile to the
Jews and there were a number of noblemen who
annoyed R. Jehiel and knocked at the door of
his study every night. But the rabbi invented a
device to prevent the noblemen from interrupting
his studies. He took an iron nail and stuck it in
the ground. And when the noblemen came and
knocked at the door of his study, the rabbi took
a hammer and hit the nail on the head. And so
skillfully was the contrivance made that at the
same time the person who knocked at the door
sank into the ground.

Now when the king came and knocked at his
door, the rabbi took the hammer and hit the
nail. Thereupon the king sank into the ground
up to his waist. Then the king knocked again,

and the rabbi, thinking it was one of the noblemen, hit the nail again, whereupon the nail
jumped up a considerable distance. The rabbi
was very much frightened and thought: "Surely
this is none else but the king." So he quickly
opened the door, bowed down before the king
and asked his forgiveness, saying that he did not
know it was his royal majesty. For as the nail
jumped up out of the ground, the king also rose
out of the ground.

Now the nobles and servants of the king who
saw what had happened to him were afraid that
he might sink entirely into the ground, so they
asked the rabbi to help him. The rabbi took the
king to the fire, administered to him many rare
drugs and finally revived him. Then the rabbi
said to the king: "My king, what is your desire
which brought you to my house at night? The
king must know that there is a wind passing in
front of my house, which causes everyone who
desires to do me harm to be swallowed up in the
earth. And if I had not come out quickly you
would have been entirely swallowed up." The
king replied: "I was half swallowed up already,
and am grateful to you for having saved me.
Now I will tell you why I came to you. I heard
a great deal about your skill in magic, and that
you have a lamp which burns without oil, and

I desired to see it." The rabbi replied: "God forbid that I should practice magic! I merely understand a little of natural properties and something of charms." And he showed the king the lamp which burned without oil. But it was like *martel*, which gives illumination like oil. When the king saw this, he took the rabbi with him to his palace and made him his chief counselor. The rabbi was rich and happy and the king held him in great esteem.

Now the king had many princes and noblemen at his court, who were jealous of R. Jehiel. They went to the king and said to him: "Your majesty, how can you endure the Jew in your palace, who regards you as unclean? If you merely touch a glass of wine, he will not drink it, not to speak of drinking from the same glass with you." But the king said nothing.

One day the king offered the rabbi wine to drink. The rabbi said: "I must not drink at this moment, but I will drink before your eyes, before I leave the table. Give me a little time." When the time came for the king to wash his hands after the meal, as is customary, the rabbi took the gold basin in which the king had washed his hands and drank the water before the king and his nobles. Then he said in the presence of the nobles: "This I may drink, but not the

glass of wine, for the Torah has forbidden it."
When the king saw this, he loved him more than
before, because he did not disdain to drink the
water in which he had washed his hands.

## 212. THE MARTYRDOM OF RABBI AMNON
OF MAYENCE

Once upon a time there lived a rabbi called
R. Amnon. He was held in high esteem by the
bishop of Mayence, for he was a great man in
every way. He was rich, learned, wise, of distinguished family—in short, he had all the good
qualities which a good Jew ought to possess, and
therefore he was respected and loved by nobles
and princes and counts and lords, who loved him
very much and delighted in his company, and
yet there was none like him in piety

One day, as he was visiting the bishop in his
palace, the nobles said to him: "Master Amnon,
if you would only embrace Christianity, our
gracious prince would make you his chief counselor, for he is very fond of you. We have often
spoken to the prince about you and asked him
to give you an honorable post, and he replied
that if you would accept his faith, he would give
you a post of great honor. Therefore we ask
you to embrace the Christian faith." But R.

Amnon refused to listen. One day the bishop himself asked him to join the Christian church, but he declined. This went on day after day, but he refused to listen to them. One day the bishop importuned him urgently to embrace Christianity, and R. Amnon replied: "I will consider the matter, and in three days I will give your lordship a reply." He did this merely in order to put the bishop off so as to have respite. When he had left the bishop, he realized what he had done in that he had told the bishop that he would consider his proposal, as if he had the remotest notion of embracing Christianity and (Heaven forbid!) deny his own God. This weighed heavily upon his heart, and he went home sad and despondent and would not be comforted. His wife asked him what he had done or what had happened to him, for it was not usual for him to be sad, but he would not tell his family anything, and said to himself: "I cannot rest until I have expiated the sin, or I will go down in sorrow to the grave."

On the third day, the bishop sent for him to hear his decision. R. Amnon replied that he would not go and that he would have nothing to do with him. The bishop sent for him twice again, but he refused to go. Then the bishop ordered him to be brought to him by force. And when he came, the bishop said to him: "What do you mean by refusing to come after I had sent for you three times? You promised to give me an answer to my proposal in three days. I therefore want your answer now." The pious man replied: "I can give you no answer to the question you asked me or are asking now. My thoughtless remark that I would take three days to consider your proposal was tantamount to a denial of my God. I will therefore suggest my own punishment. My tongue, which uttered the words, 'I will consider', shall be cut off." R. Amnon was anxious to do penance and to sanctify the name of God. Then the wicked bishop replied: "The punishment which you suggest does not appeal to me, for it is by far too light. The tongue which spoke those words, spoke nothing but the truth; but the feet, which refused to come to me, shall be cut off and the other members of your body shall also be tortured." And he ordered R. Amnon's hands and feet to be cut off, and every time they cut off a limb, they asked him whether he still refused to be converted, and R. Amnon always replied, "I do." And he said: "Make your torture more severe, for I deserve it all for the words which I have spoken." When the wicked man had accomplished his will and had tortured R.

Amnon cruelly, he ordered him to be put into a
bed, his severed limbs by his side, and carried to
his house.  When his wife and children saw him
in this state, they raised a pitiful wail, and one
can easily imagine how they felt.  But R. Amnon
said to his wife and children: "My dear wife, I
have fully deserved what was done to me, for
I was on the point of denying the Lord, but I
hope to God that He will let me expiate my sin
in this world that I may have a share in the
world to come."

When New Year's Day arrived, he asked to be
carried in his bed to the synagogue and to be
placed close to the reader.  When the reader was
about to begin the *kedushah* of the *musaf* prayer,
the saint said to him: "Wait, I want to sanctify
the name of God before I die."  And he began
the hymn, *Ubeken leka ta'aleh kedushah*, which
we still say every year on New Year's Day and
the Day of Atonement.  Then he recited the
hymn, *Unetanneh tokef kedushat ha-yom*.  When
he had finished it, he disappeared and no one
ever saw him again, for the Lord took him to the
other pious men in paradise.

On the third night after that event, he appeared in a dream to his teacher, R. Kalonymos
son of R. Meshullam, and asked him to make a
copy of the *Unetanneh Tokef* hymn, which he had

composed on that occasion and to send it to all
the communities where Jews dwelt. We still
intone the *Unetanneh Tokef* on New Years' Day
and on the Day of Atonement for his sake. May
the Lord grant us the benefit of this saint.


### 213. THE JEWISH MARTYR, THE BISHOP AND THE DWARF

Once upon a time there lived a man who had
often denied the Lord, and later repented his
deeds. And he asked himself: "How can I atone
for my sins? Penitence by fasting I cannot
endure, for I have never been accustomed to
much fasting." Finally he said: "I can do
nothing better than to sanctify the name of God.
This is the best penance I can do." Accordingly,
he went to see a bishop, who was famed for his
great piety, and said to him: "What is the
punishment of a person who makes counterfeit
money?" The bishop replied: "Burning at the
stake." The Jew said: "I deserve that punishment, for I have made counterfeit coins." He
was immediately arrested, and two days later
the bishop ordered him to be brought before him
and asked him what he meant by bringing such
charges against himself. The man replied: "It
is true, I have coined false money, for I formerly

believed in God and now I have turned away from Him and have denied His existence." When the bishop heard this, he thought that the man had reviled his (the bishop's) God and ordered him to be tortured severely in order that he should repent. But the Jew persisted in his statement. Fearing that the Jew would revile his faith still more, the bishop decided to have him killed speedily. He ordered a pillar of iron, with an iron chain attached, to be placed in the open field and made a proclamation through the land, saying, whoever wished to see a Jew burned alive should come on such and such a day to such and such a place and he would see it.

When the day announced by the bishop came, all the people of the country assembled. A fire was made around the pillar, to which the Jew was tied with the iron chain and was driven slowly around the iron pillar, until he almost burned to death. This was done to make his death a cruel one, in the hope that he might repent. When the executioner saw the horrible death that was being inflicted upon the man, he refused to be a party to it and went away, for he was touched with pity for the poor sufferer. The bishop seeing this, rose from his seat and said: "I will judge him myself for the sake of my religion," and drove him around the pillar so that the fat ran down his body. But the man persisted in his martyrdom. The bishop continued this for three days, in order to cause him all the pain possible before he died. At intervals he desisted and offered to let him go if he would repudiate his faith. But the Jew cried in every instance, "No!" So he continued driving him until he was almost dead. Then the man said to the bishop: "Listen to me, bishop, before eight days are over I will judge you as you are judging me, and everyone will see it plainly." Thereupon he began to shout: "Hear, O Israel, the Lord our God, the Lord is One," and as he pronounced the word "One," he died and was burned to ashes.

Then the bishop ordered a banquet for the people and gave them good wine to drink for the glory of the faith. As they were sitting at the table, the bishop began to laugh. When the counselors asked him why he was laughing, he said: "Why should I not laugh, the foolish Jew whom I have punished said to me that before eight days have passed he would punish me as I have punished him. That is why I am laughing." At the table sat one counselor, who was a dwarf, and he said: "Gracious prince and lord, if I had been here then, I would have advised you differently." When he was asked what he meant, he replied: "I cannot say more."

They went on eating and drinking until suddenly the bishop began to cry: "Oh, I feel hot!" He was carried into a cold cellar, but it did not do any good. Then the dwarf said to him: "The Jew told you the truth, for I will show you that the Jew is punishing you as you punished him." And the dwarf made everybody see that the Jew was driving the bishop around the pillar as the latter had done to him, and the revenge was plain to every one. Immediately the dwarf disappeared and no one knew what had become of him.

## 214. The Corpse and the Torn Sleeve

Once upon a time there lived in the city of Worms a man called R. Bunem, who assisted in the burial of the dead. One day an old man died and, as usual, R. Bunem accompanied the body to the grave. The next morning, when R. Bunem went to the synagogue, he saw at the door a man dressed in a shroud and with a wreath round his head. R. Bunem was frightened, for he believed he was a demon, and started to run away, but the man in the shroud said to him: "Do not be afraid, come here, do

you not know me?" R. Bunem replied: "Are
you not the man I accompanied to the grave
yesterday?" The other said, "Yes." Then R.
Bunem said to him: "Why did you come here,
and how are you getting along in the other
world?" He replied: "I am getting along very
well, and am held in high esteem in paradise."
R. Bunem said: "How is that? Here below we
thought you were a bad Jew. Tell me, what
pious deed have you done to deserve respect?"
The dead one replied: "I will tell you. Every
morning I rose early and read my prayers and
blessings with great devotion. Therefore I now
say the blessings in paradise and am held in high
esteem. And if you do not believe me, I will
give you a sign which will convince you. When
you put the shroud on me yesterday you tore one
of my sleeves." Then R. Bunem said: "What
does the wreath on your head mean?" He said:
"It is made of good herbs of paradise and keeps
the evil demons from doing me harm." Then he
asked R. Bunem to mend his sleeve, for he said
he was ashamed of the other spirits, who had
whole garments, while his were torn. Then the
dead man disappeared.

The moral of the tale is that every man should
say his prayers with devotion and it will go well

with him in the other world; and, moreover, one should be careful not to forget anything when dressing dead bodies.

### 215. THE MERCHANT WHO BURIED HIS MONEY IN A FIELD AND THE ADVICE OF KING SOLOMON BY WHICH HE RECOVERED IT FROM THE MAN WHO HAD STOLEN IT

In the time of King Solomon three Jewish merchants started out together on a business journey. One Friday evening they came into a forest, where they were separated and lost sight of one another. One of them continued his journey and came to a distant country to buy goods. Then he thought: "What shall I do? I am a stranger in a strange land and know no one to whom I can entrust my money." So he went out into the fields and, looking round to see that nobody was watching, he buried the money in a hollow in the ground, where corn was stored during the winter. But the man to whom the granary belonged saw from a distance the merchant hiding the money, and as soon as the merchant went away, he took it out.

After three or four days, the merchant came back to fetch his money and found it was gone. Then he cried and said: "Woe is me, what shall I do? There was no one around and yet the money has disappeared." So he went to King Solomon and complained to him. King Solomon replied: "Find out to whom the hole belongs, and go to him and tell him that you are a stranger and that you brought a great deal of money with you. Then say to him: 'I buried a part of it, but I still have a great deal with me and do not know what to do with it. Shall I bury the rest in the same place, or shall I give it to an honest man to take care of, or shall I bury it separately?' His reply will be: 'Take my advice. If the place where the other money is hidden is a safe hiding place, put the rest of your money there too.' And he will put the stolen money back, for he will reflect that when you find the other money gone you will not put any more money there. Then you go and recover the stolen money."

The merchant found out to whom the hole belonged and went to him for advice. And he advised him to put the rest of his money in the same place. The merchant said that he would follow his advice, and went to town for a walk. The man who had stolen the money thought: "If the merchant finds that his money is gone, he will not put any more there. I will therefore restore the money I have taken and then I will get the entire amount." But he did not know that the matter had been prearranged. Accordingly he put the money back and the merchant recovered his loss and went his way. The thief came back to steal the whole amount, but found nothing. Thus the merchant recovered his money through the advice of King Solomon.

### 216. How R. Meir Saved R. Judah and His Family from the Death They Deserved because They Were Remiss in Almsgiving

R. Meir was in the habit of spending four hours daily studying in the *bet ha-midrash*. One day he was surprised to find himself leaving the *bet ha-midrash* earlier than usual. And as he stood wondering at the circumstance, he heard two snakes speaking to one another. One asked the other where she was going, and the other replied: "I have been sent by the Lord to put my sign upon R. Judah and to kill him and his children." The first snake asked: "What wrong has R. Judah done?" and the reply was: "He has never in his life given alms."

When R. Meir heard this, he blackened his face and went to the house of R. Judah. No one knew him on account of his disguise, and R. Judah also thought that he was a thief. When R. Judah sat down to his meal, R. Meir seated himself at the table. The children resented his intrusion and told him to get out. But R. Meir said: "You can shout until you are dead, but I am not going until I have eaten," and against their will he sat down and ate.

When he had finished the meal, he said to R. Judah: "Now take a loaf of bread and give it to me as alms." R. Judah replied: "You scoundrel, is it not enough that I gave you food and drink? Must I give you a loaf of bread besides?" R. Meir blew out the light and his face shone like the sun. Then R. Judah thought: "There is a reason why he asked me for a loaf of bread, for otherwise why should R. Meir have come here?" And he gave him a loaf of bread for God's sake. Then R. Meir said to him: "Take my advice, send your wife and children out of the house and do not allow them to come back until tomorrow, the third hour after sunrise." R. Judah did as R. Meir had advised him and sent his wife and children out of the house, while he and R. Meir remained inside. R. Meir left the room for a moment and the snake came and wanted to kill R. Judah and his wife and children. So R. Judah cried out: "R. Meir, come and help me, for there is a snake here that wants to kill me." Then R. Meir said to the snake: "What are you doing here?" The snake replied: "God sent me to kill R. Judah and his children." Then R. Meir asked: "What has he done?" And the snake replied: "He has never given alms." Then R. Meir adjured the snake to leave the house. The snake left and R. Meir locked the door. Then he said to R. Judah: "Do not open the door until tomorrow, the fourth hour after sunrise."

In the middle of the night, as they were sleeping, the snake came back and, imitating the voice of R. Judah's wife, said: "My dear husband, open the door, for I am almost frozen." But R. Meir said: "Do not open the door, it is not your wife." An hour later, the snake came again and, imitating the voice of his eldest son, said: "Father dear, open the door, for I am almost frozen to death." R. Meir said again: "Do not open the door, for it is not your son." The snake came back several times during the night, but could accomplish nothing. When the snake saw that it could not do anything, it lay down on its belly and cried: "Woe is me, the Lord has given me a command and these people are annulling it by their prayers!" And it cried so long until it burst.

At the fourth hour after sunrise, the wife and children of R. Judah knocked at the door. Then R. Meir said: "Open the door, for the evil hour is passed. Moreover, I will show you who cried

and knocked at the door in the night." R. Judah
and R. Meir went out of the house, and there
they found the snake lying dead and its belly
split open. Then R. Meir applied to R. Judah
the following verse: "Money does not help on
the day of God's anger, but almsgiving saves
from death" (Prov. 11.4), as happened to R.
Judah. For if it had not been for the protection
of R. Meir who warned R. Judah, he and his
wife and children would have lost their lives.
That was the reason why R. Meir left the
*bet ha-midrash* earlier than usual, namely in
order that R. Judah and his family should be
saved. After that R. Judah gave generous alms.

Therefore every man should take a lesson from
this story and give alms with a kind heart, for
charity delivers from death, as is told in this
story.

### 217. THE MAN WHO WAS SOLD AS A SLAVE BECAUSE HE NEGLECTED THE STUDY OF THE TORAH

Once upon a time there lived a pious man, who
had grown old and had no children. So he prayed
to God that He might grant him a child in his
old age and promised that he would have him
trained in the study of the Torah. God heard

his prayer and gave him a son, whom he called
Saul, which means "asked."    When the son
grew up, he was trained in the Torah and became
a great master. When the old father died, the
mother said to the son: "Follow my advice, take
the money which your father left and do business
so that we may be able to support ourselves."
He followed his mother's advice and went forth
to do business.   But he saw that businessmen
cheated and swore falsely.   So he came back.
His mother asked him: "Where are the wares
which you bought?" And the son replied: "My
dear mother, I do not want to do business,
for, in business, people swear falsely and cheat
and lie.  Therefore I have no desire to carry on
business, but I prefer to study the Torah, which
is the best trade." Then the mother said: "You
are the only child I have, and if you wish to
study the Torah, I will not prevent you." So he
went away again.

When he came out into the open country, he
saw a man ploughing, and a book was lying on
the plough.  The lad went up to him and said:
"The Lord be with you." The man returned
the greeting and said: "May the Lord bless you."
The old man was Elijah the Prophet.  The lad
asked the old man: "For whom are you ploughing?" The old man replied: "I plough and I sow

and I give the corn to the poor and to the scholars." Then the lad said: "I belong to that class." The old man asked him: "Where are you going?" The young man replied: "I am going to study the Torah, and then I would like to marry a pious woman. I have a very old mother, and I should like very much that she should live to see me married." The old man replied: "There are two pious damsels in the world, one is called Hannah and the other is called Sarah. Sarah has been reserved for you, but she is three days' journey from here."

The old man took the young man into the town where the damsel lived and said to her: "Sarah, I have brought you a bridegroom." Sarah replied: "Shall I marry a man whom I do not know?" But the old man persuaded her and they made an agreement and were betrothed. They were married soon after and were very happy.

The old man left them together and went his way. After some time the old man came again and saw that they quarreled and the man was disturbed in his studies. Then the Prophet Elijah said to him: "Because you neglect your study, you will be sold as a slave for seven years." And he went his way again. The young man and his wife ran after him and cried bitterly, but they could not overtake him. The husband was sullen, and one day his wife said to him: "Why are you so sullen? Don't you like me any more? Or is it because you wish to go home to your mother and friends?" He replied: "Yes, my dear wife, I want to see my mother and friends." So they collected all that they could carry with them and started out to go to the land of his friends. On the way she said to him: "Let us sit down and rest awhile and have a bite to eat, for we are tired and have not had much to eat to-day." As he went to the brook to wash his hands, the Prophet Elijah appeared, took him away from his wife and sold him as a slave.

The poor woman sat grieving and weeping, not knowing what had become of her husband. She looked around, but saw no one. Then she said: "What shall I do? I am in a strange country and do not know where to go. I will build me a little hut and remain here. Who knows, perchance God will have pity on me and send my husband back to me." She built herself a little house and bought much corn and acquired menservants and maidservants and sheep and cattle.

Now it came to pass that a famine broke out in all lands and people died of hunger. When

'they heard that there was a woman living by
the river bank, who had a large quantity of corn
to sell, many people went to buy corn from her.
The famine occurred in the fifth year of her
husband's slavery, and the master to whom he
had been sold said: "We will go there too and
buy corn from the woman." But the slave did
not know that she was his wife, nor did he
understand what had happened to him. So they
traveled together and came to the woman. As
soon as the slave came, the woman knew him,
but he did not know her. Then she said to her
husband: "Whence do you come, what is your
wish and what is your name?" He replied:
"My name is Saul and I had a wife whose name
was Sarah, but I have been taken away from her
and do not know where she is or how she is
getting along. We were sitting together by the
bank of a river when we were separated and I do
not know where she is or whether she is still
alive." When she heard these words, she could
no longer restrain herself and began to weep and
said: "My dear husband, I am the woman whom
you left behind on the bank. The Lord, praised
be His holy name, who forsakes no one, heard
my cry and protected me from all evil. He
granted all the wishes of my heart, and I built
me a house here and am doing business with our

money and have earned great wealth." Then she asked him: "How did it happen that you disappeared so suddenly?" He replied: "Because I neglected the study of the Torah for seven days and quarreled with you, I must serve seven years as an ordinary slave. I have served five years already and have two more years to serve." So they parted again from one another, and after two years the Prophet Elijah brought him back and they lived together happily. The old mother also came to live with them and they all lived happily.

### 218. "A Bird of the Air Shall Carry the Voice"

Once upon a time a Jew was traveling across country and was attacked by a robber, who took away everything he possessed. After he had robbed him of everything, the robber said: "Now I am going to take your life, for if I let you live, you will denounce me and I shall lose my own life. Therefore I will kill you, and then I shall feel safe." But the Jew said with weeping eyes: "Let me live and I will not report you. But I tell you this: if you kill me, the birds will denounce you and you will lose your life." Then the robber said: "I see that you are making fun of me." But the Jew replied: "No, I am not making fun of you, but it says in our Scriptures: 'The birds which fly between heaven and earth will reveal the secret' (Eccl. 10.20). You see the bird on yonder tree? He will report your crime." (Some say an angel of heaven called 'Bird' carries the cry.) Then the robber grew angry and said: "You are surely making fun of me," and he killed him.

The robber went his way and came to an inn, where he asked for food and drink. The innkeeper brought him a plate of birds. When the robber saw the birds, he began to laugh. The innkeeper, who stood near the table, seeing that the guest was laughing, asked him: "Why are you laughing? Since you are laughing to yourself, it must be something clever, therefore tell me what it is about." The robber, thinking that no one would concern himself about the death of the Jew, told the innkeeper the experience he had with the Jew, and how he had made fun of him and told him that the birds of heaven would denounce him. Hence, seeing the birds on the plate, he laughed. The innkeeper thought that the Jew had foretold the truth and said to himself: "As he killed a Jew, he no doubt did other things too, and is surely a murderer. Therefore it is my duty to denounce him." And

he went to the mayor and told him that there was
a man in his inn who had committed a murder.
The mayor said to him: "Go home and I will be
there soon." The innkeeper returned home and
sat down by his guest. In a quarter of an hour
the mayor came in with three men and said to
the murderer: "You are under arrest." The
robber was very much frightened and almost
died for fear. He was thrown into prison and
tortured until he confessed to the murder of the
Jew and other murders besides. Then he was
broken on the wheel, and thus the prophecy of
the Jew that the birds would denounce him,
came true.

### 219. ADULTERY AND THE PUNISHMENT THEREOF

Once upon a time there was a wicked Jew who
lived close to the house of a rich man, who had a
very beautiful wife. The wicked man conceived
a passion for her and asked her to do his will,
promising her a great deal of money. But she
refused to listen to him and abused him for
desiring to commit the grave sin of adultery.
So he went away.

One day her husband went away on a business
trip to buy goods. And when the wicked man
heard of it, he broke in the wall on a Friday

night, violating the Sabbath, got into the house and, tying a towel around her neck to prevent her from screaming, he violated her in her own home, thus transgressing the commandment against adultery. After he had tortured her sufficiently and satisfied his evil passion, he killed her, so that she should not be able to denounce him, and transgressed the command: "Thou shalt not kill." It soon became known that he had killed the woman, so he was arrested and about to be executed. But he asked to be liberated, promising to embrace Christianity. His wish was granted. And when he had become converted, he was thrown into the water and thus he was punished by God.

Now see how many sins that man committed because of his passion for another man's wife. First he transgressed the commandment: "Thou shalt not covet thy neighbour's wife." Then he violated the Sabbath. Then he transgressed the commandment: "Thou shalt not commit adultery." Then he violated the commandment: "Thou shalt not serve other Gods before Me," as he became an apostate. So God punished him in this world, for he was cast into the water, and he was surely punished in the world to come.

## 220. The Three Daughters, or the Evil of Tale Bearing

Once upon a time there lived a pious man, who had three daughters. The first one was a thief, the second was a sluggard and the third was a liar, who never spoke the truth and who slandered people whenever she had an opportunity. One day a pious man, who had three sons, came to the city and said: "You have three daughters and I have three sons. Let us make a match between them." But the father of the girls said: "Let me alone. My daughters are not good enough for your sons, for each one has a vice." The father of the boys asked: "What are their vices?" And the other replied: "One is a thief, the second is a sluggard, and the third is a lair." The father of the boys asked: "Have they no other vices than these? If so I will cure them. Leave it to me." So they were betrothed, and he took the damsels with him and married them to his sons.

As soon as the weddings were over, he gave to the thief the keys to all his money and satisfied her greed so that she had no reason to steal. To the second he gave menservants and maidservants in plenty so that she should have nothing to do. And as to the third, he fulfilled all her wishes, so that she should not tell lies or slander anybody. And whenever the father-in-law left her house, he embraced and kissed her, for he hoped that by being good to her he would cure her of her evil quality and she would not carry on slander any more.

One day the father came to see how his daughters were getting on. So he went to the first one and asked her how she was getting along with her husband, and how she was treated by her parents-in-law. She replied: "I thank you so much, father, for having given me in marriage to this man, for I have everything that my heart desires. And moreover, I have all the keys in my hand so that I do not have to steal." Then he went to the sluggard and asked her how she was getting on. And she also said: "I am so thankful to you, father, for having brought me here, for I need not lift a hand, I have menservants and maidservants in plenty, and my husband and parents-in-law all treat me very well." Then he came to the daughter who told lies to ask her how she was getting along, and she said: "You are a fine father! I thought you gave me one husband but it seems you gave me two, the father and the son. For no sooner does my husband leave the house than my father-in-law comes in and kisses me and hugs me and wants me to do his will. Dear father, if you do not believe it, come tomorrow morning and you will see it is true."

Next morning the father came and she put him in a room where he could see what was going on. Her father-in-law came as usual and kissed her and embraced her and said to her: "My dear daughter-in-law, how are you getting on? Is there anything you want?" He did all this with the good intention of curing her of her vice, but her father who saw it, grew furious and rushed out of his chamber and killed him. Then he tried to get away, but when her two brothers-in-law came home and found their father lying dead, they killed their father-in-law. Then the slanderer began to shout: "Murder! Murder!" and they understood it was through her that the tragedy had occurred. So they killed her too, and thus through slander three persons lost their lives. Therefore did R. Huna say: "The sin of the evil tongue is greater than the three sins, murder, adultery and theft, combined."

You can see what an evil thing it is to go tale bearing and slandering and telling lies. Hell itself cannot endure a person guilty of these things. When God judges those who have been guilty of lying and slandering, He will say to hell: "Open your mouth and swallow them up."

And hell will say: "Lord of the universe, they are too much for me, for they put their mouths in the heavens and their tongue walketh upon earth" (Ps. 73.9). Then the Lord shoots at them with His arrows and then hell receives them. Thus God punishes them first and afterwards they are punished in hell. Therefore, O man, guard your mouth, for it is wholesome to your soul, and let every man speak of his own affairs only and not always mix in the affairs of others. Then you will live everywhere in honor and afterwards pass your time in joy in paradise.

### 221. The Two Robbers and Their Punishment

Once upon a time two highwaymen said to each other: "Come, let us go on the highway and murder and rob everybody who comes, so that we may get rich, too." Accordingly they dug two pits, killed everybody who came their way and threw them into the pits. This went on for a long time. One day a nobleman was riding through the forest with a large retinue, and one of them said: "I remember that there used to be a very fine leveled highroad here, and now it seems to be all ruined." They rode on and found the two robbers sitting in a pit. Finding a large sum of money in their possession, they seized them and tortured them until they confessed the many murders which they had committed. Whereupon the nobleman had them put to a shameful death.

This is the explanation of the biblical verse: "My son, if sinners entice thee to go with them, consent thou not, for their feet run to evil, to shed innocent blood" (Prov. 1.10, 16). For later on the murdered man himself stands before God and says: "Lord of the universe, Thou hast created me and hast brought me out of my mother's womb, and hast fed me with Thy loving-kindness all the days of my life, and now I have been murdered by one of Thine own creatures. Lord of the universe, avenge me on the murderer." When God hears this complaint, His wrath is kindled against the murderer and He sends another to kill him. The murderer goes to hell and has no share in the world to come, but he is punished three times every day in hell. Therefore every man should guard against murder or any other sin, for God allows no wrong to go unpunished and requites everyone according to his deeds.

### 222. THE REWARD OF VIRTUE, OR THE STORY OF THE MAN WHO NEVER TOOK AN OATH

Once upon a time there lived a rich man, who had never sworn an oath in his life. When he was about to die, he made a will and ordered his children never to take any oath of whatever kind it might be. "For," he said, "all my wealth came to me because I never took an oath in my life, and therefore God prospered me in all my doings." And the children promised to do as he desired. When he died, they divided the money among themselves fairly and without anyone of them taking an oath. Then each one went his way, except one son, who remained in his father's house.

Now in that town there were many rogues, who had learned of the instructions in the will that he should not take an oath. So one of them went to the son and asked him to return the thousand florins which, he said, his father owed him. The son denied the claim and was summoned before the court. There he was ordered to take an oath that he knew nothing of the claim. Then the son thought: "If I take the oath I shall be breaking my father's will. It were better for me to pay than to disregard my father's will." So he paid the rogue although he could have taken

an oath honestly. When the other rogues found
that he refused to take an oath, they also came
and demanded a large sum of money. In short,
they robbed him of all that he possessed. Then
more scoundrels brought claims against him,
alleged to be due to them from his father, and
swore to their validity, as the court had ordered
them to do. Accordingly he was sentenced to
pay, but he had no more money, and was put
in prison.

Now this man had a pious and beautiful wife,
who took everything that happened to her in
good part. Being too proud to take charity
because she had been rich, she was obliged to
do other people's washing in order to make a
living for herself and her family. One day she
was standing by the river bank and washing
clothes, when a ship came past and the captain
said to the woman: "Will you wash my clothes
for me?" The woman said, "Yes." And the
captain gazed at her and became enamored.
Then he asked her who she was and she told him
how she had been defrauded of her money and
how her neighbors had ruined her. The captain
said: "Here is a florin; wash my shirt for me."
She took the florin together with the other money
she had earned and released her husband from

prison. Then she went to take the shirt back to the captain, and as soon as she set foot on board ship, the captain sailed away.

When her children saw their mother being carried away in the ship, they began to cry, as can easily be imagined, and ran home and told their father that their mother had been carried away by force. When the man heard this, he lifted up his hands to heaven and praised God and begged Him to have pity upon him and his little children. The poor man took his little children by the hand and went away with them. As they traveled along, they came to a river near the sea, but there was no ferryman to take them across. So he took off his clothes and, taking the children in his arms, started to wade through the river, but the current was so strong that they were carried away. By the mercy of God, they came across a small boat, in which they crossed to the other side. Then they came to a place where there were many Jews, who had pity on him, and made him a shepherd, for they did not have one. One day, as he left his children to guard the sheep by the seashore, the ship in which their mother was passed by, and the sailors seized them and carried them away.

One day, as the poor man was guarding his

flock, he reflected how rich he had been and how he had been shamefully robbed by those scoundrels, and how miserably he had lost his wife and children so that there was nothing left for him but to be a shepherd. So thinking, he went up and down along the bank of the brook, in which he saw many dead bodies of men who had been bitten by snakes and vipers. And he thought: "It is much better for me to die than to live. I wish to God the snakes would come and kill me also." And he thought of drowning himself, thus putting an end to his misery.

Suddenly he heard a voice from heaven saying: "Go yonder and dig under that tree and you will find a rich treasure, which has been reserved for you because you observed your father's will so loyally." He dug under the tree and found an immense treasure, beyond any estimation. He was happy again and thanked God for saving him from poverty and hoped that He would also grant him the return of his wife and children if they were still alive. Then he went to the king and obtained his permission to build a new house at the seashore and to impose a tax upon all ships that passed, to be paid into the treasury of the king. Accordingly, every ship had to stop outside his house. And whenever a ship arrived, he went on board and searched for his wife and children.

Not long after, the ship in which were his wife and children came and proceeded to pay the tax. He went on board the ship to examine the wares, and found his wife and children. He knew them, but they did not know him. He asked the captain: "Where did you get this woman and the young children?" The captain replied: "I brought them from a far off country." When the woman heard the conversation, she began to weep, as she thought of her old home. And her husband could not restrain himself and also began to weep, and said to the captain: "This is my wife and you took her away in a shameful manner. I will therefore send you before the king and keep your ship here, and whatever the king decides to do with you will be satisfactory to me." But the captain begged him to save his life and promised to give him all that he posessed. So he took his wife and children and all the goods that were in the ship and let the man go. And all this came about because he had kept his father's will.

### 223. The Three Sons and the Chest Bequeathed to Them by Their Father. Herein the Parable of the Bridegroom, the Bride and the Robber

Once upon a time there lived a very pious and wealthy man, who had three sons, all of them rabbis. Before his death, he called together the heads of the community and his three sons and said: "My dear children, I leave you immense wealth, enough to last you all your life. I leave you also a locked chest, and I want every one of you to pledge that you will not open it except in case of extreme need; and when the chest is kept by one of you, one of the others shall have the key." The sons promised, in the presence of the community, to carry out their father's wishes. The pious man died, the three brothers divided the money, and were all very wealthy.

After some time, the youngest, who was a great spendthrift, lost all his money and became very poor. So he asked his brothers to open the chest and give him his share of the contents. They grieved very much at the idea of breaking their father's will. So the eldest brother said: "Rather than break my father's will, I will lend you 5,000 florins and you may pay me back or not, as you please." The youngest brother accepted the offer and took the 5,000 florins. When he spent that money too, he came back and asked to have the chest opened. Then the second brother said: "Rather than break my father's will, I will do as my elder brother did, and lend you 5,000 florins, which you may pay me back or not, as you please." And the youngest brother accepted that offer also.

When he had exhausted that amount too, he considered what he should do, and decided to wait until it was his turn to keep the key. Then he had another key made like it, so that when, after three years, his turn would come to have the chest, he could open it and take out what he wished. When the time came, he tried the counterfeit key and, seeing that it fitted, he took out the money and substituted an equal weight of stones, so that his theft should not be noticed. Then he began to do business again. The brothers thought that he had turned a new leaf and would be more careful in the future, but they did not know the secret of the chest.

In four years he used up all the money which he had taken from the chest. So he went to his brothers again and said: "I thought I would not have to come to you again, but I see that I have no luck, for I have lost everything that I had. There is nothing left to do but to divide the contents of the chest, for it is written in father's will that in case of absolute necessity the chest should be opened. Now the time has come, for I am in great need." When the brothers saw that it was inevitable, they sent for the heads of the community and carried the chest into the synagogue. Then they said: "You see that this chest is locked just as it was when our father died." And the people agreed that it was the same chest. Then the brothers continued: "Unfortunately we find ourselves obliged to open the chest, for our youngest brother insists on it although we gave him a great deal of money." And they told the people how their brother had acted towards them. Then they unlocked the chest, and found it filled with stones. The youngest brother spoke out with great effrontery: "See how they have dealt with me, friends. I see now why they refused to open the chest and always gave me money instead. That is why they are rich and I am poor. They took out the money and put stones in its stead." The two brothers were innocent and the youngest was guilty, nevertheless they looked at each other and each thought the other was guilty. The people did not know who was the thief, for they were not clever enough to find out. Then the people said: "We cannot give you a decision,

for we are not wise enough. Our advice is
that you go to the rabbi, who lives near here and
is a great scholar. He will be able to decide the
matter for you." They all went to the rabbi,
and when they came near the town where he
lived, a Jew came running towards them and
asked them whether they had seen a runaway
horse. The eldest one said: "He was white,
was he not?" The man replied: "Yes, he ran
into that forest yonder." Then the second son
asked: "Was he not blind in one eye?" And the
youngest one added: "Did he not carry two
bottles, one filled with oil and one with wine?"
And the man replied: "Yes, he ran into that
forest." As a matter of fact they had described
the horse without having seen him. The man
ran into the forest after the horse, but could
not find it. Then he pursued the three brothers,
found the inn at which they were staying and
cited them to appear before the rabbi. Then he
said: "Rabbi, I lost a horse, and I met these
three men and asked them whether they had
seen a horse and they said, 'Yes,' and gave me an
accurate description of it and told me to run
into the forest and I would find my horse. I ran
after the horse, but could not find it. I say,
therefore, that they stole the saddle-bag and let
the horse run away. I want my money, and I

want to know what they have done with my horse." Then the three brothers said: "Rabbi, we have neither seen nor heard anything of the horse." Then the rabbi said: "If you did not see the horse, how is it you described it so accurately?" They replied: "We will explain it to you. I said the horse was white because I saw the man carrying the bridle in his hands, and there was white hair sticking to it, so I surmised that the horse must be white." The second brother said: "I said the horse was blind in one eye. This I could tell from his manner of grazing. He ate the good grass and left the bad, and grazed on one side of the road only. I guessed therefore that he must be blind in one eye." Then the rabbi asked the youngest one: "How did you know that he carried two jugs, one containing wine and the other oil?" He replied: "Oil remains on the surface, wine is absorbed. Consequently it must have been carrying two jugs. We noticed the peculiar actions of the horse all along the road, but no one can prove that we saw the horse." The rabbi said that they were very clever people and dismissed the complainant.

Then he asked them what their difficulty was. They told him what their quarrel was and asked him to decide the case. Each one presented his

side of the argument and then the rabbi said:
"My dear friends, you must remain here a
while, for I cannot shake the decision out of my
sleeve." But he understood the affair very well.
Then he said: "I see that you are all very clever
men, therefore I want to ask you a question
which was sent to me from Egypt and obtain
your advice. There were two very wealthy men
in Egypt, each of whom had an only child, and
they betrothed the children to each other while
they were still in the cradle. After a while the
parents of the children died, each one leaving his
child 300,000 crowns. The boy got into evil ways
and spent all his money, being left without a
penny. On the other hand, the girl was a gem in
every way and there was none like her in beauty.
When they both reached their fourteenth year,
which was the time appointed for the marriage,
the girl sent a message to the bridegroom, asking
him to prepare himself for the wedding, as the
contract provided. But the young man sent
word, saying that he would not come and that
she should marry someone else whom she might
like, for it was enough that he had lost his own
money, and he thought it would be much better
for him to live a life of poverty by himself than
to drag her down with him. So the girl sent for
a poor young scholar and said to him: 'I wish to

marry you, but on the following condition. I will go to my former bridegroom three times and ask him if he desires to carry out our parents' will and marry me. If he refuses, you will be my rightful bridegroom and I will go with you under the wedding canopy.' The poor man was quite satisfied with these conditions and they became betrothed. After the betrothal, the girl dressed herself in silk and velvet, went to her first bridegroom and said to him: 'My dear boy, do not break the will of our parents, who joined us together. You need not worry, I have enough money and we shall be able to live quite comfortably, and instead of following loose women you will be satisfied with me.' But the young man said: 'I cannot cease from my contemptible way of living and do not wish to waste your money so that we both fall into poverty.' The girl went away, and eight days later she decked herself out in gold and silver and came again and begged him to keep their fathers' will, but he gave her the same answer as before. Eight days later she came for the third time, decked in diamonds and pearls, her bosom filled with golden crowns, and said: 'I pray you, carry out our fathers' will and marry me. We have money enough.' Then the young man replied: 'May God bless you and give you luck. Marry whomever you like, I will bear you no grudge, but I cannot commit the sin of saddening your life and losing all you have.' When the girl saw at last that the first bridegroom refused to marry her, she married the other young man. And there was a grand festivity, as is becoming when people have so much wealth. When the time came to take the bride and groom to their nuptial chamber, they had to be taken outside, for they could not spend the night in the house where the wedding took place. Now there were many robbers, who lay in wait for the bride and bridegroom and carried them away, so that nobody knew what had become of them. At the head of the robbers there was a wicked old rascal, who tried to force the bride to do his will, but she refused, saying to him: 'Will you lose all the bliss of the world to come for such a short pleasure?' Finally he had pity on her and sent her away in peace and in safety.

"Now the rabbi of Egypt asked me to decide which of these three persons was the best, the bridegroom, the bride or the robber. I do not know, but I see that you are very clever men, therefore tell me what your opinion is and then I will decide your case." The eldest one said:

"The bridegroom was the best, for he refused to squander her money." The second one said: "The bride was the best, for she was anxious to keep her father's will." The youngest brother said: "The robber was the best, for in the first place he subdued his passion and let her go home safely, and secondly he must have been a great fool not to have taken the money, for he could have kept it." Then the rabbi said: "Blessed be the Lord, who reveals the hidden. You scoundrel, you have not seen the money and yet you are greedy for it. How much more greedy you must have been for the money which you did see! Arrest the thief! for he has taken the money out of the chest." He was taken and tortured until he confessed that he had made a counterfeit key and replaced an equal weight of stone and lead for the gold that he had taken out. Thus through his wisdom, the rabbi got to the root of the matter, and as a result the youngest son remained in great poverty, while the other two brothers lived in great wealth because they kept their father's will.

## 224. STORY OF TWO YOUNG MEN WHO WANTED TO MARRY THE SAME GIRL. THEY WERE GIVEN TWO HUNDRED FLORINS EACH AND HE WHO MADE THE BETTER USE OF THEM WAS TO BE THE HAPPY BRIDEGROOM

Once upon a time there lived a very distinguished rabbi, who was as rich as any man in his time and had an only daughter, very beautiful and accomplished in every way. As both the rabbi and his wife were advanced in years, he was anxious to see his daughter married. The rabbi had a nephew, who was rich and handsome and highly educated. So one day the rabbi, being alone with his wife, said to her: "We are both old and we have only one daughter. To-day or tomorrow we shall die, and there will be no one left to protect her. To whom shall we marry her?" And his wife said: "You are right, it is indeed time that we should marry her?" The rabbi said: "I have been thinking of the matter and have decided to marry her to my sister's son, who is rich and endowed with good qualities." But the wife replied: "No, we will marry her to my brother's son, for although he is not rich, he is virtuous, handsome and educated, and we have enough money ourselves." Then the rabbi said: "I think it is better to marry her to my nephew than to yours, for we are both rich." And so they could not agree and quarreled all night.

The next day, the rabbi gave a big banquet, to which he invited friends and pious people and the two young men, and they ate and drank and made merry. After they had eaten and drunk, the rabbi asked the two lads to leave the room, and then he said: "Dear friends, we are old, and would like to marry our daughter, but my wife and I cannot agree. I want to marry her to my nephew and she to hers. We will leave it to you and will do as you say." The people asked the rabbi and his wife to leave the room, while they were deliberating the matter. When they had made their decision, they called in the rabbi and his wife and said: "Both of the young men are worthy of the damsel, although the one is poor and the other is rich. We have therefore decided that each of the two young men should be given two hundred florins and sent abroad to buy merchandise. Whoever brings home the best goods, shall marry the girl. But they must stay away a whole year before the marriage is to take place."

The rabbi and his wife were well pleased with the advice. Accordingly, they called in the two

young men, the rabbi gave each of them two
hundred florins and said to them: "I am giving
each of you two hundred florins, go abroad and
buy goods, and whichever of you buys the best
goods, shall marry my daughter." The two
young men went away together full of joy in
their hearts, for each one thought that he would
get the beautiful girl. It was as if a fried pigeon
had flown into their mouths and no one knew
anything about it. So they went away together
in peace and went over seas. They came into a
beautiful town, where there was much fine
merchandise for sale. The rabbi's nephew bought
fine goods for his two hundred florins, while
the wife's nephew bought nothing except precious
stones, for he thought they were worth the
money. Then they started on their way home.
When they were half way from home, they
spent the night in an inn, where there were
many rogues and thieves, who discovered that
they had with them money and valuables. The
young men went to sleep and in the middle of
the night the thieves broke into their chamber,
rifled their sacks and stole everything they had
there, taking away the money and the precious
stones. When the young men woke in the
morning, they found that everything had been
taken away from them. The young man who

bought the precious stones was more grieved than the other, not so much on account of the money as because he lost a beautiful damsel, for he had nothing more in his purse and was therefore at the end of his resources. But the other young man did not worry much, for he had a little money in his purse and they had not taken away all his goods. So he asked the other young man whether he wanted to go home with him. The other replied, "No." So he went home by himself with the remaining goods, but the other youth was ashamed and would not return home. When the youth came home with his goods, they asked him about his companion and he replied: "I do not know where he is, for he took a different road." So they told him that if the other youth did not come back at the appointed time they would give the daughter to him as a wife. But the wife of the rabbi grieved very much over her relative, as she did not know what had become of him. But she said nothing and thought: "There is still half a year's time. Perchance the Lord, blessed be He, will help him to get home."

We will now leave the bride and bridegroom for a while and return to the poor youth who lost all his precious stones. When his companion had left him, he felt ashamed to return home with empty hands and thought: "I will not despair, for I can still study. Therefore I will go to a *yeshibah* to study. If I lose the beautiful girl, what can I do? Maybe God will send me another one, even more beautiful." So he went to the *Nasi* of Babylon, who had about four hundred students at his *yeshibah*, all good scholars. When he reached Babylon empty-handed and in rags, no one looked at him although he was a greater scholar than all the four hundred students. When the students assembled at the *yeshibah*, he sat down behind the stove, pretending to be an ignorant man.

One day the *Nasi* read a difficult passage in the *gemara*, which the students could not understand. So he told them to explain it to him on the next day. The students went home, and during the night the ragged youth behind the stove sat down at the table, took the *gemara* and began to study very earnestly. As he was studying, Elijah came and taught him everything he desired, so that he knew more than the *Nasi* and his students put together. Then Elijah left. The youth wrote down on the table the answer to the question put to the students by the *Nasi*, and went back to his place behind the stove. In the morning, when the *Nasi* rose up, he found the answer written on the table. Never thinking

of the youth behind the stove, he asked the
students who had put it there, but no one knew.
The next day the *Nasi* read another passage,
which was even more difficult than the first.
The students studied the passage the whole day,
but could not understand it. When they retired,
the young man behind the stove came out again
and wrote the answer on the table. Early the
next morning, the *Nasi* rose up and found the
answer again written on the table. So he said:
"I see that I have bright pupils in the *yeshibah*,"
and wondered. He asked again who had written
the answer on the table, but no one knew. The
third day, the *Nasi* again read a passage, which
was pure prophecy. Again the pupils could not
understand. This time the *Nasi* made a hole in
his room so that he could see what was going
on in the *bet ha-midrash*. When all the students
retired, the ragged youth again rose up and sat
down at the table to study, and at the same time
he wrote down the answer on the table and went
back behind the stove. The *Nasi* saw all this
and wondered that he had known nothing about
the young man's ability. But he said nothing.
He came to the *yeshibah* the next day, behaving
as if nothing had happened, and the poor young
man again sat down behind the oven as if
nothing had happened. The *Nasi* again asked a

question, and the students discussed it earnestly among themselves, but found no answer. Then the *Nasi* addressed the young man behind the oven and said to him: "I order you under a penalty to give me the answer." The young man replied: "My dear master, why do you ask me? I know nothing." The *Nasi* again ordered him to give the answer and he gave it plainly, and then he explained a passage himself in such a way that no one could ask any questions. The pupils asked the master how he had become aware of the young man's knowledge, and the rabbi replied: "He is the man who wrote the answers on the table every night after I had delivered my discourse. I saw it through the hole."

Now the rabbi had a beautiful daughter, whom he offered to give the young man as a wife. The poor young man said: "No, I am not worthy of your daughter. Moreover, I am engaged to be married." And he told him all his adventure. One night as he lay in bed, he began to think of his father and mother, whom he had left behind, and remembered that the time was drawing nigh for the solemnization of the marriage. So in the morning he took leave of the rabbi and went away. The *Nasi* and all his pupils accompanied him a long way, spending

the time in homiletic discourses. Then they
turned back and the young man went his way
until he came to a dark forest. Three days and
three nights he walked in the forest until he
almost died of hunger. Suddenly he came upon
a beautiful apple tree, shook some of the apples
down and ate. No sooner had he eaten than he
became leprous. So he wept bitterly and desired
to kill himself. He went on a little further, and
saw another apple tree. So he said to himself:
"I will eat again and maybe I will die, for death
is better to me now than life." And he shook
some of the apples and ate. He was cured
and became even more handsome than before.
So he thanked God and went back to the first
apple tree and gathered many apples, and then
he went to the healing tree and took an equal
number of apples and departed, saying: "Now I
have learned enough. It will surely be of use
to me some day."

After a further journey, he arrived in the
country where his home was, and when he came
into the first town, he saw that all the people
were sad. He asked someone what was the cause
of their sadness, and the man said to him: "My
dear friend, we have a pious king, who has
suddenly become leprous, may the Lord have
mercy upon him. We have had many physicians

but they could not help him." Then the young
man said: "Dear friend, take me to the king, for I
hope with the help of God to be able to cure
him." The man replied: "The wonders of God
are great, but I do not believe that he can be
helped. For so many physicians have tried and
failed. Nevertheless, if you want to go, I will
take you to the king." So they went to the king
and asked to be announced as a person who, with
the help of God, hoped to heal the king. When
he was admitted, he fell at the feet of the king
and greeted him. The king, whose face was
covered, said to him: "Are you also confident
that you will be able to help me?" The young
man replied: "If your royal majesty will follow
my prescription, I hope with the help of God to
cure you." When the king heard him speak so
modestly, he said to him: "If you will cure me,
I will give you half my kingdom, for I prefer
death to life." Then the young man replied:
"Your majesty may rest assured, for I hope to
cure you of your illness." Then the young man
went to an apothecary, cut a slice from the
leprosy-producing apple and covered it with
sugar. Then he gave it to the king. No sooner
had the king eaten it, than he became more
leprous than before and his pain increased. So
he said: "I knew that the physician would make

it worse." The young man said: "My lord king, I told you that you must suffer a while before you will be cured." Then he went to another apothecary, cut a slice of the good apple, covered it with sugar and gave it to the king to eat. And as soon as he had eaten it, he was cured and became even more handsome than before. The king rejoiced greatly and all the people in the town with him. Then the king took the young man aside and said to him: "My dear doctor, command me and I will do anything you wish." Then the young man said: "Your majesty, I demand nothing from your royal crown that would cause you any loss. Praise God who has aided you and to whom alone belongs the strength and the power. My request of your majesty is this: There is a certain town in your dominion, called so and so, where my father and mother live. My request is that this town be given to me as a gift." The king gave him the city, and ordered the castle to be beautifully decorated for his reception. The young man then wished to depart, but the king said: "I will send you there in proper state." He put a golden chain round his neck and gave him 400 mighty horsemen to accompany him.

When the townspeople heard that their young lord was coming, they rode out to meet him and received him with great honor and gave him much gold and silver. The poor Jews also went up to the castle to pay their respects to the lord and to present him with a beautiful vessel, containing twenty ornaments of glass. The community sent as their representative the rabbi who was to have been his father-in-law, to intercede for the Jews and to be their spokesman. So he spoke and said: "Your grace, the Jews request you to accept this slight gift and to grant them your protection." The young lord took the cup and promised to be kind and merciful. Looking around, he saw his poor father, standing in torn clothes. Then he said: "Dear Jews, be reassured and observe your old faith according to your custom. But give this present to that poor ragged man, for I see that he is in great need." And he pointed to his beloved old father. "But one thing I must ask of you, whenever you have a wedding or a betrothal, let me know, for I should like to see it." Whereupon the rabbi who was to have been his father-in-law said: "This week I am going to have a wedding myself, and I will let your honor know if you wish to be present." Then the lord said: "My dear Jew, invite me and I will do you a favor in return." The rabbi took leave of the governor, wishing him long life, and went home, rejoicing that God had granted them a master who was so kind to the Jews. Then the rabbi made all the preparations for the wedding. But the poor father of the governor grieved very much, for he did not know what had become of his son, whether he was dead or alive.

When the time arrived for the wedding ceremony, they invited the lord to come, saying that the couple would be joined in wedlock. The governor told them to wait a while until he came. The messenger returned and brought a reply that the governor would soon come and that they were to wait for him. They prepared a beautiful seat for him to sit in, while the governor went and dressed himself in clothes of pure gold and gold chains and rings, went to the place where the marriage was to take place, and sat down in the seat which had been prepared for him.

When the marriage formula was about to be recited, the governor said: "Wait! I have something to say. The bride is mine. I am the other man who went away with the two hundred gold florins. And now you will see who made the better use of the money." And he told them all that had happened to him, the story of the apples and his appearance as a student. The other bridegroom had to retire in shame and he took his place, and the marriage was celebrated with joy. None rejoiced more than the poor father and mother, and none was more sad than the other bridegroom. He and his children's children continued to govern the town. Thus you see that no one can harm him whom God wishes to help. And as God helped this poor man, so may He help us also against all evil. Amen. Selah.

## 225. R. Joshua Breaks the Magic Spell Put upon His Host Who Then Becomes the Father of R. Judah b. Bathyra

R. Joshua and Rabban Gamaliel and R. Akiba were on their way to a city in Palestine called Ramah. In the course of their travel, they came to a town where they saw little children playing. They set up little heaps of earth before the gate and said: "This heap shall be for tithe and this heap for a heave offering," as they had seen the grown-ups do in Palestine, for in Palestine they still give tithe and heave offerings. When the three rabbis heard this, they said to one another: "There must be Jews in this town, let us go into the city and eat in a Jewish house." They entered the town and came to the house of a Jew. And the master of the house said to them: "Wash your hands and I will give you food."

But when he brought in the dishes, he took them first into another chamber. Accordingly the rabbis refused to eat, for they thought that he had an idol to whom he offered the food first. So they said to him: "Sir, tell us why you always take the dishes first into the other chamber before you bring them to us and put them on the table." The master of the house replied: "I will tell you. My old father lives in that chamber and I take his food to him before I put it on the table. For my father has taken a vow not to leave the chamber until Jewish sages came to see us." Then they said: "Tell your father to come out, for Jewish sages are here now." So the master of the house went to his father and told him that Jewish sages had come into the house. When the old man came out to meet the rabbis, they asked him why he had made a vow not to leave his room until Jewish sages came. The old man replied: "My son is childless, and therefore I have taken a vow not to leave the room until Jewish sages came here, in the hope that they may be able to help him." R. Joshua replied: "Bring me seed and I shall see if he has been bewitched. If so, I will help him." For R. Joshua was a member of the Sanhedrin, who had to know magic, although they were not allowed to use it against any one. But they were allowed to free a person from witchcraft.

They brought him the seed, and by means of his art he made the seed sprout and grow ears of corn, but they were empty. Then he knew that a woman had cast a spell upon him. Then he caused the woman who had cast the spell to appear before him and said to her: "Remove the spell from this man, so that he may have children, or I will denounce you as a witch." Then the woman said: "I cannot break the spell, for I have no power over it, having thrown it into the sea." Then R. Joshua adjured the prince of the sea to cast out the magic, which he did. Then he ordered the woman to disappear, while the three sages prayed for the young man, and he begot a son who came to be known as R. Judah ben Bathyra, who was a mighty man in the Torah. Then the three sages said: "Had we done nothing else by coming into this town than to bring R. Judah ben Bathyra into the world, it would have been enough."

## 226. The Evil of Selfishness

Once upon a time there lived a worthy man who was very pious and learned, and yet all the sons which he begot with his wife died. When his time came to die, he said to his pupils: "You have seen that all my sons died in my lifetime. I do not know any sin I committed except this. I had a sister who was a widow and she was ashamed to ask me to get her a husband. I knew that she was anxious to marry again, but I pretended I did not know and never gave her a husband, because I wanted to have all her money and property. Because I did this all my children died in my lifetime."

## 227. THE STORY OF KUNZ AND HIS SHEPHERD

The proverb runs: "You will be left behind as Kunz was left behind to look after the sheep." And if you ask how Kunz came to be left behind to look after the sheep, I will tell you.

Once upon a time there was a mighty king, who had a counselor called Kunz. Whenever the king needed advice, and the counselors in conference came to a decision, the clever Kunz would go to the king and say: "This is our decision." This fine gentleman always took the credit to himself, pretending that he was responsible for the advice and that the other counselors had to agree with him, for they had neither sense nor understanding. And the good

king believed what Kunz told him and considered
him as much wiser than the other counselors.

Now the other counselors noticed that the king
loved Kunz more than he loved them and they
resented it very much, for he was the least
important among them.  One day they took
counsel together how to get the better of Kunz
and humiliate him.  So they went to the king
and said: "Lord king, we beg of you to forgive us,
for we wish to ask you how it is that you think
more of Kunz and hold him in higher esteem
than the rest of us, although we know that he is
the least important among us?"   The king
replied: "I will tell you how it happens.  Whenever you come to a decision on any matter, he
reports it to me and says that the idea is his
and that you have to acknowledge every time
that he is wiser than you and that you have no
sense at all.  But I do not hold you in disrespect,
for you are all good to me."  When the counselors
heard this, they were very glad and thought:
"We will soon bring about his downfall."  Then
they said to the king: "Be assured that all which
Kunz said is a lie, for he has no sense at all.  Try
every one of us separately and you will see that
he cannot give you any advice by himself."  The
king said: "I will find out very soon," and sent
for his beloved counselor Kunz and said to him:

"My dear servant, I know that you are loyal and exceedingly wise. Now I have something in my mind that I do not wish to reveal to anyone. Therefore I want to ask you whether you can find out the truth for me, and if you do, I will reward you liberally." The clever Kunz replied: "My beloved king, ask me and I hope I can give you an answer. Tell me your secret." The king said: "I will ask you three questions. The first is: Where does the sun rise? The second is: How far is the sky from the earth? The third, my dear Kunz, is: What am I thinking?" When Kunz heard these three questions, he said: "Lord king, these are difficult matters, which cannot be answered offhand. They require time. I beg of you, therefore, to give me three days' time, and then I hope to give you the proper answer." The king replied: "My dear Kunz, your request is granted, I will give you three days' time." Kunz went away and thought to himself: "I cannot concentrate my mind very well in the city, I will go for a walk into the country. There I am alone and can reflect better than in the city."

He went out into the country and came upon the shepherd who was tending his flock. Walking along, he talked as it were to himself, saying: "Who can tell me how far the heavens are from

the earth? Who can tell me where the sun rises?
Who can tell me what the king is thinking?"
The shepherd, seeing his master walking about
wrapt in thought, said to him: "Sir, pardon me.
I see that you are greatly troubled in your mind.
If you ask me, I might be able to help you. As
the proverb says: 'One can often advise another,
though one cannot advise oneself'." When Kunz
heard these words from the shepherd, he thought:
"I will tell him. Perhaps after all he may be
able to advise me." And he said: "I will tell
you why I am so troubled. The king asked me
three questions, which I must answer or lose
my neck. I have been thinking about them and
cannot find the answer." Then the shepherd
said: "What are the three questions? Perhaps I
may be able to help you in your great trouble."
So Kunz thought: "I will tell him, maybe he is a
scholar." And he said: "My dear shepherd,
these are the three questions which the king
asked me. I must tell him where the sun rises,
how far the heavens are from the earth, and what
the king is thinking." The shepherd thought it
was well to know the answers and said to Kunz:
"My dear master, give me your fine clothes, and
you put on my poor garments and look after the
sheep. I will go to the king and he will think
that I am you and will ask me the three ques-

tions. Then I shall give him the proper answers
and you will be saved from your trouble. Then I
shall return here and you will not be in disgrace
with your king." Kunz allowed himself to be
persuaded, gave the shepherd his good clothes
and fine cloak, while he put on the shepherd's
rough garments and sat down to look after the
sheep, as though he had done it all his life.

When the three days had passed, the shepherd
went to the king and said: "Lord king, I have
been thinking over the three questions that you
asked me." The king said: "Now tell me, where
does the sun rise?" The shepherd replied: "The
sun rises in the east and sets in the west." The
king asked again: "How far are the heavens from
the earth?" The shepherd replied: "As far as
the earth is from the heavens." Then the king
said: "What am I thinking?" The shepherd
replied: "My lord king, you are thinking that
I am your counselor Kunz, but I am not. I am
the shepherd who looks after his flock. My
master Kunz was walking in the field one day
and saying to himself: 'Who can tell me where
the sun rises? Who can tell me how far the
heavens are from the earth? Who can tell me
what the king has in his mind?' He was walking
about all the time and talking in such fashion.
So I told him he should give me his good clothes

and I would give him my rough clothes; he should look after the sheep and I would, with the help of God, guess the answers to these three questions and save him. He allowed himself to be persuaded, and so he is now out in the field, dressed in my rough clothes and tending the sheep, while I am dressed in his beautiful cloak and his best clothes." When the king heard this, he said to the shepherd: "As you succeeded in persuading Kunz, you shall remain my counselor and Kunz can look after the sheep." Hence the proverb: "You will be left behind as Kunz was left behind to look after the sheep." This is what happened to him. May it go better with us.

### 228. The Rabbi Whose Wife Turned Him into a Werewolf

Once upon a time, in the land of Uz, there lived a distinguished rabbi, who was very wealthy and knew the seventy languages. He supported a great *yeshibah* and had many able students and also educated many young children. He always had at least one hundred pupils in his *yeshibah*. He also supported an organization for the poor, and many poor people had free access to his house. In short, the rabbi was a pious man and had all the virtues that a good Jew should have. But, as against this, he had a very bad-tempered wife, who could not bear with any of his actions and looked askance at all his deeds. She did not like to see a poor man enter her house.

The proverb, which says: "When the rope is too tight it snaps," was verified in the case of this pious man. He became so poor that he could no longer give any charity, nor could he do as much good for the young students as he had done formerly. Then the poor rabbi thought to himself: "What shall I do now? All the days of my life I have given freely for God's sake and have done much good to many, and now I am very poor. What shall I do? I will accept my fate willingly from the Lord, blessed be He, who does no injustice. I wonder what sin I have committed." Then he continued: "What is the good of my lamenting my poverty? There always are people who gloat over another's misfortune. There is one thing I can do. I will leave town secretly, so that no one should know what has become of me." So he called his best pupils and said to them: "My dear young men, you know well how faithful I was toward you up to now, how I supplied you with food and clothing and taught you besides. Now I will confide to you a secret, hoping that you will act towards me as I have acted towards you." The pupils replied: "Dear Rabbi, tell us your secret, for we will stand by you as long as God grants us life." So the rabbi told his pupils that he must depart, for he did not understand why he had become so poor. And he asked them to go with him. "For," he said, "I have still a few florins, which I should like to spend with you. Who knows but that God may give me wealth again, and then you will enjoy it again with me as long as you live." The pupils replied: "Dear Rabbi, whatever you desire us to do we will do willingly, and whatever we possess in money and clothes, we will share with you." So the rabbi went away with fifty of his pupils, and not a man in the community knew of his departure. When the poor people learned that their rabbi had gone, they feared greatly, and so did the little children, whom he had brought up by his bounty, as well as the other pupils who remained behind with his wife. Thus he departed together with his pupils, and wherever he came, he was received with the honor he deserved. And no one was surprised to see him traveling about, for they thought he was going to a *yeshibah* to study.

After traveling about for a year or two, their garments were torn and the money in their purses was spent, as can be easily imagined, and they became dependent upon charity. But wherever they went, people locked the doors in their faces, for nobody knew their circumstances, whether they were vagrants or students. At last the students grew tired of wandering about, and said to the rabbi: "What will be the end of our wandering? We have neither clothes nor money, and cannot help ourselves. And wherever we go, people lock the doors in our faces and look upon us as vagrants. We will therefore return to our parents. Moreover, we are getting older and wish to marry. But we will not tell anyone how you are faring or where you are." When the good rabbi heard this from his pupils, he thought for a while and then said to them: "My dear pupils, I have nothing but praise for the loyalty which you have shown to me. Therefore I beg of you to remain with me four or five days more until after the Sabbath. After that I will let you go in the name of God. Perhaps God will send us something good and we shall return home together." And the pupils replied: "Very well, dear Rabbi. We have stayed so long with you that we might as well remain a few days longer."

So they continued their travels and came to a clump of small trees. Then the rabbi said to the

pupils: "Go ahead and I will be with you soon."
The pupils went along, talking among themselves
and discussing various points of law. And the
rabbi, seeing a small spring, washed his hands
and was about to leave, when he saw a small
weasel running along with a pretty gold ring in
its mouth. He ran after the weasel until it
dropped the ring. He picked it up and saw that
the ring was of little value, but on examining
it more closely, he found an old inscription on the
inside, which he easily read. It ran as follows:
"Although I look unattractive, my value is
inestimable."

Now the rabbi was a very clever man and he
suspected that the ring must have a special
virtue. He thought as hard as he knew how to
find out what kind of charm the ring could
have, to be so valuable. Then he thought
perhaps it was a magic ring, by means of which
one could obtain one's desires, and decided to
try it. So he said: "I wish I had a girdle with
money." And before he had finished the sentence, he saw a girdle filled with gold, lying in
front of him. He became cheerful again and,
going to his pupils, he said: "My dear boys,
be of good cheer, we are going to a place where
I have a very rich friend, who will lend me
money, for he does not know that I am so poor.

I will then buy clothes for you and send you home." But he did not tell his pupils that he had found a magic ring, fearing that they might take it away from him or report him and he would lose it. The pupils rejoiced at the thought of getting new clothes and asked no further questions, having no doubt that their teacher had told them the truth. So they came to the town and after spending a day there, the rabbi dressed them in clothes of pure silk and velvet and dressed himself in clothes similar to those he had worn before. He stayed there a week or ten days, studying very earnestly with his pupils, and the people paid him all the honor which was due to him as a great scholar. One day he went into the town and bought a coach worthy of a prince, and said: "My dear pupils, come here and I will pay you back all the money which you laid out for me on the journey, and then we will go home." The pupils had no doubt that his relative who lived in the town and who was a rich man, had lent him a few thousand florins, as the rabbi had told them, so that he might return to his home with honor. They started for home together and where the people had previously shut the door in their faces, they now received them with great honor.

Now as long as the rabbi had been away from

his home the people were unhappy, but now a shout went up in the community that the rabbi had come back together with his pupils. And who rejoiced more than the poor? As soon as he had reached home he received everyone with a friendly air, for no one knew that he had gone away because of poverty; they all believed that he had gone to study. The rabbi resumed his old habits of almsgiving, opened his *yeshibah* and brought up the young children to study. On the Sabbath he was in the habit of taking a nap and then studying *tosafot* with his pupils. One Sabbath he lay down to take a nap as usual, and his wife said to him: "My dear husband, where did you get so much money? We were so poor before that you had to leave." The rabbi replied: "I had a godsend on my journey." But the wife would not believe this and she worried him so long, as women will do, until the rabbi let himself be persuaded and told her his secret. This was a mistake. For King Solomon said: "Do not confide thy secret to thy wife," for women cannot keep a secret, as happened to the good rabbi, as you will soon hear. If he had not confided his secret to his wife he would have been spared much trouble, and because he told her the secret of the ring, viz. that all one's wishes are fulfilled, he had to suffer great misfortunes.

When the evil-tempered wife heard the story, she thought: "If I had the ring, he would never get it back again," and she would have readily taken it away from him, but it could not be taken off his finger against his will. So she said: "My dear husband, let me see the ring for a while." The rabbi knew what an evil-tempered woman she was and would not give it to her, whereupon she pretended to weep and said to him: "I see you do not love me, for you will not trust me with the ring." And she plagued him until at last he gave it to her. As soon as she slipped the ring on her finger, she put her head under the sheet and said: "I wish my husband were turned into a werewolf and ran about in the woods among the wild beasts." She had scarcely uttered these words, when the good rabbi jumped out of the window and ran into the forest, called the Pemerwald (Böhmerwald), and began to devour the people and do damage, so that no one ventured to go through the forest alone for fear of the wolf which struck terror into the heart of the people. The werewolf made himself a dwelling in the forest (and took in the charcoal) to keep his lair dry. Accordingly all the charcoal burners in the forest ran away also for fear of the werewolf.

Now let us leave the wolf for a while and see

what happened in his house. When the time arrived for the rabbi to read *tosafot* to his pupils, the rabbi's wife (may her name be blotted out!) told them: "The rabbi cannot read *tosafot* to-day, as he is not well." The pupils believed her and went away. The next morning they came again, and she said: "The rabbi has gone away and has not told me where, but I believe he will be back in four years." She appeared to be very grieved, but it was only a piece of infamous acting on her part, may her name be blotted out! The poor people came to the door, but she refused to let anyone in. The poor people grieved very much at the loss of the rabbi. The infamous woman was very rich, as one can well imagine. For she was able to obtain everything she desired, hence there was no limit to her wealth. But nobody knew what had happened to the rabbi, or why he had so suddenly disappeared. Moreover, there was no one who could find out, but everyone believed he would return again, as he had done before.

We will leave the wicked woman alone and will return to the poor rabbi, running about in the forest as a werewolf, doing great damage and killing man and beast, for there is no stronger animal than the werewolf. The charcoal burners were asked if they could capture the wolf, but they replied: "No, he is much stronger than a lion and has intelligence besides." When the king heard of this, he arranged a hunt through the forest but he could not catch the wolf. They dug pits in many places but of no avail.

Now among these charcoal burners there was one whom the wolf did not hurt, but on the contrary made friends with him and spent most of its time near his hut. All other people had to avoid the forest for fear of the wolf. Now the king issued a proclamation that he who succeeded in capturing the wolf, alive or dead, would receive the king's daughter as a wife and on the death of the king would succeed to the throne. At the king's court there was an unmarried knight, who was very strong and had taken part in many tournaments. This knight arose and said: "My lord king, if you will keep your word, I will undertake to kill the wolf, for I have fought many battles and luck has always been with me. Therefore, I will try once more." The king repeated his promise on his honor. Accordingly, the knight put on his armor, feeling certain that he would succeed in killing the wolf. He went to the charcoal burner who lived in the forest and was friendly with the wolf and said to him: "Friend, show me the wolf's lair or its whereabouts." When the man saw that the knight

intended to attack the wolf, he was very much
frightened, fearing the knight would be killed in
the encounter, as had almost happened to himself.  The charcoal burner said to the knight:
"What are you doing in this forest?  If the wolf
becomes aware of your presence, you will lose
your life, great as you are."  The knight replied:
"Nevertheless, show me his lair, for I have come
here to kill him."   But the charcoal burner
continued: "Sir, I pray you, do not attempt this.
You are playing with your life."   The knight
replied: "Be quick about it, for it must be."
Then the charcoal burner said: "May God have
mercy on you," and went with him and showed
him where the wolf roamed.  The knight took
his gun and his spear in his hand and went into
the wood, thinking that as soon as he saw the
wolf, he would shoot him.  When the wolf saw
that his life was in danger, he jumped aside,
caught the knight by his throat, cast him to the
ground, and was about to kill him.  When the
charcoal burner saw this, he drove the wolf away.
The knight was not satisfied and wanted to
attack the wolf again, but the coalburner prevented him.  Nevertheless, he rushed at the wolf
a third time.   Thereupon the wolf became
enraged and wanted to tear him to pieces.  Then
the knight prayed to God to save him from the

wolf, promising that he would not attack him. The wolf released his hold and began wagging his tail in fawning fashion. He would not leave him and ran before the knight as a dog runs in front of its master. The knight was very anxious to get rid of him, for he was afraid of him, but the wolf continued to run at his side. So he took off his girdle and, tying it round the wolf, held him by it, the wolf acting as his guide in the forest. And whenever a wild beast desired to do the knight harm, the wolf tore it to pieces. And when he saw a hare or a fox, he caught it and brought it to the knight. Finally the knight brought the wolf to the king. The king and the counselors were seized with fright, for they had heard so many stories about the wolf killing people. So the king told the knight to take the wolf away. The knight replied: "You need not fear, he will do no harm to anyone who will not molest him, I pledge my life on it. On the contrary, he has caught animals for me." So the knight kept the wolf with him and took good care of him, remembering the mercy the wolf had shown to him in sparing him although he had deserved death for having made three attempts upon the wolf's life. He therefore looked after him well and gave him of the best food and drink. Whenever he went hunting, he took the wolf with him and whenever he saw a beast, the wolf caught it and brought it to him.

The king had promised that any man who brought him the wolf alive or dead would obtain his daughter to wife, and as the knight had properly earned this reward, the king kept his promise and gave him his daughter and half of his wealth besides. When at last the old king died, the young knight became king in his stead and obtained the whole land. But all the time he kept the wolf with him and did not want to abandon him as long as he lived, for the wolf had saved his life and was instrumental in his obtaining the kingdom.

One day in the winter after a heavy snowfall, the young king went out hunting and took the wolf with him. As soon as the wolf came out, he began wagging his tail and ran as if he had scented something. The king followed the wolf and saw him in the distance, digging in the snow with his feet. When the king came up, he saw that there was something written on the snow. The king was greatly astonished and said: "There is something strange about the wolf being able to write, perhaps he is a human being who has been turned into a beast by a curse, as has often happened before." .But no one was able to read the writing. He sent for all the doctors, but none could read it. Among his counselors there was one who knew Hebrew, and he told the king that it was a writing of the Jews and began to read it as follows: "My dear king, remember the kindness which I showed you when you came into my lair in the forest. I could have torn you to pieces, for I had you under me three times, and in truth would have been justified in taking your life. Nevertheless, I spared you and even helped you to become king. I have a wife who lives in a town called so-and-so (and he mentioned the name), who put a curse upon me, and unless I recover my ring, I must remain a wolf to the end of my life. But as soon as I get the ring I shall be a human being again. Remember the loyalty I have shown you, go into the town, get the ring from my wife and bring it to me for the sake of our friendship, else I will take away your life." And he gave him a sign by which he might know the ring. All this was written in the snow.

When the king heard this, he said: "I will help him again even if I lose my life in the attempt." Accordingly he took three servants with him and rode into the town which the rabbi had named and in which his wife lived. He announced that he had come to buy beautiful rings and Frankish

antiques and that he would pay any price to
obtain them. He sent for the Jews and asked
them if they had any old Frankish gold or rings
or precious stones. The Jews replied: "We are
poor people, but there is a woman in this town
who has very beautiful rings of all kinds and
precious stones." He asked the Jews to take
him to the woman, and they did so, not knowing
he was a king, but thinking he was a merchant.
When he came to the woman, he said: "My good
woman, I have been told that you have some old
curious gold rings with and without precious
stones and old Frankish work. If I like them I
will pay you a good price." And he pulled out
of his pocket many beautiful rings and said that
he had bought them on his travels. The woman
said: "I will show you what old gold I have."
And she went into her chamber and brought out
many beautiful ornaments, such as the king had
never seen. And the king was greatly astonished
to find such beautiful things in the house of a
Jewess. Among other things he saw a string of
rings, among which was the gold ring which the
wolf had described. Thinking how he might
obtain the ring, the king took the rings in his
hand and said to himself: "I wish my wolf had
the ring in his hand already." And, without
pointing to the particular ring, he said to the

woman: "What would be the price of these rings?" She replied: "So many hundred florins." The clever king concluded the bargain and bought two rings, at the same time slipping the other ring into his hand without the woman noticing it. Then he paid her the amount, took leave of her, and returned home. When he had reached home, the woman missed the ring but dared not avow it, for she did not know who the merchant was. She grieved very much and mourned like a widow, but no one knew anything about it.

When the king reached home, he ordered a great banquet and invited all the nobles of the kingdom. And as he was sitting at the table and making merry, he called for the wolf, who came in, wagging his tail with great joy, for he knew that the king had gone for the ring, but did not know whether he had brought it. The wolf kissed the king and stroked him, and when the king saw the wolf fawning so eagerly, he drew the ring out of the bag and showed it to the wolf. Had the king known the virtue of the ring, he might perhaps not have given it to him. But as it was, he took the ring and put it on one of the wolf's toes, and suddenly there stood a naked man before them. When the king saw it, he threw his mantle over him. All the nobles

who were present were frightened, but the king
said: "Fear not, the man who stands here before
you is none else but the wolf." The man rejoiced
greatly and said to the king: "My dear king, I
beg of you to grant me leave to return to my
home, for I have not been home in three or four
years." The king replied: "If it is your wish,
you may go home, but if you desire to remain
here you may stay with me and eat at my table
as long as you live, for I cannot repay you for
the kindness which you have shown me." But
the rabbi preferred to return home. The king
wanted to give him many gifts, but the rabbi
said: "My lord king, you have seen that I have
enough wealth at home, therefore I have no
need of your money. You have done me enough
good in obtaining the ring for me; for if I did
not have my ring, I would have to be a werewolf
all my life." Had the king, however, known the
secret of the ring, he would not have given it to
him so easily, for although the king possessed
many valuable things, nothing would have served
him as well as the ring. The rabbi took provisions for the journey and departed. On the
way he gathered again fifty pupils, dressed them
in black velvet and came back to his town.
When he had come near the town, he said: "I
wish that my wife (may her name be blotted out!)

be turned into a she-ass, standing in the stable and eating out of the trough with the other animals."

In the meantime the shout went up that the rabbi had come home, bringing with him fifty pupils dressed in black velvet. The community went out to meet him and received him with great honor. They would have liked to ask him where he had been all that time, but the rabbi said: "If you wish to be kind to me, do not ask me where I have been or what I have done." The rabbi pretended not to know anything about his wife, although he knew very well that she was in the stable. Accordingly, he asked his household: "Where is my wife? I do not see her, perhaps she does not like to see me bringing again fifty pupils." The people of the household replied: "If it will not frighten you, we will tell you." The rabbi said: "I shall not be frightened." The people of the house replied: "When we heard that you were coming home, we hastened to your wife to tell her the good news, but she disappeared and we do not know what has happened to her." The rabbi did not show any fear and pretended not to know. Then he said: "I believe that when she has been away so long as I, she will come back."

The rabbi resumed his former mode of life,

giving alms to the poor, maintaining a *yeshibah* and doing works of benevolence generally, so that everybody was happy again. After some time, he prepared a great banquet and invited all the people of the town. Being in good spirits, he said: "Now that God has helped me to come home in safety, I have taken a vow that I would build a beautiful synagogue and the she-ass will carry all the stones required for the building." The she-ass was his wife, but the people did not know that he had put such a curse upon her. Then the people replied: "May God give you strength to carry it out quickly in peace and in good health."

The she-ass meanwhile had been feeding and had grown very fat. Like an animal she showed no shame and mated in the open. But when the rabbi began to use her for carrying stones, she became lean again. When the rabbi saw that she refused to move, he kicked her in the side and said: "Oh, you miserable beast, remember the evil you have done to me, may the lightning strike you!" So he kept on using the she-ass very hard until she grew very thin. This went on for a long time and nobody knew what had become of his wife. When he had completed the building of the synagogue, he made again a great banquet and invited all his wife's friends. And when they were draining their cups, the rabbi told them the whole story of how his wife had made him suffer for so long and how the Lord had helped him to recover. "And now," he added, "I have cursed her that she should become a she-ass and remain such all her life."

When her relatives heard this, they became very much frightened, for they felt pity for her, and begged the rabbi to forgive her this time, saying that she would never do it again. But the rabbi would not trust her. Shortly afterwards the rabbi died and left great wealth to his children. The ring disappeared again and the woman remained all her life a she-ass. This is why king Solomon said that one should not confide his secret to his wife, for had he not revealed the secret of the ring to his wife, the rabbi would not have had the misfortune of running around wild in the forest. But he repaid her fully, for many a one digs a pit for others and then falls into it himself.


## 229. The Judgment of Solomon or the Two Mothers

It came to pass in the time of King Solomon that two women gave birth to children in one night. The infants looked so much alike that

they could not be distinguished. On the third
night, one of the women smothered her child to
death. So she slipped quietly out of her bed,
went to the cradle of her companion, took out
the living child, put the dead child in its place
and went back to her bed. The other woman
slept soundly and knew nothing of the whole
affair. When she awoke in the morning to nurse
her child, she found it lying dead in the cradle.
She became frightened, for she knew that her
child had not been ill and suspected that her
friend was responsible. So she ran quickly to
the other woman's bed and said to her: "Let me
look into your cradle and see what child you
have there, for I fear that you took my living
child and put in its stead your child, which you
had smothered." The other woman said: "It is
not true, the child is mine. What business have
you to look into my cradle?" So the two women
quarreled with one another. The one said: "The
living child is mine and the dead is yours,"
and the other said the same. At last they came
to King Solomon and the one complained that
the other had taken the living child and put the
dead one in its place. The other replied: "It is
not true, the living child is mine and the dead
is hers."

When the king heard this, he became very

much frightened, for he was still a young man, not having decided any cases yet, and this, his first case, was so difficult; for one child looked exactly like the other and he could not tell which resembled its mother. So the king said to his servant: "Bring me the executioner." When the executioner came, the young king said to him: "Take your naked sword and cut the two children asunder. We shall then be able to tell which is the real mother, for she will not allow her child to be cut in two; she will take pity on it and her natural feeling will prevent her from allowing such a thing." Then the executioner said to the women: "Come here, both of you, and may God forgive her who is in the wrong, for this is the king's decision: Inasmuch as each of you claims the living child as her own, we cannot tell which one of you speaks the truth and to which of you the child belongs. Therefore the two children will be cut in half and each of you will get half of the living and half of the dead, and you will have no reason to complain, as the one will have as much as the other." When they heard the king's decision, the real mother started crying bitterly: "Do not cut my dear child, I would rather be without it. Give it to the other woman, so that my child may remain alive." But the other woman said: "No!

Let it be cut in two that neither of us should
have the better of the other; the one is as good
as the other." When King Solomon heard that
one of the women was willing to have the
children cut in two and showed no pity for the
living child, while the other had pity and could
not suffer to have it cut up, he knew who the
real mother was and said to the executioner:
"Give the living child to the one who showed
pity, for she is the real mother. The other one
has no pity because it is not her child. She it is
who smothered her own child and took that of
the other. Let her therefore be thrown into the
water." When the woman heard the judgment,
she ran away, and the whole people of Israel
admired the wisdom which the king had shown
in making such a decision.

## 230. Solomon Playing Chess with Benaiah Son of Jehoiada

King Solomon showed also great wisdom on
another occasion. It is well known that King
Solomon invented the game of chess. One day
he played with his first counselor, Benaiah son of
Jehoiada, but the counselor could never win a
game from King Solomon, for the king knew the
game perfectly. Moreover he had invented it

and therefore he knew it better than anyone else. One day, they played again, and King Solomon again had the better of the game and the counselor was almost mated, when suddenly a great shout was heard in the street, as if two people were fighting. Solomon ran to the window and looked out into the street to see what had happened. Meanwhile the counselor took a piece called the knight off the board without Solomon's noticing it, and King Solomon lost the game. This worried him very much, for he did not believe that there was a man in the whole world who could beat him. He thought over the matter again and again to find out how he could have lost the game. He put the pieces back on the board and when he looked over the positions, he saw in his great wisdom that one piece was missing. So he said to himself: "Maybe Benaiah removed a piece while I was looking out of the window into the street and that is why I lost the game." But he thought: "I do not like to suspect Benaiah, and yet I should like to know whether he has done it. I must devise a scheme to make him confess of his own accord." The King went about, seemingly in bad humor, but made no reference to his loss of the game.

One day King Solomon, in his palace, looked out of the window and saw two men going along with sacks on their shoulders, evidently intent on committing a theft in the night, for it was quite late. The king took off his royal garments and put on plain clothes like one of his servants. Running after them, he said to them: "Good evening, dear comrades, I have learnt the trade also. Moreover, I have a few keys which will unlock the king's treasures. I have been thinking about the matter a long time but I dared not undertake the job alone, but if you will follow me we will get rich." The thieves replied: "If you have anything good, we will take care of it and do a good job." So the king said: "Let us wait a little longer till everyone is asleep so that no one may see us." When it was very late, he said: "Now is the time to go." And he led them into a chamber, which they wanted to rob. But the king said: "Not yet, we shall find something better than this." And he led them into a better room, where again they wanted to steal. But the king said: "It is not yet time, I will show you something better and we will get enough without having to carry a heavy load." And he led them into the chamber of precious stones. The king said: "Now is the time. Fill your sacks while I watch and see that no one is coming, so that we may quietly slip away." The fools allowed themselves to be persuaded, thinking it was true and not knowing that it was the king himself, and filled their sacks. Meanwhile the king locked the door and the thieves were trapped. The king went into his bedchamber again, changed his clothes, and told his servants to keep watch, for he had heard thieves in his chamber. "On your life," he said, "take care that they do not get away." And he had them watched all night so that they could not escape.

In the morning the king called the Sanhedrin. His dearest counselor, Benaiah, son of Jehoiada, was among them, and King Solomon sat with them also. Then the king said: "My dear judges, give me a right decision. What is the proper punishment for a man who steals from another, when that other is no ordinary person, but the king himself?" When Benaiah heard the king accusing someone of stealing, he thought the king meant him, for he was afraid that the king had discovered the theft of the piece. So he thought: "If I keep silent until they pronounce judgment, I shall be sentenced. I had better confess and ask forgiveness, in the hope that the king may pardon my offence. I will thus save my life." Thereupon he rose up and fell upon his face and said: "My lord king, I beg your forgiveness, for I must confess that I am the

thief. When we were playing the game of chess
and you looked out of the window, I removed
one of your pieces. I beg of you, therefore, to
spare my life, for I am making a confession."
When the king heard this he laughed, and said:
"My dear Benaiah, I did not mean you and did
not call the meeting of the court on your account.
Your deed I have long forgotten and forgiven.
The reason I called the Sanhedrin together is a
different one. I have two thieves in my chamber
who wanted to rob my most valuable apartment
and I want the decision of the court concerning
them." Thus through his cleverness King Solomon devised a method of discovering whether
Benaiah would confess. And when the king
heard it, he felt very much pleased with his
discovery of what had happened. The decision
of the Sanhedrin was that the thieves should be
hanged. The reason he devised that particular
method was that in case Benaiah had not confessed, the Sanhedrin should not have been
assembled in vain. Hence he contrived the
trapping of the thieves. This shows that King
Solomon was a very wise man and the Bible
says about him that he was the wisest of all
men, wiser even than Adam, who had a great
deal of understanding, for he gave names to

every living creature in accordance with its
nature. But King Solomon was even wiser
than Adam.

### 231. THE DANGER OF TRAVELING IN THE DARK OR THE WISDOM OF R. MEIR

We find it written that a man should always
enter under the sign *ki tob* and leave under the
sign *ki tob*. The meaning of this is that a person
traveling should so arrange his itinerary that he
should reach an inn while it is still day, for the
day is called good (*ki tob*), and should leave the
inn while it is still day, and should not reach
the inn at night nor leave it at night. There
was once an innkeeper who had his house in the
open country, and when people passed who were
too late to reach the town, they were obliged to
spend the night at the inn. When any of the
travelers was about to leave, the innkeeper would
ask him where he was going and what road he
was taking. And when the traveler said to him
that he was going a certain way, the innkeeper
would say: "I am going that way myself tomorrow." About midnight, he would wake up
the traveler and say: "Get up, it will soon be
day." The traveler would get up and go with the
innkeeper, for, in his innocence, he would feel

happy in having a companion on his way through the forest. When the traveler came out of the house he would see it was still dark and remark to the innkeeper about it. And the latter would reply: "We shall get to town so much earlier." As soon as they entered the forest, he would kill the traveler and rob him of his possessions.

Now it so happened once that R. Meir was delayed on his journey and could not reach the town in daylight; and was obliged, therefore, to spend the night in that inn. As R. Meir was sitting at the table and eating his evening meal, the innkeeper came up and asked him where he was going the next morning. R. Meir told him the truth. The innkeeper said: "I am going that way myself tomorrow." R. Meir replied: "I shall be very glad to have company." R. Meir went to sleep; and when it was midnight, the innkeeper came along and woke him up, saying, "Get up, my dear friend, it is quite late and the morning has dawned." R. Meir replied: "I am waiting for my friend, who has not yet arrived; as soon as he comes I will go." An hour later the innkeeper came and woke him again. R. Meir replied: "I am not going yet." An hour later the innkeeper came again and said: "Get up, it is very late." R. Meir replied: "I am not going yet, my friend has not arrived." The innkeeper asked him: "What is the name of your friend and where is he?" R. Meir replied: "His name is Ki Tob." What he meant was: "The day is called *tob* (good) and is the friend of man and accompanies him, but the night is no man's friend; and he refused to go in its company. The innkeeper asked: "Where is Ki Tob?" R. Meir replied: "He lives in the synagogue in my town," meaning thereby that one must first say his morning prayers with prayer-shawl and phylacteries and then start on his journey. The innkeeper went out of the house into the open and shouted: "Ki Tob!" But no one replied. The innkeeper came back and said to R. Meir: "I called Ki Tob, but he does not answer." Meanwhile the day dawned. Then R. Meir said: "Now it is time for me to go, for my friend Ki Tob is here, for the day is called Ki Tob and it has arrived. This is the best friend for a traveler.

Thus R. Meir was saved from the murderous innkeeper because he waited. Had he gone with that murderous man in the night, he would have lost his life (God forbid!). Therefore he said that all travelers should reach an inn in daytime and leave it in daytime, and no harm will befall them.

## 232. Bar Kappara and the Emperor's Son Whom He Saved from Death

Once upon a time there was a rich man called Bar Kappara, who lived in a town situated on the great sea. And he used always to walk along the seashore to pass the time, for he saw the ships coming and going and all sorts of interesting things. One day, as he was taking his usual walk, a ship arrived with many passengers, and when it came close to the shore, it ran upon a rock and foundered. A great cry arose, as can be easily imagined, and all the sailors came out with their boats to save the passengers. Bar Kappara also jumped into a little boat and tried to save whom he could. Seeing a man in the water who was half drowned, he dragged him out, and took him home with him and put him into a warm room where, after getting dry, he recovered his strength, and so his life was saved. When the man came to his senses, Bar Kappara asked him who he was and whence he came. "You must have some merit," he said, "to have survived, when all the others were drowned." The man replied: "I come from Rome. I am of royal lineage, being the Emperor's son." When Bar Kappara heard this, he clothed him from head to foot, for he had lost everything, his servants

and his clothes and his valuables, for the ship
and everything it contained in men and goods
belonged to him. He mourned for his people
bitterly and said: "I should like to return home
to my father, but I do not know how I can do so,
for I have not a single penny and am a stranger
in this land." Bar Kappara said: "Do not worry,
I will see that you return home to your father."
So Bar Kappara thought nothing of it, but went
and bought three horses, hired for him two
servants and gave him enough provisions for the
journey, for he thought: "If he is the man he
says he is, he will surely repay me. Moreover,
he can do good to the Jews, for the majority of
the Jews live under the protection of the Romans
(not to speak of the protection of God)." When
the young emperor saw the great honor Bar
Kappara had shown him and that he lent him
money besides, he wept for joy and said: "My
dear Jew, you saved me from death, you bought
me three horses, hired me two servants and lent
me money besides. The money I can return with
thanks as soon as God helps me to reach home,
for I can well afford it. But I can never in any
manner repay you for the other kindnesses you
have shown me. I hope God will repay you. But
I promise you on my honor that I will remember
them and that the Jews will benefit by your

deed, as long as I live; for if God grant me life, I shall become Emperor of Rome." Then Bar Kappara said to the young emperor: "May God grant you happiness and bliss and may all your wishes be fulfilled. Now go, in God's name, back to your empire." The young emperor kissed Bar Kappara, bade him farewell, and rode with his three horses back to Rome.

When he reached home, he was well received by his father, the Emperor, who asked him what he had done with the rest of his people. Then the son told his father the whole story of what had happened to him on the sea, how he had lost all his possessions and his servants by shipwreck and how a Jew had saved his life and had bought him the horses and hired the servants and lent him money besides. And the prince could not say enough of all the kindnesses which the Jew had shown him. The father shouted for joy at seeing his son alive and well, but he was such a wicked man that he was not pleased with the Jew's kindnesses. So he said to his son: "We have money enough, return your loan to the Jew so that he should not come here, for I do not wish to see his face." Such was the wickedness of the father. And although his son had received many kindnesses from a Jew, he was not pleased and continued to persecute the Jews all the time. The son said to his father: "My beloved father, remember the kindnesses shown me by Jews." But the father—may his name be blotted out!—refused to listen. The Jews, however, did not know that the young king was well disposed towards them.

Accordingly, the young prince sent one of his counselors with three horsemen to Bar Kappara, returning the money which he had lent him and sending him besides a sackful of money, more than one could count, and a letter saying: "Here is the money which you have lent me, but this is nothing compared to the kindness you have shown me by saving my life. It is only a return for the other kindnesses." The four knights came to the town where Bar Kappara lived and went to his house. When he saw them coming, he said to himself: "This is no doubt the money which has come from the young prince." And he paid them all due honors and asked them what they wished. They replied: "Our master, the young prince has sent us to you, and it will give him great pleasure to hear that you are enjoying good health. He sends you his kindest greetings and returns herewith the money which you lent him. He thanks you most sincerely and says that some other time he will discharge his indebtedness to all the Jews. But he would be

pleased to hear from you what interest you
expect on the money which you lent him and he
will gladly pay it." Bar Kappara answered:
"Worthy Sir, the money is a very small amount
and there was no need to go to the trouble of
sending four horses. He could have sent it with
an ordinary messenger." The counselor replied:
"My master, the emperor, cannot thank you
enough," and he pulled out a purse containing
about 20,000 florins of gold and threw it on the
table, saying: "This money has been sent to you
by our master." But Bar Kappara swore that he
would not accept any gift, but only as much as
he had lent the young prince, for he was rich
enough. The prince might give the money to
some poor Jews. The messengers urged Bar
Kappara to accept it, but he absolutely refused.
Then they said: "Our master, the prince, will be
angry with us if we bring back the money, for he
has given us strict injunctions not to bring it
back." But Bar Kappara replied: "I will on no
account take this money." Then Bar Kappara
gave the counselor two golden armlets worth
fifty crowns, and to each of the horsemen he gave
a ring worth four or five crowns. And they
returned home, brought the money back to the
young prince and told him that on no account
would the Jew accept a gift and that he said the

prince might give it to some poor Jews. "Moreover," they said, "see what presents the good Jew has given us." And the counselor showed him the armlets, and the horsemen showed him the rings.

Then the young prince went to his father and said: "Father, see what kind of a Jew he is. Not only did he refuse the presents, but he gave handsome gifts to my servants." And he showed his father the armlets and the gold rings. But the animosity of the father was so great that nothing pleased him and he continued to persecute the Jews, and the young prince could not prevent it. And still the Jews did not know how friendly the young prince felt towards them. In the meantime the Emperor was devising the most refined cruelties and gave orders forbidding circumcision and observance of the Sabbath, and issued other terrible decrees, so as to cause suffering to the poor Jews. When the Jews heard these sad decrees, they wept, put ashes on their heads and did penance. Indeed, they wished for death, for the decrees were so cruel that they could not bear them. They hoped they might be able to alter them by bribery but could not succeed, as the Emperor would not allow any Jew to come before him.

Now this decree was proclaimed far and wide

and reached the ears of Bar Kappara, who thought: "Now the time has come for me to go to Rome, to see the prince. Perchance he will remember the kindness that I have done to him and will intercede with his father in our behalf." So he got himself ready and went to Rome. When he arrived there, the Jews heard that a brave Jew had arrived, who was a great scholar and a wealthy man and had great influence; and that he had come for the purpose of annulling the decree. So the whole community went out to meet him, showed him great honor, and said to him: "Dear Rabbi, if you can do anything to annul the decree, spare no money, for we must call upon the young prince and ask him to persuade his father to remove the decree. There is nothing else we can do." Bar Kappara replied: "My dear friends, if it can be done with the help of God, then you need not worry, for I trust with His help to succeed with the young prince without spending a farthing." Bar Kappara went to the castle of the young prince, dressed in fine robes, so that he was not taken for a Jew, and announced himself as a Jew who wished to speak to his Imperial Highness. When the prince heard that a Jew wished to speak to him, he was afraid, for he knew what would happen, and it made him sad. For he feared that

his father would refuse to listen to him, and yet
he felt it was his duty to influence his father, in
view of the great kindness which the Jew had
shown him. Accordingly he allowed the Jew to
come in and when he saw what a stately man he
was, he was frightened and thought: "Maybe
this is the Jew who saved my life and was so
kind to me." But he did not know him, for the
incident had happened a long time ago. When
the Jew appeared before him, he fell on his knees
and said to him: "Most gracious prince, we
appeal to God and then to you to persuade your
father, the Emperor, to withdraw his decrees.
Remember the kindness which I showed you
when you were in the water." And he began to
weep. When the young emperor realized that
this was the man who had saved his life, he
arose from his throne, raised him up, fell upon
his neck and kissed him and wept with him:
"My dear man, if it is only possible, with the
help of God, to persuade my father, I will
certainly do so; be of good courage." And he
placed the Jew next to him and showed him
honor. But Bar Kappara replied: "I have not
come here for honors, but I beg you to see to it
that the decree be annulled. God Almighty will
surely prolong your life." The young prince
said: "Come again later, and in the meantime I

will speak to my father again." But Bar Kappara
said: "My dear prince, do not forget, for the poor
Jews are in danger of losing their lives in a
miserable manner." The prince said: "I will
leave nothing undone," and he accompanied Bar
Kappara to the door. The latter went back to
the Jews, but did not tell them whether he had
succeeded or not. He merely said that it would
all come out right, and comforted them. He
urged them to continue their pious acts and to do
penance, saying that he would do the same, in
the hope that God would have mercy upon them.
The poor Jews became very frightened, for they
understood from his words that he had not
succeeded and that the evil decree was still in
force.

Meanwhile the young prince went to his father
and invited him to dine with him. The old
Emperor replied: "Certainly, my son, I will come
and dine with you." Whilst the old Emperor
was sitting at table with his son, Bar Kappara
arrived at the gate and asked to see the young
prince. The guardsmen replied: "The prince is
sitting at table." So he offered one of the guards
a beautiful gold ring if he would announce him to
the young emperor. The guard replied: "I would
not do it for any money in the world, for the old
Emperor is dining with the prince, and if I

mentioned a Jew to him, he would take off my
head." So Bar Kappara said: "Well, then, take
this letter to the prince. He will not know what
it is about until he has read it. Then, if he asks
for me, come and tell me; if he does not ask for
me, I will leave." The guard said: "All right, I
will do what you say." Accordingly Bar Kappara
wrote a note and gave it to the guard, who was
anxious to get the gold ring, and he took it to
the young prince. As soon as the prince read the
note, he was frightened and thought: "What
shall I do? If I tell my father about it, he will
leave me. I will follow my impulse and tell the
Jew to come up. When my father sees the Jew
who has been kind to me, he will, for the sake of
his love for me, take pity on the Jews." The same
thought had passed also through the mind of
Bar Kappara, and for that reason he sent the
man to the prince to remind him of the good he
had done to him. The prince said to the guard,
"Let the man come up at once." The guard
wondered what kind of Jew he was that his
master should ask him to come up while he was
dining, but he took the message to Bar Kappara
and told him to come up at once. When Bar
Kappara came into the banqueting hall and
found all the princes seated round the table, he
fell upon his face and began to weep and said:

"Merciful prince, have pity on the poor Jews and annul the decree." When the young prince saw the Jew, he rose from his seat, took him by the hand and seated him by his side at the table, and said: "My dear father, I owe kindness to this Jew, for he is the man who saved my life. We must thank God first and then this Jew for my safety. We are much indebted to him and hence I ask you, dear father, to bear this in mind and to show him honor and to annul the decree against the Jews." And he fell on his knees before his father. When the Emperor saw the Jew, he said to himself: "This Jew has indeed saved my son's life, and if not for him, my kingdom would have passed, after my death, into strange hands, and all my possessions would be lost. I am, therefore, really much indebted to the Jew." So he said to his son: "My dearly beloved son, rise up from the ground, the Jews shall henceforth belong to you to do with them whatever you like and you need not say anything to me about it." Then he took a gold chain and put it round the neck of the Jew, and said: "Take this chain, which I give you, because you saved my son's life." When the son heard this from his father, he rejoiced and said: "My dear sire and father, I accept the Jews under my rule, so that you may have nothing further to do with them." The old Emperor replied: "I make you a present of the Jews to do with them as you like, but do not mention them before me; and show honor to this Jew, for he has done you much kindness." And with these words, the old Emperor left. When he had gone, Bar Kappara declined to take the chain, but the young prince insisted that he keep it. Then the prince and Bar Kappara sat together and called the scribes, and sent messages throughout the whole Roman Empire that the decree which had been promulgated against the Jews was now annulled. "For we realize that it is unjust. Therefore the Jews should not be oppressed, under penalty of death." And then the prince, in the presence of all the ministers, gave new assurances to the Jews, as Bar Kappara had requested him. The prince also told his counselors of the kindness which the Jew had shown him, how he had saved his life, given him money and clothes, and had bought him three horses and hired two servants to bring him home. When the counselors heard this, they said: "Such a man is worthy of all honor."

Then Bar Kappara took all the documents of guaranty, and the prince said to him: "Go and take the joyful news to your brethren and then come back to me, so that we may conclude a proper agreement and take due leave of one another." Bar Kappara went to the Jews and brought them the glad tidings and told them that the evil decree (thank God!) had been withdrawn, and how the Lord, blessed be He, had performed a miracle for him and he had sat at table with the Emperor, who honored him with the gift of a gold chain. Then he brought out the statutes and showed them to them. The Jews greatly rejoiced because Bar Kappara had succeeded so well in their behalf, and made a banquet and rejoiced as on a second Purim.

The prince, meanwhile, after dismissing Bar Kappara, whom he sent to see the Jews, ordered a robe of satin to be made. The following day he sent for Bar Kappara to appear before him. When the Jews heard of this, they were very much alarmed, for they feared that another decree was impending. But Bar Kappara said: "Fear not; I had to promise the prince that I would not depart before I saw him again. Therefore I have no fear as regards the prince. I will arrange everything well." Bar Kappara went to the prince and found him sitting round the table with all his counselors. When the prince saw him, he rose up, took him by the hand and seated him by his side. Then he said: "My dear friend, tell me what you desire, and it shall

be granted." Bar Kappara replied: "I desire
nothing in particular except that I beg you to
keep your protecting hand over my brethren
that no further oppression be their lot, and that
you will bear in mind the kindness which I
showed you." Then the prince gave him assurances again that as long as he and his children's
children lived the Jews would have no _ause for
worry, for it would be entered in the Book of
Records. It was also recorded therein that a
Jew had saved the prince's life, and therefore
the Jews should be kindly treated and, under
penalty of death, no harm should be done to
them. Then the prince ordered the satin robe
to be brought in and asked Bar Kappara to put
it on, and over it a long cloak lined with sable.
He put a gold chain around his neck and caused
him to ride through the streets on a beautiful
horse, accompanied by the sound of trumpets,
and announcement was made: "This is the man
who saved the young emperor's life." They
passed also through the street of the Jews, who
felt very happy when they saw the great honor
that was shown him, and the kindness of the
emperor. At the same time Bar Kappara showed
the Jews the new guaranties, which were much
better than the earlier ones.

The young prince also prepared a banquet of

the finest delicacies in honor of Bar Kappara and
invited his father also, although he was not very
eager to come.   But when he thought of the
kindness which the Jew had shown to his son,
he forgot his enmity and took his place among
his guests and presented Bar Kappara with a
second beautiful chain of gold that had a gold
penny attached.

Bar Kappara found favor in the old Emperor's
eyes, who asked him to stay with him and bring
his wife and children, else all the Jews would
suffer.   Bar Kappara had no choice.   He had a
beautiful residence at home, but he was obliged
to give it up and live with the young prince.
The Emperor gave him a convoy to accompany
him to his home.   When he arrived there safely,
he told his wife and children of the annulment
of the decree, which gave them great joy.   At
the same time they were sorry to leave their
native city.

The old Emperor found time weighing heavy
on his hands while waiting for Bar Kappara,
and he often sent for the Jews to inquire when
Bar Kappara was coming.   Then the news came
that Bar Kappara had arrived.   When the young
prince heard it, he went out to meet him and
received him and his wife and children in fine
style, and insisted that he must live next to the

prince's castle. So the poor Jews fared very well as long as he lived. May we fare as well and better.

## 233. R. ELIEZER BEN SIMEON SUPERINTENDENT OF POLICE

One day Eliezer the son of Simeon was walking along the street and came upon an officer of the Government who was arresting thieves, so he said to him: "Tell me, how do you manage to overcome the thieves, seeing that they are compared to wild animals, and Scripture says about them: 'He conceals himself in his hut and lies in wait against the people in order to rob them'? (cf. Ps. 10.9). It may therefore happen that you may arrest a pious man and allow the thief to go free." The officer replied: "What can I do? It is the order of the Emperor." Then Rabbi Eliezer said to him: "Come, I will teach you how to find the real thieves. Make a round of all the taverns during the fourth hour of the day, the time when people come there to eat. If you find a man asleep over his cup, find out what his occupation is. If he is a student, he has risen before dawn to study and is now drowsy and sleeps at daytime. If he is a workingman, then he worked during the night and sleeps during the day. But if he is neither a student nor a workingman, then surely he is a thief. He did not sleep during the night because he was busy robbing people in the streets and breaking into their houses. Therefore arrest him." The officer went back to the king and narrated to him how R. Eliezer had taught him to detect a thief. The king said: "Since Rabbi Eliezer knows how to detect a thief, let him also be appointed to arrest the thieves." In this way it came about that R. Eliezer was appointed to arrest thieves. When the rabbis heard of this, Rabbi Joshua, son of Korhah, sent word to Rabbi Eliezer and said to him: "You vinegar, son of wine!" He meant to say: "You had excellent parents, but you are good for nothing, because you arrest people and deliver the people of God to the king to be put to death." So Rabbi Eliezer said to Rabbi Joshua: "What am I doing? I am merely weeding out the thorns from God's vineyard, namely the wicked among the Israelites." Then Rabbi Joshua sent word to Rabbi Eliezer and said: "Leave it to God. Let Him kill the wicked Himself. Why should you arrest them? You must not do it." Rabbi Eliezer did not reply.

One day Rabbi Eliezer was met by a washerman, a man who washes clothes for hire, and the

man called him "Vinegar, son of wine," that is,
a wicked son of a righteous father. When Rabbi
Eliezer heard the impudence of the man, he
said to him: "If you speak to me like that, you
are surely a wicked man". And he ordered the
guard to arrest him. So he was taken and put
in prison. Not long after, when Rabbi Eliezer's
anger left him, he regretted that he had put the
man in prison, and went to the king, requesting
him to set the man free. But the king refused.
Then Rabbi Eliezer applied to the washerman
the scriptural verse: "He who keeps his mouth
and tongue from speech keeps his body from
suffering" (Prov. 21.23), i. e. if the man had kept
quiet and not called him a wicked son of a good
father, he would not have been put into prison.
The man was taken out for execution and was
hanged on a gallows. Rabbi Eliezer stood under
the gallows and wept aloud, for he regretted very
much what he had done. But the people said
to him: "Rabbi Eliezer, you need not weep for
the life of this man, for he and his son have
committed fornication on the Day of Atonement
with a virgin who was betrothed to another man.
A man guilty of such a crime deserves to be
stoned to death. Instead of being stoned to
death he has received his merited retribution
from God and was hanged." Then Rabbi

Eliezer put his hand on his belly and said: "Rejoice, my vitals! For seeing that I have been proven to be right in my arrest of this man on suspicion, though I did not know he was a thief, I am surely right, when I know that a man is a thief, in arresting him and handing him over for execution." Then he added: "I trust to God that the worms will not eat my vitals when I lie dead in the grave."

But although he had done right in causing the execution of the washerman, still he was not satisfied in his heart and feared he had not done right. So he went into a marble house where the winds could not reach him and took a sleeping draught. Then he had his body cut open, and a basketful of fat taken out (for he was a very fat man). The fat was kept in the sun during the months of Tammuz and Ab when the sun is hottest, and yet it had no bad odor. This assured him that the worms would not eat his body.

In the Gemara the question is asked: "How could he tell that the worms would not touch him? All that he saw was that the fat did not have a bad odor, but neither would any other fat get a bad odor unless it had flesh in it." The answer in the Gemara is: "There are small veins running through the fat which acquire a bad odor, but in the fat of Rabbi Eliezer the small veins did not acquire a bad odor." Thereupon Rabbi Eliezer quoted the verse: "Even my flesh will rest peacefully in the grave" (Ps. 16.9). The same thing happened to another man called Rabbi Ishmael, son of Rabbi Jose, whose duty it was to arrest thieves. One day the Prophet Elijah met him and said to him: "How long will you continue to do evil and hand over God's people Israel to be put to death by the king?" Rabbi Ishmael replied to the Prophet Elijah: "What can I do? It is the command of the king." Then the prophet said to him: "Your father orders you to run away to a town called Laodicea, where the king will not be able to find you."

The Gemara relates that these two men, R. Eliezer, son of R. Simeon, and R. Ishmael, son of R. Jose, were so fat that when they came up close together and faced each other, a yoke of oxen could pass through under their bellies without touching them. A high-born lady once said to them: "The children your wives have given you are not yours, for you cannot have conjugal relations with them." The rabbis replied: "Our wives' bellies are much fatter than ours." The lady rejoined: "Then I am surely right in saying that the children are not yours."

Then the rabbis said: "Our great love causes our flesh to come close together." The Gemara raises the question: "How is it possible that such worthy rabbis as they were should engage in such talk?" And the Gemara answers the question by saying that they gave the reply which they did so as to prevent slander of their children.

Although R. Eliezer, son of R. Simeon, suffered a great deal when his body was cut open, nevertheless he was still dissatisfied and feared he had done wrong in causing the execution of the washerman and of other people who might have been innocent. So every evening he put poultices on his body, which drew blood and pus; and every morning when he removed the poultices, he filled sixty buckets with blood and pus. Then his wife prepared for him sixty different kinds of food made with figs, which he ate and became well again. His wife would not allow him to go to the *bet ha-midrash*, for she was afraid the rabbis might annoy him.

Every evening R. Eliezer, son of R. Simeon, would say to his sufferings: "Come to me, dear brothers and companions!" And he would endure his sufferings all night, as just described. Every morning he would say to them: "Now, leave me that I may be able to study the Torah, otherwise

you would hinder the study of the Torah."
One day his wife heard him speak to his pains
and invite them to come to him, and she said:
"You are the cause of these sufferings yourself,
for you invite them every night. If you continue
to do it, you will waste all your father's goods on
poultices and sheets." Thereupon his wife went
away and left him alone.

At the same time it happened that sailors came
who brought sixty slaves with them, and the
slaves carried sixty girdles full of gold and gave
them to Rabbi Eliezer. They had been on the
sea, when a heavy storm arose and they prayed
to God to save them for the sake of the merits of
Rabbi Eliezer, and they were saved. When they
landed, they presented the gold to Rabbi Eliezer
because they had been saved from drowning.
And they prepared for him sixty dishes made of
figs, which he ate and became well again. Later
on his wife sent his daughter to see what the
father was doing, for she believed he was still ill,
having eaten nothing, for she had left him and
had not prepared any food. The daughter went
to see what the father was doing, and he said
to her: "Go and tell your mother, our wealth is
greater than hers." And he applied to himself the
words: "The Torah is like the ship of a merchant
which brings its master his food from distant

lands" (cf. Prov. 31.13). "So," he said, "the Torah caused this money to be brought to me from distant lands, for through the merit of my Torah these people were saved from perishing on the high seas, and therefore I received this money. And now I eat and drink and am well again."

Then he went again to the *bet ha-midrash* and sixty samples of menstrual blood were brought before him to decide whether the women were clean or not. He decided that they were and might go to their husbands without taking a ritual bath. When the rabbis heard his decision, they were very angry, for they thought it was impossible that all the women were clean. At least one among them might have been unclean. So they said to R. Eliezer: "How is it possible that not one of the women was unclean?" When Rabbi Eliezer heard this, he said: "If I was right in my decision, all the sixty women will have sons. And if my decision was not right, one of the women will have a daughter." All the women gave birth to sons, and the rabbis saw that his decision was correct, and they called all the children after his name. Rabbi remarked: "How many children in Israel the wicked king destroyed during the time that R. Eliezer was engaged in arresting thieves!" For he was not able to attend the *bet ha-midrash* and the women could not bring to him their menstrual blood.

When the time approached for Rabbi Eliezer to die, he said to his wife: "I know that the rabbis are not well pleased with me. They are angry with me because, as an officer of the law, I captured many thieves, among whom were friends of my neighbors, and they resent it. They may, therefore, not treat me properly after my death. I wish, therefore, that you put my body in the loft; and do not be afraid, for I will do you no harm."

Rabbi Samuel, son of Nahamani, said that the mother of R. Johanan had told him that she had heard it from the wife of Rabbi Eliezer himself, that he had thus lain dead on the loft for twenty-two years, and when his wife came up she pulled out one of his hairs and blood came out, for he had kept as fresh as if he had just died.

One day his wife went up the loft and saw a worm crawling out of his ear. This frightened her because she thought that the body would decompose. But her husband appeared to her in a dream and said: "Do not worry about the worm that crawled out of my ear. It is a punishment for a sin I once committed. I was once present when a scholar was insulted and, though it was in my power to do so, I made no protest.

It is as a punishment for that sin that the worm crawled out of my ear."

While R. Eliezer, son of R. Simeon, was thus lying in the loft, any persons who had a dispute would come before his door and each would present his case. Then a voice would come from the loft saying: "This man is right and the other is wrong;" and the men would then go their way.

One day the wife of R. Eliezer quarreled with her neighbor, who said to her: "May you never come to burial, like your husband." When the rabbis heard this they said: "Now the matter is urgent, for everybody knows that the pious man is dead and has lain so long on the loft without burial. Moreover, it is against the dignity of the pious man to lie so long unburied." Some say that R. Simeon, son of R. Yohai, the father of R. Eliezer, appeared to the rabbis in a dream and said to them: "A dove of mine is among you (meaning his son) and you refuse to send it back to me." When the rabbis heard this, they wanted to bury him, but the people of the town of 'Akbere would not allow them, for their town was near to that in which R. Eliezer lay, and as long as he slept in the loft no wild beast came to their town. Once, on the eve of the Day of Atonement, when the rabbis were very busy, the people of the town sent word to the people of the village of Beri, asking them to come and bury R. Eliezer. They came and put him on the bier and carried him to the cave in which R. Simeon, son of Yohai, was lying. When they came to the cave, they found in front of it a snake as round as a wheel, having his tail in his mouth and refusing to allow any one to enter. Then the people said: "Snake, snake, open your mouth and let the son come to his father." The snake opened his mouth and allowed the people to enter, so that R. Eliezer might be buried by the side of his father, R. Simeon, son of Yohai. This was the same cave in which R. Simeon, son of Yohai, and his son had been hiding.

Rabbi, being unmarried, sent word to the widow of R. Eliezer, asking her if she would marry him. She replied: "A vessel that has been used for purely holy things cannot be used for profane things." For she thought R. Eliezer was such a holy man that Rabbi was unholy compared to him. He was such a great scholar that she could not think of taking a man who was not his equal in scholarship. He replied: "If he was a greater master than I, still in learning and good deeds he was not greater than I." But she refused to marry him all the same.

### 234. WOMEN SHOULD NOT LEAVE THE SYNAGOGUE DURING THE PRAYER OF KEDUSHAH

Once upon a time there lived an old woman, who rose every morning before dawn, went to synagogue and prayed devoutly. She was a very pious woman besides and did many acts of benevolence. After she had died, she appeared to the other women in a dream, and they asked her: "How are they treating you in the other world in reward for your good deeds in this world?" She replied: "They beat me violently every day; and not only that, but wherever pious men and women are sitting together I am driven away from them and not allowed the pleasure of sitting with them."

The reason for this was because during her life in this world she left the synagogue when the *Kedushah* was recited. This was a sin for which she was obliged to suffer in the other world.

### 235. ELIJAH AND THE POOR HASID

Once upon a time there lived a pious man, who was very poor. One day, the Prophet Elijah appeared to him in the guise of a merchant and gave him two coins to engage in business, and he became very rich.   His great wealth, however, and extensive commerce, caused him to forget his goodness and piety.  The Prophet Elijah came to him again and took away the two coins, and the pious man became very poor, having lost all his money.  No one knew where the money had disappeared.  The pious man wept bitterly and grieved for the loss of his wealth.   Then the Prophet Elijah appeared again to the pious man and said to him: "Swear to me that if I return to you the two coins, you will continue to live in piety and not give yourself up to trade." The pious man gave his promise, and Elijah gave him back the two coins, which made him rich again.

The moral is that when God grants a man great riches, he must not turn away from Him, and he will maintain himself in great honor.

### 236. The Man Whose House Was Too Near the Synagogue

Once upon a time there lived a man, whose house was close to the synagogue.  Nevertheless, all his children died and no one knew why.  So he asked a wise man why his children had died, and the latter replied: "Because your house is built higher than the synagogue, making its

windows dark and extinguishing its light. Moreover it is not becoming to indulge in conjugal
love so close to the synagogue." When he heard
this, he thought it would be better to demolish
his house, and he did so. From that time on
he never lost a child.

### 237. R. GAMALIEL AND THE MAN WHO WANTED TO KNOW WHERE GOD DWELLS

One day a man said to Rabbi Gamaliel:
"Where does God live, and what is He?" Rabbi
Gamaliel replied: "I do not know." Then the
man said again: "Is this the wisdom you boast
of? You pray to God every day, and you do
not know where He is." Rabbi Gamaliel replied:
"You ask me a question about a subject which is
a journey of 500 years distant from me. For
that is the distance from heaven to earth. I will
ask you about something that you have with you
day and night, and see if you can tell me where
it is." "What is it?" said the man. "I mean the
soul," said R. Gamaliel, "which God has given
you and which you have with you day and night.
Tell me where it is and in what part of your
body it is." And the man replied: "I do not
know." Rabbi Gamaliel rebuked him and said:

"Shame on you, you frivolous man! I ask you a question about a matter which is near to you and you do not know the answer, and you want me to tell you something that is 500 years' journey from me!"

### 238. THE KING AND THE HAWK

Once upon a time there lived a mighty king who had a number of distinguished counselors and nobles and counts, as is the custom of kings, but they all treated him with contempt and did not pay him the respect due to a king.

Now the king had a young hawk which had been trained for hunting and which was able to catch many birds and hares, as we still find to-day trained hawks, which are very valuable and highly prized. The hawk never left the king, it ate from his hand and it slept in his lap, and the king was very fond of it. In the third year of his kingdom, the king made a banquet on the anniversary of his marriage to the queen and feasted all his lords, knights, counts and charioteers. When they were making merry and drinking with him he called for his hawk, for he was very proud of the bird and valued it highly. Suddenly, as the hawk was sitting there, it saw an eagle, the king of the birds, carrying food to its young. The hawk became excited, flew towards the eagle, caught it and brought it down and cast it at the feet of the king. Then the hawk returned to the king's lap, thinking that he would be very well treated for having caught such a bird. But the hawk did not know that he had done wrong in killing the king of the birds. So when the bird returned again to the king's lap, the king wrung its neck and killed it. The lords wondered very much at the king's action, but no one said anything, though all were very sorry for the bird. The king saw that all his counselors were angry, although they said nothing. So he said: "Do not wonder that I have killed the bird, and do not be displeased thereat, for such is the law of the Torah: If anyone attacks the king he is guilty of death. The eagle is the king of the birds and the hawk killed it, therefore it is right that he should lose his life. The same law applies to every man who despises the king." Then all the people marveled at his wisdom, knowing very well that he had them in mind, and from that time onwards they stood in great awe of him.

## 239. The Sincerity of R. Safra

One day Rab Safra went for a walk in the suburbs with his pupils. He was met by a pious man, a stranger, coming along the road, who thought that Rab Safra had come out to meet him, and did not know that R. Safra had merely gone out for a walk. So he said to him: "Why did you take so much trouble to lower yourself and come out to meet me?" R. Safra replied: "I do not want you to think that I came out specially to meet you. I merely came out with my pupils to take a walk." When the pious man heard this, he was ashamed for having spoken thus before R. Safra and his pupils, for he had really thought that they had come out in his honor. Then the pupils asked R. Safra why he had put the poor man to shame, which is a great sin. R. Safra replied: "Why should I have told him a lie?" The pupils said: "You might have kept silent." R. Safra replied: "If I had kept silent, he would have thought it was true, and I would not have fulfilled the verse: 'Speaketh truth in his heart' (Ps. 15.2), which means: You shall speak with your mouth that which your heart means; whereas I should not have meant what I spoke. Moreover, I should have 'stolen his heart' (cf. Gen. 31.26), i. e. I should

have outwitted him, making him think that I
had come out in his honor.   The name of the
Lord is 'Truth,' and He desires that man should
always speak the truth and never lie.   If men
observe this, the Lord sends rain in its due
season when it is needed, as the Bible says:
'Truth springeth out of the earth' " (Ps. 85.12).
Therefore people should always speak the truth
and never tell lies.

### 240. The Bandit Who Undertook to Speak the Truth

Once upon a time there was a young man who
followed a life of pleasure, eating and drinking
and gambling.   He refused to obey his pious
father and mother and associated with rogues
and thieves.   He lived in their company so long
that he became a greater thief than all his
associates.   After a time he grew tired of his wild
life and began to think: "What will be my end?
What will become of me if I continue the life
of a vagabond and a thief?  In the end I shall lose
my life."   So he said: "I will return from my
evil ways and go back to my father and mother."
And he repented of the evil deeds which he had
done and cried and wept because of his wickedness.   Then he rose up and went to Simeon, son

of Shetah, who was a very good man, and said to him: "Dear Rabbi, I have made up my mind to give up my evil ways and live a good life." Simeon, son of Shetah, replied: "Sit down at my right hand and cease your weeping and sorrow. For I will give you an easy remedy for your illness, which will help you to give up your evil deeds. My son, this is what you must do. Take care that you never under any circumstances tell a lie, and be careful that you do no injustice to anyone. If you abstain from evil and wrongdoing, you will be protected from all harm." The young man replied: "This is a very simple thing, I can easily keep it and I will do so, my dear Rabbi, as you will soon see." Then Simeon, son of Shetah, said: "If you intend to keep your promise, swear to me that you will never tell a lie or do any injustice." He did so and went home. This lasted for a while.

Next to his father's house there lived a widow, who kept a bathhouse where people went to bathe. One day the young man went to this neighbor's house to take a bath, and as he was beginning to undress he noticed in one of the chambers a great quantity of gold and silver and linen. The evil inclination overcame him and he went into the widow's chamber and stole all the silver and the gold and the linen sheets, leaving nothing behind.  When he had gathered the things up and was about to leave the house, he said to himself: "If my neighbor misses her property and raises a hue and cry and asks everyone she meets, she will come to me also and ask me whether I have seen anything. What shall I tell her? If I tell her I do not know, I shall be telling a lie, for I have the stolen property, and will thus be breaking the oath which I made to Simeon, son of Shetah.  I had better replace all the stolen things and take nothing."

Therefore, my dear friends, see what this story teaches.  Because he would not tell a lie, he did not take away the stolen goods; and because he followed the simple advice of R. Simeon, son of Shetah, he obtained the reward of heavenly bliss.

### 241. The Reward of Virtue

A man died, and not long after his death his grave was dug up by workmen in the field, and it was found that he was still alive and that the worms did no harm to his body. So R. Nahman asked him: "What good deed have you done in your lifetime to deserve such a miracle?" And the man replied: "Never in all my life have I envied anyone, and I have always stopped my ears from hearing frivolous talk. Now I am reaping the reward." And when he lies dead in his grave, he will also enjoy this privilege.

## 242. R. AMRAM OF COLOGNE AND THE STORY OF HIS BURIAL IN MAYENCE

The following story quotes some people as saying that it happened in Regensburg. This cannot be true, for from Regensburg to Mayence one must go quite a distance by land as far as the river Rhine, and then go down stream.[*]

Once upon a time there lived in Cologne on the Rhine a man named Rabbi Amram. He had a *Yeshibah* there, but he had come originally from Mayence. When he grew old, he became ill and sent for his pupils and said to them: "My dear young men, I am lying ill and about to die. I therefore ask you to carry me to Mayence and bury me next to my parents." The pupils replied: "Our dear master, we cannot do this, for it is dangerous to take you so far." Then R. Amram said: "When I die, wash the body, put

---

[*] There is no statement in the story that it happened in Regensburg. Obviously that statement was omitted in the Amsterdam edition.

it in a coffin and place it in a small boat on the Rhine and let it go by itself." When R. Amram died, the pupils washed the body, put it in a coffin and placed the coffin in a boat on the Rhine. The little boat went up the stream until it reached Mayence. When the people saw the strange sight of a boat sailing up the stream by itself, they came towards it and, finding a corpse in a coffin, they said: "This must be a holy man, who desires to be buried." But when they went to lay hands on the boat, it slipped away. The Gentiles reported the matter to the Bishop of Mayence, and the whole population came running to the Rhine, Jews and Christians together. When the Jews approached the river bank to see the great miracle, the boat moved towards them. But when the Gentiles tried to take hold of the boat they were not able, for it slipped away each time. At last it became clear that the boat wanted the Jews and not the Gentiles. Then the Gentiles said to the Jews: "Go into the boat and see what is in it." The little boat again approached the Jews, who went into it, opened the coffin and found the corpse, with a letter attached to it, wherein was written as follows: "Dear brethren and friends, Jews of the town of Mayence, know that the reason why I, Amram, have come to you, although I died in Cologne, is because I wish you to bury me next to my parents, who lie buried in Mayence. May you have much peace and long life."

When the Jews had read the letter, they all mourned and brought the coffin on land. The Gentiles attacked the Jews with great ferocity and drove them away, but they could not move the coffin from its place. Thereupon the bishop gave an order to keep watch over it, so as to prevent the Jews from taking it away. Then he built over it a huge church. The Jews begged and entreated for permission to take the body, but it was all in vain. And to this very day the church is called by the name of Amram. Every night R. Amram came to his pupils in a dream and said to them: "Bury me with my parents." When his pupils in Cologne heard this, they grieved very much and went to Mayence. When they reached Mayence, they cut a thief from the gallows, dressed him in a white shroud, took R. Amram's body from the coffin and put that of the thief in its stead, and buried R. Amram next to his parents. God protected the Jews and the matter remained a secret.

### 243. THE REWARD OF BURNING OLIVE OIL

This is about a man who had grown very old and no one could find that he had done any meritorious deed to deserve it except that he used olive oil in his lamp, which is a pious act.

### 244. THE PUNISHMENT OF TOUCHING THE LAMP ON THE SABBATH

Once upon a time a gentile lady died, and as she was about to be buried she came to life again and told the following story: "I have been in the other world and I saw the Jews in paradise, and among them I saw a woman whom I knew and who had one of her hands smeared over with a salve. I said to her: 'My dear woman, why is your hand smeared and no one else's?' Then she told me that she had once touched the candles on Sabbath, and this stigma was put upon her in paradise as a mark of disgrace." Therefore, my dear women, take care to light your Sabbath candles while it is still day, and think of the woman in paradise.

## 245. The Man Who Refused to Allow His Son to Read for the Congregation on the High Holidays

Once upon a time there lived a pious man, who was accustomed to read the prayers on New Year and on the Day of Atonement, the congregation having selected him to do this because he was a very pious man. When he became very old, he refused to read the prayers any more on New Year and the Day of Atonement, and when he was asked: "Why do you refuse to read now, after having read for so many years?" he said: "If I should read now and should die during the year, my son would claim the right to read as my successor, but he is not yet worthy to read the prayers on such holy days; therefore I will invite some one else to do the reading." And he appointed a man who was pious and wise and learned and worthy of the office.

The old man was so good that he did not want his son to succeed him in the office. For this was the reason why Eli the priest was punished, namely because, knowing that his sons were not pious, he did not rebuke them. He should have removed them from the priesthood and put others in their place, but he did not do so. Therefore he fell from his chair and broke his neck (cf. I Sam. 4.18). Therefore only old and pious men should be appointed to recite prayers on New Year and the Day of Atonement, for they know what the prayers mean.

## 246. Story of R. Matya ben Harash Who Burned Out His Eyes to Escape from Sin

Once upon a time there lived a very pious man, R. Matya, son of Harash, who was very handsome and had never looked at any woman except his own wife. One day, Satan passed by and became envious of R. Matya because he had never committed a sin. Satan thought it was impossible for a man to be without sin. Accordingly Satan went to God and said: "Lord of the universe, what is R. Matya, son of Harash, in your sight?" And God answered: "R. Matya is a very pious man." Then Satan said: "Give me permission and I will make him sin." But God said: "You will not be able to make him sin." Satan said: "Give me permission." And God gave him permission. Then Satan took the form of a beautiful woman, the like of whom was not to be seen at that time, and placed himself in front of R. Matya, son of Harash, who, when he saw her, turned away. Then Satan went over and stood facing him on the other side, and again R. Matya turned around. And whichever way he turned Satan turned also, hoping that the pious man would conceive a desire for her. Then R. Matya said: "I am afraid my evil inclination will overcome me and incite me to sin." What did the pious man do? He called one of his pupils and told him to bring him some live coals. When the pupil brought the coals, the pious man burnt his eyes out with them. When Satan saw this, he was very much frightened, for he had hoped that he would cause him to sin. Then God called the angel Raphael and said: "Go down and heal R. Matya, son of Harash." So the angel Raphael went down to R. Matya and said to him: "The Lord has sent me to heal you." R. Matya replied: "I do not wish it. What has happened has happened." The angel Raphael went back to God and said to Him: "R. Matya refuses to be healed." But God said: "Go to him and tell him that I assure him that no evil passion will have power over him." Then he allowed himself to be healed and God prolonged his life.

## 247. The Man Who Studied Nothing except the Treatise Hagigah

Once upon a time there lived a man, who during his whole life studied nothing but the treatise of Hagigah. When the man died and was about to be buried, a woman dressed in white came up to the corpse and stood in front of it. When the people saw her, they asked her who she was and what was her name. And she replied: "I am Hagigah and I am praying for this man in the other world, for he studied nothing but the treatise Hagigah all his life, and therefore he deserves that I should plead for him in the other world." In the same way all other good deeds which a man performs in this life plead for him in the world to come.

## 248. The Black King and Queen Who Had a Child That Was White

Once upon a time there lived a heathen king and a queen who were both black, and the queen bore a child which was quite white. So the king sent for Rabbi Akiba and said to him: "I and my wife are both black and yet she has born a child which is white. I will put the queen to death, for she must have been unfaithful to me with a white man." Then R. Akiba said: "Do not be in a hurry and let me ask you a question. Are the walls of your palace and the pictures painted on them white or black?" The king replied: "They are white." Then R. Akiba said: "Then your child has to be white, also. The white pictures made an impression upon your wife and therefore your child is white, for the child resembles the object to which the wife directs her attention, as we find in the story of Jacob. He put white and black rods by the troughs from which the sheep drank. They became frightened and bore speckled sheep." When the king heard this, he wondered at R. Akiba's wisdom.

Therefore every woman should have pious thoughts and she will have pious children in accordance with her thoughts.

## 249. THE OLD MAN WHO COULD NOT ABSTAIN FROM WINE

Once upon a time there lived a man who was fond of drinking wine. He had four sons, and each day one of his sons fed him, and the old man became drunk every day. One day he went out for a walk in the street and he saw a drunkard wallowing in the mud and doing all sorts of foolish antics, whilst the boys ran after him and threw stones at him. When the drunkard became sober again, the old man went up to him and asked him where he had gotten such good wine. He told him, and the old man went there and drank a great deal more than he usually did. His children, fearing that he might also demean himself and behave foolishly, went, all four of them, to the inn and took him home and put him in the cellar and locked the door, so that he should not be able to get out. After a while they went into the cellar to see what their father was doing, and they found him lying asleep on the floor with his mouth wide open and the wine running out of his throat. Then they said: "It is clear that he will not give up drinking," and they gave him all the wine he desired until he became very old and was too weak to live.*

* This story is a variant of a familiar one in which the father is carried by the children to the cemetery in a drunken state. Later they go in search of him and find him again very drunk, as it happens that an innkeeper had made a cellar in the corner of the field and the old man had found it and had drunk his fill. When the children saw this they said: "If he can find wine even in the cemetery, we had better take him home and let him drink as much as he pleases until the end of his days."

## 250. STORY OF THE WICKED KING FREDERICK WHO BEGUILED ELEVEN OF THE WISEST SAGES OF ISRAEL TO DRINK WINE WITH HIM

Once upon a time there lived a king, a mighty ruler over many lands, who was a great enemy of the Jews, and his name was Frandik (Frederick). One day he summoned all his counselors and wise men, and he summoned also eleven of the wisest scholars of the Jews to appear before him. As soon as the latter could be seen from a distance, the king and his counselors rose up and went to meet them, and received them with great honor. And the wise men wondered very much at the honor paid to them. Then the king said to them: "I love you as the apple of my eye, and I have three requests to make of you, one of which you must do, namely, you must either eat swine's flesh with me or drink wine with me, or lie with a Christian woman. You must choose one of these three courses, and by so doing you will pay me great honor, and you will find favor in my eyes." When the men heard this, they were very much frightened, and after thinking over the matter, one of them rose up, bowed before the king and, with tears in his eyes, said: "Give us three days' time and we will search in our books to see which is the best course." The

king replied: "The three days are granted." The
eleven wise men departed and debated with each
other what they should do. They finally decided
that they would drink the wine, saying that
although it is a custom, handed down by our
ancestors, not to drink wine prepared by Gentiles, yet they did not teach us that no good can
come from drinking it.

So they came to the king and said: "Our lord
the king, we have decided to spend the whole
day with you, drinking at your table." When
the wicked king heard this, he was very glad,
for he thought: "I will also make them eat
swine's flesh and commit the sin of fornication."
So the king said to them: "Order some meat
to be prepared that you are allowed to eat, so
that you may not have to eat our food." Then
he made a round table that could be revolved
slowly. In the meantime the banquet was set.
The Jewish scholars came in, and *kasher* food was
brought for them and placed on the king's table.
The king and all the lords sat together and the
eleven wise men also sat together. Before them
were all kinds of delicacies and the choicest
malmsey wine. And they all ate and drank
together, and the king carried on long conversa-
tions with them. When the king saw that they
were beginning to be filled up with wine, he

turned the table very gently so that they did not notice it. The forbidden food came in front of them, and they filled their bellies with swine's flesh. What did the king do next? He put the *kasher* food away carefully to show it to them on the morrow. When night came, he ordered beautiful beds of gold and silver to be prepared and a harlot to be placed in each one. Being very drunk, they thought the women were their wives. In the morning, the king rose early, came to their beds and said to them: "My dear friends, arise and say your prayers, for you have committed very grave sins. You ate pork of your own free will, leaving your *kasher* meat uneaten, and you committed fornication." When they saw the unclean women in their beds, they did not know how it happened, but soon realized that the king had done it intentionally. Then they repented deeply of the sins they had committed and wished they were dead. Their wish was realized and they all died an unnatural death the same year.

And all this happened to them because they had drunk of the forbidden wine. This is why the Torah has placed together the section dealing with the adulterous woman and that which treats of the Nazirite (cf. Num. 5.11–21; 6.1–21). Therefore, my dear friends, take example from this story and see how forbidden wine leads to an evil death. It is best, therefore, to keep away from much wine and thus avoid great pain.

## 251. STORY OF A MAN WHO RODE ALONE AT NIGHT AND SAW A WHOLE ARMY OF DEAD PEOPLE PULLING WAGONS FULL OF OTHER DEAD PEOPLE

One night, when the moon was shining brightly, a man was riding alone in the desert. Suddenly he saw a great number of carts full of dead people. Very much astonished, the man drew near and recognized among them a number of people who had died long ago. Then he asked these people: "Why must you draw the carts the whole night, while some of you are sitting inside?" And they said: "These carts are filled with the sins committed by us in our lifetime. We have been very free with women, therefore we must drag these carts along until we get very tired. Then they get out and we get in, and they drag the carts along until they get tired, and this continues the whole night long. There are persons appointed to beat us like beasts, while we drag the carts. For a man is punished in the other world for every sin he commits."

Therefore one should beware of committing sins.

## 252. The Dead Man Who Was Driven around a Field Which He Had Unjustly Appropriated in Life

Once upon a time a man lost his way in the great forest. In the bright moonlight, he saw a man whom he knew to be dead a long time. When he wanted to run away, the dead man called out: "Be not afraid of me, I will do you no harm," and he made himself known to him. The man said: "You have been dead so long, what are you doing here?" And the dead man said: "I will tell you. Because I took this field away by force from its owner, I have no peace, for I am driven all night long round it."

## 253. The Dead Man Who Accosted His Servant in the Field

Once upon a time a servant of a Gentile long dead was walking in the field and saw his master sitting there. The servant wanted to run away, but his master called to him and said: "Come here and fear not." The servant came to him and asked him: "What are you doing here?" The master replied: "They are driving me all over this field because I took it away by force from its owner." And he mentioned the name.

"Therefore go to my wife and tell her to return the field to him." The servant said: "Your wife will not believe me." He replied: "As a sign of the truth, let my wife come here tomorrow morning and she will find me sitting by the tree yonder." The servant told his mistress, and she said: "Did he give you a sign?" And the servant said: "Yes, tomorrow morning you will find him sitting under a tree." All his people went to the field and found him sitting there. Then they went to the cemetery and opened his grave, but found it empty. So they returned the field to the man from whom it had been taken.

## 254. The Man Whose Library Passed into Strange Hands after His Death Because He Refused to Lend His Books While He Lived

Once upon a time a pious man died and left very beautiful books behind, which the heirs sold to strange people. And the pious people grieved very much when they saw that the children had sold their father's books to strangers.

Now in that town there lived a great scholar, and he said to them: "Do not grieve that these books are going into strange hands, I will explain to you the reason. It is a punishment because he would not lend any of his books, for he used to say: 'I am an old man, the writing of the manuscript might get faded and I shall not be able to read it. Moreover, they destroy my books. Therefore I will not lend them'." One must not do so; for as a punishment for refusing to lend his books, they got into strange hands.

End.

Praise to God Almighty.

# APPENDIX

The following additional tales are taken from the Basle edition. 242 is a doublet of 5; 245 is a longer version of 126, while 182 is not found at all in the Amsterdam edition. Thus the Basle edition has 257 stories, for the most part in the same order as the Amsterdam edition except the following: Basle (B.) 158 = Amsterdam (A.) 183; B. 158 *bis* = A. 167; B. 163 = A. 169; B. 164 = A. 170; B. 165 = A 162; B. 166 = A. 168; B. 167 = A 163; B. 168 = A. 164; B. 169 = A. 165; B. 170 = A. 166.

## 182

One day R. Samuel the Pious walked across the fields in the company of two other men. Suddenly he saw the heaven opening, whereupon he said to his companions: "I see that the heaven is open. This is a good opportunity. If you prefer a petition to God at this moment, it will be granted." Accordingly all the three made their requests. One asked for handsome children; the other asked for wealth; while the pious man himself asked God to give him children (for he had not had any) who would be learned in the Torah. All their requests were granted, and when the pious man came home, his wife conceived and bore a son named R. Abraham.

Later she gave birth to Rabbi Judah the Pious. May the Lord permit us to participate in his merit. Amen. Selah.

## 242

One day the daughter of the Emperor asked Rabbi Joshua son of Hananiah: "Why is it that the food you cook for the Sabbath has a better flavor than that which you cook during the week?" He replied: "We have a spice which we put into the Sabbath food, and which gives it so good a flavor." Said the Emperor: "Give me some of the spice." R. Joshua replied: "If one observes the Sabbath, the food smells good to him, but if one does not observe the Sabbath, the food does not smell good to him. Therefore it would do you no good even though I gave you of the spice." And in this way he put him off. The moral is that one should honor the Sabbath with food and it will smell good.

## 245

Turnus Rufus the Wicked once asked Rabbi Akiba on a Sabbath day: "Tell me, my friend, why is this day any better than any other day?" Said R. Akiba to him: "My dear friend, why are

you any better than any other man?" Turnus
Rufus the Wicked replied: "What did I say to
you and what did you say to me?" Said R.
Akiba: "You said to me why is this day better
than another day and I replied why is Turnus
Rufus better than another man." Then the
wicked man said: "I am a king over all kings
and desire to be honored." Said R. Akiba:
"God is a King over all kings, Israel is His
holy people, and He desires that Israel shall
honor the Sabbath." Then the wicked man
said: "If God desires that Israel should honor
the Sabbath and do no work thereon, why does
He work Himself?" "What work does He do?"
asked R. Akiba. The wicked man replied: "He
sends rain and wind on Sabbath, and this is
work." R. Akiba replied: "It may be that He
sends rain and wind on the Sabbath, nevertheless
He desires that we should honor the Sabbath and
not do any work thereon. The work which God
Himself does on the Sabbath, He may do. For
I will tell you, Emperor. If two men live in one
court and one of them makes an *'erub*,* the other
is not required to make one and both of them
may carry things within the court, though other-

* A rabbinical device in the nature of a legal fiction to
evade the prohibition to carry articles on the Sabbath
outside of one's private precincts.

wise each of the two would make it unlawful for the other one to carry. But if a man lives by himself in a court, then though it were as large as the city of Antioch, he requires no 'erub because there is no other person to share the premises with him and make it unlawful for him to carry. Now God, may His name and remembrance be blessed for ever and ever, of whom the Bible says: 'The heavens are His throne and the earth His footstool and the whole earth is full of His glory' (Isa. 66.1; 6.3), who shares nothing with any one else, He may send rain and wind in the world, but nevertheless He desires that Israel shall keep the day holy. This can be seen from the holy manna which fell in the wilderness during the week but not on the Sabbath. A still greater proof of the holiness of the day is the river Sambation, which surges and storms and throws up stones the whole week, but on the Sabbath day it is quiet and still and does not throw up any stones. I have one more proof that God desires we should rest on the Sabbath. Smoke comes out of your father's grave during the week, but on the Sabbath there is quiet in your father's grave and no smoke comes out." Turnus Rufus departed to investigate the matter and found that R. Akiba was right.

# NOTES

# NOTES

A good deal of the material in the Notes, especially with regard to the sources of the later stories, so far as they are not indicated in Gaster's *Exempla*, was furnished by Professor Louis Ginzberg.

The figures refer to the stories.

1. Shab. 13a–b.
2. Shab. 89a.
3. Shab. 88b.

P. 4, l. 21. *974 generations*] The verse in Ps. 100.8: "The word which He commanded to a thousand generations," is interpreted by the rabbis as meaning that God's original intention was not to reveal the Law until a thousand generations of men had passed. But reflecting that humanity could not endure so long without the Law, He delayed the creation of man 974 generations and revealed the Law to Moses, 26 generations after Adam.

P. 4, l. 23. *Give Thy beauty to the heavens*] Intended as a translation of Ps. 8.2. J. P. S. version: whose majesty is rehearsed above the heavens.

4. Shab. 89b.
5. Shab. 119a.
6. Shab. 119a. For parallels see Gaster, *Exempla*, p. 210, no. 118; p. 253, no. 380.
7. Shab. 119b. For parallels see Gaster, *Exempla*, p. 210, no. 119.
8. Shab. 150b. For parallels see Gaster, l. c., p. 210, no. 117.

9. Shab. 153a.

P. 16, l. 13. *The rabbis*] M. B. פסוק, normally applied to the Bible. The reference here is to Mishna Abot, 2.10.

10. Shab. 53b.

11. Shab. 53b.

12. Shab. 31a. For parallels see Gaster, l. c., p. 202, no. 84.

P. 19, l. 3. *wise men*] Talmud, more aptly, "because their midwives lack skill."

13. Shab. 31a. For parallels see Gaster, l. c., p. 191, no. 30.

14. Shab. 31a.

15. Shab. 31a. For parallels see Gaster, l. c., p. 192, no. 31.

16. Shab. 33b. For parallels see Gaster, l. c., p. 225, no. 206.

P. 29, l. 27. *author of* . . . . *Zohar*] This statement is of course not in the Talmud.

17. Shab. 30a. *M. B.* erroneously names the chapter in Shab. where this story occurs as *Ha-Shoel*. It should be *Bammah Madlikin*.

18. Shab. 130a. *M. B.* erroneously gives the source of the story as Shab. ch. *Mefannin*. The story occurs in ch. *R. Eliezer*.

P. 31, l. 22. *One of the officers*] The Talmud has קסדור = quaestor, military adjutant, inquisitor.

19. Shab. 127b. For parallels see Gaster, l. c., p. 201, no. 79.

20. Shab. 127b. For parallels see Gaster, l. c., p. 201, no. 80.

21. Shab. 127b. For parallels see Gaster, l. c., p. 201, no. 80. At the end of this story *M. B.* has סליק מסכת שבת.

22. Ta'an. 7a. *M. B.* erroneously gives the source as Ber. ch. 1.

23. Ber. 5b. For parallels see Gaster, l. c., p. 227, no. 223.

24. Ber. 5b. For parallels see Gaster, l. c., p. 212, no. 133.

25. Ber. 5b. For parallels see Gaster, l. c., p. 222, no. 177.

P. 42, l. 14. *nephew*] In the talmudic source it says brother, but it refers to the variant R. Judah instead of R. Ada.

P. 43, l. 3. *I am ready to take an oath . . .*] *M. B.* deviates in certain details from the source. "*Auch will ich mekabel auf mich sein dass ich ihnen ihr Lohn gegeben hab*" (*M. B.* 7a), is evidently a peculiar sentence due to a misunderstanding of the original, which reads קבילנא עלי דיהיבנא ליה, "I promise that I will pay him," R. Huna having admitted that he had not paid his field laborer, whom he suspected of stealing more than his share. In *M. B.* R. Huna denies the charge.

26. Ber. 3a.

27. Ber. 6a.

28. Ber. 56a. For parallels see Gaster, l. c., p. 226, no. 215.

29. Ber. 61b.

30. Yer. Terumot 8.5, f. 40c, ed. princeps; very likely *M. B.* took it from *'En Ya'akob*, supplement.

P. 52, l. 20. *bury him*] The question was whether the butcher who had fallen from the roof shortly before the coming in of the Sabbath, should be buried immediately or should be left where he was until after the Sabbath, though his corpse was exposed to the dogs.

31. Git. 35a. *M. B.* has erroneously מסכת שבת פרק השואל. For parallels see Gaster, l. c., p. 211, no. 122. The story in the original is different. The woman herself put the coin into the jar of flour.

32. Sanh. 37b.

33. 'Ab. Zarah 10b. For parallels see Gaster, l. c., p. 218, no. 149.

P. 57, l. 21. *Severus*] *M. B.* reads אסורנים (Basle ed. אסוירונס); talmudic source has אסוירוס, probably Alexander Severus, Roman emperor.

34. 'Ab. Zarah 10b.

P. 58, l. 14. The biblical verse reads: "As the four winds of the heaven I scattered you."

35. Ta'an. 24b. For parallels see Gaster, l. c., p. 221, no. 163; p. 260, no. 409. The story in *M. B.* omits an expression here and there of the original, thus making the narrative less logical. *M. B.* has four and three legs, Talmud has three and two legs respectively.

36. Ta'an. 25a. For parallels see Gaster, l. c., p. 221, no. 163.

37. Ta'an. 25a.

38. 'Ab. Zarah 11a. For parallels see Gaster, l. c., p. 233, no. 284.

P. 64, l. 2. *Kalonika*] Talmud has Kalonymos. *M. B.* abridges the story somewhat.

Ib. l. 17. *torch*] *M. B.* שטאל קארץ. Pappenheim has "Stallkerz." It is intended as a translation of נורא in the talmudic original.

P. 64, l. 24. The verse in the Psalms reads: "thy going out and thy coming in."

39. Ta'an. 21b. For parallels see Gaster, l. c., p. 261, no. 413.

P. 66, l. 25. *I will buy them willingly* . . .] Talmud has בהני שקלינהו, which means: "This is what I paid for them." This makes better sense.

40. Ta'an. 24a.

P. 67, l. 21. *Yokreh*] Talmud has יוקרת, but the correct

reading is ידקרת = Yodḳart. See Malter, *Ta'anit* (Schiff Library of Jewish Classics), p. 177; id. *The Treatise Ta'anit* (Publications of the Amer. Acad. for Jewish Research), p. 103.

P. 68, l. 1. *How can I show pity . . .*] Talmud has: "How can a man who had no pity for his own son and daughter have pity for me?"

41. Ta'an. 24a.

42. Ta'an. 24a. For parallels see Gaster, l. c., p. 263, no. 417.

43. Ta'an. 22a. For parallels see Gaster, l. c., p. 260, nos. 405 and 406.

P. 72, l. 14. *Khuza*] *M. B.* has חוזאי; Talmud חוזאה. See Malter, l. c., p. 158. Rashi says מבי חוזאי.

44. Ta'an. 21a.

P. 73, l. 10. *my bed*] Amsterdam ed. of *M. B.* has איין בעט. Basle ed. more correctly has מיין, which corresponds to the talmudic reading פורייאי and makes better sense.

45. Ta'an. 20b.

46. Ta'an. 20b.

P. 77, l. 10. *golden chair*] Talmud has נוהרקא = carriage.

47. 'Ab. Zarah 18a. For parallels see Gaster, l. c., p. 234, no. 292.

P. 79, l. 20. *who is mentioned . . .*] *M. B.* has: "*der im Hurban* (destruction of the Temple) *steht.*"

P. 82, l. 25. *commentary*] Rashi gives the story, which is merely alluded to in the Talmud. Beruriah, wife of R. Meir, protested against the statement of the rabbis that women have not stability of character. R. Meir insisted on the truth of the statement, and to prove it persuaded one of his pupils to make an effort to seduce her. She finally consented and, realizing what she had done, she committed suicide. R. Meir could not stand the disgrace and went to Babylon.

48. Sanh. 39a. For parallels see Gaster, l. c., p. 196, no. 55.

P. 83, l. 3. *Emperor*] *M. B.* has קיסר: Talmud has כופר = heretic, unbeliever.

49. Sanh. 39a.

50. Sanh. 39a.

P. 85, l. 14. *Emperor*] *M. B.* קיסר: Talmud כופר, as in story 48, q. v.

51. Sanh. 90b.

P. 87. *M. B.* seems to have misunderstood the point of the daughter's logic if Rashi is right. According to Rashi the point is that God makes man (not Adam) out of water (טפה סרוחה), hence He can surely make him again out of clay or earth. The talmudic story is very succinct.

52. Ta'an. 23a. For parallels see Gaster, l. c., p. 264, no. 422.

P. 87, l. 22. *bake a cake*] Talmud has עג עונה = drew a circle. Rashi says: שורה עגולה כמו עונה שהיא עגולה. *M. B.* evidently misunderstood his text and took עונה literally.

P. 89, l. 14. *for the good of the greatest number*] Another instance of misunderstanding of his source on the part of the author of *M. B.* Talmud has שאין מתפללין על רוב הטובה, which means: "it is not proper to pray for the cessation of too much good."

P. 90, l. 14. *weakened*] Talmud has מתחלל = profaned.

Ib., l. 17. *even though the son has sinned*] *M. B.* again misunderstood a word in his source. מתחטא does not mean "to have one's sin forgiven," but "to act petulantly."

53. Ta'an. 23a. For parallels see Gaster, l. c., p. 264, no. 422.

54. Ḥul. 7a. For parallels see Gaster, l. c., p. 212, no. 128; p. 243, no. 331.

P. 97, l. 5. *cut off their hoofs*] Talmud has קטילנא להו = I will kill them.

55 (erroneously numbered in *M. B.*, 58). Yer. Shek. 5.1, fol. 48d = Bab. 18b. *M. B.* no doubt took it from *'En Ya'akob*, whose explanations of the laconic text are woven into the story. For parallels see Gaster, l. c., p. 228, no. 235.

56. Ḥul. 59b. For parallels see Gaster, l. c., p. 187, no. 7.

57. Ḥul. 59b. For parallels see Gaster, l. c., p. 187, no. 9.

58. Ḥul. 60a. For parallels see Gaster, l. c., p. 187, no. 8.

59. Ḥul. 60a. For parallels see Gaster, l. c., p. 187, no. 10.

60. Ḥul. 105b.

61. Ḥul. 105b.

62. Ḥul. 105b.

P. 105, l. 14. *three things*] This statement in the Amsterdam ed. makes no sense, as no three things have been mentioned. The talmudic source mentions three things of which the two rabbis were careful, two of which are omitted in this edition, no doubt for elegance' sake, but the conclusion was retained with the number three in it. This is due to the fact that the Basle edition has all the three mentioned in the Talmud as well as the concluding admonition, which is not in the Talmud.

63. Ḥul. 105b.

64. Yoma 35b. For parallels see Gaster, l. c., p. 203, no. 91.

P. 107, l. 4, *the rich and the poor*] Talmud has עני, עשיר, ורשע. The wicked (רשע) must have fallen out in *M. B.* (Basle ed. same as Amsterdam), for at the end of the story the רשע is mentioned.

P. 107, l. 25. *winter*] *M. B.* has תקופת טבת, which denotes the winter solstice.

65 (erroneously numbered in *M. B.*, 68). Git. 47a. *M. B.*

erroneously indicates the talmudic chapter as *ha-Nizaķin.*
It should be *ha-Sholeaḥ.*

66. B. M. 84a. For parallels see Gaster, l. c., p. 227,
no. 224.

P. 114, l. 8. *and followed them up with* . . .] Talmud has
ומפריקנא ליה עשרין וארבעה פירוקי = "I answered him," not
"he answered."

Ib., l. 12. *How then can I know* . . .] Seems like a
misunderstanding of the source. Talmud has אטו לא ידענא
דשפיר קאמינא = "Do I not know that my statement is
correct?" In other words R. Johanan had no doubt he
was right, but he wanted an opponent to sharpen his mind.
From *M. B.* we get the impression that since R. Eliezer
ben Pedat always sided with him, R. Johanan was not
sure of his position. Amsterdam ed. has: *"weiss ich denn
ob ich den peshat* (interpretation) *recht sag."* Basle ed.
has: *"weiss ich dass ich den peshat recht sag."*

67. Ket. 66b. For parallels see Gaster, l. c., p. 213,
no. 135.

P. 116, l. 14. *according . . . the camel eats* . . .] Talmud
has simply לפום גמלא שיחנא = "as the camel so is his load."
*M. B.* evidently took the word פום (= mouth) literally,
according to the camel's mouth so is his load. Rödelheim
ed. (R) has *ist* instead of *esst* (עסט). See Grünbaum,
*Jüdisch-deutsche Chrestomathie,* p. 397.

P. 116, l. 20. *As surely as I should like* . . .] *M. B.*
אזוי וואר זאל איך זעהן . . . דאז איך דיא זעלביני פרוי . . . , which
means literally: "May I so surely see the rebuilding of
Zion as I am sure that I saw the woman . . ." It is really
a form of oath.

68. Ket. 62b. For parallels see Gaster, l. c., p. 217,
no. 148.

69. Ned. 50a. For parallels see Gaster, l. c., p. 217,
no. 148.

P. 120, l. 11. *mattresses*] *M. B.* טפּילבֿן; Pappenheim, *Pfühlben.*

Ib., l. 11. *She combed the straw*] Talmud has הוה קא מנקיט; R. Nissim: משׁערותיה; היה מלקט התבן משׂערו; Rashi: ליה תיבנא.

Ib., l. 14. *a golden bodice . . .*] *M. B.* נילדן לייבלן. Talmud ירושלים של has רמינא ליך ירושלים דדהבא. Rashi explains תכשׁיט של; R. Nissim: זהב, בתי נפשׁ שׁמצויירות בכל עניני ירושלים זהב שׁירושׁלים מצוייר בה.

Ib., l. 17. *ordinary person*] *M. B.* שלעכטער מאן. זונשׁט איין שׁלעכטער = *schlichter.* Talmud אידמא להון כאנשׁא. שׁלעכטער

P. 121. The story is slightly different in the Talmud, details being left out in *M. B.*, which refers to the same story in no. 68.

70. Ned. 50a.

P. 122, l. 5. *a large piece of wood*] Talmud גווזא. Rashi תיבה, so R. Nissim. Jastrow, *Talmudic Lexicon*, p. 219, s. v. גווזא I, trunk, stem.

This story in *M. B.* is a combination of the talmudic text and the commentaries of Rashi and R. Nissim (ר'ן). The stories of the Roman *matrona* and of Turnus Rufus are only alluded to in the talmudic text, the details being supplied in Rashi and R. Nissim without giving the sources.

P. 124, l. 1. *disputing*] *M. B.* מפקיח זיין, evidently a mistake for מקפח, which occurs in R. Nissim's account of the story: שׁהיה ר' עקיבא מקפחו בקראי. The same word מפקיח occurs in *M. B.* in the same sense a few lines below.

P. 125, l. 1. *in a previous story*] see no. 34.

71. Ned. 50b.

P. 125, l. 14. *four shillings*] Amsterdam ed. of *M. B.* erroneously reads פיל (= many) instead of פיר (= four) of the Basle ed., which is correct and corresponds to the talmudic reading.

72. Ned. 62a. For parallels see Gaster, l. c., p. 205, no. 109.

73. Ket. 62b.

P. 128, l. 12. *sifting*] M. B. Amsterdam ed. בייטלט, Basle ed. רעדיד.

74. Ket. 62b.

P. 128, l. 25. *Hakinai*] Talmud has בן חכינאי, son of Hakinai, which is correct, since the reference is to Hananiah.

75. Meg. 27b. For parallels see Gaster, l. c., p. 260, no. 408.

76. Meg. 27b.

P. 130, l. 21. *Rab 'Anan*] Tal. has Rab, and M. B. in the sequel also has Rab. R. Joseph and R. Johanan and R. 'Anan are not in the talmudic text. Where did M. B. find them?

77. 'Er. 21b. For parallels see Gaster, l. c., p. 220, no. 160.

P. 131, l. 25. *ha-Garsi*] The explanations of the name are taken from Rashi.

78. Ned. 49b.

P. 134, l. 5. *See how much . . .*] Talmud slightly different. He said to the man who brought him the garment, "See how much money I have here, but I do not like to have enjoyment in this world." חזי מאי איכא מיהו לא ניחא לי דאיתהני בהדין עלמא.

79. Giṭ. 7a. In the Talmud the story is told without any detail, and the name is Ḥanina b. Gamaliel and not Ḥananiah, as in M. B. All it says is בקשו להאכילו דבר גדול שנאבר מהם אבר מן. Rashi explains: ומאי ניהו אבר מן החי השחוטה ומפני אימתו חתכו עבדיו אבר מן החי והביאו תחתיו שלא יבין. The detail that Ḥanina b. Gamaliel had a premonition that there was something wrong with the food is not directly stated in the text.

80. Mak. 24a. For parallels see Gaster, l. c., p. 229, no. 240.

81. Suk. 53a. For parallels see Gaster, l. c., p. 215, no. 139a; p. 216, no. 142. *M. B.* has אליה רוף and אחיה בן. שׁיטא. In I Kings, 4.3 they are called אליחרף and אחיה, both being בני שׁישא. I use the correct names in the translation.

82. Ḳid. 82b.

P. 137, l. 10. *hosts*] *M. B.* has erroneously, "*der Herr von die ganze Welt.*"

P. 137, l. 12. *a roebuck* . . .] Talmud has לא ראיתי צבי קייץ וארי סבל ושועל חנווני, "I have never seen a deer engaged in gathering fruits, a lion carrying loads, or a fox keeping a shop."

83. B. B. 11a. For parallels see Gaster, l. c., p. 204, no. 100. The moral at the end of the story is not in the talmudic text. This applies in most instances. See Introduction.

84. B. B. 11a. For parallels see Gaster, l. c., p. 204, no. 101.

P. 139, l. 9. *Of the family of the Hasmoneans*] This fact is found in Rashi ad loc. It is of course incorrect. Monobaz was a king of Adiabene, who, with his son of the same name, embraced the Jewish faith. See Josephus, *Antiquities*, XX, 2, 1, sq.

P. 139, l. 13. *forefathers*] *M. B.* has פריינד ( = friends), no doubt a mistake, though Basle ed. has the same.

P. 140, l. 12. *He who preserves his life* . . .] The J. P. S. translation reads: "And he that is wise winneth souls." *M. B.* gives a different translation to bring out the point of the story.

P. 139, l. 16. "*And for thee shall be the charity*"] J. P. S.

has: "And it shall be righteousness unto thee . . ." *M. B.* renders it to suit his point.

P. 140, l. 21. *"The glory of the Lord will gather thee in"*] J. P. S.: "the glory of the Lord shall be thy rearward." *M. B.* renders it to suit his point.

85. Yoma 83b. For parallels see Gaster, l. c., p. 238, no. 315.

P. 141, l. 19. *a wicked man*] the idea of wickedness is not contained in the name Kidor itself, which, if divided into two parts, *Ki dor* (כי דור), means "for generation." The idea of wickedness comes from the rest of the verse, which is associated with *Ki dor*.

86. Tanḥuma, Balak 15. For parallels see Gaster, l. c., p. 220, no. 158. The heading in *M. B.* is: "Tractate Ḥullin, ch. *Kol ha-Basar*," no doubt referring to fol. 106a. But there is only a brief allusion to the story there, no details being given at all. Rashi gives the salient facts, but no more. The details as found in *M. B.* can only have come from Midrash Tanḥuma as indicated. This would seem to suggest that the author of the headings in *M. B.*, citing the sources, was some one other than the compiler of the stories. Perhaps he was the same as the translator of them into Judeo-German.

The story in *M. B.* is essentially the same as in the source except that two interesting expressions have been left out. Concerning the innkeeper or rather shopkeeper (חנווני), as the Midrash calls him, the original says that he sold both *kasher* and *terefah* meat (בשר טהור ובשר חזיר) so that he might not be known as a Jew (quite modern!), and when a Jew came in he gave him beef, and to a Gentile he gave swine's flesh. His test was whether the customer washed his hands or not. The customer in question had a similar 'complex', he was also a "crypto-Jew" (בצנעה יהודי אני), and hence he did not wash his hands. But he

was overcome with compunction and dread (עמדו שערותיו
נבהל ונחפז) when he discovered that he had eaten pork.
One wonders if these touches are not due to a later hand,
possibly of Marrano days. *M. B.* tells the story quite
without the color of the original.

87. Yer. Meg. 1. 13, fol. 72b. No doubt *M. B.* took it
from *'En Ya'akob*, supplement.

88. Sanh. 44b. For parallels see Gaster, l. c., p. 243,
no. 332. The story is not found in the talmudic text,
but in Rashi, who must have taken it from the Jerusalem
Talmud, which has the story with some variations in
Sanh. 6.9 and Hag. 2.2.

P. 149, l. 17. *atonement for me*] *M. B.* has "auf euch"
(אייך), which makes no sense. אייך (Basle ed. same) is no
doubt a misprint for מיך. The original in Rashi proves it.

P. 149, l. 27. *the rule being*] *M. B.* has, "*als mir finden in
Pasuk*" = as we find in the [biblical] verse. But the
rule in question, though derived from the Bible, is, in
the form quoted, talmudic and not biblical.

89. Pes. 57a.

P. 150, l. 14. *King Jannaeus*] Jannaeus is not mentioned
in the Talmud, which says simply מלכא ומלכתא = the king
and the queen. Rashi says מלכי בית חשמונאי = the kings of
the Hasmonean dynasty.

90. Ta'an. 23a.

91. Ta'an. 23b.

P. 155, l. 17. *Hanan*] *M. B.* has חנין.

Ib. *M. B.* has חנין דאס איז טייטש דער זיך פיר בארג, which
gives the impression that חנין means "one who hides
himself." This is due to a misprint, for the Basle ed. has
correctly חנין הנחבא דש אישט טייטש חנין דער זיך פר בורג.

92. Ket. 67b. For parallels see Gaster, l. c., p. 227,
no. 228. In the heading *M. B.* (Amsterdam) has errone-

ously מציאה אשה as the title of the talmudic chapter instead of מציאת האשה. Basle edition is correct.

93. Ket. 67b. For parallels see Gaster, l. c., p. 228, no. 229.

94. Ta'an. 21a. For parallels see Gaster l. c., p. 190, no. 25; p. 205, no. 102.

P. 159, l. 8. *ants*] *M. B.* און מייסן. Pappenheim, *Ameisen;* Talmud נמלים.

P. 162, l. 7. *"his earth as swords . . ."*] J. P. S.: "His sword maketh them as dust, His bow as the driven stubble." Note the peculiar interpretation of *M. B.* (really Talmud) to bring out the allusion.

95. Erroneously numbered in *M. B.*, 96. Tanhuma, Mishpatim, 5.

In the heading *M. B.* gives the source as *'En Ya'akob* commentary, f. 153c. The story is in fact given in Ibn Ḥabib's commentary, in *'En Ya'akob*, on *'Ab. Zarah 11a, where the source is given as above, Tanḥuma, Mishpatim. The reference is to ed. Venice 1567 (שכ"ז) and the same ed. is meant, though it is not mentioned, in heading of No. 205. This gives us a terminus a quo for the date of the *M. B.*

P. 165, l. 19. *"To him who is despised . . ."*] I gave the J. P. S. translation in the text. The words in *M. B.* are not clear: הערט איר קינדר ישראל צו דען פאר שעמטן (שמעטן Basle) לייבן צו דען און פר ווערדינן אלי פעלקר (צו קנעבטן Basle inserts) צו הערן, אם לעצטן זיא ווערן קומן דיא קינינן אונ' דיא הערן אונ' זיא ווערן זיך נינן צו אים.

P. 166, l. 4. *the guidance of a ship . . .*] In the original the reading is נתח לאסטרטלירוס אנונה אלא אם כן נטל זיינו שלו = Have you ever given his allowance to a military chief unless he has his armor on him? Where did *M. B.* get his interpretation of the passage? It might help us to deter-

mine the date of the compilation if we knew. The Homburg
ed. of *M. B.* omits this story.

96. Ta'an. 19b. For parallels see Gaster, l. c., p. 202,
no. 85.

P. 168, l. 25. *shone*] ולטה נקרא שמו נקדימון שנקדה חמה בעבורו,
a play upon the words Naḳdimon and *nakad*, which means
in Hebrew to shine.

P. 169, l. 3. *Gibeah*] should be Gibeon, cf. Josh. 10.12.

P. 169, l. 4. *Amalek*] in the Talmud the reference is to
Deut. 2.25, which refers to Sihon.

97. Ber. 34b. For parallels see Gaster, l. c., p. 221,
no. 167.

98. Ber. 34b.

P. 170, l. 17. *Into the ground*] not in the Talmud.

99. Tosafot to Ta'an. 9a. For parallels see Gaster,
l. c., p. 205, no. 104. *M. B.* has erroneously in the heading:
"Tosafot to Berakot, ch. 1," מס׳ ברכות פרק ראשון הביא תוספות.
A slightly different version in Pesiḳta, ed. Buber, 96a and
Tanhuma Reëh, 10; cf. also Enelow, *Menorat ha-Maor*,
I, 53–54, where the source is likewise Tosafot and not the
Midrash, as assumed by the editor.

100. Rashi, or rather pseudo-Rashi, to Ta'an. 8a; *'Aruk,*
s.v. חלד. *M. B.* names Rashi in the heading, and not
*'Aruk,* although Rashi gives the story merely in summary
fashion, while the details are found in *'Aruk.* The fact
is that whoever inserted the headings in *M. B.*, possibly
the compiler or the translator (see notes to No. 86), read
the story neither in Rashi nor in *'Aruk,* but in *'En Ya'akob,*
who names Rashi and Tosafot as telling the story briefly
and then refers to *'Aruk* as giving a longer version, which
is then reproduced.

P. 174, l. 20. *a human being or are you a demon*] *M. B.*:
"*bist du ein Geheuer oder bist du ein Ungeheuer*"; *'Aruk:*
מן בני אדם אתה או מן מזיקים.

P. 175, l. 14. *ketubah*] marriage contract. *ķiddushin*] betrothal, legal and legitimate marriage.

P. 176, l. 6. *Shadkanim*] pl. of *shadkan*, marriage broker.

101. Ta'an. 20a. For parallels see Gaster, l. c., p. 202, no. 89.

P. 178, l. 2. *Pasuķ*] *Pasuķ* (= פסוק) refers, strictly speaking, to a biblical verse. Here it is applied erroneously to a saying of a rabbi of the Mishna, R. Eleazar b. Simeon.

P. 197, l. 7. *R. Simeon*] no doubt a mistake for R. Eleazar b. Simeon. However, the correct reading in the Talmud would seem to be R. Simeon b. Eleazar, cf. Malter's edition of *Ta'anit* in *Publications of the Academy for Jewish Research*, New York, 1930, p. 80, l. 8 and note; p. 81, l. 6 and note. Wm. has R. Simeon b. Eleazar as well as R. Eleazar (Grünbaum, 403).

102. Ta'an. 20b.

103. B. B. 10a.

104. Git. 68a. For parallels see Gaster, l. c., p. 260, no. 404; p. 207, no. 114.

P. 186, l. 13. *ḥalizah*] the ceremony in default of a levirate marriage; cf. Deut. 25.5–11.

P. 186, l. 27. *reward in this world*] A widely prevalent rabbinic doctrine that a wicked man is rewarded in this world for any good deeds he may have to his credit and punished in the next for his wicked deeds. See Albo, *'Iķķarim*, ed. Husik, IV, part 1, p. 100 ff.

105. Ber. 33a. For parallels see Gaster, l. c., p. 221, no. 164.

106. Ķid. 81a.

107. Tosafot to Ķid. 80b, catchword כי. For parallels see Grünbaum, p. 406. It is the famous story of the "Matrona of Ephesus." Cf. Krauss, הגרן, IV, 27–28.

108. Ḳid. 81a. For parallels see Gaster, l. c., p. 268, no. 442.

109. B. M. 85a. *M. B.* does'not finish the story and ends abruptly. Talmud adds that as a result of the envy of the sages the fire once scorched his legs and thereafter his nickname was, "Shorty with the scorched legs" (קטין חריך שקיה).

110. B. B. 3b. For parallels see Gaster, l. c., p. 230, no. 250.

P. 198, l. 11. *Judah son of Bota*] Talmud has Baba son of Bota. *M. B.* changes the name to Baba later on, p. 198, ll. 22 and 25 and p. 119, l. 6. The story in *M. B.* is abridged. The words of the girl in *M. B.* are not clear. In the Talmud she says: כל מִי דאתי ואמר מבית חשמונאי קאתינא עבדא הוא דלא אישתיירא מינייהו אלא ההיא ינוקתא וההיא ינוקתא נפלה מאיגרא לארעא = Any one who says that he is a descendant of the Hasmoneans is a slave, for no one survived but a young girl and she fell (threw herself) down from the roof. I am not sure whether the last words, "and—roof", are those of the girl or of the narrator. At the end of the story *M. B.* gives the Bible (עשרים וארבע = 24 [books]) as authority for Herod's rebuilding of the Temple!

111. Ḳid. 81a. For parallels see Gaster, l. c., p. 213, no. 136.

P. 200, l. 11. *I would throw . . . drown you*] Talmud has: שותינהו לדמך כתרתי מעי.

112. Ḳid. 81a.

P. 201, l. 1. *thrown you down . . . died instantly*] Talmud has, as in preceding story: שויתיה לדמך כתרתי מעי.

113. Giṭ. 45a.

P. 201, l. 8. *'Elos*] Talmud has 'Eles, עיליש.

114. Sanh. 93a. For parallels see Gaster, l. c., p. 191, no. 28.

115. Sanh. 109b.

P. 207, l. 4. *washerman* . . .] In the Talmud it simply says: ההוא כובס אקלע להתם אמרו ליה הב ד' זוזי אמר להו אנא במיא דעברת יהב חמניא א'כ יהב ליה אמרו עברי במיא. The words: דער נינג איבר דיא בריק און פארט אך איבער דען וואשר, have nothing corresponding to them in the Talmud. It is not clear to me what the point of the story is unless it is simply an indication of the topsy-turvy character of Sodomite justice that if one crossed the water without using the bridge he had to pay more. But in that case the additional words of *M. B.* quoted above spoil the story. The washerman must have said: "I got across without using the bridge." Rashi says: דעבר במיא עובר ברגליו בטים. Hence translate: "who waded through the water."

116. Ned. 40a. For parallels see Gaster, l. c., p. 224, no. 197.

117. Ned. 9b.

118. Sotah 8b.

119. Pes. 112b.

P. 214, l. 1. *Naza*] Talmud has שכנציב = Shekanzib, a place in Babylonia, see Jastrow, *Lexicon*, s.v. Did *M. B.* have a different text? The story of R. Papa is not given in the talmudic text, but is found in Rashi and Rashbam.

120. Ber. 18b.

P. 216, l. 6. *hail*] in the Talmud the second year had שדפון = blasting of the grain by the wind, and not hail.

121. Ber. 18b.

P. 217, l. 6. *saddle-bag*] Talmud has זוזי = money.

122. Ber. 27b. For parallels see Gaster, l. c., p. 221, no. 169. *M. B.* has Eliezer for Eleazar.

123. Ned. 66b.

P. 221, l. 21. *two lentils*] In his commentary on the Talmud Rashi is not certain whether טלפי had two meanings, רגלי בהמה and עדשים or whether the mistake was that she took the word תרי, a couple, literally. *M. B.* adopts the second.

124. Meg. 7b.

P. 222, l. 23. *Raba*] Talmud has Rabbah.

125. Ket. 103a.

P. 225, l. 10. *they exclaimed*] In *M. B.* it was the rabbis who prayed that the celestials might win out over the terrestrials, while in the Talmud it was the maid who prayed thus as she had prayed the opposite before. *M. B.* is contradictory in saying in the immediate sequel that the rabbis did not cease praying that Rabbi might not die.

P. 225, l. 20. *rent the back of his garment . . .*] *M. B.* has: קרעיה ללבושיה. Talmud has דא מאכט ער קריעה הינטר זיך ואהדריה לקרעיה לאחוריה = he rent his garment and turned the rent so that it was on his back.

P. 225, l. 23. *had a dispute . . . have won*]. Talmud reads more picturesquely: אראלים ומצוקים (Rashi: צדיקים ומצוקי ארץ) אחזו בארון הקדש נצחו אראלים את המצוקים ונשבה ארון הקדש. *M. B.* paraphrases this figure of speech.

126. Sanh. 65b. For parallels see Gaster, l. c., p. 188, no. 15.

127. Ḳid. 31a. For parallels see Gaster, l. c., p. 223, no. 188.

128. B. B. 58a. For parallels see Gaster, l. c., p. 237, no. 311; p. 256, no. 391.

129. Meg. 16a.

P. 233, l. 10. *steps*] Talmud has אינרא = roof, here and in other places too.

130. Ber. 32b. For parallels see Gaster, l. c., p. 194, no. 45.

131. Hag. 4b.

P. 235, l. 4. *Dima*] Talmud has Bibi (ביבי). *M. B.* obviously confused Bibi with Domeh (דומה) who is men-

tioned in the same story as the שומר הפתים (Rashi ad loc.):
‏.והדר משלימנא לדומה‎

P. 235, l. 26. *Ecclesiastes*] An error for Proverbs. Note
peculiar translation of the verse.

132. 'Er. 54b. For parallels see Gaster, l. c., p. 222,
no. 179.

P. 236, l. 26. *generation*] M. B., Amsterdam ed., ‏נבירד‎,
Basle, ‏נבירט‎. Talmud ‏דָּרְךְ‎ from ‏דָּר‎. ‏דָּרָא‎ = generation.

133. Ber. 20a. For parallels see Gaster, l. c., p. 227,
no. 222. Berakot contains only the story of R. Johanan.
The rest of the story in *M. B.* about the wife of Elisha the
high priest is not given in Ber. 20a. Many versions of this
legend are given by Horowitz, ‏תוספתא עתיקתא‎, V, 43–45 and
57–66. The story in *M. B.* is almost identical with the
legend given on pp. 49–50 from ‏שערי דורא‎, Niddah 23;
cf. also ‏תוספתא עתיקתא‎ II, 11–15 and 34–39.

134. Many versions of the legend are found in the
Midrashim and later writings but without the homiletical-
moralizing addition of *M. B.* Cf. Horowitz, ‏תוספתא עתיקתא‎,
IV, 4, 15–16 and V, 57–58. Cf. also note on *M. B.* 248.
For parallels see Gaster l. c., p. 227, no. 222. *M. B.* has
erroneously, Ber., ch. 3.

135. B. M. 59b. For parallels see Gaster, l. c., p. 212,
no. 125.

P. 246, l. 2. *figure of speech*] *M. B.* reads ‏כביכול‎, ‏וױדר‎
‏נירעט‎ (= ‏נירעט‎ . . . ‏וױדר‎. ‏הקב'ה ניט נירעט‎ = "one must not say this
of God") is intended as an interpretation of the rabbinic
expression ‏כביכול‎, for which see Jastrow, *Lexicon*, s.v. ‏יכול‎.

P. 247, l. 22. *taḥanun*] a special prayer during which
one rests his face in the hollow of his elbow so as to exclude
all foreign thought. Talmud refers to this prayer as
‏לטיפל על אפיה‎ = to fall on one's face. *M. B.* renders it

תחנות זאנן. Perhaps it is a mistake for תחנון, for תחנות has a different meaning.

136. R. Baḥya in his commentary on Exodus 25.2. There is no evidence that *M. B.* drew on Tanḥuma, Terumah, 2, which Baḥya himself cites as his source. The story is found also in *Hibbur Ma'asiyyot* (hereafter cited as *Ḥ. M.*) end, a work known to *M. B.* For parallels, see Gaster, l. c., p. 255, no. 386.

137. Abot, 6.9.

P. 251, l. 3. *Bible*] note rabbinic interpretation of the verse.

138. Ms. Oxford, in Gaster, l. c., Hebrew part, p. 194, no. CCCIII.

139. *Ḥ. M.*, Commandment V, last story. For parallels see Gaster, l. c., p. 240, no. 323; 261, nos. 413 and 413a.

140. *'Aseret ha-Dibberot*, commandment VII, 2 and ed. Jellinek, 81–83. For parallels see Gaster, l. c., p. 254, no. 384.

141. Tanḥuma Bereshit, 7; where, however, it is Hadrian, and not Alexander, who claims divine honors. For parallels see Gaster, l. c., p. 185, no. 3.

142. Yer. Peah I, 15c. For parallels see Gaster, l. c., p. 224, no. 190. *M. B.* no doubt took the story from *'En Ya'akob*, Additions to Vol. I.

143. Ms. Oxford in Gaster, *Exempla*, Hebrew part, no. CCCV, where the hero is called R. Johanan; cf. ibid., English, p. 238, no. 316; and Ginzberg, *Legends*, V, 148, note 49.

P. 268, l. 28. *trouble*] *M. B.* ממון, Basle מומן, no doubt a mistake. The Hebrew source has המקום יצילך מן הרעות העתידות לבא עליך. Similarly below.

144. Tanḥuma, ed. Buber, Introduction, 157. For parallels see Gaster, l. c., p. 268, no. 441b. Cf. Ginzberg, *Legends*, VI, 286, note 31.

145. *H. M.* 8. For parallels see Gaster, l. c., p. 235, no. 304. Cf. Ginzberg, *Legends*, VI, 258–259.

146. A combination of *Ḥ. M.* 14 and '*Aseret ha-Dibberot*, ed. Jellinek, 80–81. For parallels see Gaster, l. c., p. 213, no. 134, and Ginzberg, גנזי שעכטער, I, 235–237, 238–240.

147. B. M. 84b. The hero in the Talmud is R. Eleazar b. R. Simeon. *M. B.* seems to have elaborated the story. Ḥanina seems to be a favorite name with *M. B.* He uses it also in no. 143 instead of Johanan found in his source. Cf. also note on no. 169.

148. Yalkut Ruth 607, whose source is Ruth Zutta, ed. Buber, 55.

149. 'Er. 53b. For parallels see Gaster, l. c., p. 239, no. 317; p. 228, no. 236.

150. Suk. 52a.

P. 299, l. 5. *will have the privilege*] *M. B.*, Amsterdam, מכח is corrupt. Basle ed. reads correctly זוכה.

151. Suk. 52a.

152. "This is to my knowledge," writes Dr. Ginzberg, "the earliest story about a *dibbuk*, which is first met with in the writings about Luria and his pupils. The nearest to that given in *M. B.* is the one told about Luria and Vital in the different versions of שבחי הארי, which, however, were published later than the *M. B.*" See, for parallels, Gaster, l. c., p. 248, no. 349.

153. Beẓah 16a continued with Shab. 119b and 119a. Cf. Gaster, l. c., p. 195, no. 51.

P. 304, l. 21. *concealment*] a play upon לעלם, as if from עלם.

P. 305, l. 17. *departs*] a play on וינפש, explained to mean ווי אבדה נפש.

154. San. 104a–104b. The heading in *M. B.* is Ekah R. which is a mistake. The story in Ekah R. 1.2 is similar to,

but not identical with, that in *M. B.* The heading belongs as a matter of fact to no. 155. Cf. following note.

155. Ekah R. 1.2.

156. Chalaz, ספר המוסר, ed. Mantua, IV, 23b–29a. Also found in Ben Sira, ed. Constantinople (c. 1580); cf. *ZHB*, X, 159.

157. A more elaborate version is found in *Brandtspiegel*, VI, 8d–9b, but to my knowledge (writes Dr. Ginzberg) not found in Hebrew sources earlier than *M. B.* Cf. Gaster, l. c., p. 248, no. 355, who refers to *Sefer ha-Musar*. This must be a misprint, as the story is not found there.

158–183. Most of these legends concerning R. Judah Ḥasid and his father R. Samuel are found in a Hebrew Ms. (now in the Frankfort library) described by Adolph Brüll in Brüll, *Jahrbücher*, IX, 9–71, hereafter referred to as B., followed by the number of the story in the Ms.

158. = B. 13.

159. = B. 4.

P. 319, l. 23. *fandel*] Basle פאנדיל, pandel, perhaps same as *Pardel*, a leopard.

160. = B. 12.

161. Not in Ms. B. or anywhere else. The nearest parallel is the legend about Abu Aaron of Babylon in *Ahimaaz Chronicle*, ed. Neubauer, 112.

162. Not found in any other source.

163. = B. 14.

164. = B. 25.

165. = B. 10.

166 (erroneously marked in *M. B.*, 100). = B. 22.

167. = B. 35.

168. Not in B. or anywhere else. Cf. the story of the *homunculus* with the word אמת on his forehead in ספר הקנה, 36a, ed. Koretz.

169. Not in B. Seems to be a German folktale. It does

not contain anything specially Jewish, though R. Judah
and his son-in-law R. Ḥanina (a favorite name in *M. B.*,
cf. note on no. 147) are the heroes.

170. ספר הגן of R. Isaac b. Eliezer, IV. Not in B.

171. = B. 34. Cf. Gaster, l. c., p. 245, no. 339.

172. = B. 32.

173. = B. 21.

174. = B. 15.

175. = B. 16.

176. = B. 17.

177. = B. 18.

178. = B. 19.

179. Not in B. or anywhere else. Cf. Gaster, l. c., p. 245,
no. 338. Notwithstanding certain Jewish features at the
end of the legend, the story seems to be a German folktale.
Note that nos. 174–180, with the exception of no. 179,
follow in *M. B.* the same order as in B.

180. = B. 20.

181. = B. 2.

182. = B. 4.

P. 395, l. 7. *ḥibbut ha-keber*] lit. pressing of the grave;
according to a popular superstition, punishment in the
grave, of sinners and persons who forget their names
after death.

183. = B. 36.

184. Ibn Yaḥya, *Shalshelet ha-Ḳabbalah* (הרמב'ם ורש'י),
ed. Venice, 49b.

P. 397, l. 4 *Bouillon*] *M. B.* has ליון (Lyons?)

185. Ibn Verga, *Shebet Yehudah* (ה'יו), ed. Wiener, 39,
and from there *Simḥat ha-Nefesh*, 54b, where the place is
correctly given as Spain and not Turkey, as in *M. B.*
A similar very much elaborated story is given by D.
Günzburg in *REJ*, XVII, 48–49, from a Yemenite Ms.
G. did not notice, however, that Ibn Verga makes it

quite impossible to take the Ms. very seriously. He wrote about a century before the event is said to have taken place.

186. Chalaz, *Sefer ha-Musar*, III, end. This is also the same as Adhan in בנאות דשא. to which Gaster, l. c., p 250, no. 371, refers. *Simḥat ha-Nefesh*, ed. Amsterdam, 33b, very likely used *M. B.*

187. Ekah R. l. 4. Cf. Gaster, l. c., p. 235, no. 303.

188. A shorter Hebrew version from a Cambridge Ms. is given in *Bet ha-Midrash* VI, 137–139. Cf. Vogelstein and Rieger, 296–298 and Landau, *Beilage z. Allg. Zeit.*, 1906, no. 269.

P. 410, l. 19. *Sabbath Goyah*] a gentile woman who lights the fire in Jewish houses on the Sabbath.

P. 416, l. 20. *R. Simeon. . . descent*] no doubt misplaced. It should follow "checkmated him," above, p. 415, l. 16.

189. *Ḥibbur Yafeh* = *Bet ha-Midrash* V, 138–139. Cf. Gaster, l. c., p. 262, no. 414.

190. *Ḥ. M.*, 15. Cf. Gaster, l. c., p. 236, no. 307.

191. *'Aseret ha-Dibberot*, Commandment II, 2 and ed. Jellinek, 71. Cf. Gaster, l. c., p. 251, no. 376.

192. *Sefer Yuḥasin* in Neubauer, *Anecdota*, I, 171–72; *Bet ha-Midrash*, VI, 130–131; cf. Jellinek, Introduction, 32.

193. *Kol Bo*, 18. Cf. Baer, *'Abodat Yisrael*, 112 and Gross, *Gallia Judaica*, 73.

194. *Alphabet ben Sira*, ed. Steinschneider, 4b ff. Cf. Gaster, l. c., p. 253, no. 381; p. 269, no. 449.

195. *Ḥ. M.*, 1. Cf. Gaster, l. c., p. 215, no. 139.

196. Ms. Oxford in Gaster, l. c., Hebrew part, p. 193, no. cccii; cf. ibid., English, p. 236, no. 306 and Kaidanower, קב הישר, 25 = *Bet ha-Midrash*, VI, 143–144.

197. *Bet ha-Midrash* IV, 146, in משלים של שלמה המלך. Cf. Gaster, l. c., p. 258, no. 401.

198. *Bet ha-Midrash*, IV, 148–50, in משלים של שלמה המלך. Cf. Gaster, l. c., p. 259, no. 402.

**199.** *Bet ha-Midrash*, IV, 150–151, in משלים של שלמה המלך.
Cf. Gaster, l. c., p. 259, no. 403.

**200.** Ḥ. M., 18 and *Bet ha-Midrash*, VI, 133. Cf. Gaster, l. c., p. 214, no. 137.

**201.** No source known to me (writes Ginzberg). On the "plant man", cf. Ginzberg, *Legends*, V, 50, note 148.

**202.** Shorter version in Ziyyoni, ויחי, and R. Elijah ha-Kohen, *Shebet Musar*, 35, 114b. Cf. also Zacuto, *Yuḥasin*, ed. Filipowski, 230 and Ketubot 103a.

**203.** No Hebrew source known. Cf. Gaster, l. c., p. 264, no. 422 and p. 265, no. 423, where *Niflaot* is no doubt a misprint for *Niflaim Ma'asekah*, a later book based on *M. B.*, and the reference to *Sha'are Yerushalayim* is incorrect, as nothing of the kind is to be found there.

**204.** Ms. Oxford in Gaster, l. c., Hebrew part, p. 195, no. ccciv. Cf. also ibid. English, p. 237, no. 313.

**205.** Rashi, Ta'an. 18b. Cf. Malter ad loc. The first part alone is from Rashi, the rest from the Talmud. Cf. Gaster, l. c., p. 190, no. 22. *M. B.* has תענית הביא רש"י דף קל"ו. This refers to the Venice ed. 1567 of the *En Ya'aḳob*. Cf. note on No. 95.

**206.** Yoma 82b. The reading R. Tarfon is incorrect and was caused by a confusion with Yer. Yoma, 8.4, fol. 45a.

**207.** Yoma 82a–82b.

**208.** A German folktale!

**209.** *'Aseret ha-Dibberot*, Commandment IV, 10; ed. Jellinek, 74–75. Cf. Gaster, l. c., p. 237, no. 312.

**210.** Not known to me (writes Ginzberg). Did the author of *M. B.* use a Ms. of *Shalshelet ha-Ḳabbalah* where the legend was given?

**211.** *Shalshelet ha-Ḳabbalah*, 57a–57b.

P. 513, l. 6. *martel*] *M. B.* מארטל. *Sh. H.* חוטר מאיר כמו שמן.

**212.** In many editions of the German and Italian

*Maḥzorim;* cf. Davidson אוצר, II, 200 and *Shalshelet ha-Ḳabbalah,* 56b–57a (סמ'נ ורמב'ן).

213. Not known to me (writes Ginzberg).

214. ספר הגן, II; addition to *Sefer Ḥasidim,* ed. Wistinetzki, 427.

215. '*Aseret ha-Dibberot,* Commandment III, 3 and ed. Jellinek, 87–88, and in many other places; cf. Gaster, l. c., p. 206, nos. 111 and 112, and p. 240, no. 324. Only in *M. B.* Solomon catches the thief. The beginning does not properly belong to this story but to that of '*Aseret ha-Dibberot,* Commandment VIII, 1, which, in ed. Jellinek, precedes this one.

216. *Ḥ. M.* 13. Cf. Gaster, l. c., p. 238, no. 314.

217. '*Aseret ha-Dibberot,* ed. Jellinek, 84–86, but not in the longer recension. Cf. Gaster, l. c., p. 241, no. 327.

218. מוסרי הפילוסופים, ed. Loewenthal, where read איבקוש = Ibycus instead of אינקוש. Cf. Gaster, l. c., p. 265, no. 431.

219. ארחות צדיקים, XIV; כד הקמח, I, 86b (חמדה), ed. Breit. Cf. Ginzberg, *Legends,* VI, 43, note 235.

220. '*Aseret ha-Dibberot,* Commandment IX, 1; *Bet ha-Midrash,* V, 145. At the end some quotations from 'Arak. 15b. Cf. Gaster, l. c., p. 216, no. 143.

221. '*Aseret ha-Dibberot,* Commandment VI, 1. Cf. Gaster, l. c., p. 254, no. 382.

222. '*Aseret ha-Dibberot,* Commandment III, 4, and in a shorter version, ed. Jellinek, in *Bet ha-Midrash,* I, 72–73. *M. B.* seems to have used both sources. Cf. Gaster, l. c., p. 252, no. 378.

223. The clever detection of the thief as told here is an old Solomon tale found in many Hebrew sources, for ex., '*Aseret ha-Dibberot,* Commandment VIII, 1, and cf. Ginzberg, *Legends,* VI, 286, note 30. The first part of the story is not known to me (writes Ginzberg) from other sources. Cf. Gaster, l. c., p. 206, nos. 111, 112.

224. Almost identical with Ms. Oxford, published by Israel Lévi in *REJ*, XXXIV, 67 ff. Cf. Gaster, l. c., p. 242, no. 330.

225. Yer. Sanh. 7.11, fol. 25d; abbreviated in *Ḥ. M.* 3. Cf. Gaster, l. c., p. 255, no. 388.

226. *Sefer Ḥasidim*, ed. Wistinetzki, 132.

227. A German tale, found also in Grimm, *Kinder-und Hausmärchen*, III, 237 (3d edition). Cf. Grünbaum, *Jüdisch-deutsche Chrestomathie*, 443–444; also Gaster, l. c., p. 269, no. 443.

228. The story, though told of a rabbi, is a typical German folktale.

229. The biblical story of the wise judgment of Solomon (I Kings, 1.4).

230. The story is hardly a genuine Solomon tale. It is more likely a German folktale. Cf. Gaster, l. c., p. 265, no. 426.

231. Ber. R. 92.6. The introductory sentence is from Ta'an. 10b. Cf. Gaster, l. c., p. 222, no. 181.

P. 603, l. 7. *Ki tob*] "that it is good;" cf. Gen. 1.4

232. Kohelet R. ll. 1–2, very much elaborated.

P. 606, l. 5. *great sea*] the Mediterranean.

233. B. M. 83b–84b. Cf. Gaster, l. c., p. 203, no. 95.

P. 625, l. 13. *Your father*] Talmud reads: אבוך ערק לאסיא את ערק ללודקיא.

P. 627, l. 12. *They had been on the sea*] The reason of the gift is given in Rashi. Tosafot gives it in the name of the Midrash.

P. 631, l. 25. *still in learning . . .*] Talmud, more logically: נהי דבתורה נדול ממני אבל במעשים טובים מי נדול ממני.

234. *Sefer Ḥasidim*, ed. Wistinetzki, 132.

235. Luzzatto, *Kaftor va-Feraḥ*, Ber. 1, ed. Amsterdam, 7b. Cf. Gaster, l. c., p. 235, no. 302.

236. *Sefer Ḥasidim*, 150.

237. Luzzatto, *Kaftor va-Feraḥ*, Ber. 1, 16b, from Midrash Tehillim, 8.5.

238. Luzzatto, *Kaftor va-Feraḥ*, Ber. 9, 25a, taken without acknowledgment from Onkeneira, *Ayyuma ka-Nidgalot*, ed. Berlin, 12b–13a.

239. Rashi, Mak., end; Luzzatto, *Kaftor va-Feraḥ*, Shab. 9, 29b. Cf. Gaster, l. c., p. 235, no. 300.

240. Luzzatto, *Kaftor va-Feraḥ*, Ḥag. 1, 43a; cf. Ginzberg, in Husik, '*Iḳḳarim*, III, 290, note 1; *Simḥat ha-Nefesh*, 43d; and comp. also the small ס׳ חסידים (Warsaw, 1866), 13a–13b.

241. Luzzatto, *Kaftor va-Feraḥ*, Shab. 13, 34a, where *Tanna debe Eliyahu* is given as the source, by which is meant not the Mishna that goes by that name, but *Ḥuppat Eliyahu*. Cf. ed. Horowitz, 53, who has no reference to the use of *Ḥuppat Eliyahu* by Luzzatto.

242. *Shalshelet ha-Ḳabbalah*, 37a; cf. J. E., s.v. Amram of Mayence. The author of the article did not know that the very same story is told of R. Eleazar b. Nathan (cf. Brüll, *Jahrbücher*, IX, 44) and hence the assumption that the Amram legend is only a Jewish rendering of the Christian St. Emmeran legend becomes rather dubious.

243. *Sefer Ḥasidim*, ed. Wistinetzki, 166.

244. *Sefer Ḥasidim*, 86.

245. *Sefer Ḥasidim*, 389.

246. '*Aseret ha-Dibberot*, Commandment VII, 1, and ed. Jellinek, *Bet ha-Midrash*, I, 79–80. *M. B.* might also have used Yalḳuṭ I, 161, where the story is given from Midrash Abkir (reference not found in ed. princeps!).

247. Luzzatto, *Kaftor va-Feraḥ*, Ḥag., end, 71a. A different version in Aboab, *Menorat ha-Maor*, 213; cf. Ginzberg, גנזי שעכטער, 2.

248. Luzzatto, *Kaftor va-Ferah*, Niddah 3, 83b–84a. On the early sources containing this legend, cf. note on No. 134. Luzzatto very likely is based on Aboab, *Menorat ha-Maor*.

249. Luzzatto, *Kaftor va-Ferah*, B. B. 1, 99a = Ms. Oxford, published by Israel Lévi in *REJ*, XXXII, 60. Older versions in Gaster, l. c., p. 236, no. 305.

250. Luzzatto, *Kaftor va-Ferah*, B. B. 1, 98a–98b.

251. *Sefer Hasidim*, 48.

252. *Sefer Hasidim*, 37.

253. *Sefer Hasidim*, 37.

254. *Sefer Hasidim*, 178.